A
J
£2.50

Fiat 124 Sport 1966-74 Autobook

By Kenneth Ball
Associate Member, Guild of Motoring Writers
and the Autopress Team of Technical Writers.

Fiat 124 Spyder, Series AS   1966-69
Fiat 124 Spyder, Series BS   1969-72
Fiat 124 Coupé, Series AC   1967-69
Fiat 124 Coupé, Series BC   1969-72
Fiat 124 Coupé, Series CC   1972-74
Fiat 124 Coupé, Series CCI   1972-74
Fiat 124 Spyder, Series CS   1972-74
Fiat 124 Spyder, Series CSI   1972-74

Autobooks

Autopress Ltd. Golden Lane Brighton BN1 2QJ England

The AUTOBOOK series of Workshop Manuals is the largest in the world and covers the majority of British and Continental motor cars, as well as all major Japanese and Australian models. For a full list see the back of this manual.

CONTENTS

ISBN 0 85147 471 3

First Edition   1971
Second Edition, fully revised   1972
Third Edition, fully revised   1973
Reprinted   1973
Fourth Edition, fully revised   1974
Reprinted   1974

© Autopress Ltd 1974

925

Printed and bound in Brighton England for Autopress Ltd by G Beard & Son Ltd   B

ACKNOWLEDGEMENT

My thanks are due to Fiat (England) Ltd. for their unstinted co-operation and also for supplying data and illustrations.

I am also grateful to a considerable number of owners who have discussed their cars at length and many of whose suggestions have been included in this manual.

Kenneth Ball
Associate Member, Guild of Motoring Writers
Ditchling Sussex England.

INTRODUCTION

This do-it-yourself Workshop Manual has been specially written for the owner who wishes to maintain his car in first class condition and to carry out his own servicing and repairs. Considerable savings on garage charges can be made, and one can drive in safety and confidence knowing the work has been done properly.

Comprehensive step-by-step instructions and illustrations are given on all dismantling, overhauling and assembling operations. Certain assemblies require the use of expensive special tools, the purchase of which would be unjustified. In these cases information is included but the reader is recommended to hand the unit to the agent for attention.

Throughout the Manual hints and tips are included which will be found invaluable, and there is an easy to follow fault diagnosis at the end of each chapter.

Whilst every care has been taken to ensure correctness of information it is obviously not possible to guarantee complete freedom from errors or to accept liability arising from such errors or omissions.

Instructions may refer to the righthand or lefthand sides of the vehicle or the components. These are the same as the righthand or lefthand of an observer standing behind the car and looking forward.

CHAPTER 1

THE ENGINE

1:1 Introduction

Since the model was introduced in 1966, engines of four sizes have been fitted to the Fiat 124 Sport. The basic construction of the engines is the same and any differences between the four versions are those associated with alterations in bore and stroke dimensions.

The following table gives the essential details of the four engines:

1438 cc	80 x 71.5 mm	90 bhp
1608 cc	80 x 80 mm	110 bhp
1592 cc	80 x 79.2 mm	108 bhp
1756 cc	84 x 79.2 mm	118 bhp

The complete engine is shown in **FIG 1:1** and transverse and longitudinal sections in **FIGS 1:2** and **1:3**. Detailed specifications of the engines will be found in **Technical Data** at the end of the manual.

The valves are located in the cylinder head, operated by twin overhead camshafts driven by a toothed rubber belt. The head is constructed in three parts, as shown in **FIG 1:13**, comprising head proper, containing the combustion chambers, and two upper boxes housing the camshafts.

The cast iron cylinder block includes the crankcase and houses the five bearing crankshaft. The fuel and oil pumps together with the ignition distributor, are driven by the rubber timing belt by way of an auxiliary shaft on the side of the block.

1:2 Removing the engine

All normal servicing procedures applicable to a front mounted engine can be carried out with the engine in the car including decarbonizing, checking and setting tappet clearances, make-and-break points, cleaning and resetting sparking plugs, adjusting drive belts, changing air and oil filters, carburetter adjustments and oil and water changing, etc. For more extensive maintenance, it will be necessary to remove the engine from the car following this procedure.

First, raise the car to a suitable height or, alternatively, place it over a pit to give the necessary headroom. If neither pit nor lift is available, chock the rear wheels and raise the front on a jack enabling stands to be placed under the front wheels. Drain the radiator, auxiliary tank, cylinder block and heater system of water. Drain the oil from the sump.

Next, disconnect the battery leads, then the HT leads from the ignition coil to the distributor and the LT lead to the make and break. Disconnect the alternator and starter cables, the low oil pressure (grey) and excess temperature water (green) transducer wiring, identifying the latter for later reconnection if necessary.

Uncouple the accelerator rod, sliding it out of the ball joint on the dash relay lever, and the choke cable from the carburetter. Disconnect the fuel line to the pump of the petrol tank, and then disconnect the fuel line at the pump.

FIG 1 : 1   The 1438 cc engine

Unbolt the exhaust pipe from the manifold and remove the gasket. Loosen the hose clips on the connections to the radiator and to the air conditioning heater and uncouple the hoses from the engine. Disconnect hose to auxiliary tank.

It may now be more convenient to unbolt and remove the radiator from the chassis to give more room for operations. Take out the two upper screws attaching the radiator to the body, then slide the radiator off the lower support bracket.

From inside the car, remove the gearshift lever (see **Chapter 6, Section 6 : 3**) and take off the transmission cover.

Next, working from beneath the car, disconnect the flexible coupling from the gearbox drive shaft by removing the nuts and bolts 2 (see **FIG 1 : 4**), leaving the coupling on the propeller shaft. Disconnect the speedometer drive cable. Unhook the clutch withdrawal fork return spring 3 (see **FIG 1 : 5**), unscrew the locknut and nut 1, 2, and remove the adjusting rod 4 from the clutch fork 5.

Unbolt and remove the engine flywheel cover. Remove the fixing bolt securing the exhaust pipe support clip to the bracket at the rear of the transmission. Unbolt and remove the heat shield and then the starter motor from the front end.

Support the engine and gearbox unit on a substantial garage jack, preferably using the special support bracket, A.70509, remove the four bolts securing the gearbox to the engine—an articulated wrench, A.55035, is designed for this operation—and unbolt and remove the cross-member supporting the gearbox from the chassis floor 5 (see **FIG 1 : 4**).

Ease the gearbox to the rear of the car to separate the clutch shaft from the bearing in the rear end of the crankshaft. Lower and remove the gearbox from under the car

(see **FIG 1 : 6**). The starter motor can then be removed from the engine compartment.

Hook the lifting bar A.60541, to a hoist and pass the front sling under the thermostat housing and the rear sling under the crankcase. Unbolt the engine from the front support pads and lift the engine clear by means of the hoist. Transfer to the bench or, more preferably, to the special support stand Arr.22204.

1 : 3 Dismantling the engine

Remove the support brackets from the crankcase. Remove the oil dipstick. Dismantle the clutch assembly by removing the six bolts and washers attaching it to the flywheel.

Remove the air filter by unscrewing the wingnut and remove the cover.

Disconnect and remove the sparking plugs and unbolt and remove the distributor (see **FIG 1 : 7**). Store in a clean dry place. Extract and store the oil pressure and water temperature transducers.

Unbolt and remove the alternator and extract the Vee-belt coupling, the fan, generator and water pump. Unbolt the fan and pulley from the water pump and then remove the pump (see **FIG 1 : 8**).

Lock the crankshaft from turning by applying the special fitting A.60305 to the starter ring (see **FIG 1 : 9**) then unbolt and remove the alternator and fan drive pulley at the opposite end of the crankshaft. Note that this is keyed to the shaft so that the timing mark shall be properly located (see **FIG 1 : 10**).

Disconnect the accelerator rod from the carburetter throttle lever. Unbolt and remove the water outlet cover housing the thermostat, remove the thermostat and then unbolt the lower half of the outlet from the cylinder block.

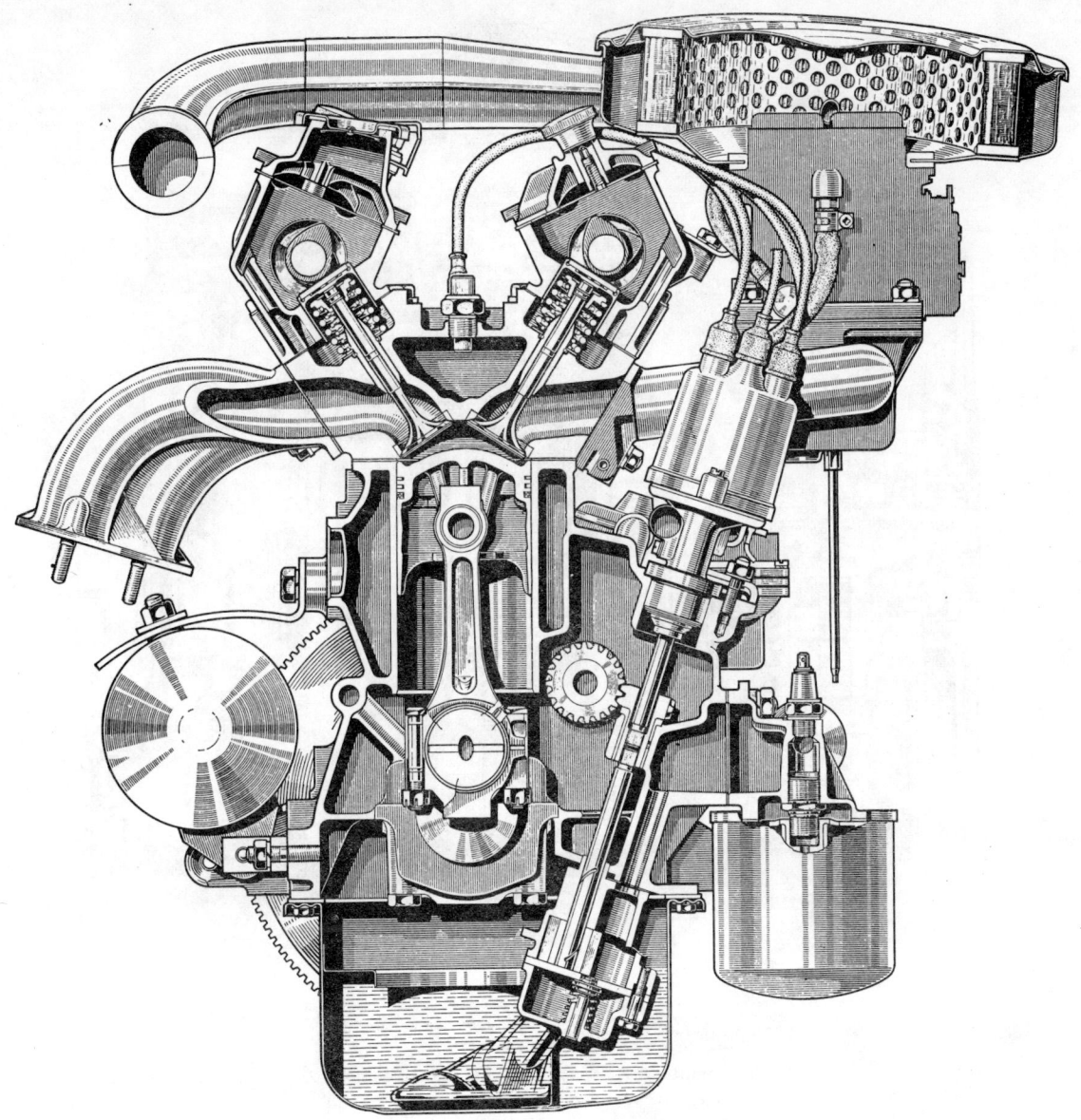

FIG 1:2   Transverse section through 1438 cc engine

Loosen and remove the fuel delivery pipe to the carburetter, and take off the carburetter. Undo and remove the oil filter.

Unbolt and withdraw the fuel pump. As each joint is broken, carefully preserve and store the gaskets and washers. Make a note of every stage not detailed in these instructions so that, when reassembling, the parts are returned to their original positions. Do not rely on memory alone.

Next the cylinder head should be removed by unscrewing the 10 hexagonal bolts in the order shown in **FIG 1:12** and lifting off. Then unscrew the knurled bolts and lift off

the two coverplates over the camshaft housings, which may be removed after withdrawing the ten securing bolts (see **FIG 1:13**).

Unscrew the covers at the rear of the camshafts and withdraw the camshafts to the rear after removing the single bolt by which the drive sprocket is secured (see **FIG 1:14**). Extract the tappets and adjusting shims, storing them in order so as to ensure correct replacement. Remove the inlet and exhaust manifolds.

If the engine is now turned upside down, the sump and its joint washer may be removed, also the front timing gear cover. Unbolt and remove the drive sprocket from

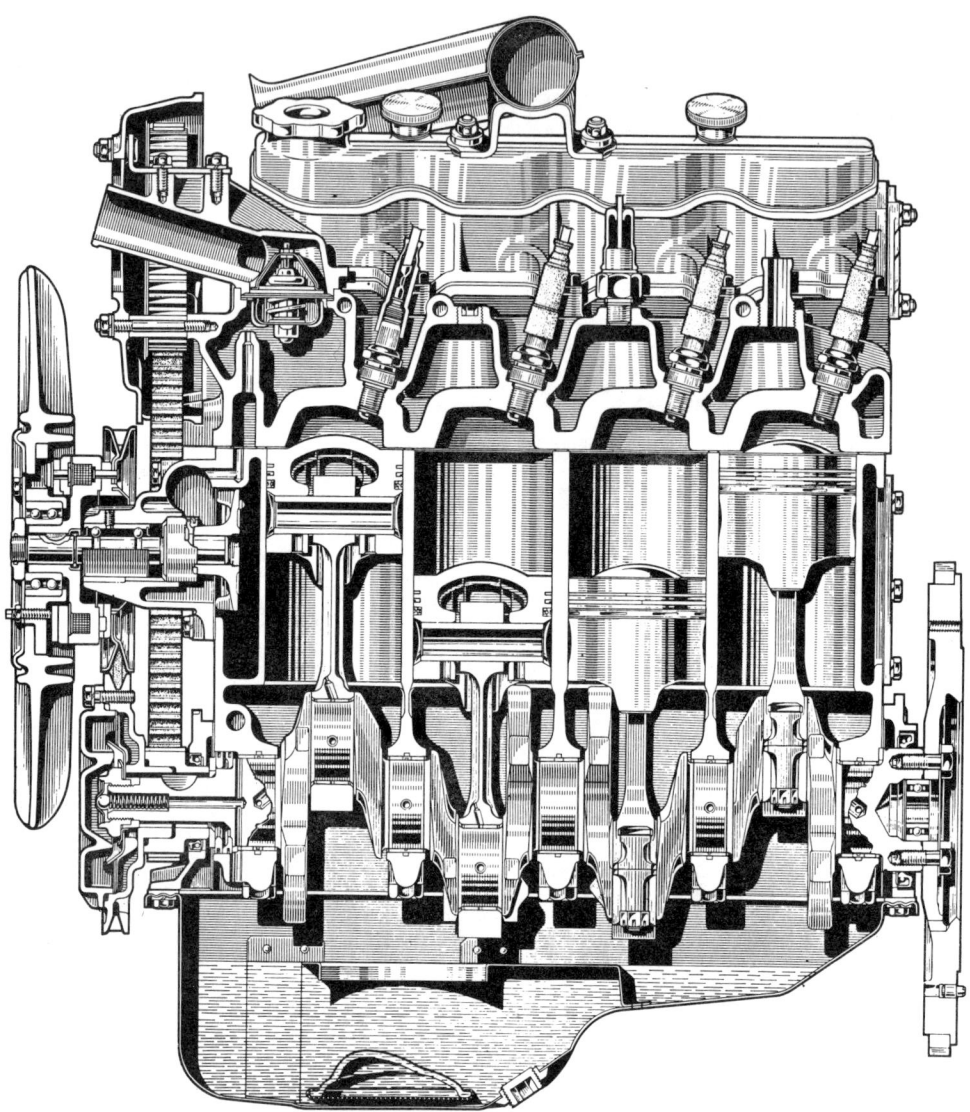

FIG 1 : 3   Longitudinal section through 1438 cc engine

the crankshaft and at the other end unbolt and remove the flywheel and withdraw the ballrace with the puller A.40006/1/3 as shown in **FIG 1 : 15**).

Remove the upper driving gear of the oil pump from its spindle, unscrew the bolts attaching the pump to the crankcase and withdraw the pump complete with its section pipe.

Before unbolting the connecting rod caps, make sure that they are numbered in order to ensure their correct replacement, then push them up and remove them with pistons through the top of the cylinder bores.

Remove the bolts securing the rear coverplate of the crankcase (see **FIG 1 : 16**) and take it off with its gasket. Remove the bolts securing the main bearing caps and extract the caps and shells. Lift out the crankshaft and

then the remaining halves of the bearing shells. Remove the thrust bearing half rings in the rear main bearing (see **FIG 1 : 17**).

1 : 4 Servicing the cylinder head

The cylinder head is in aluminium with cast iron valve seat inserts and is shown in **FIG 1 : 18**, which in conjunction with **FIG 1 : 19** shows how the camshafts and their housings are attached and operate. This latter diagram also shows very clearly the method of adjusting valve tappet clearances by means of adjusting shims in the sunken head of the tappet. The component parts of the valve assembly are shown in **FIG 1 : 20**.

With the head on the bench, clean it thoroughly and remove all traces of carbon before dismantling the valve

12

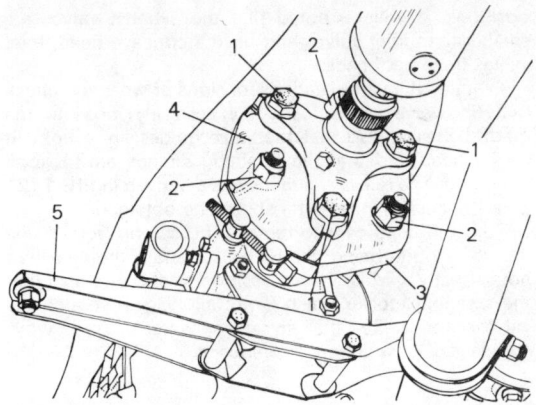

FIG 1 : 4 Flexible coupling between propeller shaft and gearbox

Key to Fig 1 : 4 1/2 Coupling nuts and bolts 3 Tool A.70025 4 Flexible coupling 5 Crossmember

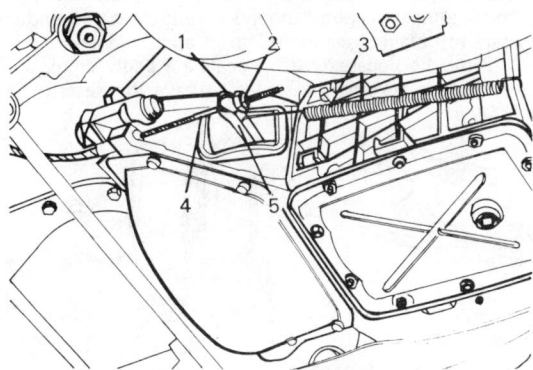

FIG 1 : 5 Clutch release controls

Key to Fig 1 : 5 1 Adjusting nut 2 Locknut 3 Return spring 4 Flexible cable 5 Clutch fork

FIG 1 : 6 Removing transmission

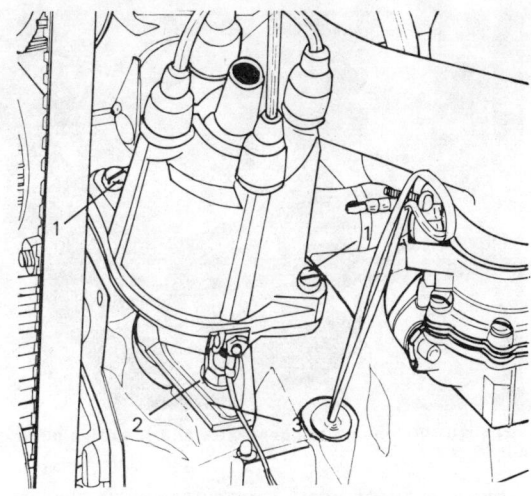

FIG 1 : 7 Distributor fitted to engine

Key to Fig 1 : 7 1 Cap fixing screws 2 Bracket fixing nut 3 Distributor bracket

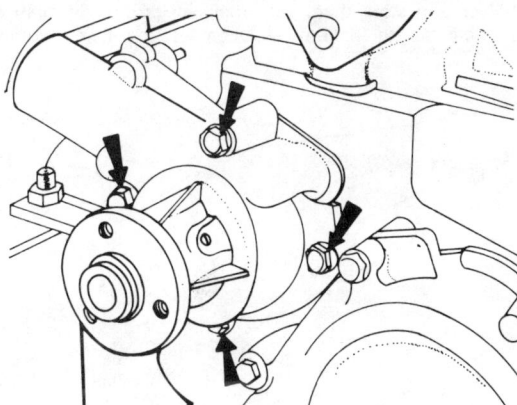

FIG 1 : 8 The water pump showing securing bolts

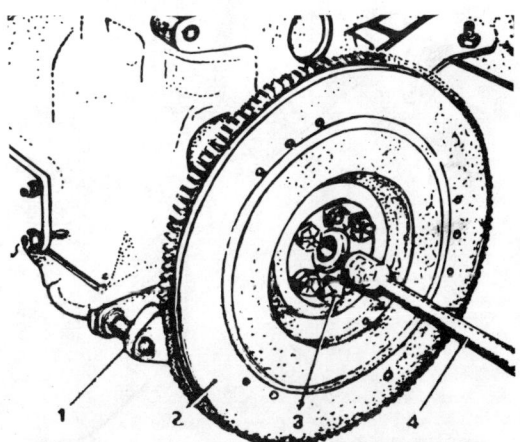

FIG 1 : 9 Flywheel and starter ring gear

Key to Fig 1 : 9 1 Locking tool A.60305 2 Flywheel 3 Fixing bolts 4 Socket wrench

FIG 1 :10 Removing the generator and fan drive pulley nut

assemblies, taking great care not to score the soft aluminium surfaces.

Using a suitable compressing tool release and remove the valve collets, cups and springs, then withdraw the valves and store them with their accessories in such a manner as to ensure replacement in their original positions. It will be noted that the exhaust valves are smaller than inlet valves and have a concave head. Inlet valves have flat heads.

Examine the valve seatings for signs of wear and check that the valve stems are not excessively loose in the guides. Ensure also that the valve guides are a tight fit in the head and that the retaining circlips are in good condition. The relevant dimensions are given in **FIG 1 : 21** and if necessary new parts should be obtained.

Turn the head over to remove the carbon from inside the valve ports being careful not to strain the camshaft housing studs while in this position. Make sure also that the scraping tool or brush is not allowed to scratch the valve seatings. See that any oil or water passage ways are clear of obstructions or deposits.

1 : 5 Valves and valve gear

The valves should be cleaned with a wire brush or emerycloth and checked for condition, particularly for accuracy in the stem. If the seats are in good condition they should be lightly ground in with a carborundum paste to obtain a seating width of approximately 2 mm.

It may be necessary if the seats are badly worn, or if new valves are being installed to have the seats recut.

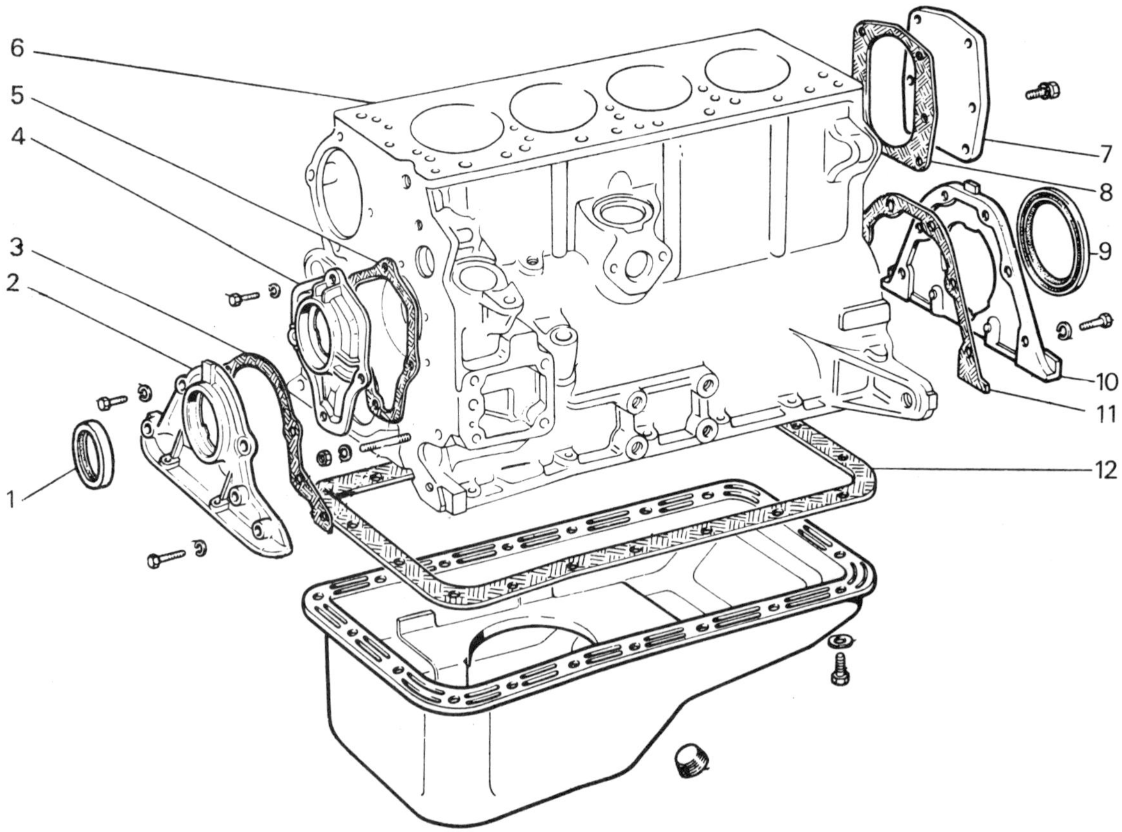

FIG 1 :11 Exploded view showing cylinder block seals and gaskets

Key to Fig 1 :11 1 Sealing ring 2 Cover 3 Gasket 4 Cover 5 Gasket 6 Cylinder block 7 Cover 8 Gasket 9 Sealing ring 10 Cover 11 Gasket 12 Sump gasket

This is a job normally assigned to a service station, but the relevant information required is given in **FIG 1:22**.

Next it will be necessary to check the valve springs. It will be seen that there are two springs to each valve, wound in opposite directions and they should be renewed as a pair if either fails to measure up to specifications as detailed in **Technical Data**.

When all parts have been checked the valves may be reassembled in their correct positions in the head and the springs and cups fitted. Do not omit the oil sealer which is fitted over the inlet valve guide. Refit the camshaft housings and then replace the valve tappets and their adjustment shims and refit the camshaft.

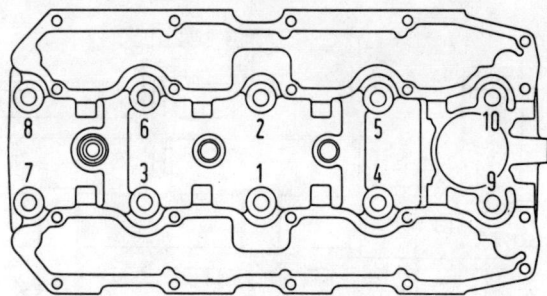

FIG 1:12 Sequence for tightening and loosening cylinder head bolts

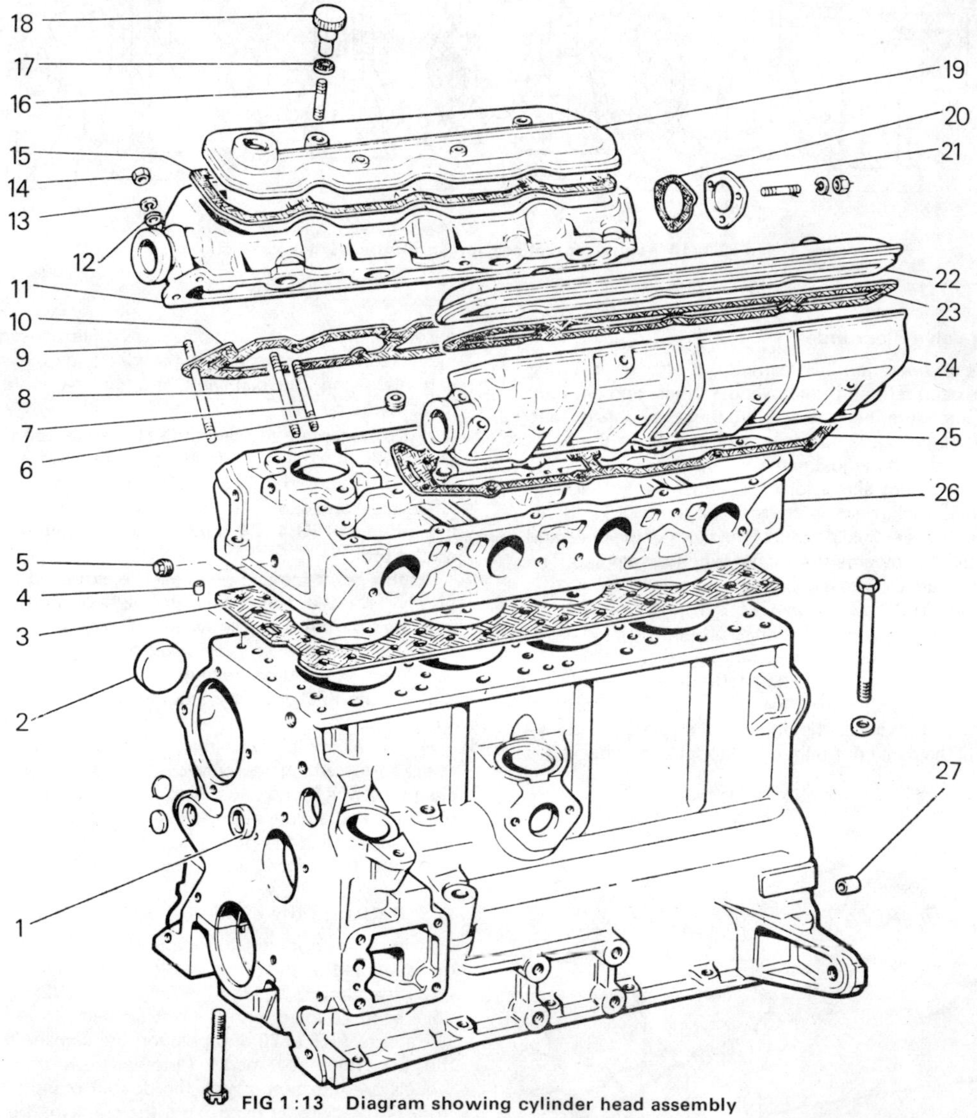

FIG 1:13 Diagram showing cylinder head assembly

Key to Fig 1:13 1 Plug 2 Plug 3 Head gasket 4 Dowel pin 5 Plug 6 Plug 7 Stud 8 Stud 9 Stud 10 Gasket 11 Camshaft box 12 Washer 13 Split washer 14 Nut 15 Cover gasket 16 Stud 17 Sealing ring 18 Knurled knob 19 Cover 20 Gasket 21 Cover 22 Cover 23 Gasket 24 Camshaft box 25 Gasket 26 Cylinder head 27 Dowel pin

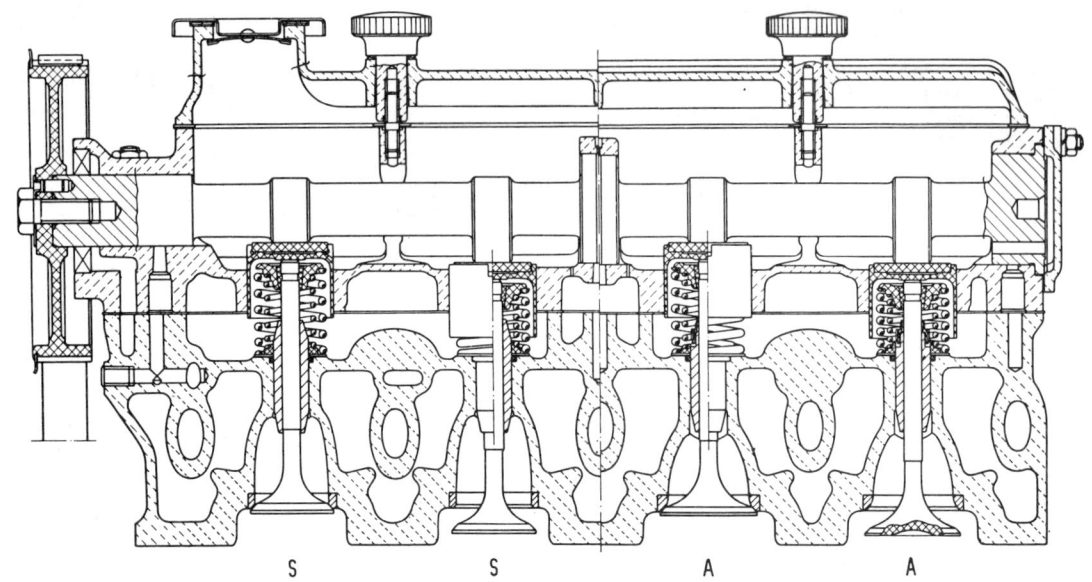

FIG 1 : 14   Longitudinal section through cylinder head

Key to Fig 1 : 14   A Inlet   **S** Exhaust

Setting valve clearances

This is an operation best carried out after the cylinder head has been refitted to the cylinder block, and contrary to the procedure necessary with most overhead twin camshaft engines it is not necessary to remove the camshafts to make the adjustments.

The adjustment shims, or cap plates, are available in 30 different thicknesses in steps of .05 mm (.0019 inch). The thickness is etched on one of the faces of the plate and this should be towards the tappet when assembled. The correct clearances with a cold engine are as follows:

1438 and 1608 cc	Inlet .45 mm (.017 inch)
	Exhaust .50 mm (.019 inch)
1592 and 1756 cc	Inlet .45 mm (.017 inch)
	Exhaust .60 mm (.0.23 inch)

To check and adjust the clearances proceed as follows:

Remove the two camshaft covers and rotate the crankshaft until the cam controlling the tappet to be checked is

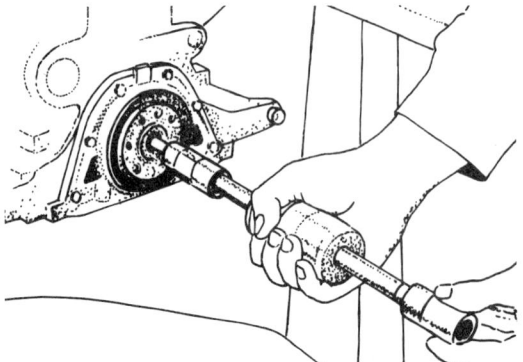

FIG 1 : 15   Withdrawing transmission drive shaft ball-race

perpendicular to the tappet, i.e. valve closed. Then measure with a feeler gauge the clearance between the cap plate and the camshaft and make a note of the measurement.

If it is necessary to adjust the clearance turn the camshaft until the valve is fully open and insert the tool A.60318 as shown in **FIG 1 : 23** to hold down the tappet while the camshaft is further rotated in the direction of the arrow in **FIG 1 : 24** until the cam meets the stop A on the tool.

At this point the cap plate can be extracted by means of an air jet applied through the slot in the tappet indicated by the black arrow in **FIG 1 : 23**.

If the clearance as previously measured was greater than the correct measurement, it will be necessary to fit a new plate thicker by the amount of the difference, and vice versa.

As an example, if an inlet valve clearance is being checked for which the correct value is .45 mm and the clearance was found to be .65 mm, the clearance is .2 mm too great and a plate must be used which is .2 mm thicker (or 4 sizes) than the plate just removed.

Repeat this procedure for each valve.

1 : 6 Refitting the cylinder head

It is most important to ensure that the valves do not get damaged at this time, and once the head has been fitted the camshafts MUST NOT BE TURNED until they have been coupled with the driving belt.

Refer to **FIG 1 : 25** and position the camshafts so that the two reference marks (arrowed) on the sprocket wheels are registering with the double pointer 1 on the front of the cylinder head. Turn the crankshaft until Nos. 1 and 4 pistons are at TDC.

Insert two dummy studs into two of the holes in the cylinder block for the cylinder head securing bolts (holes

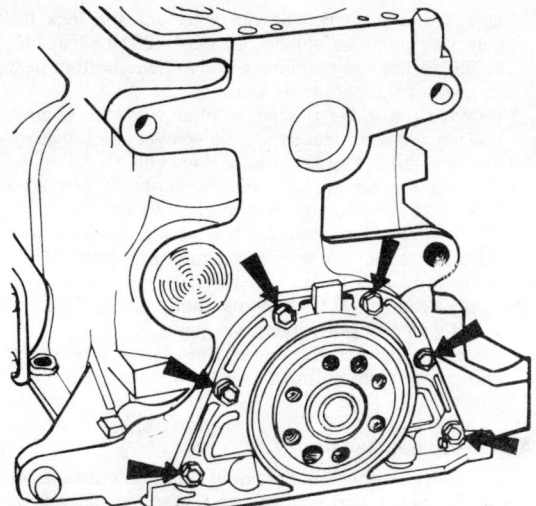

FIG 1 : 16   Removing rear crankcase coverplate

FIG 1 : 17   Removing half rings of crankshaft thrust bearing

8 and 9 are convenient for this purpose—see **FIG 1 : 12**). Fit a new cylinder head gasket.

Very carefully position the head on the block using the dummy studs as pilots and by hand only start in the securing bolts and remove the dummy studs.

The cylinder head bolts must be progressively tightened according to the sequence shown in **FIG 1 : 12** in not less than two stages. At the first stage tighten to a torque of 29 lb ft (4 kg m) and then to the specified value of 48.5 lb ft (6.7 kg m).

Fitting the timing belt:

Fit the belt round its various sprockets as shown in **FIGS 1 : 25** and **1 : 26** and apply a spring balance such as A.95698 (11 in **FIG 1 : 25**) to the hole in the upper righthand arm of the idler with a load of 60 lbs (27 kg), then tighten nuts 7 and 9 to clamp the idler.

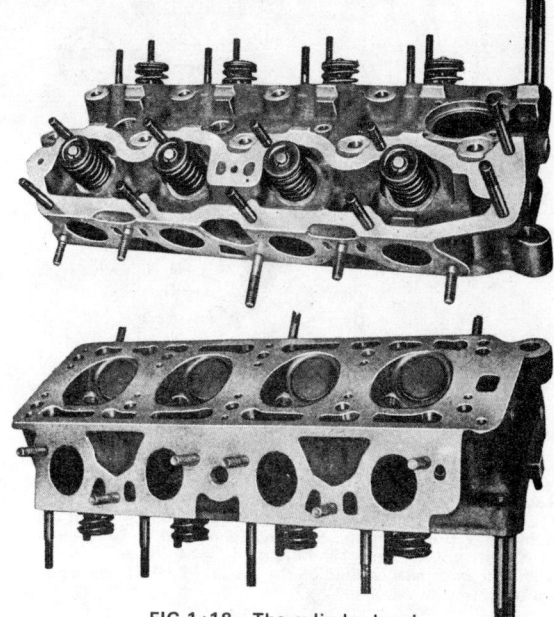

FIG 1 : 18   The cylinder head

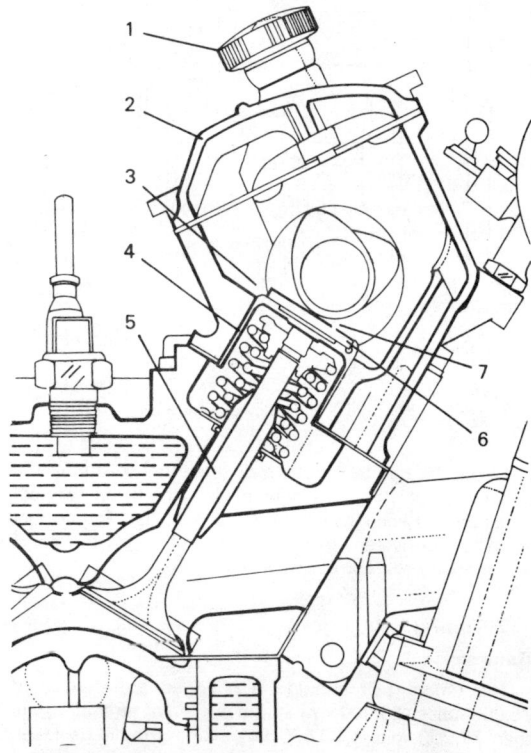

FIG 1 : 19   Cylinder head section through inlet valve

Key to Fig 1 : 19
2 Camshaft cover adjusting shim or cap plate
4 Tappet
7 Clearance

1 Camshaft cover fixing screw
3 Slot in tappet for extracting shim
5 Inlet valve
6 Adjusting

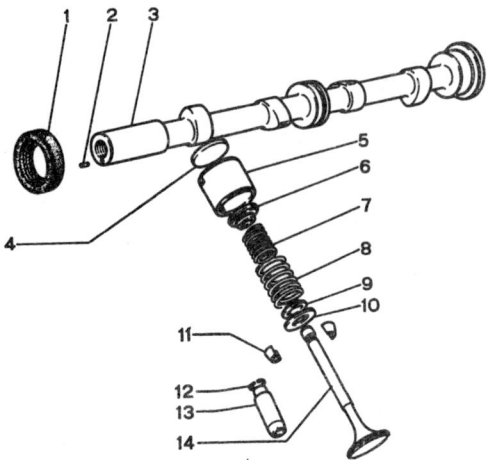

FIG 1:20   Details of valve assembly

Key to Fig 1:20   1 Sealing ring   2 Peg   3 Camshaft
4 Cap plate   5 Tappet   6 Upper spring cup   7 Inner
spring   8 Outer spring   9 Lower spring cup   10 Washer
11 Collet   12 Circlip   13 Valve guide   14 Valve
Note that an oil seal is fitted on the top of the inlet valve guide
not shown in illustration

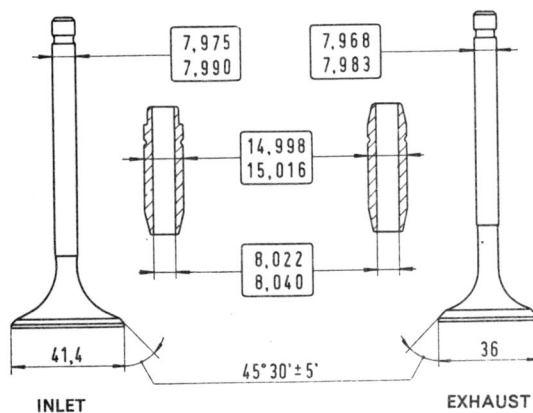

INLET   EXHAUST
FIG 1:21   Main data for valves and guides

Check the belt tension two or three times, turning the
engine about three quarters of a turn in the correct
direction between each check. Check also for correct
valve timing by seeing that the two marks on the gears
are opposite the corresponding pointers.

1:7 Timing belt

Renewal:

The timing belt should be changed at intervals of
25,000 miles (40,000 km) and in any event after not more
than 37,000 miles (60,000 km). Care should be taken
when handling the belt not to bend it to acute angles
lest it suffer damage.

1 Draw off part of the water in the cooling system and
   remove the radiator upper hose and the top section
   of the air duct. Remove the timing gear cover.

2 Check that the valve timing is correct and lock the
   camshaft gears by means of tool A.60319 (4 in **FIG
   1:25**). Apply the handbrake and engage bottom gear
   to prevent the engine turning.

3 Remove the lower protection plate from the engine.
   Loosen the alternator mounting screws and tensioner
   nut, and remove the alternator drive belt.

4 Slacken the timing belt idler locknuts (7 and 9 in
   FIG 1:25) and remove the toothed belt.

5 Fit the new belt and fix the spring balance tool
   A.95698 to the hole in the upper righthand arm of the
   idler (11 in **FIG 1:25**).

6 Apply a load of 60 lbs as shown and then tighten nuts
   7 and 9 to clamp the idler.

7 Check the belt tension two or three times, turning the
   engine about three quarters of a turn between each
   check.

Adjusting belt tension:

This may be done with the engine in the car as follows:
Repeat item 1 above, then use the spring balance as
described in 5 and 6.

Check the tension as previously instructed, replace the
parts removed and refill the cooling system.

Auxiliary drive shaft:

The shaft in the crankcase which drives the distributor
and the oil and fuel pumps is carried on two lined steel
bushes and is driven by the timing belt as shown at 7 in
FIG 1:26.

Spring-type belt stretcher:

Starting from engine No. 42577 a spring-type stretcher
has been fitted for adjustment of the timing belt tension.
The procedure for renewing a timing belt will be similar
to that outlined above, but note the following sequence
for tension adjustment (see **FIG 1:27**).

Loosen the nut 3 and screw 4. The spring 6 will now
cause the stretcher to tighten the belt.

Tighten up nut 3 and screw 4 to lock the stretcher.
Now unfasten and lock the stretcher two or three times,
each time turning the crankshaft half to three quarters of
a turn in its normal direction of rotation.

Check the timing of valves and auxiliary drive shaft.

It should be noted that the correct torque for the nut 3
is 34 lb ft (4.7 kg m).

1:8 Pistons and connecting rods

First, remove all carbon deposits from the crown of
the pistons and from the ring grooves. Extract the piston
rings and examine them for wear or cracks. Clean out the
oilways. Examine the movement of the piston on the
gudgeon pin to determine the amount of wear. The
gudgeon pin is a shrink fit in the little-end of the connecting rod and can be removed only in a hydraulic press
with the aid of the special mandrel A.60308 while the
piston/conrod assembly is supported on fixture A.95605.

Examine the big-end half-shells for scoring or excessive
wear. Hone out fine marks; otherwise replace the shells.
Insert the pistons in the cylinder bores and check for
clearance. This should be not less than .0031 nor greater
then .0039 inch measured at a point at right angles to
the gudgeon pin 2 inches below the piston crown.

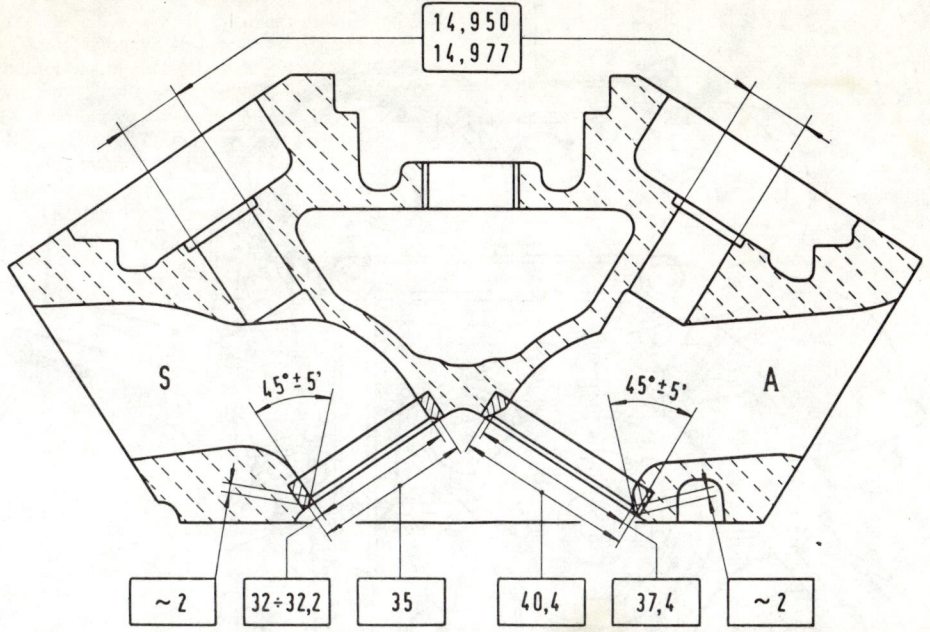

$$\boxed{\begin{array}{c} 14,950 \\ 14,977 \end{array}}$$

S   45°±5'   45°±5'   A

| ~ 2 | 32÷32,2 | 35 | 40,4 | 37,4 | ~ 2 |

FIG 1:22   Main data on valve seats and valve guides in cylinder head

Standard pistons are graded in three classes according to the effective diameter measured at 52.25 mm from the piston crown. They are also graded in three categories by the gudgeon pin bore. The letters and numbers of these grades are stamped on the underside of the piston bosses as shown in **FIG 1:29**.

Standard gudgeon pins are graded into three categories represented by numbers marked on the pins. The correct pin clearance in the piston boss must be .00031 to .00102

inch and this is obtained by using pins and pistons of the same numerical group.

Details of the dimensions of pistons and gudgeon pins will be found in **Technical Data**.

If cylinder wear necessitates a rebore or the fitting of a new liner, the work should be passed to an approved Fiat dealer with the necessary equipment. It is a specialist job necessitating skills and equipment outside the experience and capacity of the average owner-mechanic.

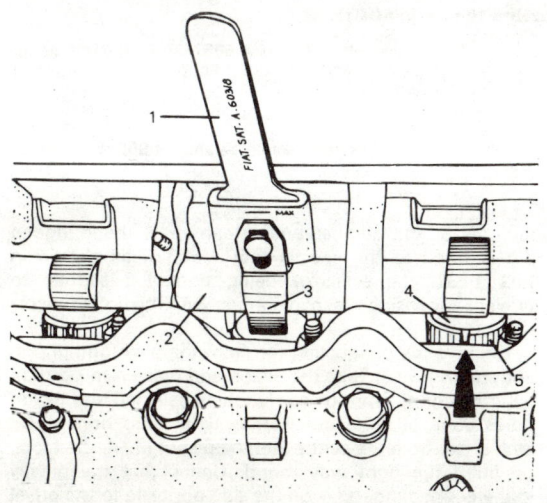

FIG 1:23   Tappet clearance adjustment, 1

Key to Fig 1:23   1 Tool A.60318   2 Camshaft   3 Cam
4 Cap plate   5 Tappet   Arrow shows slot in tappet for
extracting cap plate

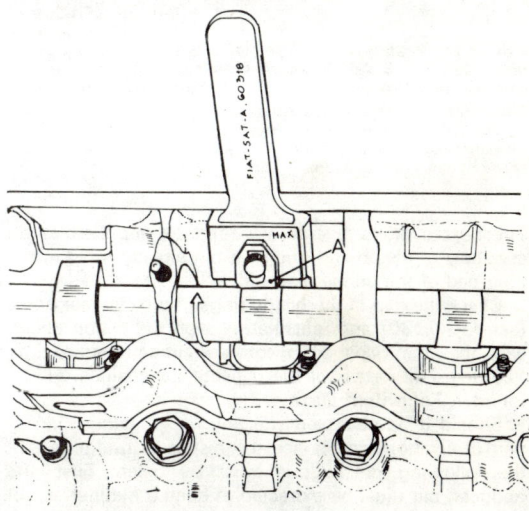

FIG 1:24   Tappet clearance adjustment, 2

Holding down the tappet with Tool A60318
To free the cap plate, rotate the camshaft in the direction of the
arrow until the cam meets the stop A on the tool

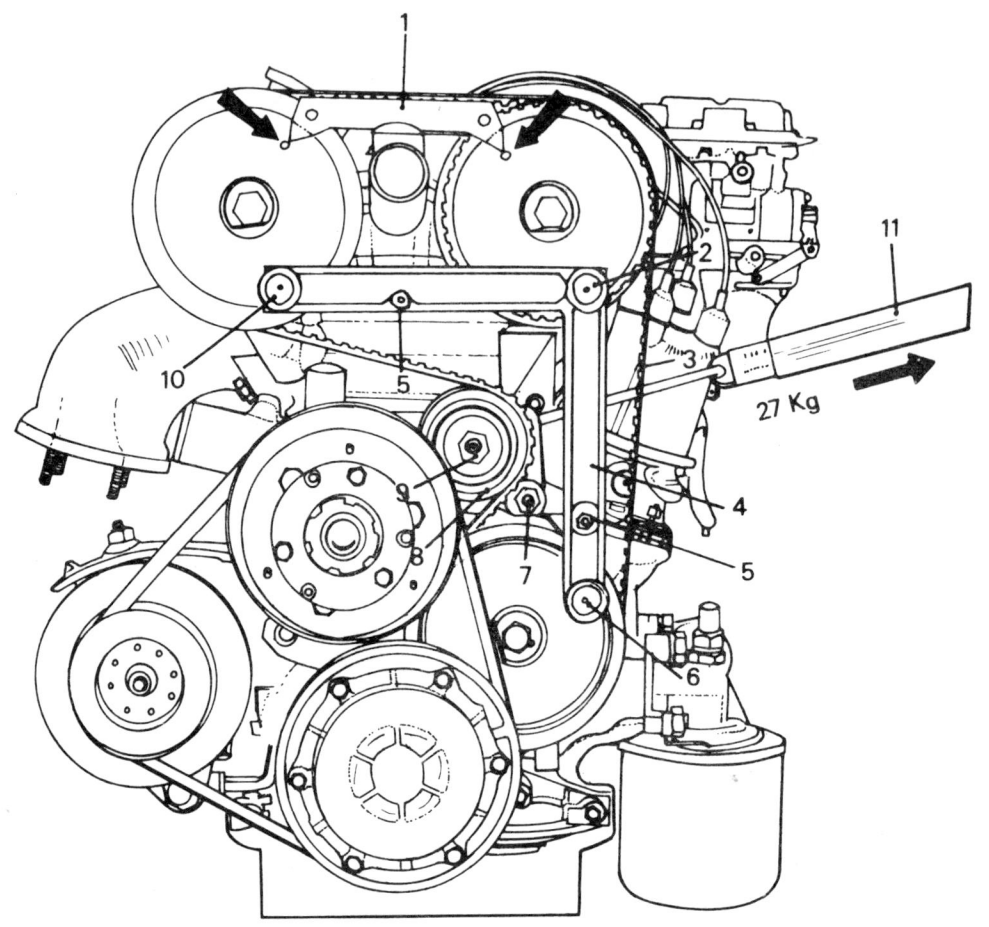

FIG 1:25   Fitting and adjusting the timing belt

Key to Fig 1:25   1 Fixed pointer   2 Inlet camshaft gear locking screw   3 Toothex belt   4 Tool A.60319   5 Fixing nuts for tool A.60319   6 Auxiliary drive shaft gear locking screw   7 and 9 Idler clamping screws and nuts   8 Idler pulley   10 Exhaust camshaft gear locking screw   11 Spring balance A.95698 used to adjust belt tension

The two arrows at the top of the illustration show the marks on the gears opposite their corresponding pointers on the cylinder head to give correct valve timing.
The arrow at the side shows the direction of the 27 kg (60 lb) load to be applied to the idler using spring balance **A.95698** to ensure correct timing belt tension.

The next oversize piston will then be supplied as an assembly of piston and gudgeon pin already fitted in the little-end of the connecting rod.

Check the gap of the piston rings in the cylinder bores (see **FIG 1:30**) and refit the rings on the piston taking care that the gaps are displaced circumferentially by 120 deg. Full details of the relevant dimensions will be found in **Technical Data.**

Should it be necessary, for any reason other than as part of a rebore, to replace the piston or gudgeon pin, the following precautions must be taken. First, the gudgeon pin must be extracted in such a manner as not to distort or bend the connecting rod. Secondly, the new piston must be of the same class as the one it replaces and thirdly, it must be of exactly the same weight.

The connecting rod, with cap removed, must then be heated in an oven up to 240°C, and left for about 15

minutes at this temperature. Meanwhile, the gudgeon pin is fitted to the special tool A.60325 as shown in **FIG 1:31**, the setscrew being tightened slightly to prevent expansion when in contact with the hot connecting rod.

Remove the connecting rod from the oven and grip it, upright, in a vice. Take the piston and place it in position over the connecting rod so that the small-end and piston bores coincide. Remember, the piston boss bore is .08 inch offset from the centre and the piston must, therefore, be fitted the right way round. Check that the oilway in the connecting rod is on the side opposite to the offset (see **FIG 1:32**).

Now insert the gudgeon pin on the mandrel into the piston bore and push home until the shoulder of the tool is in contact with the piston boss (see **FIG 1:33**), holding the piston hard against the small-end of the

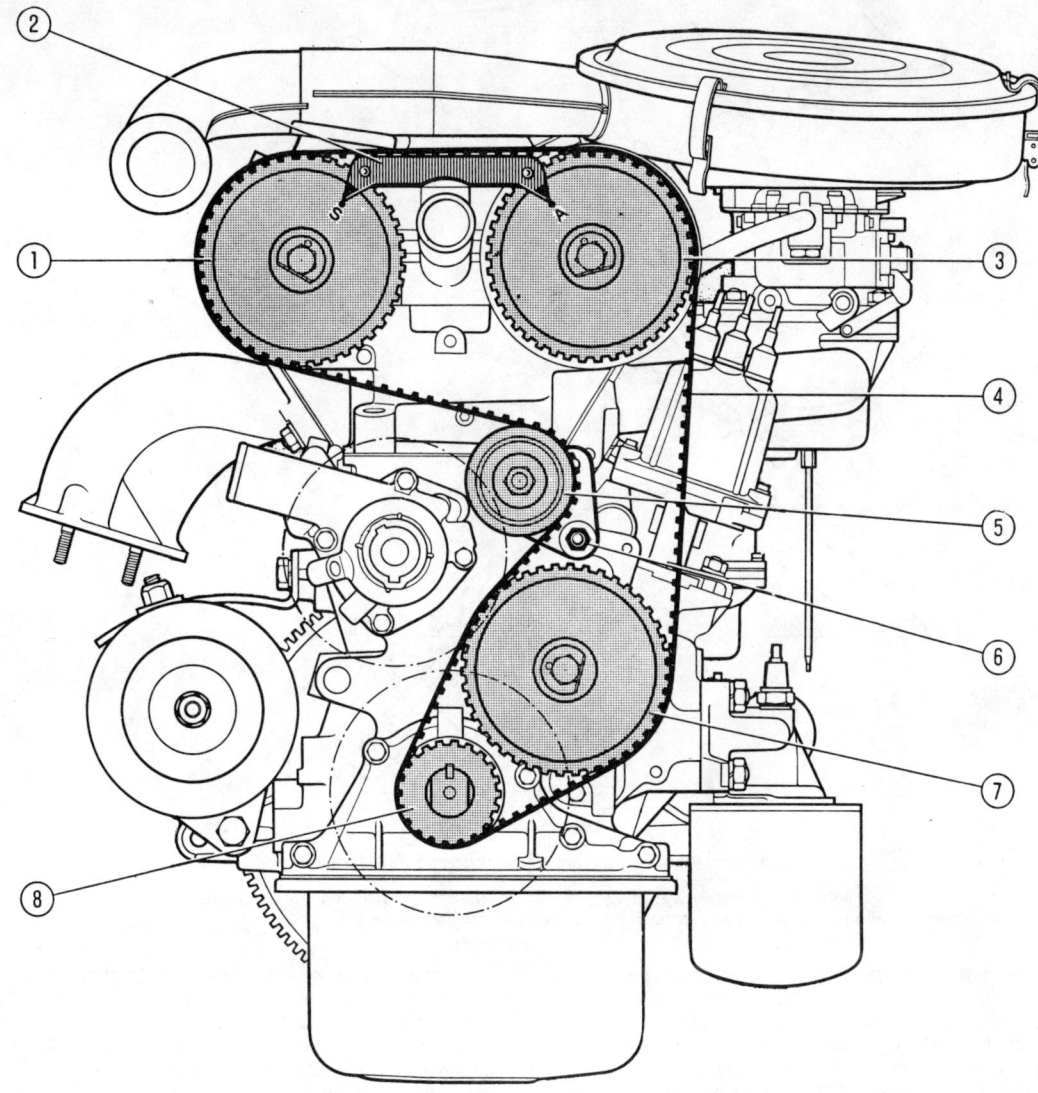

FIG 1 : 26 Timing gear and auxiliary drive

Key to Fig 1 : 26 1 Exhaust camshaft gear 2 Fixed pointer 3 Inlet camshaft gear 4 Toothed belt 5 Idler pulley 6 Idler clamping nut 7 Auxiliary drive shaft gear 8 Crankshaft gear

connecting rod so that it abuts against the connecting rod in the direction of insertion of the gudgeon pin.

Allow to cool, loosen the setscrew and withdraw the tool. The assembly must then be checked in a special fixture, A.95605, as shown in **FIG 1 : 34** and a torque wrench applied to the nut on the right and tightened to a torque of 9.4 lb ft. This corresponds to an axial thrust of 882 lb and the gauge will, naturally, indicate some deflection. On removal of the thrust, however, if the installation has been satisfactory, the gauge should return to its original reading showing that there has been no movement of the gudgeon pin within the small-end bushing.

1 : 9 Servicing the cylinder block

The cylinder block and crankcase is a single casting. Thoroughly degrease the unit and blow through all the oilways until they are clear. Inspect the cleaned block for any signs of damage or cracks and check that the upper face is clean, flat and free from corrosion marks.

Examine the surfaces of the bores. Remove fine scores, if present, with blue-back emerypaper and then check the diameter of the bore at three different levels and the bores themselves for circularity. This is done with a special dial gauge, A.96136, scaled in thousandths of a

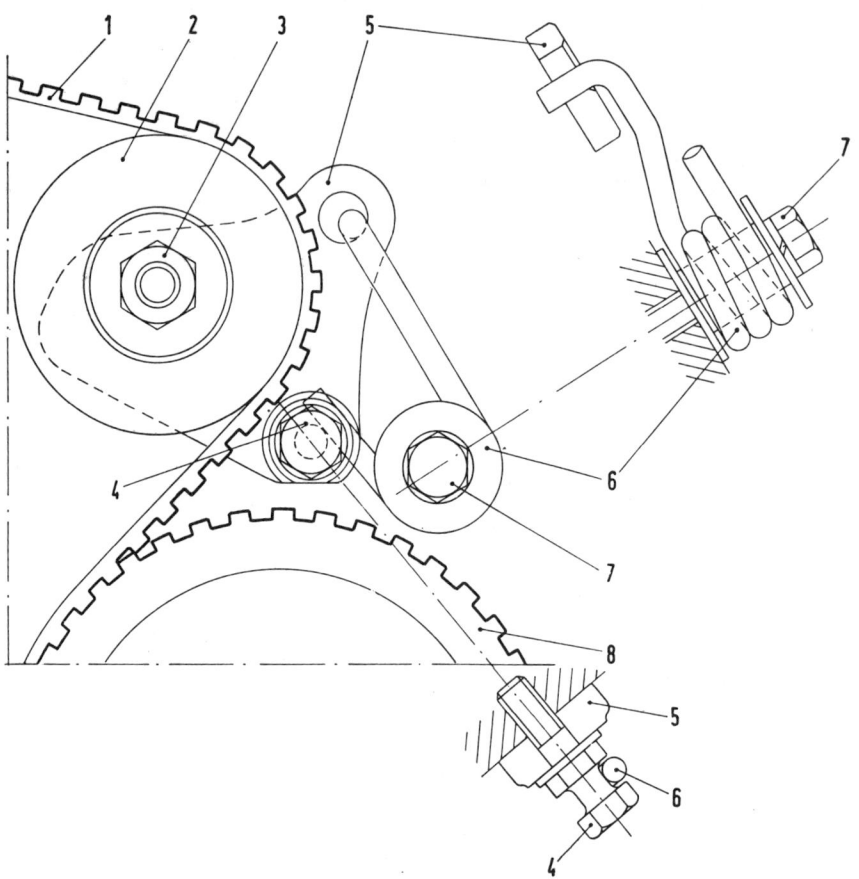

FIG 1:27 Fitting diagram of spring type belt stretcher

Key to Fig 1:27   1 Toothed belt   2 Pulley with double-row ballbearing   3 Belt stretcher pivot and spring end rest   5 Belt stretcher   6 Stretcher spring   7 Spring spacer retaining screw   8 Auxiliary drive shaft gear

millimetre. If there is any appreciable difference in the diameter—in excess of .01 mm—between top and bottom measurements, or the bore is in excess of .01 mm out of round, the bore will have to be honed to suit the next oversize of piston and new pistons fitted. If the wear in either direction exceeds .15 mm, reboring will be necessary or, if the rebore necessitates an increase in diameter over the limits for oversize pistons, a new dry liner will have to be fitted. All of these operations are specialist skills and should be entrusted to a Fiat service agent.

Note that the class of bore and piston may change from cylinder to cylinder in the same block and the bore classification letter is stamped on the sump joint face of the block adjacent to the cylinder.

Similarly, if the top surface of the block is not flat as checked on a surface plate, or with a straightedge and feeler gauge applied diagonally across the block, re-grinding will be necessary. This operation, too, should be entrusted to a Fiat agent.

1:10 Crankshaft and main bearings

Degrease and examine the crankshaft for signs of wear on the journals or cracks on the journals or webs. If any are present, install a new crankshaft. Slight scoring on the journals may be removed by honing with a very fine carborundum stone but, if the scoring is deep or the journals are more than .002 inch out of round, the shaft will have to be reground and undersize shells fitted. This, again, should be entrusted to a Fiat agent.

If possible, check the crankshaft for alignment by swinging it in a lathe between centres and then measuring the eccentricity at the five bearing surfaces. Alternatively, swing the crankshaft on knife edges by the two end journals over a surface plate and check the eccentricity on the three inner journals. This should not exceed .001 inch.

Thoroughly clean all oilways. It will be necessary to remove the end plugs in the webs to clear the diagonal oilways.

Examine the starter ring gear on the flywheel. If the teeth are broken or worn, the ring gear will need renewing. The ring in a shrink fit on the flywheel and has to be removed in a hydraulic press. The new ring is then heated to about 250°C and then pressed home on the flywheel. It sometimes helps if the flywheel is placed in a refrigerator for a while before fitting the ring gear.

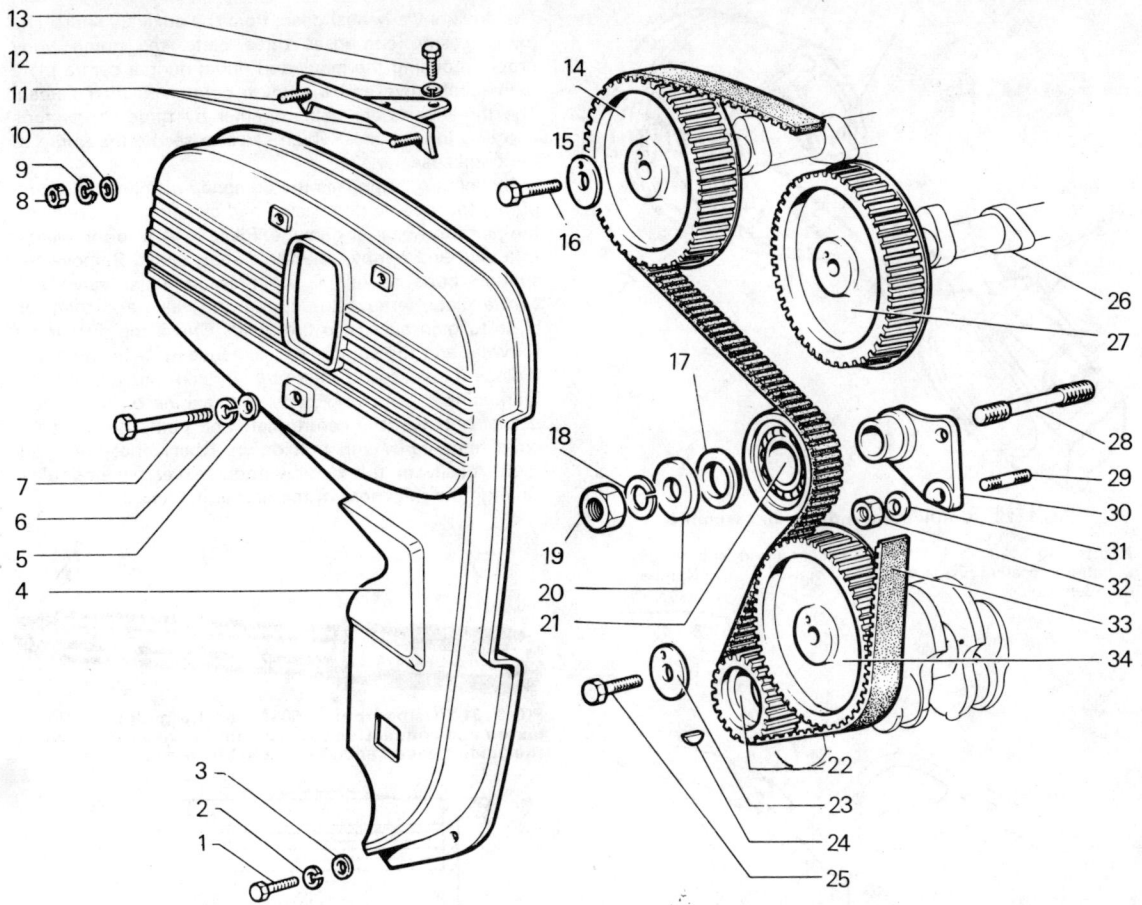

FIG 1:28   Diagram showing layout of timing belt and wheels

Key to Fig 1:28   1 Screw   **2** Split washer   **3** Washer   **4** Cover   **5** Washer   **6** Split washer   **7** Screw   **8** Nut
9 Split washer   **10** Washer   **11** Bracket   **12** Split washer   **13** Screw   **14** Camshaft pinion   **15** Retainer plate   **16** Screw
17 Spacer   **18** Split washer   **19** Nut   **20** Washer   **21** Idler pulley disc   **22** Crankshaft pinion   **23** Retainer plate   **24** Key
25 Screw   **26** Camshaft   **27** Camshaft drive pinion   **28** Stud   **29** Stud   **30** Bearing housing for tensioner   **31** Retainer ring
32 Nut   **33** Toothed belt   **34** Auxiliary shaft pinion

Examine the clutch plate facing on the flywheel and check for flatness. Remove any score marks with a smooth file, finishing off with a fine carborundum stone.

If any of the bearing shells are scored or badly worn, change them for the same class unless the journals themselves have been reground. The shell surface must never be scraped or adjusted in radius. To check wear, use the Plastigage method.

This comprises a short length of calibrated plastic thread inserted between the journal and shell during bearing assembly and the bearing cap bolts are tightened to a torque of 60 lb ft. Afterwards, the cap bearing and shell is removed and the degree of flattening of the thread measured with a special gauge, supplied as part of the Plastigage kit, to give the clearance. This should not exceed .0037 inch.

Finally, reassemble the crankshaft in the crankcase, tightening the cap bolts to a torque of 60 lb ft and check

that it rotates freely and without binding at any point. Check crankshaft end play with a dial gauge and, if it exceeds .014 inch, replace the thrust rings with oversize rings. These are available in standard (.090 to .092 inch) and oversize (.095 to .097 inch) thicknesses. When fitting, make sure that the grooves on one side of the rings face outwards.

Check that the metal-reinforced seals at each end, in the timing gear and rear crankcase covers, are in good condition and replace if at all suspect.

A sealed ballbearing is seated on the rear end of the crankshaft supporting the clutch shaft. Check for noise and, if necessary, extract with the ram puller, A.40006/1/3 and replace.

Finally, bolt the flywheel back onto the crankshaft (see **FIG 1:9**) tightening the bolts to a torque of 59 lb ft, with the reference mark on the periphery in line with crankpins 1 and 4. Turn while checking the degree of

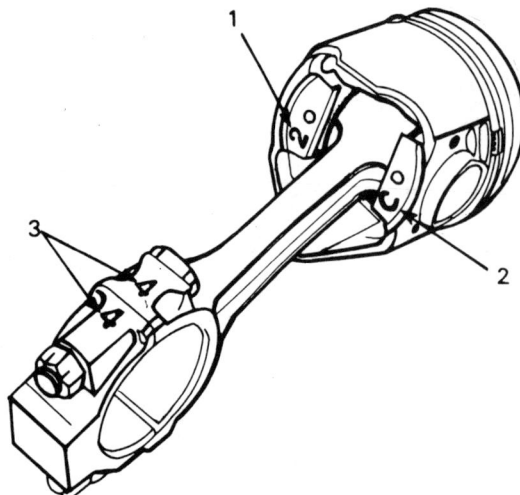

FIG 1 : 29   Connecting rod/piston assembly

Key to Fig 1 : 29   1 Number indicating gudgeon pin group
2 Letter indicating piston diameter group   **3** Number of
cylinder in block

The drive is via helical gears from the auxiliary shaft. The pump casing comprises three parts, the pump body proper, housing the gears and outlet duct, a centre plate with relief valve and a suction cone with filter screen. The three parts are held together by three short studs and two longer ones which serve to secure the pump to the crankcase.

Inspection comprises the complete dismantling of the pump, thoroughly degreasing and cleaning and checking the parts for wear or damage. Place it, shaft downwards, in a vice and remove the three short studs. Remove the suction cone to reveal the pressure relief valve and centre plate, remove the spring and valve and then the plate to gain access to the gears. Check the gear faces for wear and the spindle for clearance in its bushing and replace if necessary. Thoroughly clean and reassemble, lubricating the moving parts with engine oil. Fit a new gasket between the centre plate and pump body, fit the cone temporarily and bolt down. Check that the gears rotate easily in the body without excessive end play. Change the thickness of the gasket if necessary.

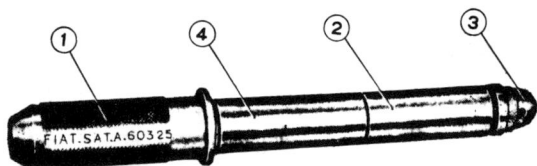

FIG 1 : 31   Using tool A.60325 to fit gudgeon pin in piston and connecting rod. The pin 4 is secured between the guide sleeve 2 and the handle 1 by the setscrew

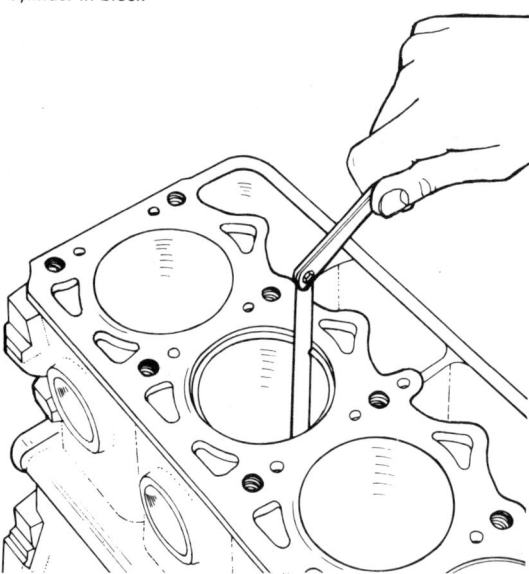

FIG 1 : 30   Measuring piston ring gap

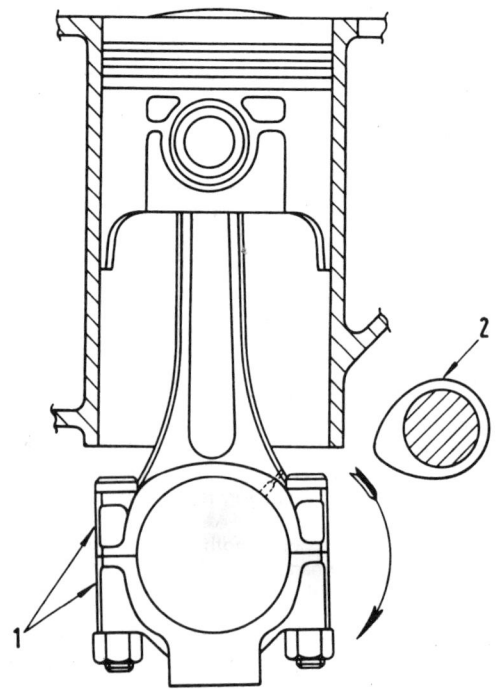

FIG 1 : 32 Piston assembly fitted to cylinder bore (viewed from front of engine)

Key to Fig 1 : 32   1 Cylinder number   **2** Auxiliary shaft

flange runout with a dial gauge placed about 1.25 inches from the shaft centre. The runout must not exceed .001 inch.

Always use new oilway plugs, checking that they are of the same weight as those they replace, driving them into position with tool A.86010 and staking them with a punch.

1 : 11 Oil pump

The oil pump is of conventional type·comprising a pair of spur gears rotating in opposite directions within a close fitting casing, the oil being transferred from one side to the other via the unmeshed teeth of the gears.

Remove the suction cone and thoroughly clean. Inspect the filter to ensure that it is not clogged. Clean the oil pressure relief valve and the spring, which should have a free length of 1.58 inches.

Reassemble and check that the gears move freely. Finally, reinstall in the crankcase and tighten down the bolts.

1:12 The oil filters

The fullflow oil filter consists of a metal container holding a cartridge-type filter element. A valve is provided to bypass the filter element if it should become choked.

The cartridge should be renewed every 6000 miles, access being obtained by removing the filter body with tool A.60312 as shown in **FIG 1:35**.

The filter support casting can be unbolted from the crankcase for the purpose of cleaning the inlet and outlet ducts. Attached to this casting is the transducer which closes a switch to illuminate the warning lamp on the dashboard if the oil pressure should fall below 9 lb/sq inch.

Centrifugal oil filter:

This is mounted on the forward end of the crankshaft and is shown in section in **FIG 1:36**. It consists mainly of a cover 1, a pulley hub 7, an annular deflector 2 and a regulating valve comprising the ball 4 and spring 5.

The oil arrives through two longitudinal channels in the crankshaft and is forced into the peripheral region of the filter by the deflector 2 where radial ribbing on the inner face of the pulley and cover collects the impurities and returns the oil to the centre of the assembly. From here, overcoming the action of the spring 5, it passes into the crankshaft, through the hollow fixing nut 3 and eventually returns to the sump through holes in the front bearing cap 14.

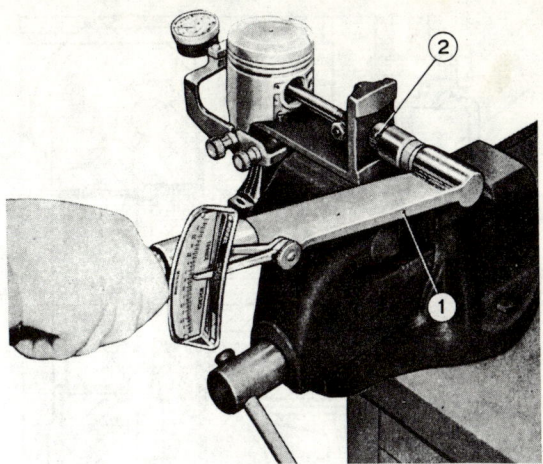

FIG 1:34   Testing gudgeon pin fit with tool A.95605

Key to Fig 1:34   1 Torque wrench   2 Nut on stem of tool

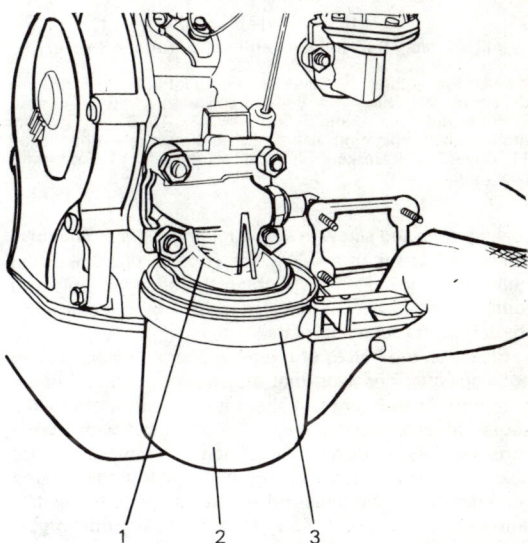

FIG 1:35   Removing the oil filter with tool A.60312

Key to Fig 1:35   1 Filter adaptor   2 Filter casing
3 Strap spanner A.60312

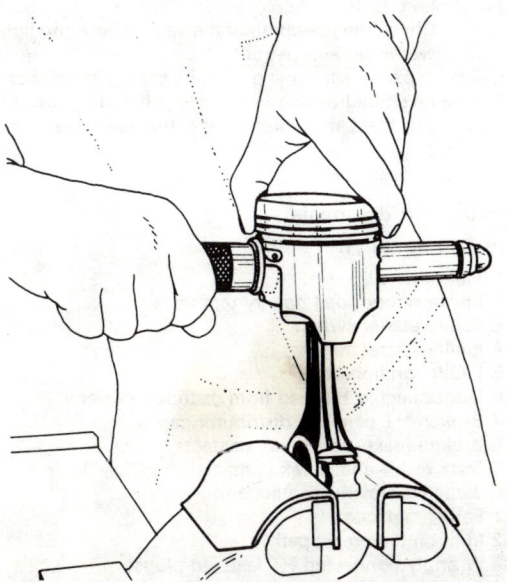

FIG 1:33   The gudgeon pin is in place when the shoulder of the tool is in contact with the piston boss

Regular cleaning of the centrifugal filter should be carried out at each service. Remove the front cover by taking out the six bolts, clean out the accumulated sludge and wash in paraffin before reassembling. If the sealing rings are at all doubtful they should be renewed and the ball 4 should be checked for freedom of movement.

1:13 Reassembling the engine

Reassembly of the engine is carried out by reversing the procedure for dismantling.

Fit first the auxiliary shaft into the front and rear bearing bushes which are a press fit in the block, after smearing the surfaces with clean engine oil. Then fit the

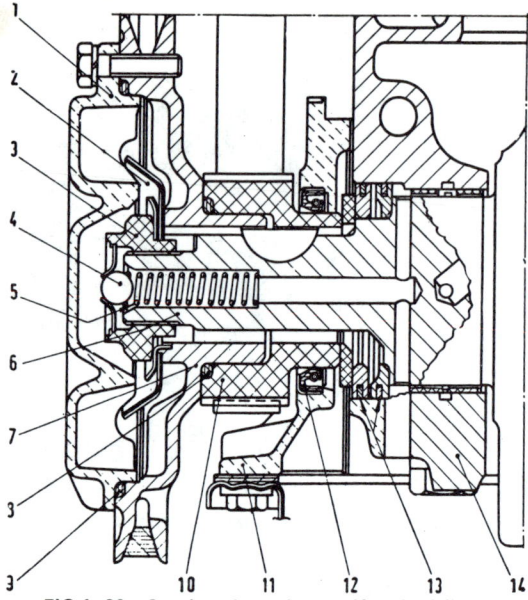

FIG 1:36 Section through centrifugal oil filter

Key to Fig 1:36   1 Cover of centrifugal filter   2 Annular deflector   3 Nut   4 Ball   5 Spring   6 Crankshaft   7 Pulley hub   8 and 9 O-rings   10 Driving gear for toothed belt operating camshafts and auxiliary drive shaft   11 Cover   12 Gasket   13 Oil seal rings   14 Front main bearing cap

sealing rings and screw in a new retaining plate. The drive pinion is fitted with a key which ensures that it is fitted only in the one position. Tighten the securing bolt to a torque of 31 lb ft (4.2 m kg) and lock by bending over the tab of the retaining plate.

Place the top halves of the main bearing shells in their housings after checking that they are in good condition, otherwise fit new ones. If there is any doubt about the degree of wear present, check the clearance with Plasti-gage and if it is more than .0059 inch (.15 mm), undersize bearings must be fitted and the crankshaft journals ground accordingly. Fit the thrust rings and complete the installation of the crankshaft (see **Section 1:10**) not forgetting to lubricate the bearing surfaces. The bearing cap bolts should be tightened progressively to 59 lb ft (8.2 kg m) all the while rotating the shaft. Fit new metal/rubber oil seals to the front and rear coverplates.

Fit the drive pinion for the toothed belt to the crankshaft and the centrifugal oil filter, tightening the nut securing the pulley to a torque of 80 lb ft (12.2 kg m).

Oil the pistons before inserting them in the top of the cylinder bores, noting that the cylinder number on the connecting rod faces the left when viewed from the front and the oil hole in the rod towards the auxiliary shaft.

The reference numbers stamped on the big-end caps will ensure that they are fitted in the correct positions. Fit new self-locking nuts and tighten to 37 lb ft (5.2 kg m).

When installing the oil pump, in order to ensure that the oil pump driving shaft is flush with the distributor drive shaft, the latter should be fitted temporarily complete with distributor and drive pinion before refitting the oil pump. Always use a new gasket.

Always use a new gasket when replacing the sump and tighten up the securing bolts diagonally to a torque of 5.8 lb ft (.8 kg m). Make sure while tightening that the gasket is not displaced.

Instructions for fitting the cylinder head and the toothed belt driving the camshafts were given earlier in **Sections 1:6** and **1:7**.

To refit the distributor:

Turn the engine until No. 1 piston is approaching TDC on the compression stroke, i.e. both valves closed, and the timing mark on the fan driving pulley is opposite the uppermost of the three reference lines on the drive housing.

Check that the contact breaker gap is between .016 and .018 inch, then turn the shaft until the rotor is opposite No. 1 contact in the cap (the cylinder numbers are marked in the cap) and the points about to open. Insert the shaft into the auxiliary drive gear and secure the distributor in place with its bracket and nut. Further instructions on timing the ignition will be found in **Chapter 3**.

Refit the fan and pulley on the water pump spindle, replace the alternator and fit the belt over the three pulleys. Adjust the belt tension before clamping the alternator to give $\frac{1}{2}$ inch movement in the middle of the longest run.

1:14 Refitting the engine in the car

This operation is a reversal of the removal procedure detailed in **Section 1:2** and should not present any special difficulty. Great care must be taken when re-coupling the engine to the transmission to ensure that the clutch shaft is correctly inserted in the slots in the driven plate (see **Chapter 5**).

When all the electrical cables have been reconnected and the carburetter controls re-established, the sump and the cooling system should be re-filled and the engine started. Check the operation of the various warning lights and for water, oil and petrol leaks.

After a period of running at full working temperature, the engine should be allowed to cool off and the cylinder head fixing bolts re-tightened and the valve clearances checked.

1:15 Fault diagnosis

(a) Engine will not start

1 Flat battery
2 Loose or corroded battery terminals
3 Faulty starter switch
4 Faulty starter motor
5 Faulty ignition coil
6 Disconnected HT lead from distributor to coil
7 Broken HT pencil in distributor cap
8 Broken make-and-break contacts
9 Dirty make-and-break contacts
10 Jammed moving contact arm
11 Faulty capacitor
12 Ignition timing slipped
13 Wrongly connected HT leads to plugs
14 Choked fuel line or carburetter jets
15 Faulty fuel pump

16 Empty fuel tank
17 Air lock in fuel line
18 Jammed starter pinion
19 Open circuit in starter solenoid circuit

(b) Engine fires then stalls

1 Idling out of adjustment
2 Choke not out
3 Slow-running adjustment too slow
4 Dirty or over-gapped plugs

(c) Engine runs but without power

1 Ignition timing slipped
2 Automatic advance feature not operating
3 Valve springs weak
4 Distributor cam worn
5 Make-and-break gap too small
6 Tappet clearances wrong
7 Burnt valves

(d) Engine runs but fades at speed with load

1 Fuel starvation through faulty pump
2 Fuel starvation through wrong needle valve setting
3 Fuel starvation through choked filters
4 Fuel starvation through choked line from tank

(e) Engine fires erratically on idling

1 Wrong idling jet setting
2 Faulty plugs
3 Weak valve spring on one or more cylinders
4 Wrong tappet adjustment on one or more cylinders

(f) Engine 'spits'

1 Water in carburetter
2 Leaking head gasket

(g) Engine 'pinks'

1 Wrong octane fuel
2 Ignition too far advanced

(h) Engine overheats

1 Shortage of water in radiator
2 Slipping fan and pump belt
3 Ignition too far retarded
4 Gasket blown in head

(j) Engine spits back into carburetter

1 Weak inlet valve spring
2 No clearance on inlet valve tappet
3 Sticking inlet valve stem
4 Transposed HT plug connections

NOTES

CHAPTER 2

THE FUEL SYSTEM

2:1 The fuel pump

The fuel pump which is mounted on the lefthand side of the engine, is a mechanically operated diaphragm-type driven by a cam on the auxiliary shaft. The exploded view given in **FIG 2:1** shows the component parts of the pump and will assist in servicing this item.

To remove the fuel pump, first disconnect the two fuel supply pipes, inlet from the tank and outlet to the carburetter, noting that if the former is not first released at the tank it will be necessary to plug the end to prevent loss of fuel by syphoning. Unscrew the two bolts securing the pump to the crankcase and lift off. Clean off all external dirt and oil and dismantle completely.

Wash all parts in fuel and see that all sludge is removed from the filter gauze and the casing. Examine the diaphragm for any trace of cracking or hardening and check that the return spring and that of the operating lever are not weak or deformed. Renew any defective parts.

When reassembling always use new seals and gaskets and smear the lightly with grease before fitting. Place the gaskets and insulator over the studs on the crankcase, then fit the pump, checking that the lever is free on its spindle and making correct contact with the face of the cam. Refit the fuel pipes.

Later cars may be fitted with an electric fuel pump.

2:2 The fuel tank

This is located on the righthand side of the boot as shown in **FIG 2:2** and holds 10 gallons of fuel including a reserve of a little more than one gallon which will be indicated by a fuel reserve warning lamp on the instrument panel.

To remove the tank, first disconnect the battery, then drain out all fuel from the drain plug. Remove the strap clamping screw, detach the strap and lift out the guard plate. Disconnect the fuel supply pipe and the breather pipe. Disconnect the earthing and fuel gauge cables. Remove the tank.

Reinstallation is a reversal of the above procedure.

2:3 Weber 34 DFH carburetter

This is the first of the types of carburetter which may be fitted to the 1438 cc engine. It has a double down-draught body with a differential throttle opening control whereby the secondary throttle is opened by a pneumatic device dependent upon the position of the primary throttle and the depression in the primary duct.

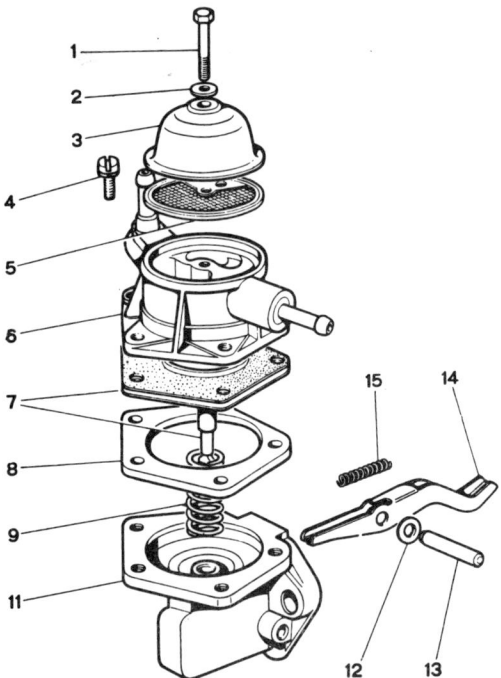

FIG 2:1   Exploded view of fuel pump

Key to Fig 2:1   1/2 Cover fixing screw and washer
3 Cover   4 Cover body screw   5 Filter   6 Upper body
7 Diaphragm   8 Spacer   9 Spring   10 Lower body
12/13 Washer and pivot pin   14 Operating lever   15 Lever
return spring

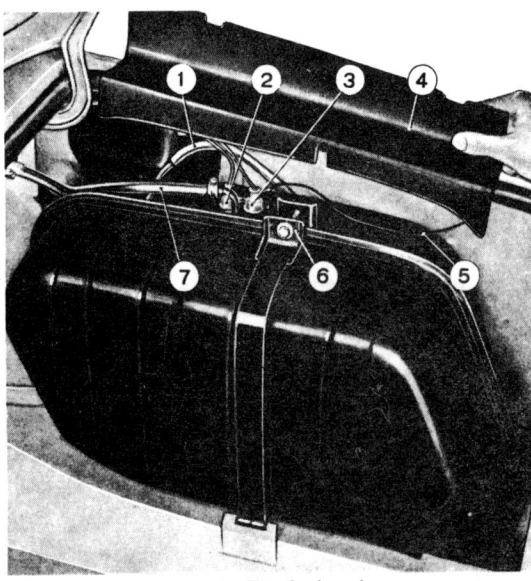

FIG 2:2   The fuel tank

Key to Fig 2:2   1 Breather pipe   2 Protecting cap of fuel
gauge cable terminal   3 Protecting cap over terminal of
fuel reserve warning-lamp cable   4 Guard plate   5 Earthing
cable of fuel gauge   6 Tank retaining strap   7 Fuel line
to fuel pump

Other main features include a diaphragm-type accelerator pump, a device for consuming fumes from the crankcase and an extra fuel device operating on both barrels when the throttles are wide open.

Reference to **FIGS 2:3** and **2:4** will assist in following a short description of the operation of this type of carburetter.

The fuel from the pump passes through the needle valve 1 and enters the float chamber 17 from which it flows through the main jets 16 to the well 15. It is now mixed with air entering through the air corrector jet 5 and the orifices of the emulsion tubes 14 and passing through the nozzles 9 it reaches the carburation area consisting of the auxiliary venturi 10 and choke 11. Also shown in this diagram is the enrichment circuit for the secondary barrel. Fuel from the float chamber passes through the calibrated orifice 3 and mixes with a controlled quantity of air entering through 4 and then flows through the duct and bush 6 and 7 through the nozzle 8 into the secondary barrel during high speed operation.

The sketch at bottom left shows the linkage controlling the opening of the secondary throttle. The tab 26 of the sector 22 mounted on the primary throttle shaft 23 makes contact at wide throttle openings with the arm 27 of the idle lever 21, thus freeing the lever 28 mounted on the secondary throttle spindle and permitting its operation as illustrated in **FIG 2:4**.

The two small drawings on the right of **FIG 2:3** show the device for aspirating gases from the crankcase. This consists of a rotating shutter 31 fixed on the primary throttle spindle 23 which admits the gases to the area beneath the throttle butterfly 24 through the inlet tube 29 and the groove 32. When the throttle is in the idling position a calibrated quantity is still admitted through the orifice 30.

Progressively opening the throttle 24 in **FIG 2:4** causes the rod 39 on the end of the free lever 40 to close the valve 36 in the vapour discharge duct 35 so that when the primary throttle is fully open the depression in the primary duct acting through the passage 49, lifts the diaphragm 50 and by means of the rod 51 opens the secondary throttle.

Accelerator pump (see FIG 2:5):

The action of opening the throttle 41 moves the cam 62 against the roller on the end of the lever 61 and so presses in the diaphragm 60 which injects a supply of fuel into the carburetter primary duct through the passage 63, delivery valve 55 and pump jet 56. The spring 59 absorbs rapid throttle openings and prolongs fuel delivery.

Any excess fuel delivered by the pump returns to the float chamber through the bush 78.

Starting (see FIG 2:6):

When the choke control is pulled fully out for starting the engine from cold the lever 65 moves into the position A causing the choke butterflies 64 to block the air intakes and at the same time partially opens the primary throttle 24 through the rod and lever 67 and 68. The choke 10 consequently delivers the rich mixture required for starting.

As soon as the engine is running the depression acting on the diaphragm 69 partially opens the choke butterflies, thus permitting the engine to run on a rich mixture.

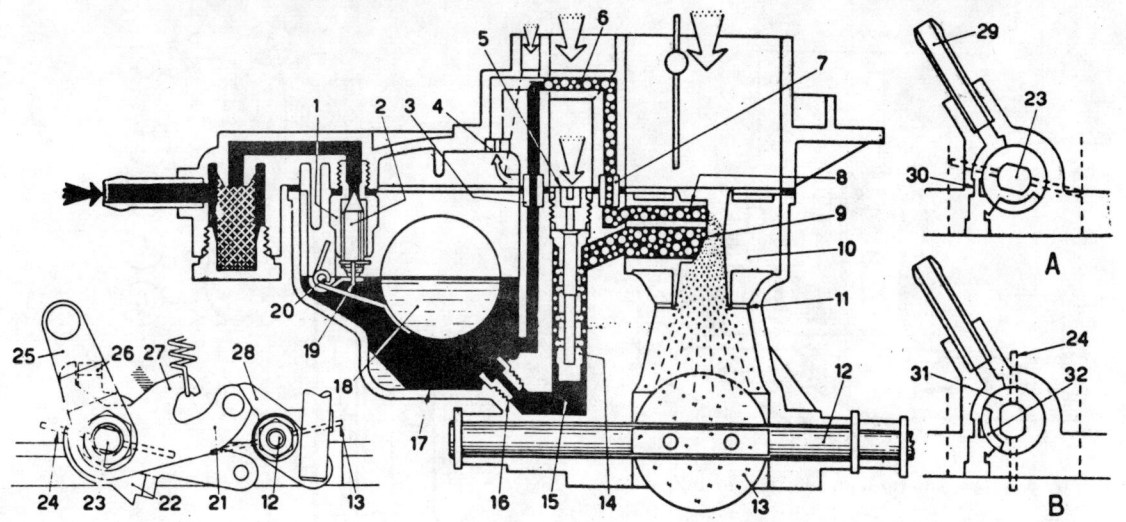

FIG 2:3   Section through carburetter. Weber 34 DHS end view

Key to Fig 2:3, 2:4, 2:5 and 2:6   1 Needle valve   2 Needle   3 Calibrated orifice   4 Calibrated orifice   5 Air corrector jet   6 Enrichment duct   7 Calibrated orifice   8 Enrichment nozzle   9 Main nozzle   10 Auxiliary venturi   11 Main venturi   12 Throttle spindle, secondary   13 Throttle valve, secondary   14 Emulsion tube   15 Fuel well   16 Main jet   17 Float chamber   18 Float   19 Float arm   20 Float spindle   21 Idle lever   22 Sector   23 Primary shaft   24 Primary throttle   25 Throttle control lever   26 Tab   27 Hook   28 Lever   29 Tube   30 Calibrated orifice   31 Rotating valve   32 Slot   33 Calibrated orifice   34 Idle jet   35 Duct   36 Valve   37 Duct   38 Duct   39 Operating rod   40 Lever   41 Lever   42 Progression holes   43 Idle supply orifice   44 Idle volume control screw   45 Duct   46 Duct   47 Idle jet   48 Calibrated air orifice   49 Depression duct   50 Diaphragm   51 Operating rod   52 Depression duct   53 Progression holes   54 Lever   55 Check valve   56 Delivery nozzle   57 Check valve   58 Spring   59 Spring   60 Diaphragm   61 Lever   62 Cam   63 Duct   64 Choke valves   65 Lever   66 Spring   67 Link   68 Lever   69 Diaphragm chamber   70 Tab   78 Idle supply orifice

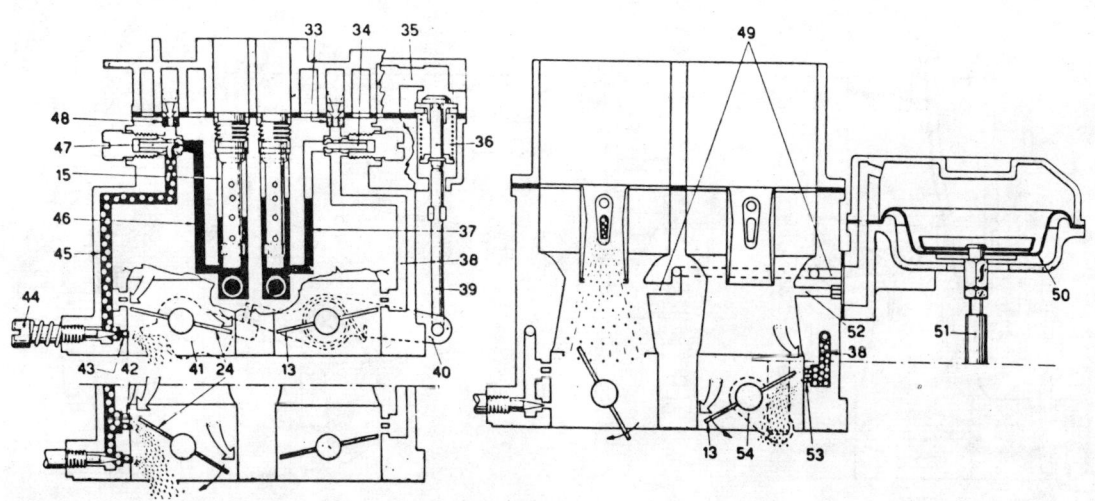

FIG 2:4   Section through carburetter, side view

Key to Fig 2:4   See Key to Fig 2:3

FIAT 124 SPORT

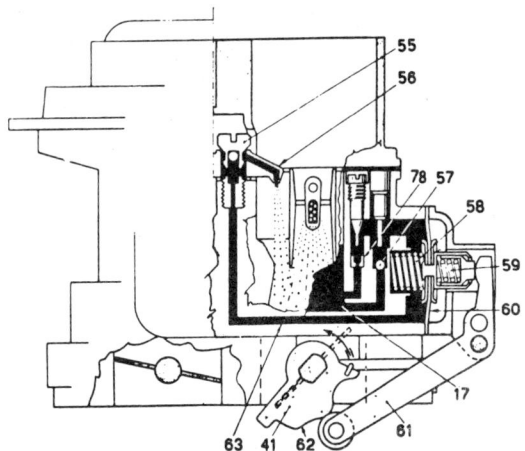

FIG 2:5 Section through acceleration pump

Key to Fig 2:5 See key to Fig 2:3

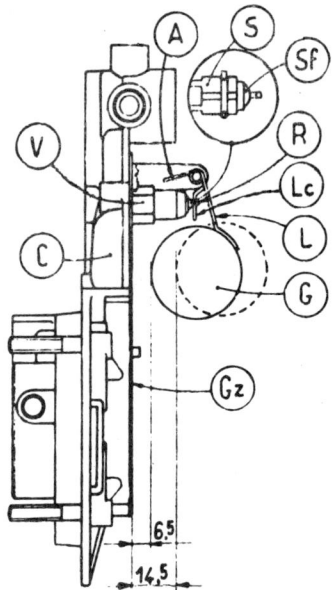

FIG 2:7 Adjusting the float level

Key to Fig 2:7 **A** Float mounting arm **C** Carburetter cover **G** Float **Gz** Gasket **L** Float mounting plate **Lc** Spring plate **R** Return spring hook **S** Needle **Sf** Ball **V** Needle valve

As the engine warms up the choke control knob should be progressively pushed in until, when full working temperature is reached, the lever 65 is in position B when the choke is fully open and the throttle returns to its normal idling position.

The speed of the engine when idling is controlled by means of the adjusting screw 44 in **FIG 2:4**.

2:4 Setting the float level

In the event of trouble which is believed to be due to an incorrect fuel level in the float chamber, and before making any adjustments make sure that the float is of the correct weight (11 gr), that it is not dented or pierced and that it is able to revolve freely on its spindle. Check also that the needle valve V is firmly screwed in and that the ball on the needle seats securely in its housing (see **FIG 2:7**).

Hold the carburetter cover C vertically as shown so that in this position the spring plate of the float will be in light contact with the ball, and the distance between the float and the cover must be 6.5 mm when the gasket is firmly in position. From this position the float should be free to move 8 mm to its fully open position and this movement should be ensured by suitably bending the arm A. Check that the hook R allows free movement of the needle.

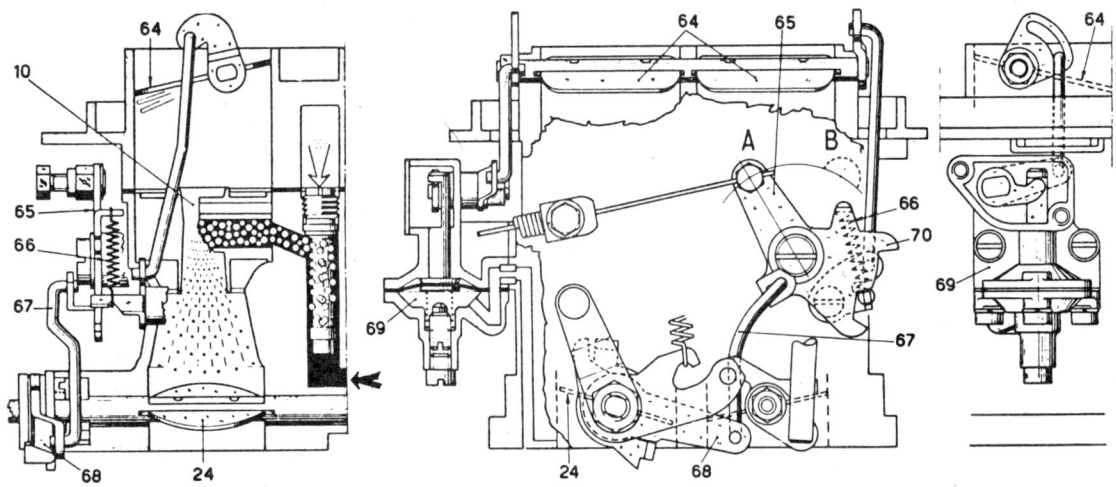

FIG 2:6 Sectional diagram showing controls at 'START' position

Key to Fig 2:6 See Key to Fig 2:3

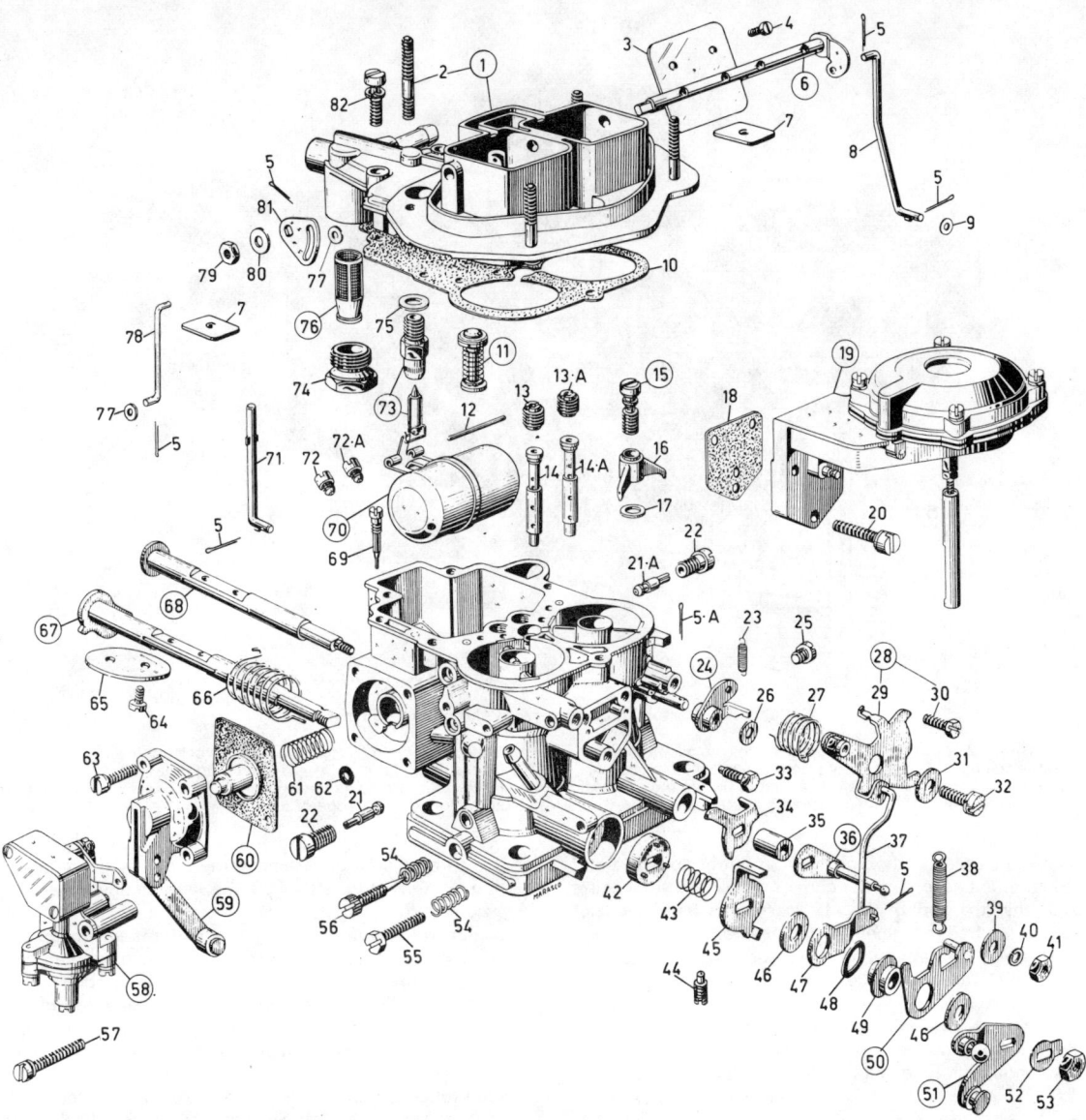

FIG 2:8 Exploded view of Weber 34 DHS carburetter

Key to Fig 2:8   1 Carburetter cover including: 2 Stud   3 Starter valve   4 Fixing screw   5 Splitpin for 8   6 Starter valve spindle   7 Dust excluder   8 Starter operating rod   9 Washer   10 Carburetter cover gasket   11 Float chamber breather valve 12 Float spindle   13 Primary air corrector jet   13A Secondary air corrector jet   14 Primary emulsion tube   14A Secondary emulsion tube   15 Pump control valve   16 Pump jet   17 Pump jet gasket   18 Gasket for 19   19 Automatic advance device   20 Fixing screw   21 Primary idle jet   21A Secondary idle jet   22 Idle jet carrier   23 Starter valve spring   24 Control lever for 8   25 Inspection screw for secondary idle jet   26 Washer for 24   27 Spring for 24   28 Starter control lever complete with: 29 Lever   30 Cable fixing screw   31 Washer for 29   32 Fixing screw for 29   33 Outer cable fixing screw   34 Primary spindle operating lever   35 Distance piece   36 Secondary valve control lever   37 Fast idle operating rod   38 Spring for 50 39 Washer for secondary spindle   40 Spring washer   41 Nut   42 Shutter   43 Spring   44 Secondary valve adjusting screw   45 Primary spindle control lever   46 Washer for 50   47 Fast idle control lever   48 Friction washer   49 Bush for 50 50 Lever   51 Throttle control lever   52 Lockwasher   53 Nut   54 Adjustable screw spring   55 Primary valve adjustable screw 56 Carburetter idle adjustable screw   57 Fixing screw for 58   58 Overchoking control   59 Pump cover   60 Pump diaphragm 61 Pump spring   62 O-ring   63 Fixing screw for 59   64 Fixing screw for 65   65 Butterfly valve   66 Primary spindle return spring   67 Primary spindle   68 Secondary spindle   69 Plug for pump discharge duct   70 Float   71 Operating rod for 11 72 Main primary jet   72A Main secondary jet   73 Needle valve   74 Filter plug   75 Gasket for 73   77 Washer for 78 78 Operating rod for 58   79 Nut   80 Serrated washer for starter spindle   81 Control lever for 58   82 Carburetter cover fixing screw

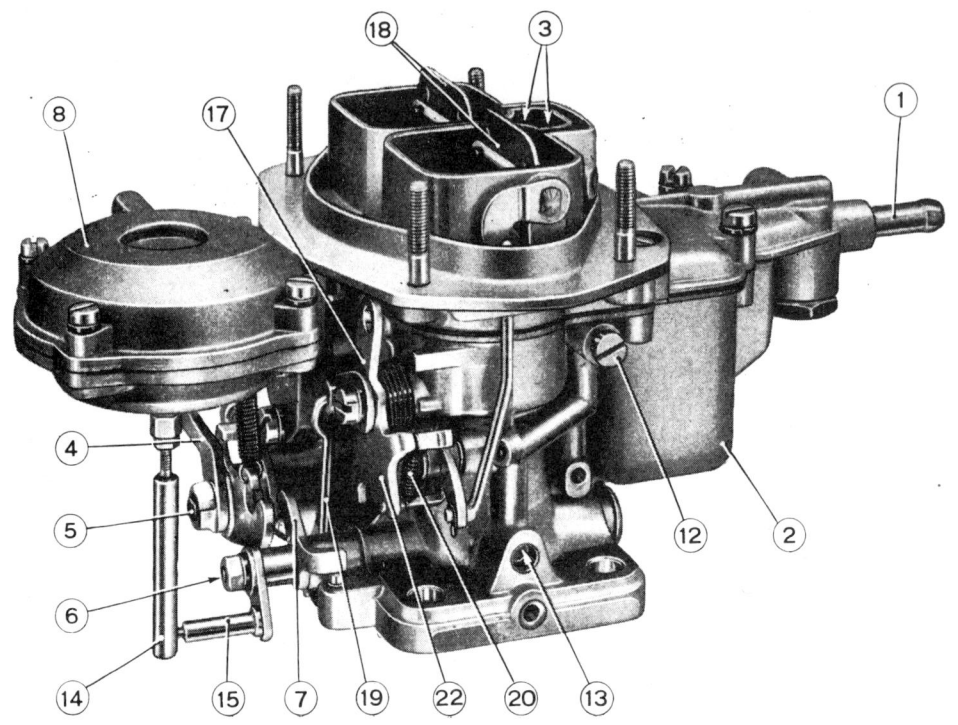

FIG 2:9 Carburetter seen from the choke control side

Key to Fig 2:9   1 Fuel line connection   2 Float chamber   3 Air corrector jet   4 Differential throttle control lever   5 Primary throttle spindle   6 Secondary throttle spindle   7 Secondary throttle differential control lever   8 Diaphragm device   12 Idling jet   13 Progression holes   14 Diaphragm device rod   15 Secondary throttle spindle actuating lever   17 Choke control lever   18 Choke valves   19 Primary throttle starting link   20 Choke valve return spring   22 Lobe of lever (17)

If the closed position of the float is not correct, bend the tongue L to obtain the correct measurement, making sure that the spring plate Lc is smooth and does not hinder the free movement of the needle.

Replace the carburetter cover ensuring that the float can move easily and does not rub on the walls of the float chamber.

The float level should be checked whenever a new float is fitted or the needle valve changed. The gasket also should be renewed at the same time.

2:5 Weber 34 DHS carburetter

This model is fitted to later 1438 cc engines and is only very slightly different from the type 34 DFH described above. An exploded view of the complete carburetter is given in **FIG 2:8** and any changes in specification will be found in **Technical Data** at the end of this Manual.

Overchoking when starting up is prevented by a vacuum operated device which provides automatic opening of the choke throttle plates.

The two external views of the carburetter at **FIGS 2:9** and **2:10** show the position of the various jets and adjusting screws.

2:6 Dismantling and reassembly

To dismantle the carburetter, first remove the air cleaner, disconnect the fuel line and uncouple the choke

and throttle controls. Remove the blow-by gas connection at the carburetter. Loosen and remove the nuts securing the carburetter to the intake manifold and withdraw the carburetter together with the sealing gasket. Transfer the carburetter to the bench. Remove the cover to the float chamber and drain free from petrol.

Thoroughly wash the body with a cleaning fluid and dry off. (Carbon tetrachloride is probably the most effective and safest fluid to use). Working on a bench covered with clean paper, proceed to dismantle the carburetter, remove all jets and blow through the ducts with dry compressed air. Swill all small parts with cleaning fluid and dry. Examine all parts for signs of wear or damage and replace as necessary. Reassemble using new gaskets throughout, checking that the jets are unobstructed. Do not insert metal wire or probes into jets or the bore may be damaged, upsetting the calibration.

When finally reassembled, lubricate the bearings with a spot of light oil and then reassemble on the manifold, applying a little sealant on the gaskets to ensure that the joints are leakproof. Couple up the throttle and choke controls, fit the blow-by gases tube, connect the fuel lines and, finally, install the air cleaner.

2:7 Routine maintenance

Routine maintenance is confined to periodical cleaning of the carburetter, removing all dirt and scale from the float chamber and blowing out main, pilot and starting

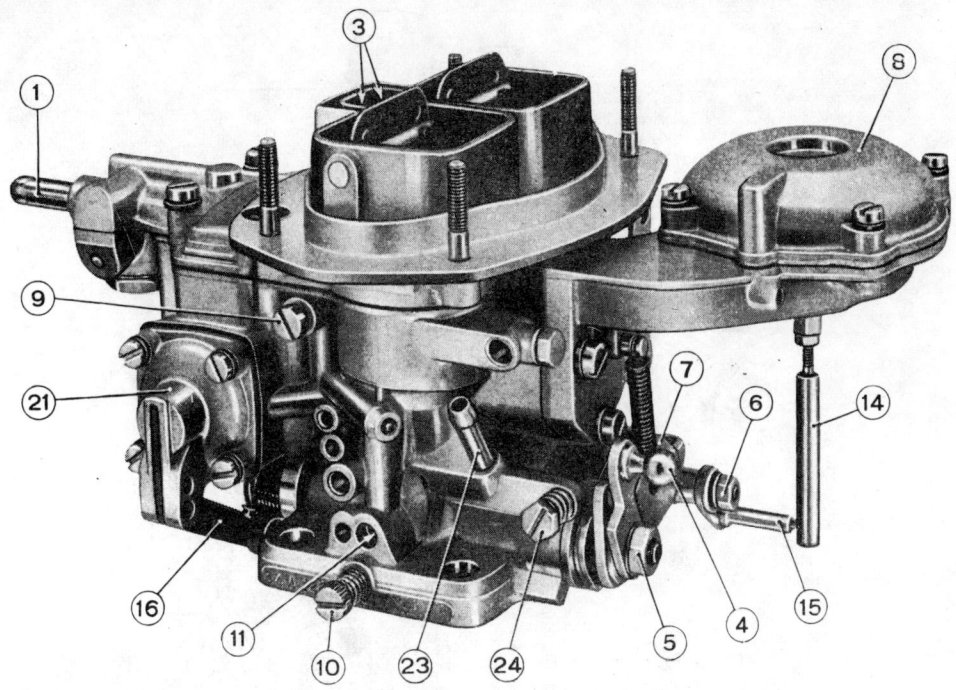

FIG 2:10 Carburetter seen from pump side

Key to Fig 2:10   1 Fuel line   3 Air corrector jets   4 Differential throttle opening lever   5 Primary throttle spindle   6 Secondary throttle spindle   7 Secondary throttle differential opening control lever   8 Diaphragm device   9 Idling jet   10 Idling jet adjusting screw   11 Progression holes   14 Diaphragm device rod   15 Secondary throttle control lever   16 Accelerator pump lever   21 Accelerator pump   23 Crankcase gas suction connection   24 Slow-running adjustment screw

jets. To clean the strainer, unscrew and take off the plug adjacent to the fuel line connection on the float chamber, remove the strainer and blow clear. If it is distorted or torn, replace.

If the carburetter tends to flood, check that the needle valve is in good order and then check the float level as described in **Section 2:4**.

2:8 Tuning for slow-running

Start the engine and run until it has reached normal working temperature. Open the throttle by means of the slow-running adjustment screw 24 in **FIG 2:10** until the engine is running smoothly.

By operating the idling jet adjusting screw 10 bring the engine to its maximum speed at the existing throttle opening and then close the slow-running screw by half a turn. Again reset the idling screw for maximum speed and continue this sequence until the engine is turning at its slowest speed consistent with smooth running. This gives the correct setting for the idling jet and the throttle stop may be opened slightly to give a normal tickover speed of about 600 rev/min.

2:9 Twin carburetter installation

All cars that are fitted with a 1608 cc engine have, as their standard equipment—two dual barrel carburetters of Weber type 40 IDF 10/11. This model is very similar to

the types 34 DFH or 34 DHS described earlier and is shown in exploded diagram of **FIG 2:11**. Details of jet sizes and choke dimension will be found in **Technical Data** and provided that these are correct the only item of servicing apart from cleaning is the synchronization of the twin carburetters. This is done by observing the following procedure:

Remove the air cleaner and disconnect the accelerator link from the lever 21 which controls all four throttle butterflies. Operate this lever by hand to make sure that the shafts are working freely and returning to their fully closed position.

Slacken off the locknuts of the four air correction screws 48 and fully close the four screws to cut off the air correction, then secure the locknuts.

Close up fully the four idle mixture metering screws 41, then turn them back by one complete turn.

Turn back the idle adjusting screw 4 in **FIG 2:12** and the screw 5 adjusting the tuning of the carburetters, then press down on the lever 1 in order to compress the spring of the reaction rod 6 and turn the screw 5 until it contacts the arm of the lever 7 which controls the throttle butterflies in the rear carburetter.

Now bring the idle running setscrew 4 into contact with the main lever 1 and give it one more complete turn.

Start up the engine and by means of a suitable instrument such as Synchrotest check the four carburetter throats for an even intake depression. If on any one

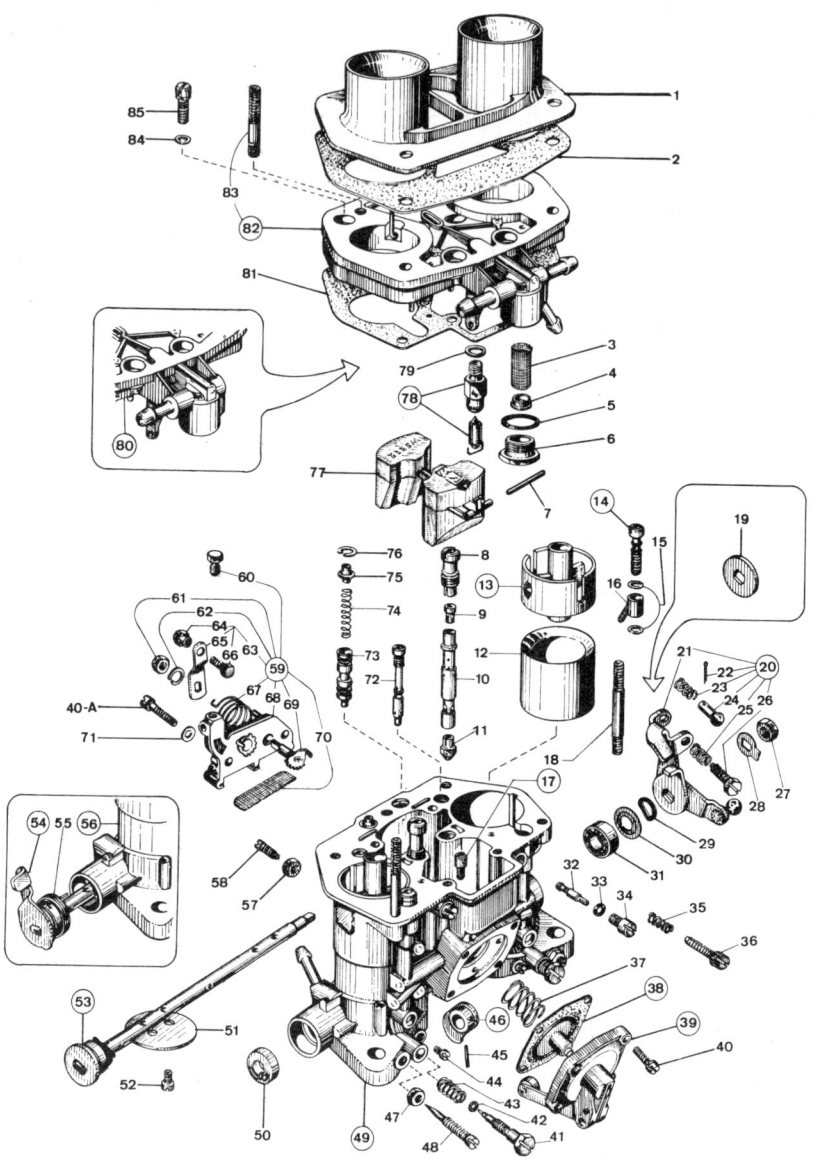

FIG 2:11 Exploded view of Weber 40 IDF 10/11 carburetter

Key to Fig 2:11   1 Air horn   2 Gasket for 1   3 Filter   4 Plug for 3   5 Gasket for 4   6 Filter inspection plug   7 Float fulcrum pin   8 Emulsion jet carrier   9 Air restrictor jet   10 Emulsion tube   11 Main jet   12 Venturi   13 Secondary venturi   14 Pump inlet valve   15 Gasket for 16   16 Pump jet   17 Pump inlet and outlet valve   18 Screw   19 Washer   20 Butterfly control complete with: 21 Lever   22 Splitpin   23 Spring for pin   24 Pin   25 Spring for screw   26 Screw   27 Fixing nut   28 Locking washer   29 Corrugated washer   30 Spring washer   31 Ball bearing   32 Idling jet   33 Gasket for idling jet carrier   34 Idling jet carrier   35 Spring for adjusting screw   36 Adjusting screw   37 Diaphragm return spring   38 Diaphragm   39 Pump cover   40 Fixing screw   40A Starter cover fixing screw   41 Idling adjusting screw   42 Gasket   43 Spring   44 Progression hole inspection plug   45 Cam locking pin   46 Pump operating cam   47 Nut for air adjusting screw   48 Air adjusting screw   49 Carburetter body   50 Sealing plug   51 Butterfly valve   52 Fixing screw   53 Main spindle   54 Main spindle   55 Valve return spring   56 Carburetter body   57 Nut for diffuser fixing screw   58 Diffuser fixing screw   59 Starter control complete with: 60 Outer cable fixing screw   61 Lever fixing nut   62 Spring washer   63 Lever complete with: 64 Cable fixing nut   65 Lever   66 Cable fixing screw   67 Lever return spring   68 Starter cover   69 Starter control spindle   70 Filter   71 Washer for fixing screw   72 Starter jet   73 Starter valve   74 Spring   75 Starter spring guide and stop   76 Spring ring and stop for spring   77 Float   78 Needle valve   79 Gasket   80 Carburetter cover   81 Gasket   82 Carburetter cover complete with: 83 Stud   84 Washer for 85   85 Cover fixing screw

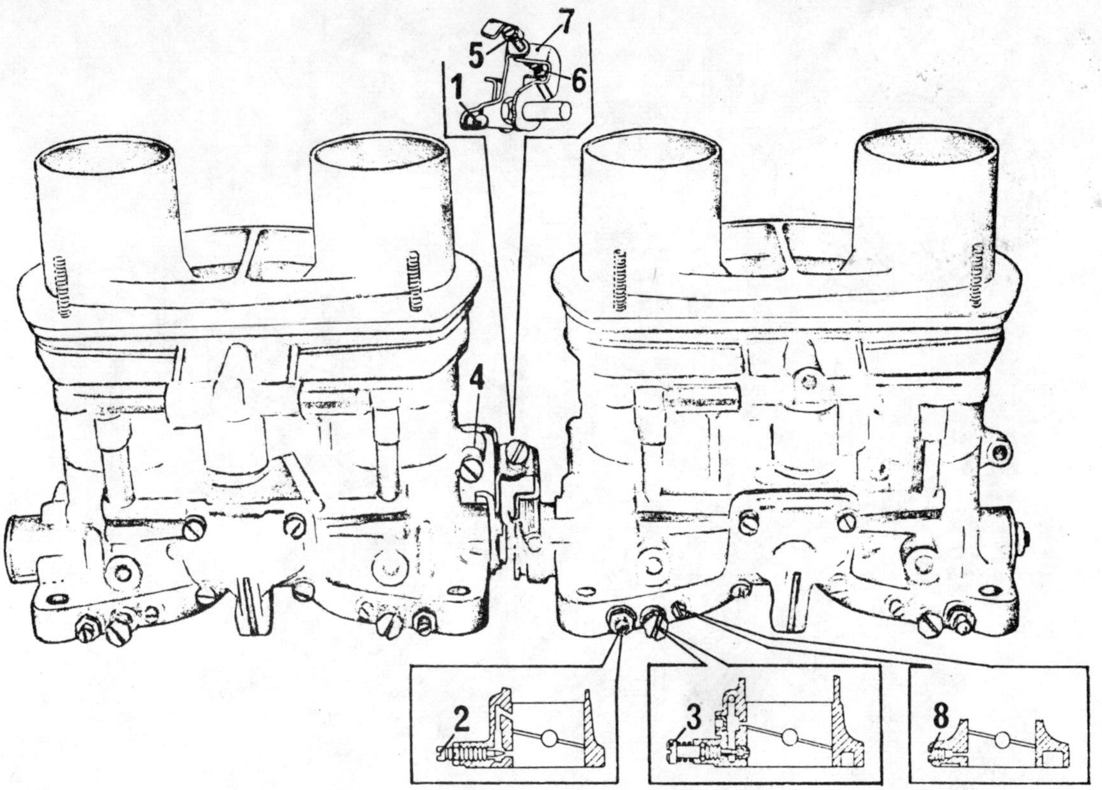

FIG 2:12   Synchronizing twin carburetters

Key to Fig 2:12   1 Throttle control lever   2 Air correction screw   3 Idle mixture metering screw   4 Idle running setscrew
5 Carburetter link screw   6 Reaction rod spring   7 Rear carburetter throttle control lever   8 Vacuum outlet plug

carburetter it is found that one throat shows a lower value than the other, turn back the air correction screw 2 until they are equal and secure the locknut.

Repeat this operation on the other carburetter but note that one of the air correction screws on each carburetter must remain closed.

Next it is necessary to obtain the same vacuum reading at all four air intakes by means of the screw 5 which controls the linkage between the two carburetters.

Turn the idle running setscrew 4 to bring the engine speed to approximately 900 rev/min and adjust the idle mixture metering screws to obtain the best mixture in each cylinder. A further check with the Synchrotest will show if the four throats are still showing the same vacuum and if they are not, the adjustment given above should be repeated as necessary.

Reconnect the accelerator link to the lever 1 and refit the air cleaner.

If it is found that the sparking plugs become fouled in the course of a lengthy operation it may be helpful to change plugs from Champion MGY to N9Y as a temporary measure.

2:10 Adjusting float level

The procedure for setting the float level on these carburetters is the same as that described earlier, but

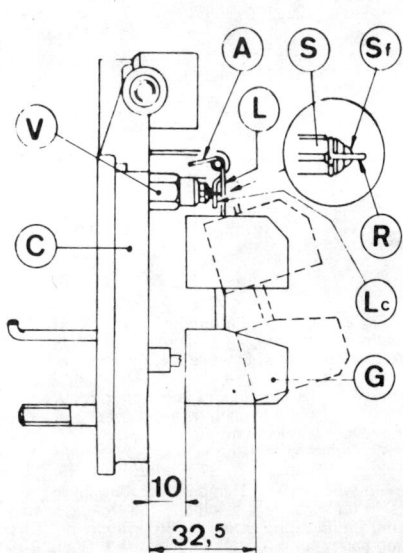

FIG 2:13   Setting float level on type 40 IDF 10/11

Key to Fig 2:13   A Tab   C Cover   G Float   L Float arm   Lc Needle arm   R Hook   S Needle   St Ball   V Needle valve

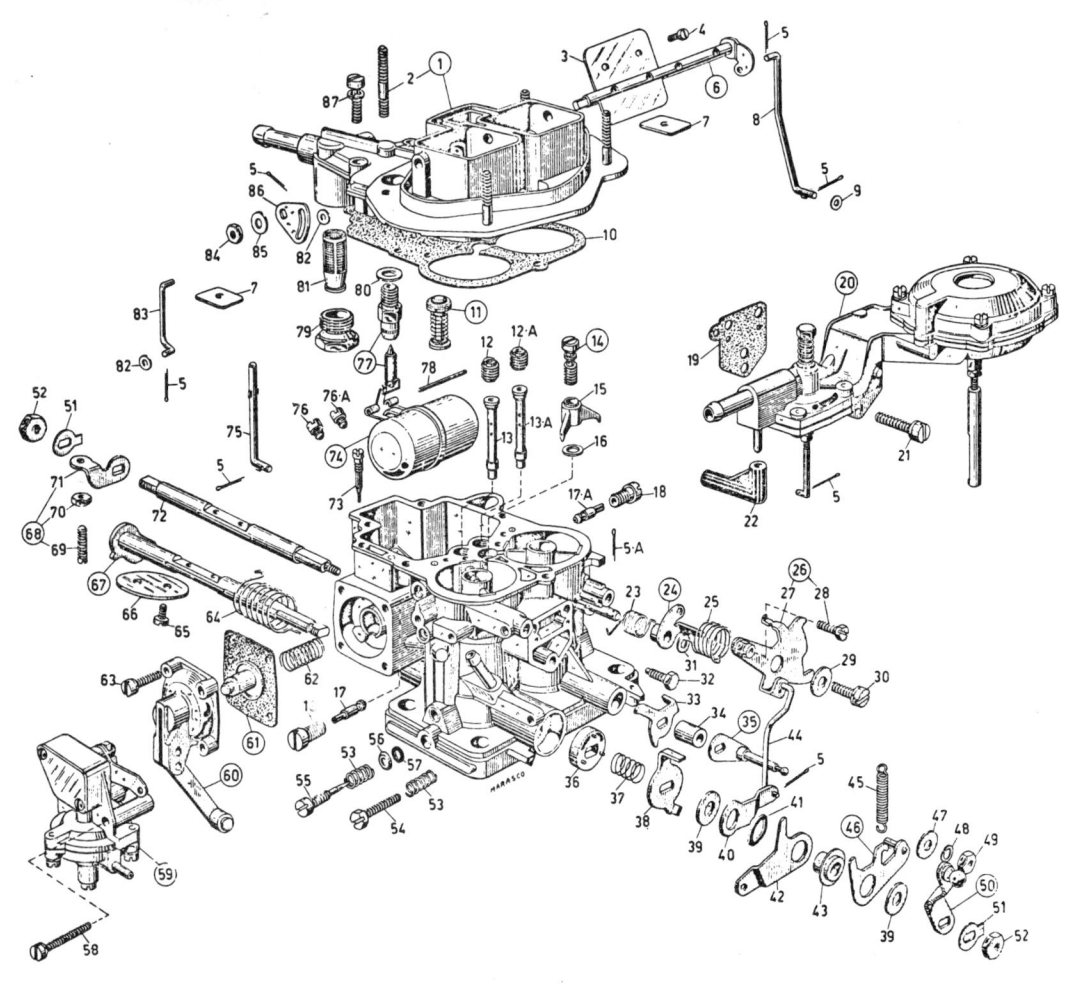

FIG 2:14   Exploded view of Weber type 32 DHSA carburetter

Key to Fig 2:14   1 Carburetter cover complete with: 2 Stud   3 Choke valve   4 Fixing screw   5 Splitpin for rod
5A Splitpin for spindle   6 Choke spindle   7 Dust cover   8 Starter operating rod   9 Washer   10 Cover gasket
11 Float chamber breather valve   12 Primary air jet   12A Secondary air jet   13 Primary emulsion tube   13A Secondary emulsion
tube   14 Pump discharge valve   15 Pump jet   16 Gasket   17 Primary idling jet   17A Secondary idling jet   18 Idling
jet carrier   19 Diaphragm assembly gasket   20 Diaphragm assembly   21 Fixing screw   22 Overchoke device
connection   23 Regulating spring for choke valve opening   24 Operating lever for 6   25 Spring   26 Choke valve
operating lever complete with: 27 Lever   28 Cable fixing screw   29 Washer for 26   30 Fixing screw for 26   31 Washer for
same   32 Outer cable fixing screw   33 Secondary spindle operating lever   34 Distance bush   35 Secondary butterfly operating
lever   36 Shutter   37 Spring   38 Primary spindle operating lever   39 Distance washer   40 Fast idling lever
41 Friction washer   42 Damper operating lever   43 Bush for lever   44 Fast idling operating rod   45 Spring for lever   46 Lever
47 Washer for secondary spindle   48 Spring washer   49 Nut   50 Butterfly operating lever   51 Locking washer   52 Nut
53 Spring for adjusting screw   54 Primary butterfly adjusting screw   55 Volume control screw   56 Cup   57 Gasket for 55
58 Fixing screw for overchoke device   59 Overchoke device   60 Pump cover   61 Pump diaphragm   62 Pump spring   63 Pump
cover fixing screw   64 Primary spindle return spring   65 Butterfly fixing screw   66 Butterfly valve   67 Primary spindle
68 Secondary butterfly opening lever, complete with: 69 Screw   70 Nut   71 Lever   72 Secondary spindle   73 Pump
discharge duct and screw   74 Float   75 Float chamber breather valve operating lever   76 Primary main jet   76A Secondary
main jet   77 Needle valve   78 Float spindle   79 Filter plug   80 Gasket for 77   81 Filter element   82 Washer for rod
83 Overchoke device operating rod   84 Nut   85 Corrugated washer   86 Overchoke device operating lever   87 Carburetter
cover fixing screw

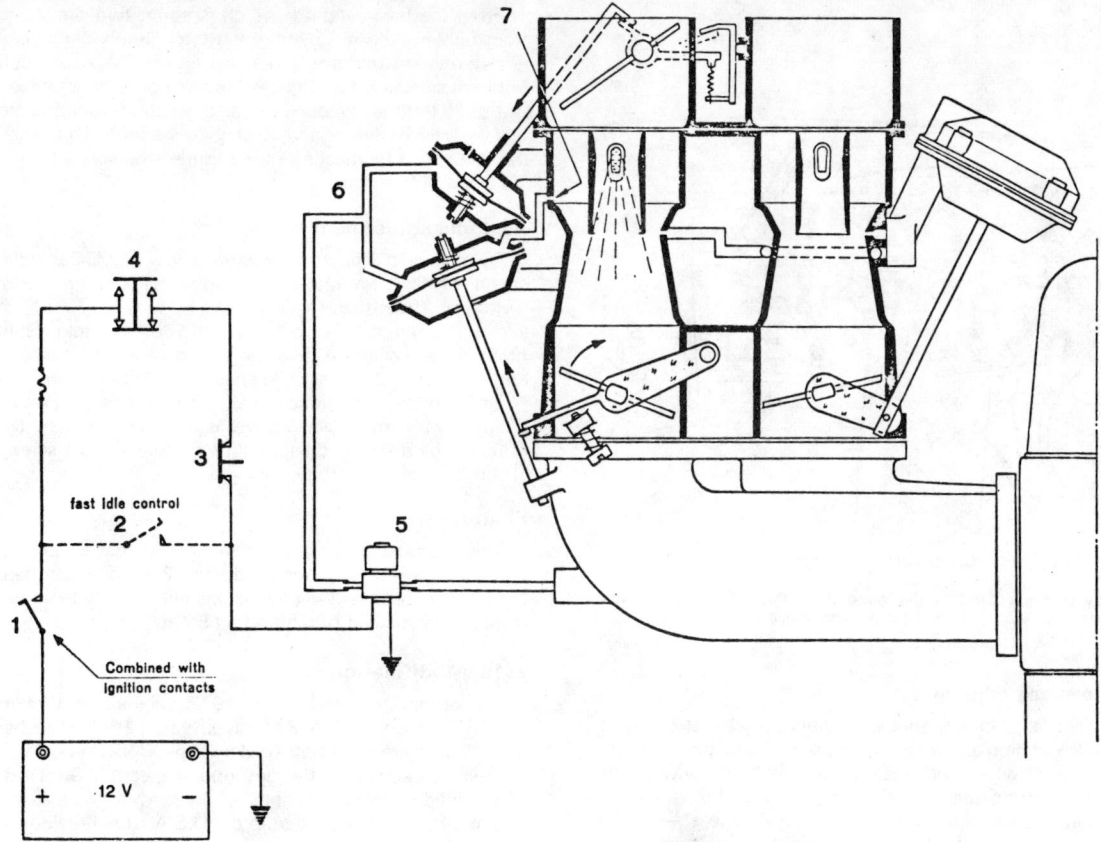

FIG 2:15 Schematic diagram of the 32 DHSA carburetter

Key to Fig 2:15   1 Switch combined with ignition contacts   2 Switch for fast idle   3 Switch, closed when clutch is engaged   4 Switch closed when 3rd and 4th gears are engaged   5 Electrovalve   6 Diaphragm capsules   7 Bypass orifice

reference to **FIG 2:13** will show that the construction is slightly different and the dimensions are changed.

2:11 Emission control

In order to comply with the stringent regulations currently in force in the United States of America and elsewhere, special carburetters and highly accurate testing and adjustment techniques have been evolved. The equipment required to test the installation on these cars and to ensure a permissible level of contaminated emission is beyond the scope of the owner/driver and for this reason he is instructed not to attempt any adjustments to the settings made by the manufacturer.

Provided that regular attention is paid to valve tappet clearances and the condition of the fuel and air intake systems and also the ignition and exhaust systems, the maintenance operations recommended by the manufacturer, performed by authorized agents using specified parts and instruments will ensure that the permissible limits are not exceeded.

Gases from the crankcase are prevented from escaping into the atmosphere by a device mentioned in **Section 2:3** and the devices incorporated in the Weber carburetter type 32 DHSA which is fitted to Fiat cars for the American market will control satisfactorily the pollution from the exhaust gases. This carburetter is shown exploded in **FIG 2:14**.

2:12 Weber 32 DHSA carburetter

A schematic diagram of this carburetter and its air pollution control system is shown in **FIG 2:15**, from which it will be seen that it incorporates two vacuum operated diaphragm capsules 6 which prevent the main throttle and choke valves from closing when decelerating, depending upon the setting of the switches 3 and 4, and so prevent the over-rich mixture normally produced at this time. The switch 3 closes when the clutch is engaged while switch 4 is closed when third and fourth gears are engaged. The electro valve 5 intercepts the depression between the inlet manifold and the two capsules.

Switches 1 and 2 are made when the ignition is turned on and for fast-idle control respectively. The bypass orifice 7 admits an air-bleed to neutralize the vacuum action on the diaphragm when the electro valve 5 closes.

The carburetter also includes a vacuum operated control for the auxiliary throttle opening and an internal device limiting the enrichment provided by the idle-speed mixture adjusting screw.

FIG 2:16 Carburetter adjustment, type DHSAI

Key to Fig 2:16 1 Idle mixture control screw 2 Fast idle
control screw 3 Throttle stop screw

Idle speed adjustment:

This adjustment should preferably be made by a
service station equipped with an exhaust gas analyzer
the use of which will ensure not only conformity to the
carbon monoxide emission regulations, but also the
maximum fuel economy in operation. In the absence of
this equipment it is possible to obtain an acceptable
setting as follows:

Start the engine and make sure that it is at full working
temperature.

Using the throttle stop screw (see **FIG 2:16**) find the
smallest throttle opening at which the engine will run
smoothly and then adjust the idle mixture screw to
obtain the fastest running at the smallest opening
consistent with evenness.

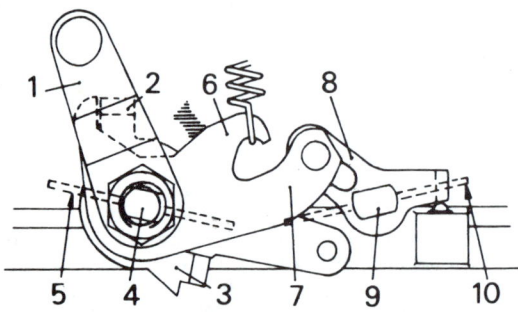

**FIG 2:17 Showing the mechanism for the differential
opening of the throttles**

Key to Fig 2:17 1 Primary throttle lever 2 Extension tab
3 Sector plate 4 Primary throttle spindle 5 Primary
throttle plate 6 Idle lever arm 7 Idle lever
8 Secondary throttle lever 9 Secondary throttle spindle
10 Throttle plate

From the basic setting, which is about two turns out
from fully in—do not overtighten the idle mixture screw
in determining this position—slowly turn the screw out
until the smoothest and fastest engine speed is obtained.
Although this may be done by ear, an accurate tachometer
will be of assistance and it may be necessary to reset
the idle speed by means of the throttle stop screw to the
specified 850 rev/min.

Fast idle adjustment:

By means of the throttle stop screw obtain an idle
speed of 850 rev/min, then press the electric press
switch on the lefthand valance and by means of the fast
idle screw adjust the fast idle to 1600 rev/min. Still
holding the switch in, blip the throttle and see that the
engine returns to its fast idle speed of 1600 rev/min.

Under these conditions the CO content of the exhaust
should be 3% and if an analyzer is available this may be
obtained by a slight adjustment of the idle mixture screw
at the base of the carburetter.

Float level:

This is adjusted in the same manner as that described
for the 34 DFH carburetter in **Section 2:4** and illustrated
in **FIG 2:7**, but the two dimensions will be 6 and 14 mm
respectively instead of 6.5 and 14.5 mm.

2:13 Modification

On certain late 1971 and 1972 cars either Weber
34DCHE or Solex C34 PAIA type carburetters may be
fitted. These are both very similar to the Weber type DFH
in their operation and the description given in **Section
2:3** will be largely applicable.

Since 1973 cars exported to the U.S.A., that previously
had twin carburetters, are now fitted with double-barrel
single units to conform to the 1973 U.S. standards of
emission control.

2:14 Fuel evaporation system

As a further item of pollution control equipment a gas
vapour recirculation system is used on American models
which is designed to prevent fuel vapours from being
passed to the atmosphere. The fuel tank has a sealed
filler and is vented through a cannister filled with activated carbon to the inlet manifold.

When the engine is stopped fuel vapours are stored in
the cannister, but when it is running a further air intake
to the cannister admits a fresh air supply which, in
passing through, purges the fuel vapours from the carbon
and they pass on into the combustion system.

2:15 Weber carburetter type 34 DMS

This carburetter, which is fitted to 1973 models with
1600 and 1800 engines, is very little different from the
type DHS described earlier in this Chapter. The main
point of difference is in the method adopted for the
differential opening of the secondary throttle, which is
not in any way dependent upon the depression of the
inlet but is purely mechanical.

Refer to **FIG 2:17**. When the accelerator pedal
is depressed, the primary throttle control lever 1 is moved
and also the sector plate 3 which is fixed on the primary
throttle shaft 4. Thus the tab 2 of sector 3 moves through

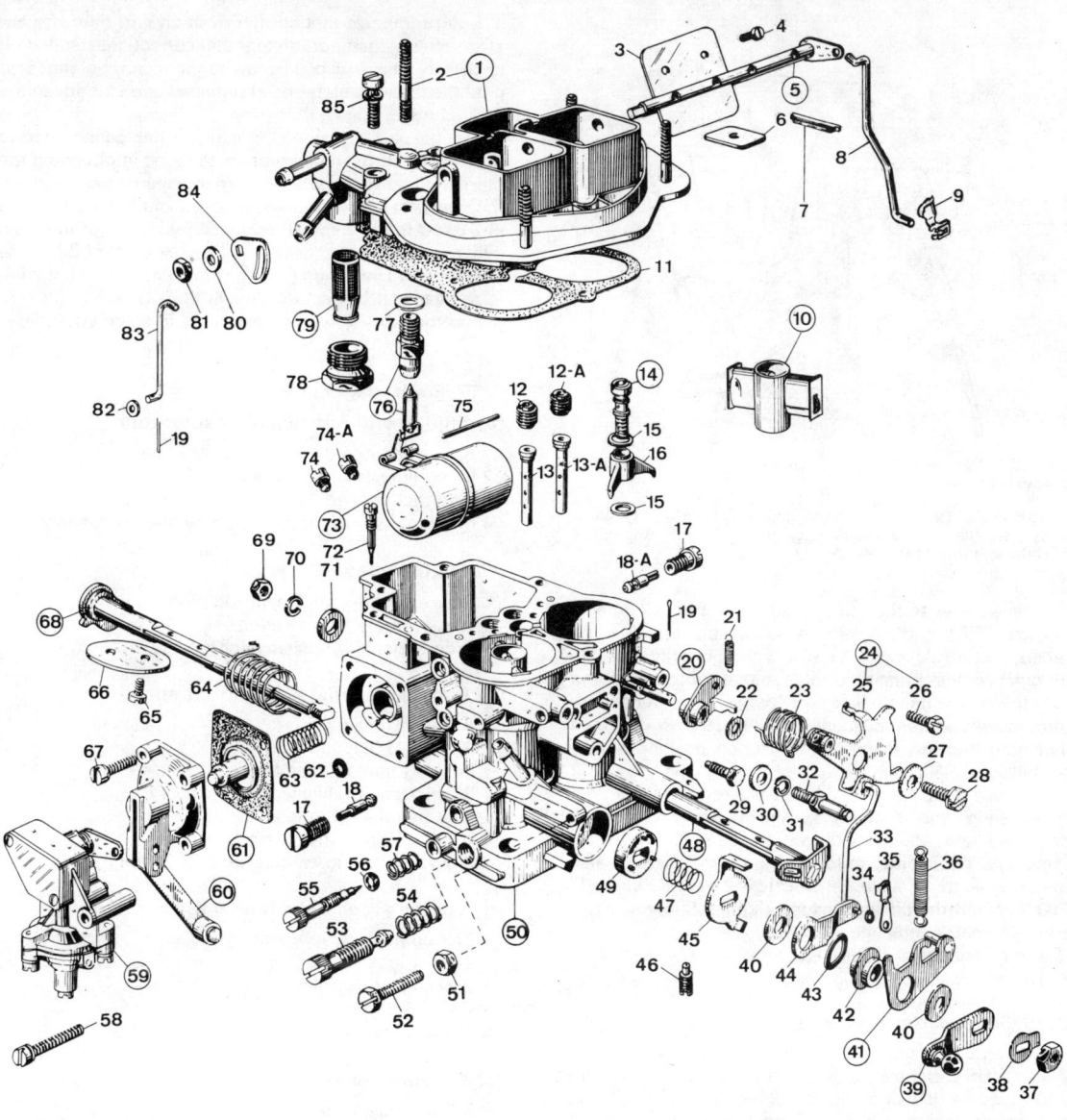

FIG 2:18   Components of the Weber 34 DMS carburetter

Key to Fig 2:18   1 Top cover   2 Stud   3 Choke plate   4 Screw   5 Choke spindle   6 Dust excluding plate   7 Sealer
8 Choke control rod   9 Lever   10 Auxiliary venturi   11 Gasket   12 Primary main air jet   12A Secondary main air jet
13 Primary emulsion tube   13A Secondary emulsion tube   14 Pump valve   15 Gasket   16 Pump jet   17 Idle jet carrier
18 Primary idle jet   18A Secondary idle jet   19 Splitpin   20 Choke control lever   21 Return spring   22 Washer
23 Return spring   24 Throttle control lever assembly   25 Lever   26 Screw   27 Washer   28 Screw   29 Cable clamp
screw   30 Washer   31 Spring washer   32 Spring anchor pin   33 Fast idle control rod   34 Gasket   35 Clip   36 Spring
37 Nut   38 Lock washer   39 Primary throttle lever   40 Spacer   41 Idle lever   42 Bush   43 Friction washer   44 Fast
idle lever   45 Sector plate   46 Stop screw   47 Spring   48 Secondary throttle spindle   49 Shutter   50 Carburetter body
51 Nut   52 Primary throttle adjust screw   53 By-pass idle screw   54 Spring   55 Idle mixture screw   56 Gasket
57 Spring   58 Screw   59 Over choking control   60 Pump cover   61 Pump diaphragm   62 Gasket   63 Spring
64 Primary throttle return spring   65 Screw   66 Throttle plate   67 Screw   68 Primary throttle shaft   69 Nut   70 Spring
washer   71 Washer   72 Plug for pump discharge   73 Float   74 Primary main jet   74A Secondary main jet   75 Float
pivot pin   76 Needle valve   77 Gasket   78 Filter plug   79 Filter   80 Friction washer   81 Nut   82 Washer   83 Choke
control rod   84 Choke control lever   85 Screw

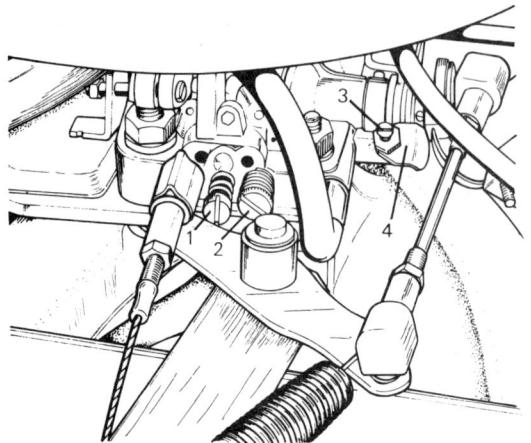

FIG 2:19 Adjusting idle speed on Solex C34 E1ES 5 carburetter

Key to Fig 2:19   1 Idle volume metering screw
2 By-pass idle volume metering screw   3 Throttle stop screw
4 Throttle stop screw lever

the same angle as the throttle plate 5 before it contacts the arm 6 of the idle lever 7 which in turn operates the secondary throttle lever 8, spindle 9 and butterfly plate 10. In practice the primary throttle moves through about two-thirds of its total travel before the secondary throttle commences to open. The linkage is so designed that both throttles reach the fully open position simultaneously.

The operation of the DMS carburetter at starting, accelerating and running is similar to that already described and adjustments will be carried out in the same way. The procedure for setting the float level is also the same as that detailed in **Section 2:4** and shown in **FIG 2:7**, but the dimensions are slightly different, viz. 7 and 14.5 mm.

The components of the carburetter are shown in **FIG 2:18**.

2:16 Solex carburetter type C34 EIES 5

This type of carburetter, which is very similar to the Weber DHS described earlier, is fitted to later 1600 and 1800 models. It has a slightly different method of idle adjustment which should be described, as a similar layout will be found also on some Weber carburetters.

Refer to **FIG 2:19**. Idling speed is adjusted by means of the primary throttle stop screw 3, while mixture strength is regulated by the volume control screw 1 which controls the amount of fuel admitted to mix with the air drawn in by the engine.

First set the throttle stop screw 3 so that the engine runs without missing. Use the screw 1 to give the fastest

steady running at this throttle position and then use the stop screw again to obtain the correct idle speed. If necessary these two last operations can be repeated until the fastest steady speed obtained corresponds to the desired idling speed.

The by-pass idle metering screw 2 has been added to emission controlled carburetters to assist in obtaining the correct idle mixture when using an exhaust gas analyzer. In these cases the throttle stop screw must remain locked **shut** and the idle speed regulated by means of the main idle control screw 1, using the by-pass control 2 for fine adjustment. The action of this screw may not be apparent to the ear, but its use will enable the CO rate to be kept below the 4.5% maximum permitted in some countries.

2:17 Fault diagnosis

(a) Engine will not tick over smoothly

1 Slow-running adjustment set too fine
2 Idling adjustment incorrect
3 Idling jet choked
4 Ignition and leaking pistons may also be suspect

(b) Engine idles too fast

1 Slow-running adjustment too high
2 Weak throttle return spring
3 Excess friction in accelerator linkage

(c) Engine dies under load or at speed

1 Restricted main jet
2 Restricted fuel valve
3 Sticking float in chamber
4 Restriction in fuel line
5 Low petrol level in tank
6 Weak spring in fuel pump
7 Blocked filters in carburetter or fuel pump

(d) Engine stops with fuel in tank

1 Broken pump diaphragm
2 Vapour lock in fuel line
3 Blockage in fuel line
4 Choked filters
5 Choked main jet

(e) Carburetter floods

1 Sticking fuel valve
2 Float punctured
3 Float arm bent

(f) High fuel consumption

1 Wrong main jets
2 Fuel leaks in line or at joints
Check also sparking plugs, distributor timing and under-inflated tyres

CHAPTER 3

THE IGNITION SYSTEM

3 : 1 Operating principles

The ignition system for the 124AC.000 engine is conventional for a car with a negative earthed system. That is to say, it comprises ignition coil, distributor and breaker with centrifugal advance feature, sparking plugs and HT leads.

Maximum engine performance under all conditions of load and engine speed is dependent on several factors. These include cylinder head temperature, grade and temperature of the fuel vapour, compression ratio of the engine and the interval before top dead centre at which ignition commences. Some are a function of engine design based on predicted engine and ambient vapour temperatures and the cooling system is devised to achieve these temperatures when running under normal conditions. The variables are engine speed and load and these are dealt with by a centrifugal device in the distributor which increases the interval between ignition and top dead centre as the speed increases.

Beneath the insulated plate carrying the HT distributor rotor arm is a plate linked to the shaft by a pair of spring loaded centrifugal weights and having at its lower end the cam operating the make-and-break contacts. As the shaft speed increases, the weights, moving out of centre against the tension of the spring under centrifugal force, rotate the cam on the shaft in the same direction as the shaft rotation. The contacts are, therefore, opened a few degrees earlier with increases in engine, and consequently shaft, speed, the advance with speed being approximately linear up to 3500 rev/min after which it remains at the maximum of 30 deg. (that is 10 deg. fixed advance plus 20 deg. variable advance) at higher rev/min (see **FIG 3 : 1**).

The ignition coil is wound as an auto-transformer. That is to say, the primary and secondary windings are connected in series, the common junction being connected to the positive terminal of the battery through the ignition switch. The opposite side of the primary winding is connected to the negative polarity earth through the make-and-break contacts which are shunted by a small capacitor. The far end of the secondary winding is connected to the HT distributor. While the contacts are closed, current flows through the primary winding magnetising the core and setting up a fairly strong magnetic field. Each time the contacts open, the battery current is cut off and the field collapses, inducing a high current in the primary winding and a high voltage in the secondary. The primary current is used to charge the capacitor and the flow is high and instantaneous. It is

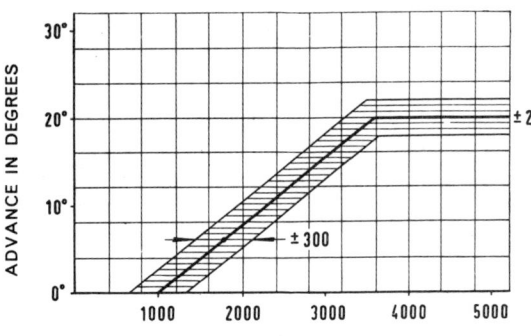

FIG 3:1 Graph showing degree of advance with speed effected by centrifugal control

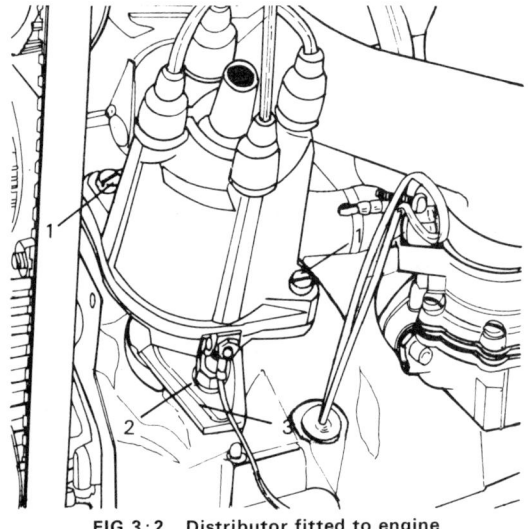

FIG 3:2 Distributor fitted to engine

Key to Fig 3:2   1 Cap fixing screws   2 Securing nut
3 Bracket

this high current peak which induces the surge in the secondary winding to produce the sparking voltage across the plug points. Without the capacitor, the current peak would be much smaller and the sparking voltage much reduced, to a point at which it might not even ignite the fuel vapour in the cylinder.

The capacitor, therefore, serves the dual purpose of minimising contact breaker point wear and providing the high charging surge to give the necessary punch to the spark.

3:2 Distributor maintenance

Distributor maintenance is confined to periodical checks of the make-and-break contact gap and to the condition of the interior of the distributor cap, the HT contacts, rotor and HT carbon pencil in the centre of the cap. The gap should be between .018 and .020 inch measured by feeler gauge when the moving arm pad is at the peak of the cam on the distributor shaft. The adjustment is made by loosening screw 4 (see **FIG 3:3**) on the

fixed arm plate and retightening in the new position when the plate and fixed contact has been reset.

The inside of the distributor cap 1 must be clean, free from moisture and carbon dust and with no signs of cracking or the formation of tracking carbon paths. The HT pencil in the centre must be unbroken and free to move against the spring in the housing. Lubrication is confined to the application of a spot of light oil on the shaft and to the pivots of the weights, both of which are accessible by removing the cap 2 of the rotor assembly. No oil should be applied to the make-and-break mechanism which must be perfectly clean and dry.

3:3 Removal of the distributor

To remove the distributor from the engine, first disconnect the HT leads to the sparking plugs and unscrew and remove the distributor cap. Disconnect the LT lead to the make-and-break terminal which can be seen above the securing bolt 2 in **FIG 1:9**. Unbolt and remove the nut 2 and clip (see **FIG 3:2**) securing the distributor in place on the engine and lift the distributor clear of the shaft bearing hole.

Time may be saved in setting up after maintenance if the precise position of the rotor in relation to one of the terminals is noted and the engine crankshaft is not altered while distributor maintenance is being carried out.

Always cover the exposed entry into the crankshaft with clean, lint-free rag to prevent the entry of dirt or swarf while the distributor is being serviced.

3:4 Dismantling the distributor

Unscrew the two cheese-head screws retaining the rotor cap and remove the cap. Dismantle the weights and springs. Beneath the distributor mounting is a collar secured by a pin. Remove the pin and slide the collar off the shaft. The shaft may now be withdrawn from the distributor. Disconnect and remove the capacitor. Dismantle the make-and-break. Wash all metal parts in a suitable cleaning fluid and dry.

Examine the shaft and rotor for signs of excessive play or wear. Renew if necessary. Examine the fixed and moving contacts of the make-and-break, clean and remove pits or high points with a smooth file or carborundum stone or, if too badly burned or worn, renew completely. **Never use emerycloth when cleaning the points as particles of emery may become embedded in the relatively soft contact face material.**

Check the cam faces for signs of wear or scoring. Polish out light scores with a smooth carborundum stone or replace if too badly worn.

Examine the insulation of the rotor cap and distributor cap for signs of tracking or carbonization and replace if any are present or suspected. Check the conditions of the rotor contact arm, HT pencil and HT contacts in the distributor cap. Replace if these show signs of burning or the HT pencil is too short.

Check the condition of the cam follower on the moving contact arm of the make-and-break and replace if the wear is such as to alter the timing of the ignition by more than 2 deg. This is a little difficult to check but, broadly speaking, if follower wear is such that the setting of the contact gap necessitates the fixed plate being close to the limit of adjustment, ignition timing will almost certainly be affected outside the set limits.

Examine the condition of the weights and springs. The springs must not be over-extended (i.e. the coils must be closed together when at rest) and the weights must be an easy, but not sloppy, fit on the pins.

Check the capacitor. If an insulation test set, such as a 'Megger', is available, it can be used to check the insulation resistance between the terminal and case. This should be of the order of .5 megohm or better at 100 volts. The best check, however, is to charge the capacitor from a DC source (the battery if no other is available, or the terminals of the 100 V, insulation tester) and leave for about 5 minutes. The terminal and case of the capacitor should then be shorted and, if the capacitor is healthy, a noticeable spark should result. If the capacitor needs replacement, the capacity of the replacement unit should be .2 to .25 microfarad at 50 Hz.

3:5 Reassembling

Reassemble the distributor and set the make-and-break gap at .16 to .18 inch. If a small spring balance is available with a scale of up to 2 lb, check the pull of the moving arm pressure on the fixed contact. This should be about 20 oz.

Before replacing the rotor cap, check that the movement of the flyweights about their pins provides the necessary movement of the cam on the distributor shaft and that the action is free. Apply a spot of oil to the pivot points and to the shaft before insertion in the mounting bushing. Insert the shaft into the bushing and replace the collar, securing it with the pin. Check for end-play which should not be noticeable. Fit and reconnect the capacitor across the make-and-break contacts.

Examine the HT leads from the distributor cap and, if at all perished, replace them, fitting the rubber overshoes at the cap end and the shrouded connectors at the sparking plug end, with the cable-bunching washers at the intermediate positions.

3:6 Replacement, meshing of driving spindle

If the crankshaft position has not been altered since the distributor was extracted, turn the rotor to the approximate position it was and insert the spindle into the skew gear at the bottom of the distributor shaft housing. With the splines engaged, turn the crankshaft until the mark on the generator drive pulley is opposite the 10 deg. or 5 deg. reference line (see **FIG 3:4**) on the camshaft drive cover (see **Technical Data**).

Withdraw the distributor until the shaft splines are just clear of the skew gear and rotate the shaft slightly one way or the other until the contacts are just about to open on clockwise rotation. Push the shaft home and secure the distributor in place by the clip and nut. Rotate the crankshaft through 180 deg. and check that the contacts commence to open the next time the mark is opposite reference point 1. If this is not the case, release the distributor and repeat the procedure until the correct meshing is obtained. For small discrepancies, fine adjustment can be obtained by slackening the clip and slightly rotating the lower half of the distributor until properly set and then tightening the clip.

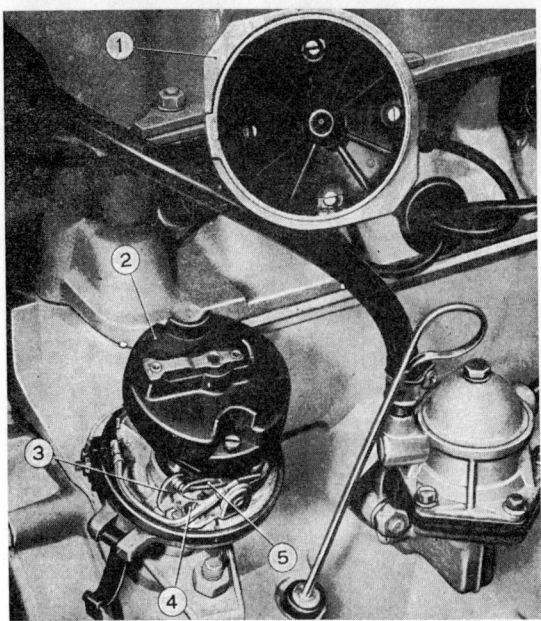

FIG 3:3   Distributor with cap removed

Key to Fig 3:3   1 Cap   2 Rotor arm   3 Fixed contact arm   4 Adjusting screw   5 Moving contact arm

FIG 3:4   Timing the ignition

Key to Fig 3:4   1 10 deg. BTDC   2 5 deg. BTDC   3 TDC   4 Timing mark on pulley

It is essential to see that the clip is fully resting on the flange of the casing and that the nut is tightened down to prevent inadvertent twisting of the distributor in service.

Should the crankshaft position have been altered, it is necessary first to set the crank at top dead centre for cylinder No. 1 on the compression stroke (that is, with both inlet and exhaust valves closed) by removing the camshaft covers and examining the position of the cams. Then turn the crankshaft back 10 deg. or 5 deg., whichever is applicable, by means of the crankshaft pulley until the reference mark on the pulley is again opposite to the appropriate timing mark.

Now turn the rotor of the distributor until the rotor arm is opposite to terminal 1 (the cylinder numbers are marked on the distributor cap) check the contact position as before, insert the distributor shaft home in the skew drive gear and secure. Replace the camshaft covers.

Clip the distributor cap back into place and connect the HT leads to the respective sparking plugs. Finally, reconnect the capacitor lead and the LT lead from the ignition coil, terminal D, to the LT terminal on the distributor.

3:7 HT cables

The HT cables between the distributor and the coil and sparking plugs are of standard pattern and either the low resistance core or high resistance core cables can be used without affecting engine performance. The high resistance core cables are preferred in that they minimize radio interference both on the internal radio, if fitted, or with radio or television sets in the vicinity.

Any indication of deterioration of the insulation should be countered by complete renewal of all HT cables. Similarly, if trouble is experienced in wet weather, the plug shrouds should also be renewed.

3:8 Sparking plugs

Sparking plugs, as provided, are of Marelli pattern, Type M14-19 (CW24OLP). The British equivalent is Champion Type M14-19 (N9Y). The thread is metric M14 x 1.25. The gap setting for optimum performance is .019 to .023 inch.

Misfiring or uneven firing at low speeds may be due to faulty plugs. Check that they are clean, that the gap is set to the spacing mentioned above and that the insulation is clean and dry on the exterior and free from deposits of carbon in the interior. The usual deposit from a satisfactory plug running at the right cylinder temperature is hard and fawn.

Heavy carbon deposit can be the result of an over-rich mixture, over-cool running or oil leakage past the piston rings. The latter is usually indicated by a moist, as well as black, deposit. Cracked insulation or looseness in the plug seating can also be the cause of loss of power and irregular running. The life of a plug, though long, is not indefinite and, for best performance, plugs should be changed every 10,000 miles.

When cleaning and adjusting the gap, always bend the outer electrode and never the inner one. Use a proper sparking plug wrench, preferably a torque wrench set to 32 lb ft torque.

Garages possessing plug cleaning equipment will sandblast and check for gas tightness for a small charge but the cost of new plugs is so small that it is usually better to renew than to service.

3:9 Fault diagnosis

(a) Engine will not fire

1 Low battery volts
2 Dirty make-and-break points
3 Faulty condenser
4 Broken make-and-break spring
5 Broken or disconnected HT lead
6 Broken or disconnected LT lead
7 Faulty ignition switch
8 Condensation in or on distributor cap
9 Broken carbon pencil in distributor cap
10 Wet or cracked plug insulators

Low battery volts may not show across the battery terminals on open circuit but, if a cell is poor, when the starting current (of the order of 160 to 300 amps depending on ambient temperatures) is flowing, the volts across the ignition coil may drop to below 9, the minimum for creating a healthy spark. Even with a good battery, on a very cold day the starting current can be high enough to prevent ignition until just after the starter motor has been switched off, an excellent reason for not keeping the starter switch closed for more than a second or so. A series of short starts is far more likely to get the engine to fire.

(b) Engine misfires

1 Faulty plug or plugs
2 Carbon track on distributor cap
3 Moisture on sparking plugs
4 Faulty HT lead to plug
5 Too large a gap on one plug
6 Plug contacts bridged by carbon deposit
7 Plug loose in engine

(c) Poor acceleration

1 Engine too far retarded
2 Centrifugal weights seized up
3 Centrifugal spring or springs broken or disconnected
4 Distributor base clamp loosened
5 Excessive gap on make-and-break

CHAPTER 4

THE COOLING SYSTEM

4:1 Principle of operation

The water cooling system for the 124AC.000 engine is conventional in that it comprises a radiator, water pump and fan, the radiator also being the heating source of the air conditioning system.

The radiator, forward mounted behind the engine grille at the front of the body, is a vertical tube pattern the rows of tubes being aircooled by horizontal rows of gills. Water is circulated between the cylinder jacket and the radiator by a belt-driven pump of the centrifugal vane type mounted centrally immediately above the crankshaft. An extension of the shaft forward carries the hub to which is bolted both the driving pulley and the fan.

A thermostat mounted between the radiator, water pump and engine restricts the flow until the water in the jacket has reached a certain temperature at which the engine can function efficiently. A two-stage cooling system is incorporated whereby water is allowed to circulate around the cylinders without passing through the radiator via a bypass connection, the transition to circulation through the radiator being a progressive one as the thermostat valve opens.

Ram air passing through the radiator when the car is in motion assists cooling while the fan on the pump shaft tends to accelerate the cooling air flow at speed and maintains a stream of air through the radiator gills while the car is stationary.

The heating source in the air conditioning system is also a water tube radiator, mounted horizontally and deriving its hot water circulation from a port in the rear of the cylinder head, returning to the front radiator via an inlet to the pump adjacent to the cylinder block inlet. This flow can be controlled from the driving compartment by a valve.

The capacity of the system, including the heater, is 13 pints and the system is pressurized by a spring-loaded radiator cap to achieve a boiling point of around 120°C. Expansion of the contents is taken care of by an overflow pipe from the filler cap housing exhausting into an auxiliary header tank mounted over the lefthand front wheel in the engine compartment.

A warning device situated at the rear of the cylinder block illuminates a lamp on the right of the speedometer dial should the temperature of the cooling water reach a dangerous level. The pairs of fan blades are not mounted at right angles to each other and this is intentional, it being claimed that quieter operation is achieved by the arrangement.

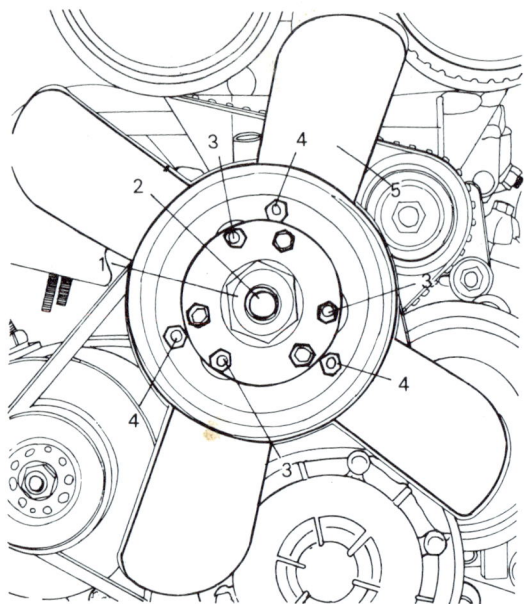

FIG 4 : 1 Electromagnetic fan and alternator drive belt

Key to Fig 4 : 1 1 Fan hub locking nut 2 Water pump spindle 3 Electromagnet air gap adjusting screws 4 Fan securing screws 5 Fan

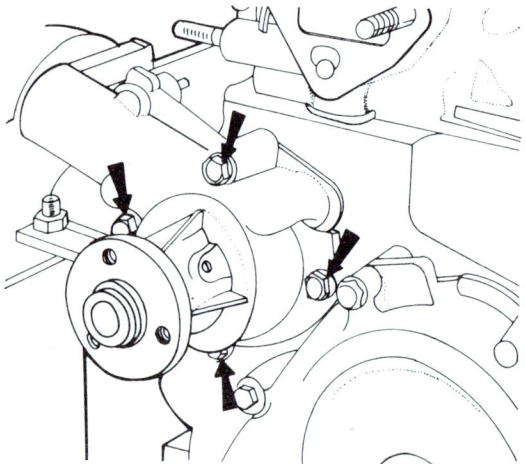

FIG 4 : 2 Removing the water pump

4 : 2 Cooling system maintenance

Maintenance of the cooling system is confined to periodical flushing of the radiator, refilling with antifreeze solutions for cold weather, checking that the fan is securely attached to the pump shaft and that the belt tension is properly adjusted. At frequent intervals, the hose connections should be examined for water leaks, particularly in view of the pressure that builds up in the system during normal running, and tightened as necessary.

Draining of the radiator is effected by opening the cock on the lefthand side at the bottom of the radiator and by removing the filler cap. As the thermostat prevents circulation of water between the cylinder block and radiator while cold, it is preferable to run the engine first until the thermostat opens, so allowing the block to drain through the radiator cock as well. The last remnants of cooling water can be removed from the cylinder jacket by unscrewing the plug on the righthand side of the cylinder block.

Draining of the air conditioning radiator is effected by moving the lower of the two heater controls in the cab to the right as far as it will go and, if this is done before opening the radiator cock, the water will be drained out simultaneously by suphon action.

Before changing to antifreeze, ensure that all rust has been removed by cleaning through with sodium bicarbonate solution, one ouce of bicarbonate to each pint of water. The radiator and waterways should be filled with the solution and the engine run for about ten minutes to circulate and heat it and then left for about another 30 minutes before draining and flushing.

Any good antifreeze solution incorporating an inhibitor may be used providing that it has been made up in accordance with the instructions on the container. Don't forget the contents of the auxiliary tank when changing from fresh to antifreeze solution or vice versa.

Maintenance of the air conditioning system is limited to ensuring that the controls are all operational and that the rain water drain is not clogged.

Check the belt tension at regular intervals and tighten as necessary until there is $\frac{1}{2}$ inch movement in the centre of the longest run. It is also good practice to check the operation of the warning lamp by disconnecting the cable at the transducer and earthing it to the adjacent metal. This will disclose a burnt-out lamp cable open-circuit which would nullify an overtemperature warning.

Regular maintenance and frequent visual inspections of the cooling system can often disclose faults, and conditions leading to faults, before they have assumed serious proportions.

4 : 3 Water pump removal and dismantling

To remove the water pump, first drain the system. Disconnect the hose connection from the thermostat bypass. (This will already have been done if the engine has been completely dismantled as outlined in **Section 4 : 1**).

Loosen the driving belt by slackening the generator upper clamp nut and then unbolt and remove the fan (see **FIG 4 : 1**). Unbolt and remove the pump from the cylinder block (see **FIG 4 : 2**). It may be necessary to remove the two top screws securing the radiator to the side brackets and to rock it back to get the necessary clearance for these operations.

Transfer the pump to a bench and secure it in a vice (see **FIG 4 : 3**). Then, using a puller A.40026, withdraw the impeller from the shaft. Remove the setscrew 3 (see **FIG 4 : 4**) which retains the bearing in place and withdraw the spindle complete with bearing and pulley hub.

Using a puller or a small press, remove the hub from the spindle. **Both impeller and hub are interference fits on the spindle and are not keyed to it in any way.** The packing 5 can now be driven out of the pump body with an ordinary drift.

Clean all parts thoroughly and, in particular, remove any scale from the impeller vanes and pump body. Examine carefully for any signs of excessive wear or cracks and replace as necessary. Check that the contact face of the pump is perfectly flat where it beds down on the crankcase.

4:4 Reassembling the pump

Refit the pump body with new packing, pressing it well home into the seating. Refit the hub onto the shaft with a press ensuring that it is an interference fit and the end of the boss is flush with the end of the shaft. Repack the bearing with grease and fit the bearing and spindle back into the pump body, taking care to see that the recess for the setscrew is opposite to the hole in the pump body. Insert the setscrew and stake in place with a punch.

Check that the impeller is still a tight interference fit on the shaft (the shaft diameter should be not less than .0007 inch nor more than .002 inch greater than the bore diameter of the impeller) and then force the impeller onto the spindle in a hydraulic press using spacer A.60314 as shown in **FIG 4:5**. Press home until the clearance between the impeller and pump body is .02 inch (see **FIG 4:6**).

Finally, check that the shaft rotates on its bearing easily and without end play and that there is no excessive noise while doing so.

4:5 Radiator and filler cap

The radiator sits on a bracket attached to the chassis at the bottom and is secured in place by studs and nuts to brackets on either side at the top. Elastic pads, washers and spacers are provided to give a measure of flexibility in the mount and these must always be re-used or replaced when refitting the radiator after a service overhaul.

To remove, open the drain cock and take off the filler cap and, when the radiator has been drained, disconnect the two hoses, one at the top and the other at the bottom and remove the overflow pipe to the header tank. Remove the nuts and lift out the radiator.

To check the radiator for leaks, blank off the outlets, fill with water and then pressurise to 14 lb/sq in with test pump and gauge, Ap.5066. The test can also be applied to the whole cooling system if desired.

If a leak is indicated by the gauge needle falling back after pumping has ceased, locate the leak and, if small, repair by soldering. Extensive leaks are best dealt with by replacing the radiator as it is not possible to guarantee complete watertightness for long after such repairs.

The filler cap seals and pressurizes the contents of the radiator and cooling system. Should the cooling water boil, the seal overcomes the pressure of the upper spring (see **FIG 4:8**) releasing the contents to the overflow pipe and header tank. On cooling, the contents contract and lowers the pressure within the system to below ambient atmospheric. The lower valve opens to draw water back from the header tank into the system. If, for any reason (loose filler cap or faulty lower gasket, etc.), the system is not sealed, the system will not be so efficient and there may be a persistent loss of water content through evaporation.

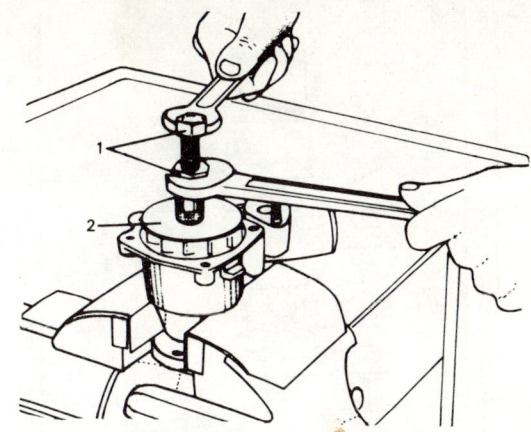

FIG 4:3   Removing water pump impeller 2 from spindle using puller A.40026 1

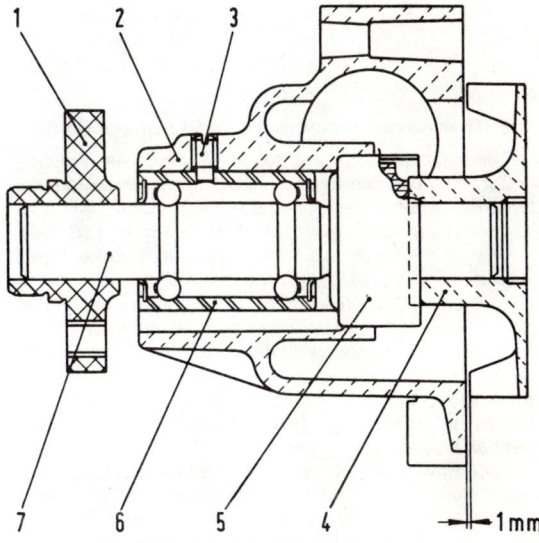

FIG 4:4   Section through water pump

Key to Fig 4:4   1 Fan pulley hub   2 Pump body
3 Bearing setscrew   4 Impeller   5 Packing   6 Bearing
7 Spindle
Assembly clearance between impeller and pump body: .0039 in (1 mm)

Always take great care in removing the filler cap after the engine has been running for any length of time or the overtemperature warning has operated. The pressurized system enables the water temperature to rise above 100°C, the boiling point at normal ambient pressure. If the filler cap is removed at this temperature, the lowering of pressure will enable the contents to flash into scalding steam which will emerge with high velocity and, possibly, disastrous results to the person concerned. A safe rule is not to remove the filler cap so long as the overtemperature warning is showing.

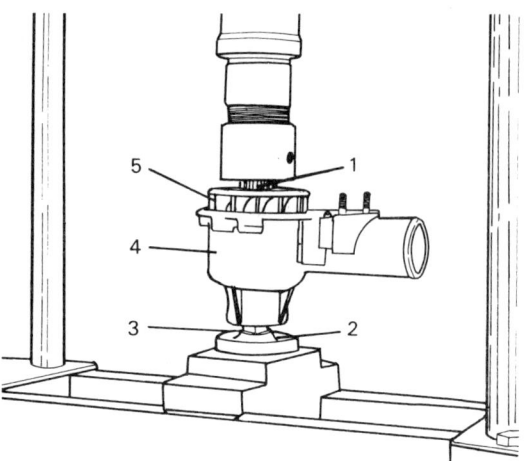

FIG 4:5 Using hydraulic press to fit impeller to pump

Key to Fig 4:5   1 Spacer A.60314   2 Fan pulley hub
3 Spindle   4 Pump body   5 Impeller

4:6 Thermostat maintenance and replacement

. The thermostat is mounted in a three-way junction unit in the hose connections between the lower radiator tank, the radiator header and the pump outlet.

This layout is shown diagrammatically in **FIG 4:9.**

With this layout, water is circulated by the pump around the cylinder jacket and the bellows when the valve is closed, so preserving a more uniform cooling of the cylinder block and, at the same time, communicating the water outlet temperature direct to the bellows. As the bellows expand, the lower valve partly opens and the upper valve commences to close. The water flow is now divided, part circulating direct round the cylinder block and part through the radiator.

At maximum temperature, the lower valve is fully open and the upper valve closed, shutting off the direct flow. All cooling water then circulates through the radiator. In this way, the thermostat opening is a variable with both engine jacket temperature and radiator water temperature, the two being balanced to achieve a steady engine temperature regardless of the temperature of the cooling flow of air or the load on the engine.

The setting at which the valve commences to open is fixed during manufacture and cannot be adjusted. If any doubts exist as to the correctness of thermostat setting, a check can be made by extracting the thermostat from the system and immersing it in a bath of water which can be heated while the water temperature is checked by a thermometer. When the water reaches 85°C (185°F) the valve should start to open and, at 100°C (212°F) it should be fully open. If this is not the case, replace the thermostat.

A puncture in the bellows will result in the valve remaining fully open, circulating water through the radiator all the time. This is a 'fail-safe' system, the only disadvantage then being that the engine takes considerably longer to reach the temperature for efficient operation.

As a small amount of air is locked in the lower hose from the radiator sump to the thermostat lower face by the valve being closed when filling the radiator, this must be allowed for by either topping-up the radiator after an initial run or, more usually, by adding an extra quarter-pint of water to the header tank.

4:7 Air conditioning maintenance

The air conditioning system can be understood by the diagrammatic view in **FIG 4:10.** The air intake is part of a metal tray in the hood panel of the body 3. This forms a chamber fitted with deflectors to discharge any rain entering the intake to a drain in the engine compartment. The central outlet from the chamber gives directly into the intake 4 of the radiator housing which is provided with shutter that can be opened or closed from the control 10 inside the car.

The radiator housing is bolted to the underside of the instrument panel and contains the radiator with water connections and a control valve 7, opened and closed by the lever 10. Clipped to the underside of the radiator housing is the fan housing, containing the accelerator fan controlled from the switch 11, and provided with an adjustable shutter 8 which controls the entry of air from the system into the car interior. A bypass duct from the radiator housing channels air to the windscreen deflectors 2, for demisting, each deflector being separately adjustable.

The heater water delivery line 6 is connected to the outlet from the cylinder head. The return flow line 5 is connected to the righthand flanged inlet to the circulating pump visible in **FIG 4:6.**

The fan is mounted on two rubber pads in the housing and is used for ventilation in warm weather and for the warming and circulation of fresh air within the car during cold weather. It also assists in the demisting of the

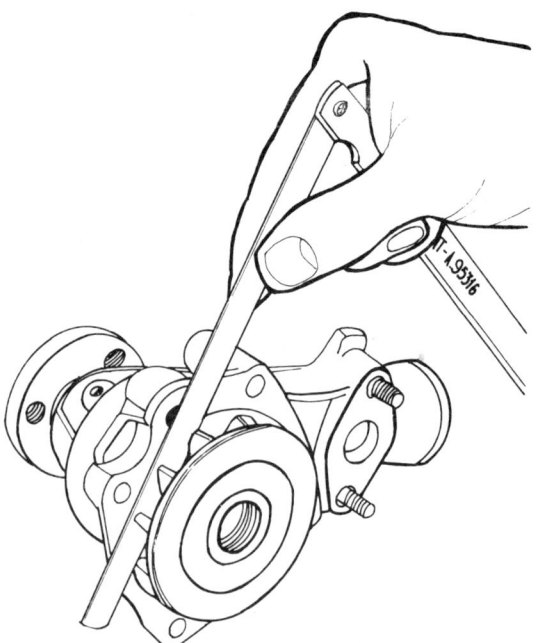

FIG 4:6 Checking clearance between impeller and body with .04 inch feeler gauge

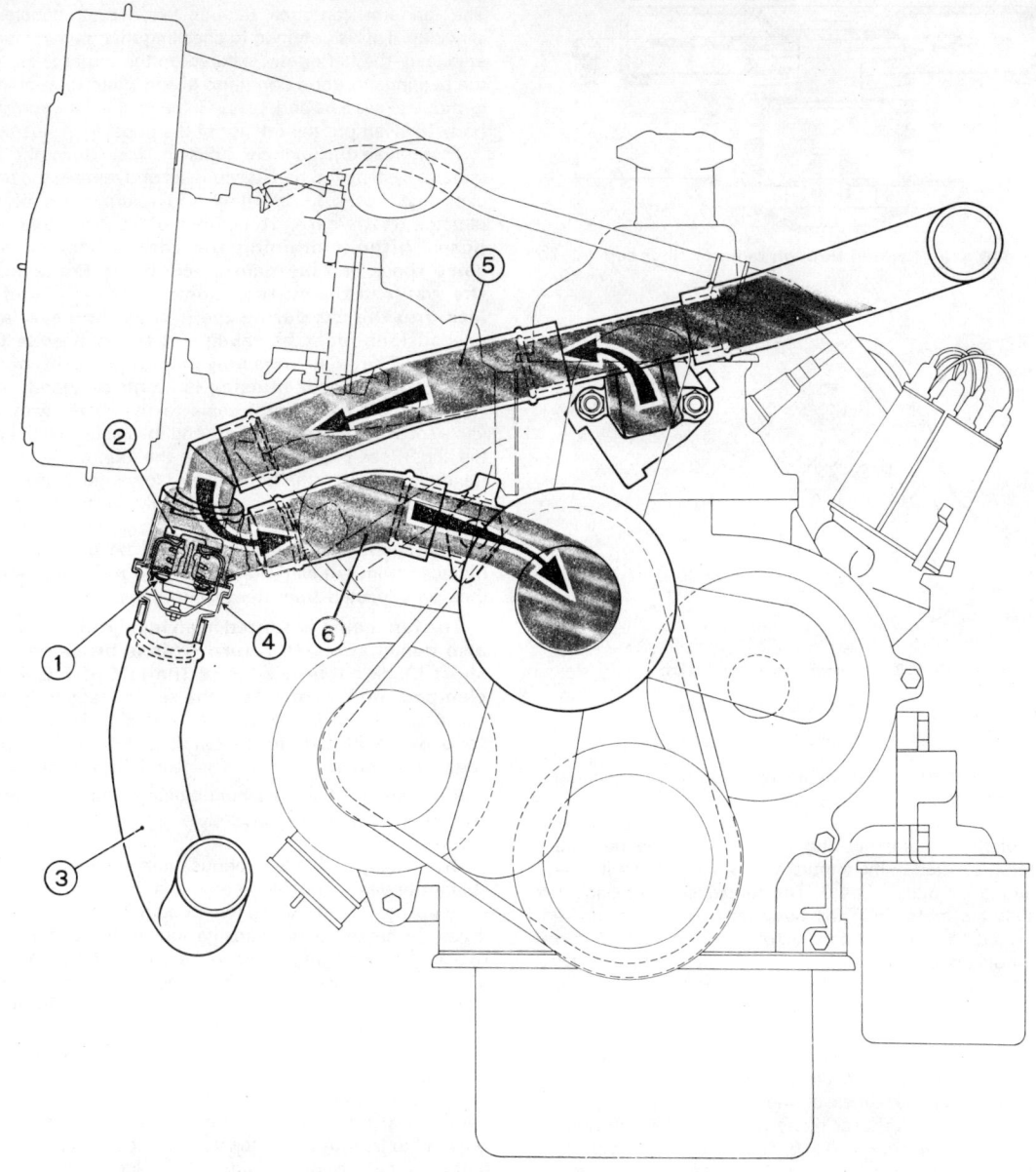

FIG 4:7 Cooling circuit diagram

Key to Fig 4:7   1 Lower thermostat valve   2 Upper thermostat valve   3 Return pipe from radiator   4 Connection housing thermostat   5 Pipe from cylinder head   6 Water pump suction pipe

windscreen when the car is stationary or travelling too slowly for the introduction of ram air.

The radiator housing (see **FIG 4:11**) is a moulded plastic body 1 to which is secured, by four nuts and bolts, the radiator 5, with the inlet 6 and outlet 7, water pipes and control valve 9, with operating lever 8. The shutter 4 is hinged at the forward end to rise and fall under the

control of a cable, linking it with the lever on the dashboard, securing by the clip 2. The pierced lugs for bolting the housing to the underside of the dashboard and the air sealing pad around the housing opening are clearly visible. At the forward end of the picture is the slotted entry to the ducts supplying the air to the two demister outlets. In the centre lower part can be seen one of the

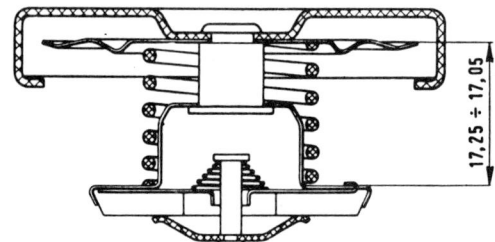

FIG 4:8 Section through radiator filler cap

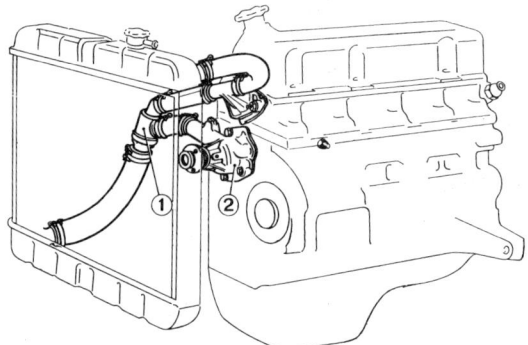

FIG 4:9 Thermostat installation

Key to Fig 4:9   1 Thermostat   2 Pump

four clip seatings which enable the fan unit to be secured to the underside of the housing.

The fan unit (see **FIG 4:12**) is a close fit to the underside of the radiator housing and contains the fan and motor 4, secured in the annular collar 3, integral with the moulding by metal clips 2. The rubber support pads 1 insulate the motor from the body for reduction of noise and vibration. The curved deflector in the front part of the figure directs the flow of air, via the slotted entry in the radiator housing, to the diffuser ducts. At the rear can be seen the hinged discharge shutter for distributing the air to the inside of the car.

The two diffuser outlets are mounted on the dashboard proper and can rotate to direct the stream of demisting air to the required zones of the windscreen. They are connected to the diffuser ducts by rubber sealing rings which can be seen in **FIG 4:10**. The ducts themselves are push fits into the sealing rings and are retained in position by the radiator housing rear support flange with slotted entries.

The upper of the two lever controls regulates the position of the shutter (see **FIG 4:11**), and the lower lever, the control valve regulating entry of hot water to the radiator. Beneath the dashboard can be seen the fan housing with air outlets regulated by the discharge shutter. When closed, all the air is deflected upwards to the demisters. By adjusting both valves, almost any desired inflow of cool, warm or hot air can be obtained.

To remove the system from the car, first disconnect the electrical connections to the fan motor, a black and yellow cable, at the control switch. Remove the four clips securing the fan unit to the housing and lower away.

The fan unit can then be transferred to a bench for servicing. This is confined to checking that the fan blades are clean, the fan tightly secured on the motor shaft and the bearings in good condition giving silent rotation and without excessive end play. Remove the fan from the body to clean out the interior of the housing.

To remove the radiator housing, first, drain the car radiator system and then disconnect and remove the hose clips and hoses to the flow and return pipes of the radiator. **With care, it is possible to remove the hoses without draining the car radiator system since these can be maintained above the level of the water in the system. Some water is bound to leak into the car during the process however and precautions must be taken not to let it soak the carpets. The hose ends may be plugged with corks while the radiator housing is being serviced.**

Disconnect the control cable to the valve, with the valve set in the closed position, and the cable sheath from the clip 9 (see **FIG 4:11**). Loosen the four nuts retaining the radiator within the housing and lower away from the housing. Transfer to the bench. Finally, loosen the cable sheath anchor clip and extract the air intake shutter control cable. The housing can then be unbolted and removed from the car. The air ducts to the diffusers can then be extracted from the sealing rings.

The fan, being mounted in an insulating housing, also needs an earth return. This is provided by a short black cable, visible to the left of FIG 4:12, clamped under only of the nuts securing the radiator to the body. Check that this is replaced to provide an adequate earth connection when reassembling the unit or the fan will not run.

Reassembly of the air conditioning unit is a simple reversal of the above procedure and should give no problems.

Dismantling of the various components is also straightforward. The fan motor can be dismantled by unscrewing the nuts on the two through-bolts after which it can be broken down into the four main components, two end plates, armature and field coil, the latter also including the brush holders and brackets.

The valve can be dismantled after removing from the radiator by unscrewing the two nuts attaching it to the fixing studs and then the two studs attaching the inlet pipe flange to the mating flange on the valve. The outlet pipe, which is welded by a clip to the inlet pipe, must then be unbolted from the radiator outlet flange if this, too, is required to be moved but the valve itself can be extracted without breaking the second seal.

Dismantling of the valve is then simple but, on reassembly, take care to see that the rubber seal is inserted and does not overlap between the flanges or the valve will leak.

The air inlet shutter can be removed by unscrewing the two nuts and washers fixing the hinge to the radiator housing. The air distribution shutter is retained in place by two screws and washers and spring hinges.

A general inspection of the complete system should include a check of the electrical connections to and from the fan motor, the condition of the commutator and brushes, the connections to and from the fan switch and a check that the switch itself is not faulty. The radiator should be carefully inspected for incipient cracks or

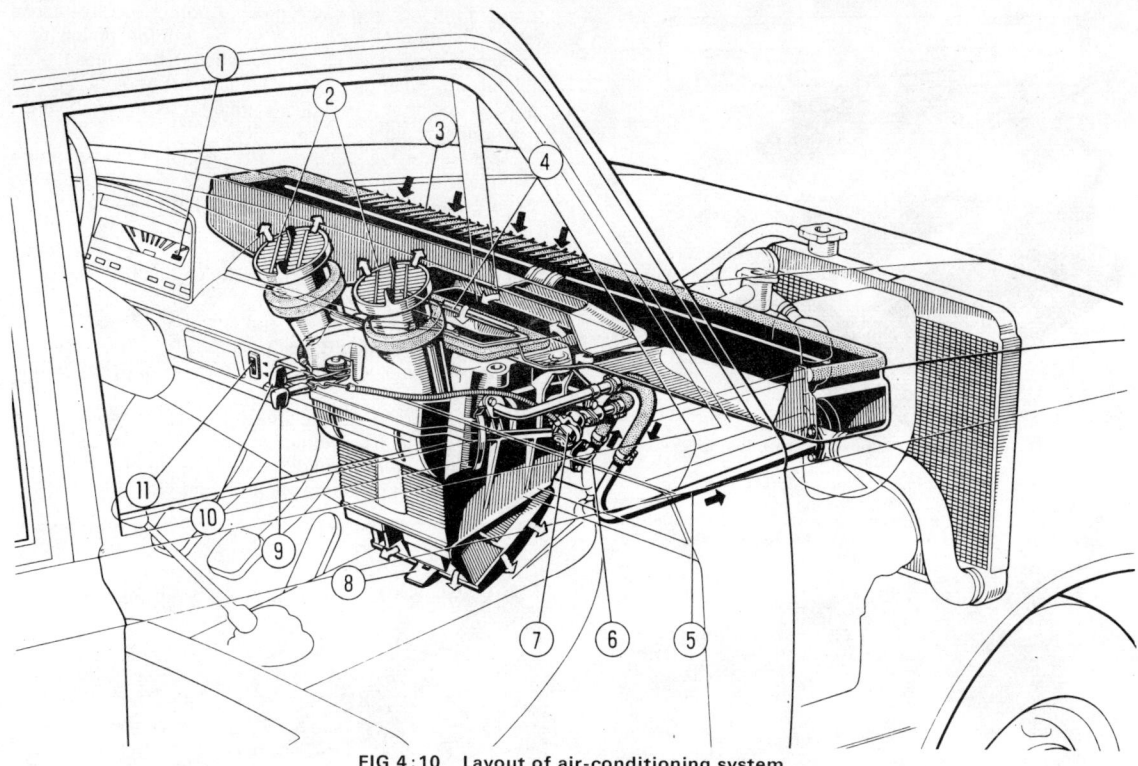

FIG 4:10   Layout of air-conditioning system

Key to Fig 4:10   1 Engine temperature warning light   2 Adjustable diffuser to direct air onto windscreen or inside car   3 Air intake slots in hood panel   4 Air intake shutter to direct external air into heater   5 Heater water return line   6 Heater water delivery line   7 Heater water control valve   8 Shutter to admit air to car interior   9 Lever operating valve (7)   10 Lever to control air shutter (4)   11 Heater fan switch

pinhole leaks, dents, etc., and, on reassembly, the joints for watertightness. The water hoses must be examined for signs of deterioration and the unions to the pipes for proper sealing.

When reassembling the unit in place in the car, take care to insert the gasket between the radiator housing and the inlet duct, and also the gasket between the fan housing and the radiator housing, and to position them properly before tightening the screws or fitting the clips.

After reassembly, open the valve and run the engine for a while to circulate the water through the heating radiator and then make a final check for all hose connections for watertightness.

Coupé:

On the Coupé model the switches and levers controlling the heating and air conditioning have been moved to a position between the front seats as shown in **FIG 4:13**.

4:8 Overtemperature warning

The overtemperature warning transducer is mounted at the top of the block on the rear distributor side of the engine. Its position can be seen in the two diagrams in **FIG 4:9**.

The transducer comprises a temperature-operated contact which closes when the water content of the

cooling system exceeds 100°C. The contacts earth the cable from the warning lamp on the dashboard which is energized from the battery positive via the ignition switch. If the cooling water temperature exceeds 100°C, the red warning light will come on at the righthand side of the speedometer. Switching off the ignition extinguishes the lamp **but it is important to appreciate that it does not alleviate the condition. Do not, therefore, take it for granted that it is safe to remove the radiator cap after the engine is stopped just because the warning light is extinguished.**

The warning lamp may become illuminated through a genuine alarm or through a fault in the electrical system. Dealing first with possible faults, the lamp will light if (a) an earth fault occurs on the green cable between the transducer and the instrument panel, or (b) if the contacts of the transducer have welded together or its internal insulation has failed. Conversely, the lamp will not light to give a warning when the water is over-temperature if there is an open circuit in the line, the lamp filament has burned out or fuse No. 1 on the fuseboard has blown. Always check the fuse first but this is simple since the same fuse supplies, among other circuits, the windscreen wiper and air conditioning fan motor. Check that each of these are operating before attempting to replace the warning lamp or look for an open-circuit. If both these are operative, remove the cable from the

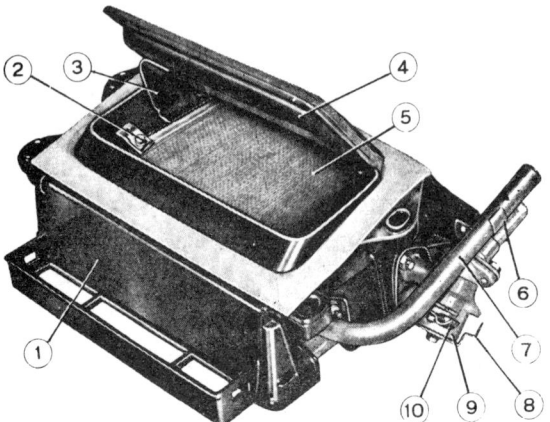

FIG 4:11   Radiator housing of car heater

Key to Fig 4:11   1 Fan housing   2 Fixing clip for cable
operating shutter (4)   3 Support   4 Air inlet shutter
5 Radiator   6 Hot water inlet pipe   7 Water outlet pipe
8 Valve lever   9 Valve   10 Clamp for valve cable

FIG 4:12   Fan housing showing fan motor 4 partly
removed from collar 3 in which it is retained by clips 2 on
mounting pads 1

transducer and earth it to the engine metal. If the lamp
does not light, then remove the bulb and insert a new one.

If the lamp remains alight with the ignition on and the
radiator cool (that is, should it come on when the engine
is switched on for the first time after standing) first,
disconnect the lead at the transducer. If the lamp remains
alight, examine the cable run for an earth fault. If it does
not, the fault is in the transducer and it must be replaced.
It is not possible to repair or readjust a transducer.

Possible causes of an overtemperature warning are
insufficient circulation through a slipping pump or fan
driving belt, leakage of water from the cooling system, a
faulty thermostat remaining in the closed position (this is
rare), a choked radiator or a failure in engine lubrication.
The latter should, however, be advised by the oil-pressure
warning lamp but it is possible that a bulb failure could

prevent the warning being given. Another possible cause
of overheating is a slipping of the ignition timing to a
fairly retarded state. This, too, should be noticed by a
falling off in engine performance but it may not be
appreciated that a retarded engine tends to overheat on
load rather rapidly.

There is always, of course, the normal overtemperature
condition arising out of long traffic jams in hot weather,
or long hauls in low gear at fairly high engine speeds.
These can be countered by suitable precautions, such as
switching off the engine while waiting for the traffic
queue to move rather than to let the engine tick over or, in
the case of the long haul on a steep gradient, to run the
engine at about half its full-out speed, remembering that
the maximum torque develops at 3500 to 3800 rev/min
though the maximum power output may be around
5600 rev/min.

The overtemperature warning is not, therefore, only a
warning of fault conditions developing but a useful
indication of driving conditions which are not conducive
to good engine performance and long life.

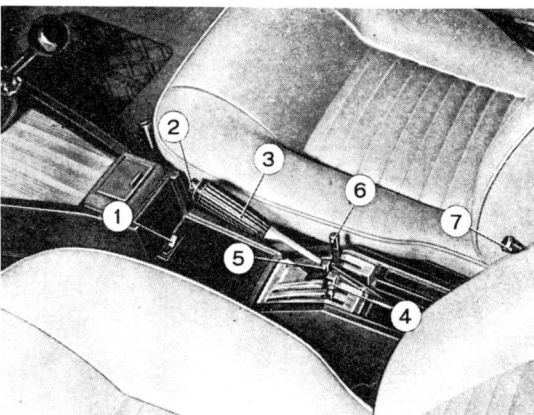

FIG 4:13   Air conditioning controls on Coupé model

Key to Fig 4:13   1 3-position fan control switch
2-3 Handbrake lever   4 Ventilation air control lever
5 Heater control lever   6 Heater-air control lever

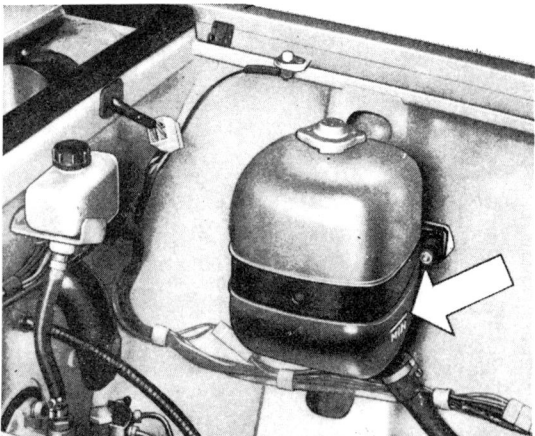

FIG 4:14   Auxiliary header tank showing position of
minimum contents mark

4:9 Electro-magnetic fan

On early engines, fitted to cars up to chassis No. 0000251, the fan was a press fit on to the water pump spindle, but on later engines it was located by a key and locked with a nut as shown in **FIGS 4:1** and **4:15**.

Maintenance:

After the first 1000 to 1300 miles check that the air gap (Y in **FIG 4:15**) between the body and the armature is .25 to .35 mm. If necessary adjust as follows:

1 Unscrew the locknuts 8 of the three adjusting screws.
2 Adjust the screws as required, checking the air gap each time with a feeler gauge opposite each screw as it is adjusted.
3 Lock the nuts and make a final check.

At 12,500 miles, carefully clean the contact ring 5 with a dry cloth. Unhook the retaining spring, slip off the brush holder and check the wear on the brush and the condition of the brush spring. If either part is defective it should be renewed.

Faults:

If the water temperature gauge indicates 89°C (192°F) or above and the fan clutch has not engaged, the thermostatic switch may be defective. A new switch should be obtained, but as a temporary expedient the two leads may be connected to the same terminal which will cause the fan to run continuously.

If this does not make the fan clutch engage, there may be an open circuit in the windings. The remedy is to obtain a new pulley complete with magnet and brush ring. As a temporary measure the following procedure will cause the fan to run continuously.

Unscrew the locknuts 8 on the three air gap adjusting screws 9 and tighten up the screws to a moderate extent until the armature adheres to the body of the magnet. Lock up the three locknuts.

4:10 Fault diagnosis

(a) Too frequent topping up of radiator

1 Leakage from joints or hose junctions
2 Faulty filler cap seal
3 Leak in heater system for air conditioning
4 Leaking drain cocks or valves
5 Leaking cylinder head gasket

The last is a serious condition occurring after an engine overhaul through failure to check cylinder head nut tightness after a few hours running. It usually is accompanied by loss of power and occasionally by excessive

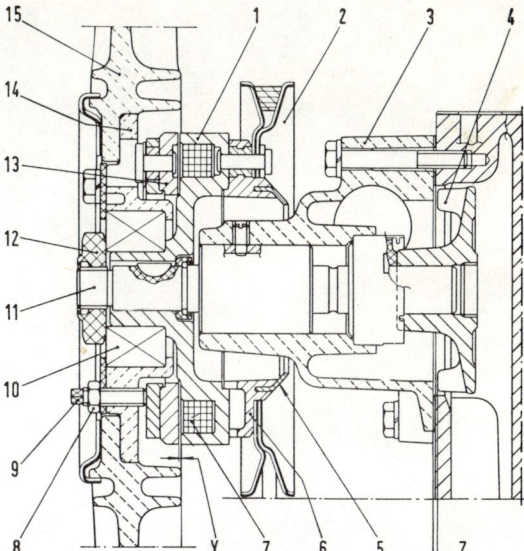

FIG 4:15 Section through water pump and electro-magnetic fan clutch

Key to Fig 4:15   1 Pulley hub and body of electro-magnet   2 Pulley   3 Pump body   4 Pump rotor   5 Contact ring   6 Contact ring hub   7 Magnet coil   8 Locknut   9 Magnet air-gap adjusting screw   10 Fan bearing   11 Water pump spindle   12 Nut   13 Armature of electro-magnet   14 Fan hub   15 Fan   Y = .25 to .35 (.0098 inch to .0137 in)   **Z** = 1 mm (.0394 in)

condensation from the exhaust. Immediate strip down and a new gasket is imperative if further damage is to be avoided.

(b) Operation of overtemperature warning

1 Broken or loose fan belt
2 Low water level in radiator
3 Obstruction in radiator passages
4 Faulty thermostat
5 Fault on overtemperature transducer or cable

(c) Engine will not warm up

1 Faulty thermostat
2 Ambient temperature too low

(d) Air conditioning not operating

1 Air lock in radiator system
2 Broken or disconnected shutter cable
3 Broken or disconnected valve cable

NOTES

CHAPTER 5

THE CLUTCH

5:1 Construction and operation

The clutch is of the dry single plate type with a diaphragm pressure spring, and with a spring cushioned hub as part of the driven plate. The hub and hub-plate are coupled, through six helical springs, to the cushion disc which is integral with the segmented driven plate faced on both sides with bonded asbestos brake material (Ferodo). This ensures smooth engagement between the engine and the gearbox drive shaft by damping out cyclical acceleration and retardation torques. The special diaphragm pressure spring maintains a constant load on the pressure plate irrespective of the degree of clutch wear on the friction facings.

The drive from the engine is communicated to the gearbox drive shaft by clamping the driven plate between the pressure plate, part of the clutch withdrawal mechanism, and a machined facing on the engine flywheel. This pressure is applied by the diaphragm riveted at three points to the clutch cover against spring rings which act as a fulcrum around which the diaphragm bells when the centre section, divided into a group of eighteen radial segments, is deflected by the clutch withdrawal flange. This belling has the effect of releasing circumferential pressure on the pressure plate and, consequently, on the facing ring.

A view of the clutch and clutch housing is shown in **FIG 5:1**. The same view is shown diagrammatically and with an end view to show the clutch withdrawal lever in **FIG 5:2**.

Operation of the clutch withdrawal mechanism can better be understood by reference to **FIG 5:2** together with the detail of the section through the fork lever and throwout sleeve in **FIG 5:3**. The diaphragm 1, pivoted about the spring rings 2, and secured by the rivets 3, to the clutch cover 4, in the rest state applies pressure to the annular plate 5, to clamp the friction surfaces of the driven plate 6, to the machined facing on the flywheel 7. The engine torque is therefore transmitted via the cushion springs 8 to the hub 9 on the splined shaft 10 and to the gearbox.

Depression of the lever 11, acting against the withdrawal fulcrum 12, moves the pins 13, towards the flywheel taking with them the throw-out sleeve 14. This applies pressure to the friction ring 15 which, acting on the clutch withdrawal plate 16, supported on arms 17 from the clutch cover, forces the inner ends of the

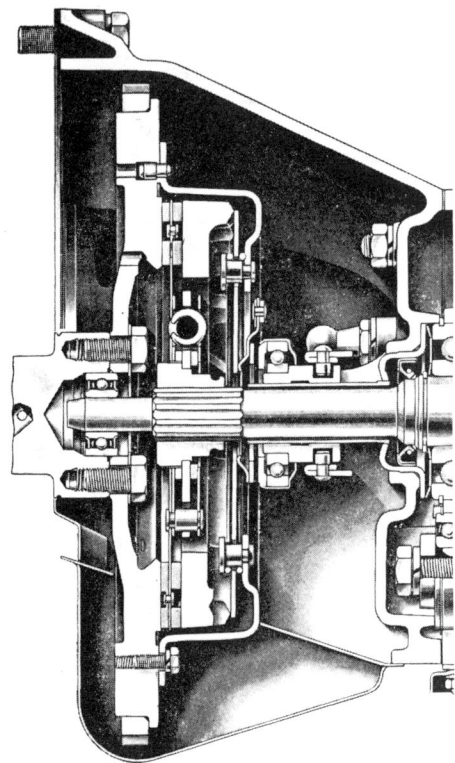

FIG 5:1 Sectional side view through clutch and bell-housing

diaphragm segments to the left causing the outer periphery to bell to the right, releasing the pressure on the driven plate.

The clutch withdrawal lever 11 is actuated by a Bowden cable 18 (see **FIG 5:3**) against the tension of the return spring 19. The other end of the cable is linked to the clutch pedal and adjustment of travel is by means of the nut and locknut 20.

5:2 Maintenance

In the ordinary way, routine maintenance is confined to examination of the linkage between the pedal and the clutch lever, ensuring that the Bowden cable is well lubricated in the sleeve, the bearings of the pedal control shaft are not worn or dry and that the free travel of the pedal is correctly set. There should be about $\frac{3}{4}$ inch free play on the pedal before commencement of clutch withdrawal this corresponding to a gap of .07 inch between the throw-out sleeve and the friction ring. Less than this may result in excessive wear on the withdrawal mechanism and may also introduce unnecessary noise while running. Adjustment is made by loosening the locknut 2, and adjusting nut 1 (see **FIG 5:4**) on the screwed pullrod at the end of the Bowden cable and then adjusting the nut 1, until the correct amount of free play is obtained at the clutch pedal. Secure this setting by the locknut but, in doing so, make sure that the grommet in

the lug through which the cable sheath is inserted is properly seated or the reaction of the sheath to the cable pull will not be satisfactory. If necessary, replace the grommet.

The clutch pedal is mounted on bushings on a pivot pin common to the footbrake (see **Section 10:12**). It is, of course, essential that the clutch and brake pedals shall operate independently, be free on the pivot pin and bushings and that the clutch return spring is in place and not over-extended. It is not sufficient to depend on the clutch fork return spring at the other end of the Bowden cable to counter the weight of the pedal. Always replace weak or broken springs.

Maintenance of the clutch proper can only be done after removal of the gearbox. The procedure is detailed in **Section 6** and necessitates the jacking-up of the car to gain access for working.

5:3 Servicing

Providing the the maintenance outlined in the previous paragraphs has been carried out, the clutch and linkage need no routine servicing.

5:4 Clutch removal and dismantling

With the engine jacked up and the gearbox removed, the clutch on the flywheel will be revealed on the flywheel as in **FIG 5:5**. The bellhousing enclosing the clutch and withdrawal mechanism is removed as part of the gearbox assembly taking with it the splined driven shaft and leaving the driven plate clamped between the two clutch facings but otherwise unsecured. **The realignment of this plate with special tool A.70081 is an essential part of reinstalling the gearbox and unless done properly and with due care and attention, damage to the clutch may result.**

To remove the gearbox, it will have been necessary to disconnect the clutch throw-out mechanism. The clutch withdrawal lever will still be in position and this is removed by pulling the lever to the left until the spring clip securing the fulcrum end to the ball joint 12 (see **FIG 5:3**) slips clear. The pins engaging the slot of the throw-out sleeve may then be disengaged by pulling the lever still farther out and slipping the lever clear of the throw-out sleeve. Remove the sleeve and the friction ring.

Mark the clutch cover and the flywheel with a small dab of paint so that on reassembly, the clutch will be in the same relative position.

Remove the bolts securing the clutch cover to the flywheel and transfer the complete assembly to a flat jig plate, to simulate the flywheel. The driven plate will be freed when the clutch cover bolts are removed and will come away as a separate component. Take care that it does not slip to the ground while so doing.

The two assemblies will then appear as in **FIG 5:6**.

First examine the driven plate and check that the cushion springs are all in place, intact and in good condition. Check the condition of the hub splines and the general condition of the friction plate, particularly at the six points where the periphery meets the central member.

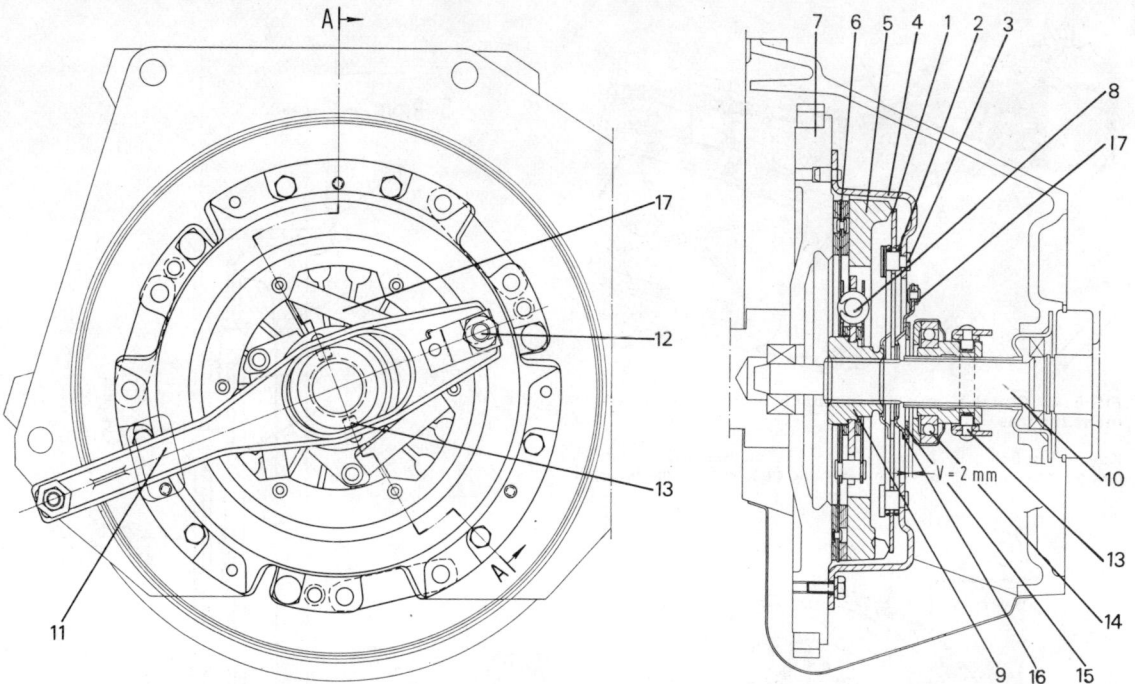

FIG 5:2 Diagrammatic view and section through clutch assembly

Key to Fig 5:2 1 Diaphragm 2 Spring rings 3 Rivet 4 Clutch cover 5 Annular pressure plate 6 Driven plate
7 Flywheel 8 Cushion spring 9 Drive hub 10 Gearshaft 11 Throwout lever 12 Fulcrum 13 Pins 14 Throwout sleeve
15 Friction ring 16 Withdrawal plate 17 Clutch strap

Examine the Ferodo facings and check that they are not excessively worn or heavily scored. Check that all the rivets are in place and that none are proud of the surface. Check the condition of the rivets securing the two parts of centre assembly. If there is any suspicion of weakness, completely replace the driven plate.

Generally speaking, it is not advisable to attempt to reface the driven plate with new friction material. The fitting is a specialist skill and it is easier to renew the whole plate.

Next, examine the pressure plate assembly, checking first that the pressure plate is smooth and free from scoring on the contact face. A section through the assembly is shown in **FIG 5:7**.

The facing on the pressure plate is .35 inch from the level of the clutch cover mounting surface. So, for check purposes, it is necessary to insert a ring 7 inches in diameter by .35 inch thick between the jig plate and the pressure plate in order that the clutch withdrawal force can be checked.

First of all, examine all rivets and rivet holes for signs of cracks or looseness. Check that the three arms supporting the clutch withdrawal flange are secure at both ends and properly centre the flange. Check that the diaphragm retaining clips 5 (see **FIG 5:7**) are holding the diaphragm and pressure plate in close contact and that the diaphragm itself is secure on the spring rings 4 and rivets. Examine the eighteen segments for signs of wear or cracking.

Finally, place the assembly face downwards on the ring on the jig plate and apply a load in the direction of

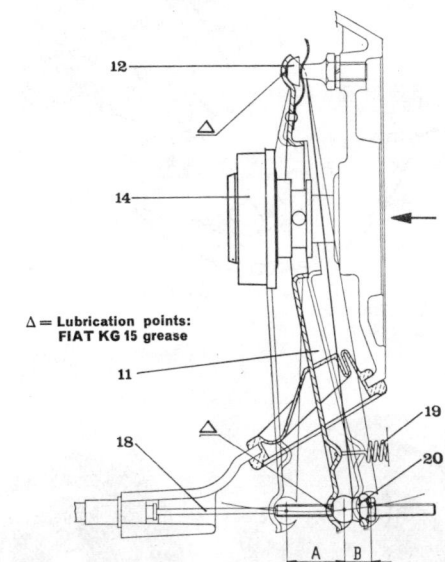

△ = Lubrication points: FIAT KG 15 grease

A = 1.18″ (30 mm). Declutching travel corresponding to a .055″ (1,4 mm) shift of clutch disc.

B = .59″ (15 mm). Shift of clutch withdrawal lever due to wear of driven plate.

FIG 5:3 Diagrammatic view of clutch withdrawal mechanism

Key to Fig 5:3 11 Throw-out lever 12 Fulcrum pillar 14 Throw-out sleeve 18 Bowden cable 19 Clutch fork return spring 20 Adjusting nut and locknut

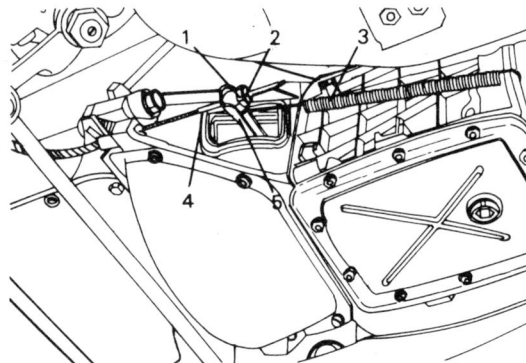

FIG 5:4 Clutch throw-out mechanism showing adjustment for free play

Key to Fig 5:4 1 Adjusting nut 2 Locknut 3 Clutch fork return spring 4 Bowden cable and pullrod 5 Fork lever

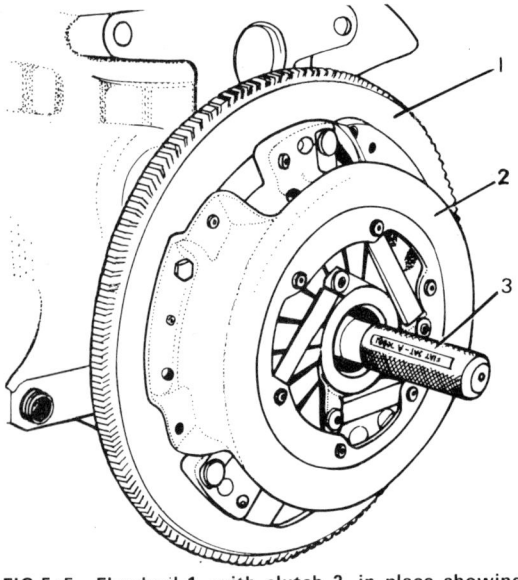

FIG 5:5 Flywheel 1, with clutch 2, in place showing use of tool A.70081 3

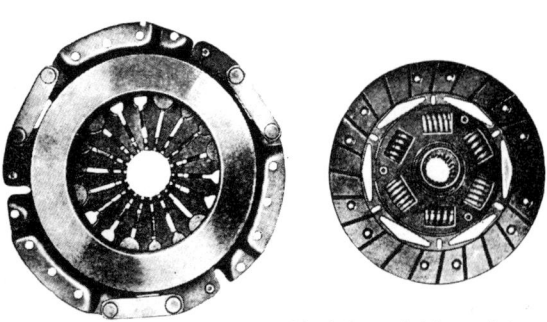

FIG 5:6 Pressure plate assembly, left, and driven plate removed from flywheel for inspection

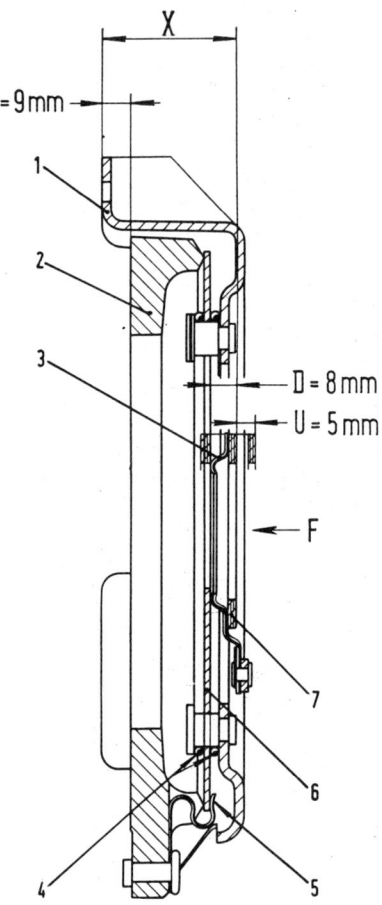

FIG 5:7 Section through pressure plate assembly showing points for setting check

Key to Fig 5:7   1 Clutch cover   2. Pressure plate   3 Clutch withdrawal flange   4 Diaphragm spring rings   5 Diaphragm retainer clip   6 Diaphragm   7 Friction ring
X=1.62 inch±.05 inch   **F**=728 lb±55 lb   **S**=.35 inch
D=.31 inch   **U**=.19 inch

the arrow to the centre withdrawal flange. Increase the load to 728 lb and note that the flange has been lifted from the jig plate. Check that the withdrawal travel 'D' is .31 inch and that the corresponding movement of the pressure plate is .062 to .066 inch.

If the measurements are different from the above or a lighter load produces the same deflection, replace the complete clutch cover assembly. Since the assembly is a riveted one, it is not advisable for the owner mechanic to dismantle and reconstruct it. Replacements are available from the Fiat agent on an exchange basis.

Do not endeavour to lift or carry the assembly by the withdrawal flange as this may strain or damage the suspension arms.

5:5 Reassembly, refitting and plate alignment

To reassemble, first insert the end of tool A.700081 in the driven plate hub from the projecting end and then fit it into position on the flywheel with friction ring in contact with the flywheel facing. Ensure that both faces are clean and free from grease or oil. The end of the tool will be supported in the flywheel hub bearing.

Replace the coverplate assembly in its original position on the flywheel, checking that all the dowels are home and then insert studs and lockwashers, tightening them down to a torque of 7.25 lb ft. Again make sure that both faces are clean and free from grease and oil.

In the bellhousing of the gearbox, fit, first, the withdrawal throw-out lever and throw-out sleeve on the gearshaft sleeve, lubricating the surface with engine oil, insert the pins in the collar of the throw-out sleeve and push the fulcrum end spring onto the ball-head fulcrum. Secure the lever in place by re-installing the clutch fork return spring.

Clean and refit the friction ring on the same shaft and then raise the gearbox on the hydraulic jack so that the gearshaft is in line with the flywheel. Remove the centring tool from the clutch assembly and carefully insert the end of the gearshaft into the space it has vacated making sure that the splines on the end of the shaft marry with those on the hub of the driven plate. Centre the friction ring on the clutch withdrawal flange, push the gearbox home with the gearshaft now in the flywheel centre bearing and secure in place by means of the four bolts and spring washers tightened with special wrench, A.55035.

It will be found necessary to incline the gearbox assembly slightly, with the rear end lower than the front, to get the gearshaft to enter the clutch and flywheel assembly and into the ballbearing on the crankshaft. The operation must be carried out with great care and precision.

Replace the lower bellhousing cover and secure by the studs and washers. Finally couple the clutch throw-out cable to the clutch fork lever and adjust for travel.

5:6 Replacement of the clutch Bowden cable

In the event of breakage of the cable linking the clutch pedal with the clutch fork lever, complete replacement of the Bowden assembly is preferable to attempting to renew the inner cable alone. The procedure is straightforward comprizing the extraction of the old cable and the installation of the new one in exactly the same position. The grommet in the bracket at the clutch end for terminating the sheath must be renewed at the same time.

The layout of the clutch cable release system is shown in **FIG 5:8**, together with pedal travel dimensions.

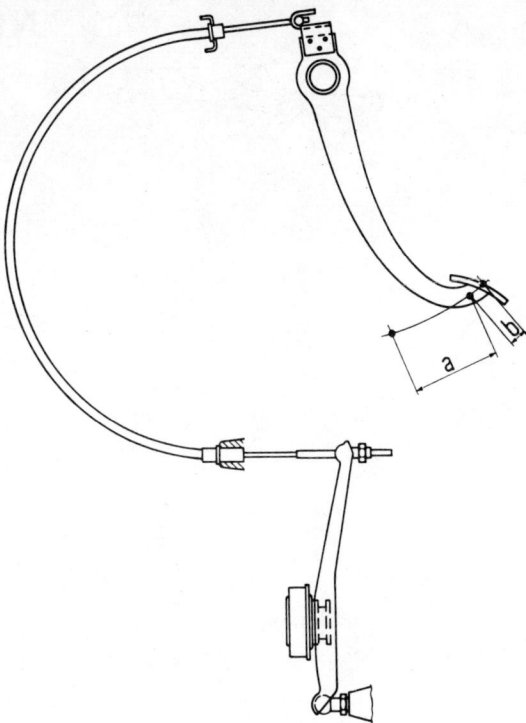

FIG 5:8 Details of clutch operating cable (1973)

Key to Fig 5:8 **a** = 3.9 inch (98.5 mm). Max. release travel **b** = .98 inch (25 mm). Free travel

5:7 Fault diagnosis

(a) Clutch will not disengage

1 Broken Bowden cable
2 Adjusting nut worked loose
3 Stretched Bowden cable
4 Broken pins on withdrawal lever
5 Failure or breakage of fulcrum pillar

(b) Clutch will not engage

1 Insufficient pedal free play
2 Weak or broken clutch return spring
3 Ruptured diaphragm
4 Badly worn friction facings
5 Oil or grease on facings

(c) Noises with clutch engaged

1 Throw-out bearings worn or dry
2 Insufficient free travel on clutch pedal
3 Throw-out fork spring broken or disengaged

NOTES

CHAPTER 6

THE GEARBOX

6:1 Construction and operation

The gearbox fitted to Coupé models is of the conventional type with four forward gears and a reverse gear. The forward gears are all synchromesh. The wheels are of helical pattern, permanently meshed to give quiet operation. The reverse gear is obtained by a sliding intermediate spur gear between gears on the layshaft and mainshaft.

The gearbox is in three parts: a forward bellhousing within which are contained the clutch and clutch lever, a central section with the synchromesh gear trains, selector forks and rods, and a rear cover for the gear selection mechanism and reverse gear. The three alloy castings are bolted together to form a single unit, the bellhousing and gear sections each having a bottom inspection cover (see **FIG 6:1**).

The main gear components comprise a mainshaft, a layshaft and the selector forks and rods. The mainshaft is supported at the front end in needle bearings in the gearshaft (which transmits the drive from the clutch to the layshaft) and in ballbearings at the rear and in the centre where it passes through the wall between gearcase and the cover.

The drive from the gearshaft 1 (see **FIG 6:2**) is transmitted to the layshaft 2, via the first pair of helical gears 3, at the forward end of the gearbox. Adjacent to the drive gear and integral with the gearshaft is the tooth wheel 4, which is engaged with the inner teeth of the sliding sleeve 5 to provide the direct top gear drive.

In all other gears, the drive is via the layshaft and through one of the three pairs of helical gears 6, 7, 8, the driven gear of each pair being a sliding fit on the mainshaft with each having a tooth wheel, on the side adjacent to the sleeve, as an integral part. Gear selection is by movement of one of the two sliding sleeves 5, 9, which are splined to a central hub keyed to the mainshaft. The internal splines of the sleeve, when the latter is moved left or right, mesh simultaneously with the tooth wheel of the adjacent driven gear and those of the hub to provide a positive drive to the mainshaft and beyond while leaving the remaining pairs of helical gears free to rotate without taking load. The synchronizing feature is provided by a tooth wheel 10, interposed on the shaft between the sleeve hub and a driven gear. The tooth wheel is friction driven on one side by the driven gear and locked by dogs on the other, immediately prior to engagement with the tooth wheel by the sleeve, to ensure that

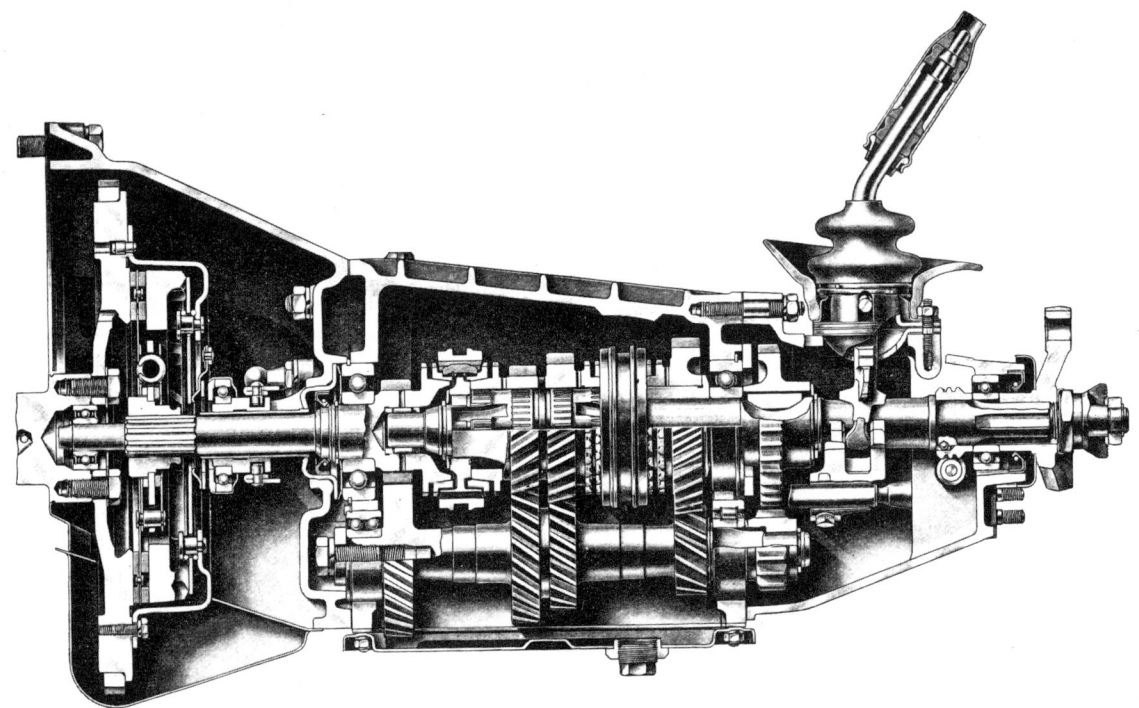

FIG 6:1   Sectional side view of clutch and gearbox assembly

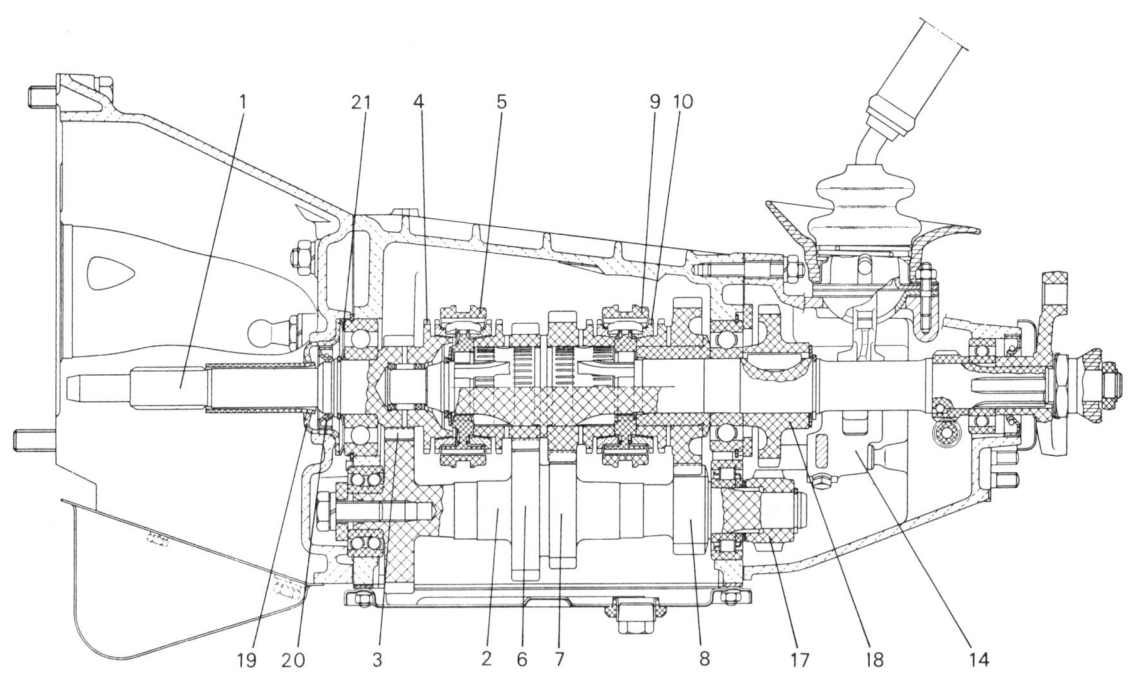

FIG 6:2   Diagrammatic section through clutch and gearbox

Key to Fig 6:2   1 Gearshaft   2 Layshaft   3 First pair of helical gears   4 Tooth wheel   5 Third/fourth gear sliding sleeve
6 Third gear helical pair   7 Second gear helical pair   8 First gear helical pair   9 First/second gear sliding sleeve   10 Tooth
wheel   14 Reverse gear striker rod   17 Driving reverse spur gear   18 Driven reverse spur gear   19 Centre cover with O-ring
20 Oil seal   21 Belleville spring washer

both the sleeve and the driven gear are at the same speed of rotation before positive meshing.

The sleeves are moved by forked arms, embracing the circumferential groove of the sleeve, mounted on striker rods passing through the wall of the gearcase into the covered area where they are selected and moved by the end of the gearshift lever 11 (see **FIGS 6:3** and **6:4**). Engagement of the lever 11, with the upper rod 12, enables the first or second gear to be selected by movement of sleeve 9, in either direction. Engagement of the lever with the lower rod 13, enables the third gear to be selected or, alternatively, the direct drive to be engaged.

Engagement of the lever with the third striker rod 14, moves the intermediate spur gear 15, on its shaft 16, into mesh between the spur gears 17 and 18, on the layshaft and mainshaft respectively, to provide a direct drive but with reverse rotation.

Positive movement of the striker rods in each direction is ensured by a spring-loaded ball positioning device while a secondary set of rollers forms a safety feature preventing the simultaneous movement of both sleeves into gear.

On Sport models the gearbox has five forward speeds, the fifth ratio being in effect an overdrive and it is housed in the rear cover together with the reverse gears and selector bars. In general the instructions for servicing the fourspeed box will apply, but material points of difference will be found at the end of this chapter and in **Technical Data**.

6:2 Maintenance

Maintenance of the gearbox is confined to periodical checking on the oil level and topping up with SAE 90 EP, or equivalent grade oil. Filling is done through the hole on the righthand side of the gearbox, viewed from the rear, closed by a screw plug. The oil must reach the bottom level of the hole. The content of the gearbox when full is 2.4 pints but there is no necessity for draining and refilling during the life of the car unless there has been some mechanical failure within the gearbox. Similarly, after a complete overhaul, the old oil can be re-used if it is not obviously contaminated.

The gearlever, being a direct drive, needs no adjustment but, in time, the ball joint may become slack. This can be rectified by replacing the dome washer as detailed in **Section 6:7**.

It always pays to keep a good ear to gearbox noise as this can disclose incipient troubles before they reach a dangerous stage. A light finger applied to the end of the gearlever will sense any damaged or chipped gears while the car is running. While no sound should come from the gearbox in any of the forward gears, there will always be a degree of whine with the reverse since gears are not helical and even the best of spur gears are not dead silent in operation.

6:3 Removing the gearbox from the car

Gearbox overhaul is essentially a bench process necessitating removal of the complete unit from the car. Proceed as follows.

Working from inside the car, first remove the upper part of the gearlever. How to do this is described in **Section 6:7**. Raise the car on stands to give good working

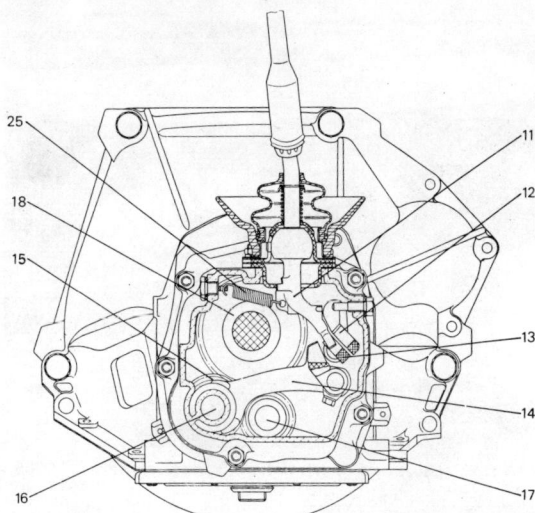

FIG 6:3 Transverse section through gearlever and selector rods

Key to Fig 6:3   11 Operating end of gearlever
12 First/second gear striker rod   13 Third/fourth gear striker rod   14 Reverse gear striker rod   15 Intermediate reverse spur gear   16 Reverse intermediate gear shaft   17 Driving reverse spur gear   18 Driven reverse spur gear
25 Gearlever spring

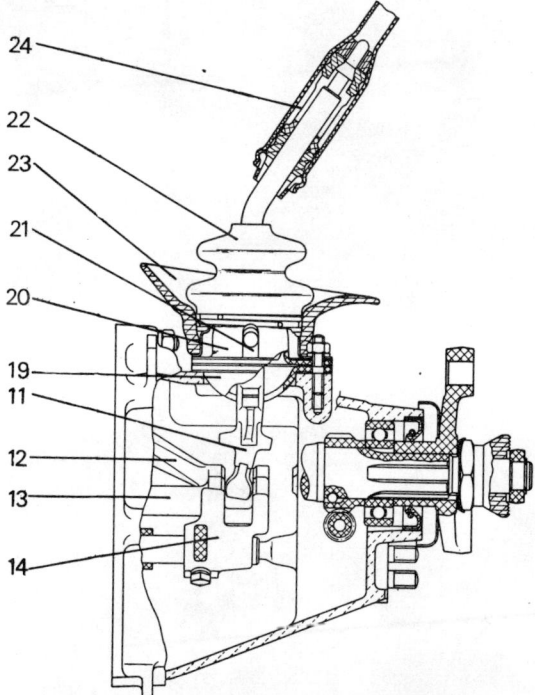

FIG 6:4 Coverplate with gearlever assembly

Key to Fig 6:4   11 Operating end of gearlever
12 First/second gear striker rod   13 Third/fourth gear striker rod   14 Reverse gear striker rod   19 Lower half-cover   20 Upper half-cover   21 Ball and pin   22 Rubber boot and spring   23 Grommet   24 Gearlever stub and joint

FIG 6:5 Lowering gearbox from car on support A.70509

FIG 6:6 Gearbox clamped to support Arr.22206. 12 on stand Arr.22204

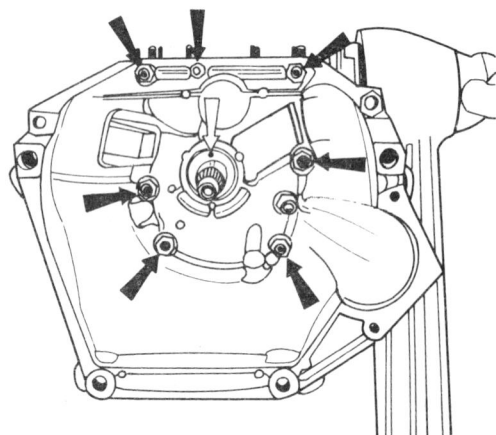

FIG 6:7 Interior view of bellhousing showing seven attachment nuts (black arrowed) and oil drain hole (white arrow)

clearance under the body and then loosen and remove the three bolts securing the flexible coupling on the crankshaft to the spider on the mainshaft. Unscrew and withdraw the speedometer drive from the rear cover. Unbolt and remove the clutch withdrawal Bowden cable. Unbolt and remove the flywheel cover and, at the same time disconnect the heavy duty earth cable connection which is made by the rear lefthand bolt securing the cover.

Remove the bolt securing the exhaust pipe support to the bracket on the rear cover and also the starter motor heat shield which is attached to the exhaust manifold with two nuts and lockwashers. Remove the three bolts securing the starter motor to the bellhousing, disconnect the heavy duty lead to the motor and the solenoid control cable and remove the starter.

Using a hydraulic jack and special support attachment A.70509, take the weight of the gearbox and then remove the four bolts securing it to the engine block. Offset spanner A.55035 has been designed for this operation. Unbolt the crossmember from the underside of the body (see **FIG 1:4**) and remove the two bolts and two nuts securing the member to the gearbox.

Ease the gearbox free of the clutch by moving it back on the garage jack and lower to clear the front suspension (see **FIG 6:5**). Withdraw from under the car and transfer to the bench or, preferably, support Arr.22206/12 mounted to one arm of the stand Arr.22204 (see **FIG 6:6**).

6:4 Dismantling

Thoroughly clean the exterior of the gearbox using, for preference, one of the proprietary cleaning materials, and dry off. Then unscrew the drain plug and drain the oil from the gearbox into a clean container. If it is not obviously contaminated, it may be used to refill the box after maintenance overhaul has been completed.

Turn the gearbox over and remove the coverplate with drain plug and gasket. Disconnect the clutch fork return spring, ease the fork clear of the fulcrum and clutch throw-out sleeve, and remove fork lever, sleeve and friction ring. Unbolt and remove the bellhousing from the gearcase together with its gasket. There are seven retaining nuts which are arrowed in **FIG 6:7**.

At the same time, remove from the gearshaft the centre cover 19, oilseal 20 and spring washer 21 (see **FIG 6:2**). Remove the fixing bolts of the third/fourth gear selector fork to enable the sleeve 5 to be engaged with a gear at the same time as sleeve 9 is engaged with another, so locking the shafts to facilitate further dismantling.

Slide off the dust cover at the end of the mainshaft and extract the snap ring retaining the flexible coupling centring ring in place. Use expanding pliers A.81101 for this purpose (see **FIG 6:8**). Remove the centring ring with universal puller A.48005 (see **FIG 6:9**), flatten the tabwasher, undo the nut and take the spider off the shaft. Remove the speedometer drive support with gasket from the rear cover.

Unscrew the two nuts retaining the coverplate over the three detent ball springs and remove balls and springs. **Note that the reverse gear detent ball spring 1 (see FIG 6:10) is different from the remaining two and take steps to avoid transposing them when reassembling.**

The next step is to remove the rear cover. First, remove the stop screw 4 (see **FIG 6:12**) from the case and then

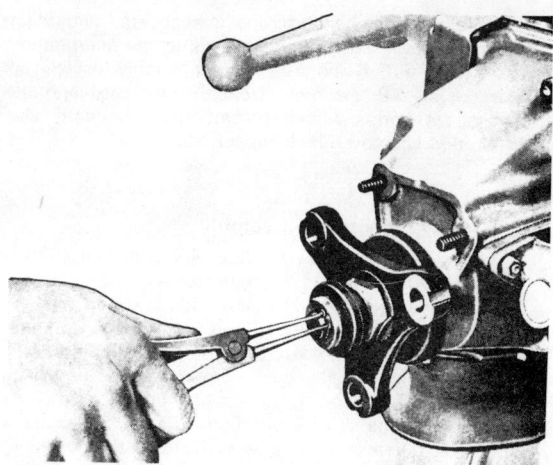

FIG 6:8 Removing snap ring retaining the centring ring on the mainshaft with expanding tool A.81101

FIG 6:10 Detent ball springs with cover removed. The reverse gear spring 1, is of different compression strength to the 3rd/4th gear spring 2, and 1st/2nd gear spring 3. Do not transpose on reassembly

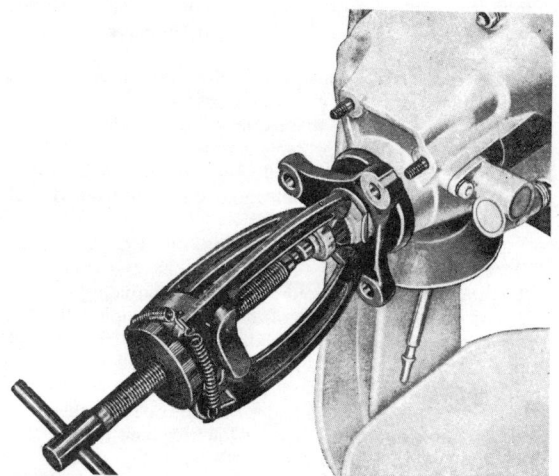

FIG 6:9 Removing centring ring with universal puller A.48005

FIG 6:11 Removing rear cover casting from gearbox showing the five retaining nuts, arrowed

unbolt the six nuts and spring washers retaining the cover on the gearbox (see **FIG 6:11**). Push the gearlever stub away from the side with the stop screw to disengage the lower end from the striker rods and then part the rear cover from the gearbox. Remove the gearlever from the rear cover by unscrewing the three nuts and spring washers at the base and by disconnecting the lever return spring 2 (see **FIG 6:12**). Slide the rear ballbearing 8 and speedometer drive gear from the mainshaft 7 (see **FIG 6:13**). Slide the reverse gear selector rod and fork 3 and 6, out from its seating and remove the intermediate spur gear 5 from the spindle.

Using expanding pliers A.81101, take off the snap ring retaining the reverse driving gear (see **FIG 6:14**) and slide the gear and spring washer clear of the layshaft. Take off the snap ring retaining the driven gear of the reverse train, **first compressing the spring washer with tool A.70158 as shown in FIG 6:23**, remove the

spring washers, driven gear and then extract the Woodruff key.

With the gears still locked, unscrew the bolt, with spring and flat washer, from the end of the layshaft (see **FIG 6:14**) and extract the double row ballbearing. Remove the ballbearing at the other end of the layshaft and then carefully withdraw the layshaft from the gearbox (see **FIG 6:16**). Remove the third/fourth selector rod from the case, undo the bolt securing the first/second selector fork to the rod, remove this rod next and, finally, extract both selector forks from the gearbox.

As the rods are removed from their bearings, the selector safety rollers will be released. Carefully note how these are located and preserve for reinstallation in the same manner on reassembly.

Remove the mainshaft intermediate ballbearing retainer plate and then **carefully** withdraw the gearshaft and ballbearing through the gearbox casing (see **FIG 6:17**).

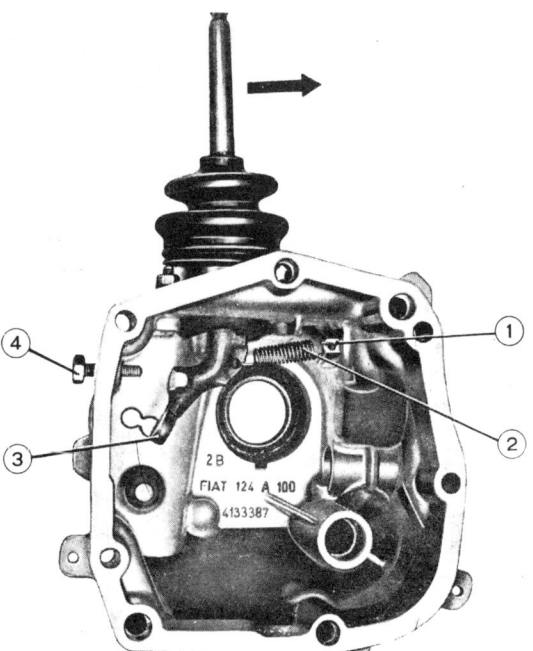

FIG 6:12 Interior view of rear cover with gearlever 3, gearlever centring spring 2, anchor screw 1, and side travel stop 4

FIG 6:13 Gearbox partly dismantled showing reverse gear train with intermediate gear 5, fork lever 6, and bolt 4, striker rods 1, 2 and 3, and speedometer drive 7 with ballrace 8

In doing so, the needle bearing with retainer rings supporting the end of the layshaft in the end of the gearshaft will come apart and all the needle rollers, twenty-three in number, will be released. These must be carefully collected and stored with the retainer rings for reassembly later.

Withdraw the intermediate ballbearing and this will allow the mainshaft, with all components in place, to be tilted for removal from the gearcase.

Transfer the mainshaft to a bench, covered with clean paper, and proceed to dismantle it into the components as shown in FIG 6:18. Add to the assembly, the reverse gear spindle 49, extracted from the gearcase and the component parts of the layshaft and gearchaft, also dismantled and laid out as section.

6:5 Inspection and reassembly

Thoroughly clean the interior of the gearcase, bell-housing and cover and examine for signs of damage, cracks or damaged threads on the studs. If any are present, change the part involved. Thoroughly clean all ball-bearings in a suitable solvent, dry in a jet of compressed air and examine for damaged races or cracked or broken balls. Check for smooth running and change if there is any suspicion as to their condition. Clean and examine the needle rollers and the roller surfaces on the mainshaft and gearshaft. Examine the joint faces of the casings to check for oil leakage past the gaskets and remove any burrs that may be present with a smooth file.

Examine the oil breather on the front cover to ensure that it is not blocked. Replace any oil seals that are defective. Better still, replace all oil seals by new ones at each overhaul.

Turning, next to shafts, examine each one carefully for surface damage, corrosion or signs of circumferential wear. Check that the splines are clean cut and not worn and that the hubs slide freely on them.

Check the mainshaft between centres using a dial gauge and ensure that the runout does not exceed .001 inch at the worst point.

Examine all the gear teeth for (a) signs of damage or wear to the gears themselves and (b) the wear lines on the gear faces occasioned by normal mating. These should be smooth, well polished and extending the full width of the gear teeth. Backlash must not exceed .004 inch when new or .008 inch maximum.

Inspect the two sliding sleeves for wear where the forks encircle the groove and where the splines mate with those on the outer periphery of the hub (see FIG 6:19).

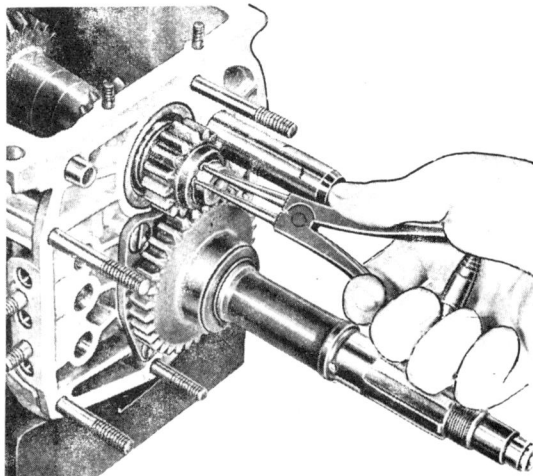

FIG 6:14 Removing snap ring from layshaft with expanding tool A.81101

Check the condition of the dogs and the retaining springs. Examine the synchronizing rings for wear, particularly on the external teeth of the tooth wheel. Replace any component which is worn, damaged or suspect.

Check the condition of the selector forks and the striker rods, particularly where the end of the gearlever engages the ends of the rods. Examine the detent springs and balls and replace any part that is not entirely satisfactory.

When the examination has been completed and the necessary replacements obtained, reassembly may be commenced.

First, reassemble the gears on the mainshaft. While this is being done, refer to **FIG 6:18** constantly to ensure that the components are in the right order and have been fitted to the shaft the right way round. Lightly oil the surface of the shaft before mounting the gears and sleeves.

Slide the third gear 34 and synchronizing ring 33 onto the mainshaft from the gearshaft end and follow up with the hub 30, sliding sleeves 32 and three dogs 26, secured in position by the two springs 31, 28. The component parts of the hub and sleeve assembly are shown in **FIG 6:19 and it is important to remember, when assembling, that the hooked ends of the two springs must not be inserted into the same dog.** Secure in place with the washer 23, and snap ring 24. The fitting is shown in **FIG 6:20**.

From the other end of the shaft, fit the second driven gear 35, and synchronizing ring 36, the hub, sliding sleeve and dogs 38, 40 and 21 with retaining springs 37 and 39, the synchronizing ring 41, firstspeed driven gear 42 and bush 43. Carefully insert into the gearcase (see **FIG 6:21**).

Working from the rear end of the shaft, insert the intermediate ballbearing and drive it home in the housing. This bearing 8 (see **FIG 6:18**) and the reverse intermediate gearshaft 49, are secured in place by the retainer plate 11. Insert the gearshaft, fit the plate and secure with the screws 9, staking them in place with a punch (see **FIG 6:22**).

Fit the ballbearing 4 and spring washer 3, to the gearshaft and, with the assistance of tool A.70158 and a press (see **FIG 6:20**) insert the spring retaining clip 2, as

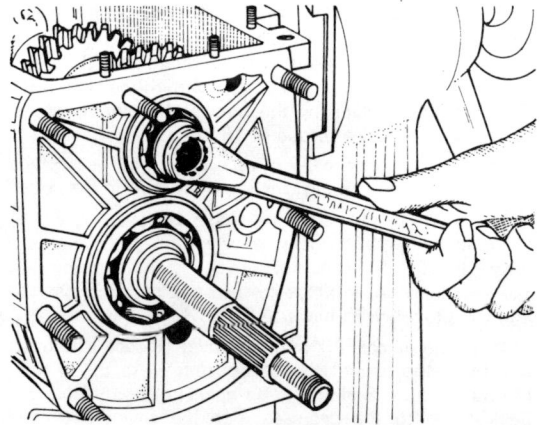

FIG 6:15 Removing bolt from layshaft with gears locked

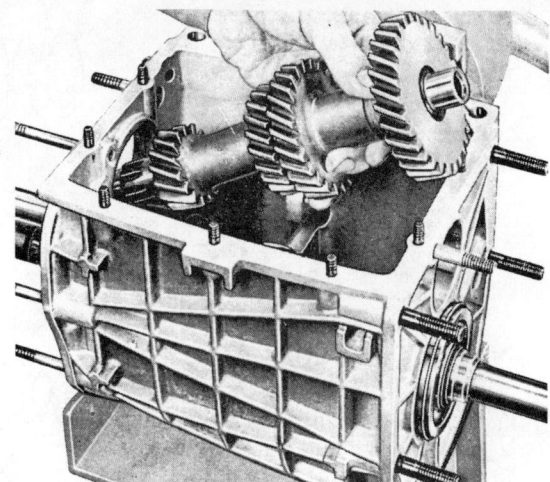

FIG 6:16 Withdrawing layshaft from gearcase

FIG 6:17 Withdrawing gearshaft showing tooth wheel, synchronizing ring, first helical drive gear and ballbearing

already effected on the mainshaft synchronizing ring, in the groove on the shaft.

Install the inner thrust ring 5 (see **FIG 6:18**) in the recess of the gearshaft, grease the interior surfaces of the recess and install the 23 needle rollers by pressing them into the grease coating and insert the outer ring 7. Taking care not to disturb the needle rollers, insert the gearshaft into the main case and slide it over the end of the mainshaft interposing the fourth gear synchronizing ring 27, and spring washer 29, between them.

Fit the first and second gear selector fork onto the sliding sleeve 39, insert the selector rod into position from outside the gearcase, through the boss of the selector fork and into the opposite bearing, fixing the locating roller for the bar into position while doing so, and secure the fork to the rod by the bolt and spring washer.

Fit the third and fourth gear selector fork onto the sliding sleeve 32, install the selector rod and locating roller **but do not, at this stage, secure the fork to the roller.**

Insert the layshaft into the case, fit the front double-row bearing 55, and the rear roller bearing 53, lock the

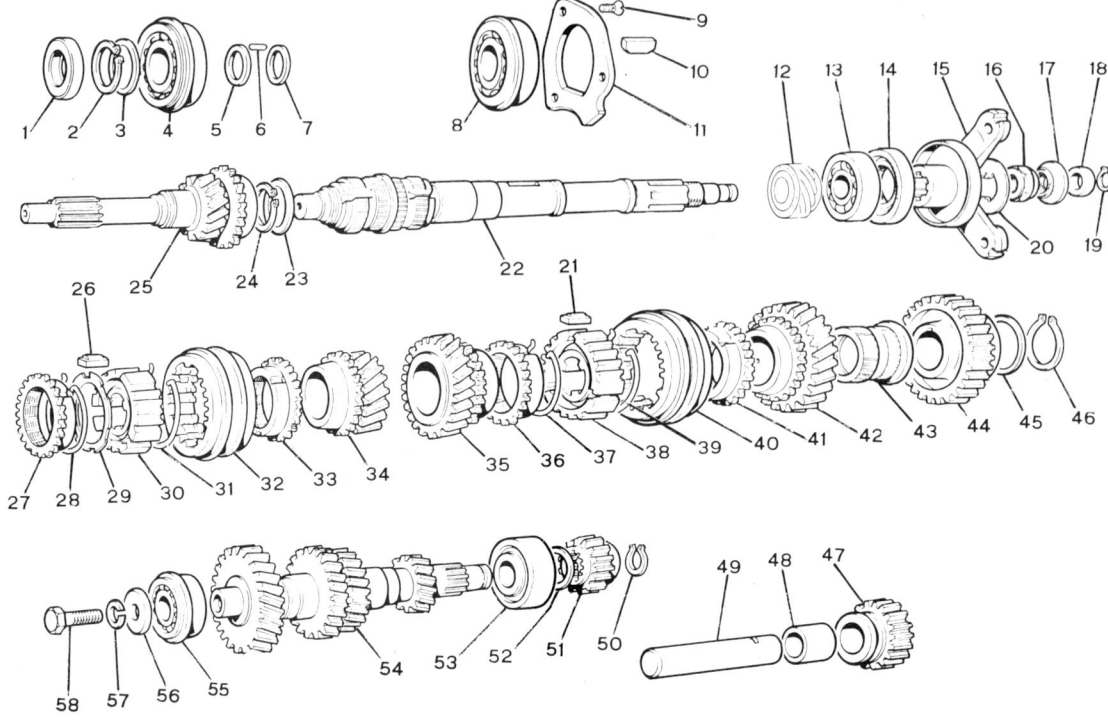

FIG 6:18 Components of gearbox laid out to show relative positions

Key to Fig 6:18 1 Centre cover oil seal   2 Snap ring   3 Spring washer   4 Gearshaft ballbearing   5/7 Needle bearing thrust rings   6 Needle rollers   8 Intermediate ballbearing   9 Retainer plate screws   10 Reverse-gear-to-mainshaft key   11 Retainer plate   12 Speedometer drive gear   13 Mainshaft ballbearing   14 Rear cover oil seal   15 Spider   16 Lockwasher and nut   17 Sealing ring   18 Centring ring   19 Snap ring   20 Oil seal   21 Dog   22 Mainshaft   23 Washer   24 Snap ring   25 Gearshaft   26 Dog   27 Fourth gear synchronizing ring   28/31 Dog retaining springs   29 Belleville spring washer   30 3rd/4th gear hub   32 Sliding sleeve   33 3rd gear synchronizing ring   34 3rd gear   35 2nd gear   36 2nd gear synchronizing ring   37/39 Dog retaining springs   38 1st/2nd gear hub   40 Sliding sleeve   41 1st gear synchronizing ring   42 1st gear   43 1st gear bush   44 Reverse driven gear   45 Spring washer   46 Snap ring   47 Reverse intermediate gear   48 Bush   49 Intermediate gearshaft   50 Snap ring   51 Reverse driving gear   52 Spring washer   53 Layshaft rear roller bearing   54 Layshaft with driving gears   55 Layshaft front double row ballbearing   56 Flat washer   57 Spring washer   58 Layshaft bearing retainer bolt

shaft against turning by engaging two gears on the mainshaft and fit and secure the stud 58, spring washer 57 and flat washer 56, at the front end, tightening the stud to a torque of 68 lb ft. At the opposite end, fit the reverse gear 44, to the mainshaft 22, by means of the key 10, and secure by the spring washer 45, snap ring 46, using tool A.70158 (see **FIG 6:23**). **Take care to ensure, in this operation, that the spring washer is properly centred and does not catch on the shoulder of the undercut on the shaft.**

Next, fit the spring washer 52, and reverse driving gear 51, to the layshaft and secure in place by the snap ring 50, using expanding pliers A.81101. Insert the reverse selector rod locating roller in its seating and fit the selector fork on to the rod securing it with the bolt and spring washer. Fit the intermediate gear 47, with the grooved collar in the selector fork arms, on its bushing 48, and simultaneously, insert the selector rod in its guide in the main casing and the gear on the intermediate gearshaft.

Install the speedometer drive gear 12 (see **FIG 6:18**) on the mainshaft together with the ballbearing 13, ready for the fitting of the rear cover. The end view will then be as in **FIG 6:13**.

On the bench, assemble the gearshaft to the cover and attach the lever return spring to the anchor screw 1 (see **FIG 6:12**).

Holding the gearlever over in the direction of the arrow, slide the cover onto the fixing studs at the rear of the crankcase, with the gasket in between, release the gearlever and check that it now engages with the selector rods. Then secure in place by the nuts and spring washers tightened down to a torque of 18 lb ft.

Install the speedometer drive support and gasket and secure by nut and spring washer to the stud in the cover.

Attach the flexible coupling spider 15 (see **FIG 6:18**) to the mainshaft with lockwasher and nut and tightened to a torque of 58 lb ft, fit the dust cover 17, and centring ring 18, securing both in place by the snap ring 19, inserted into the groove with pliers, A.81101.

Drive the oil seal 20, into the cover 19 (see **FIG 6:2**) and fit to the rear of the bellhousing, with the sealing O-ring in place. Slide onto the gearshaft and secure the bellhousing to the gearcase with the seven nuts and washers tightened to a torque of 37 lb ft, except for the smaller nut for which the setting is 18 lb ft.

The gears can now be unlocked and the third and fourth selector fork secured to the selector rod with the bolt and spring washer.

Reinstall the selector rod detent balls and springs and secure the coverplate and gasket by two nuts and spring washers.

Refit the lower cover and gasket to the gearbox, tightening the ten nuts and spring washers to a torque of 7 lb ft. Reinstall the clutch throw-out sleeve and thrust bearing and the throw-out fork lever, securing in position with the return spring.

Turn the gearcase, bottom up, and fill with SAE 90 EP grade oil up to the level of the filler hole. As already mentioned, the capacity of the gearbox is 2.4 pints. Screw the filler plug into place and turn the gearbox right way up. Leave for a while and then check all gaskets, bearing seals and filler plug surround for signs of oil leakage.

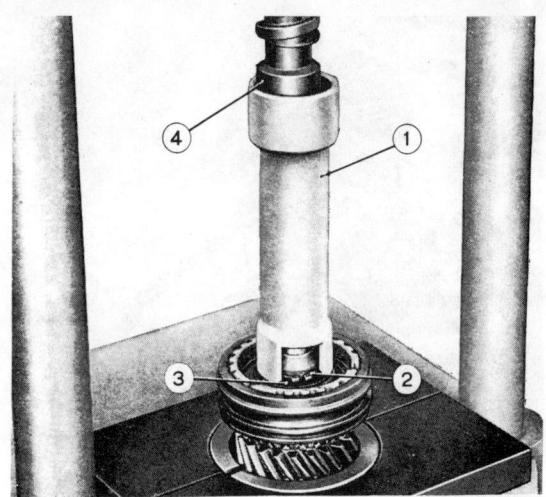

FIG 6:20 Fitting snap ring on mainshaft with tool A.70158 1 in press 4. The snap ring 2, is backed by a spring washer 3

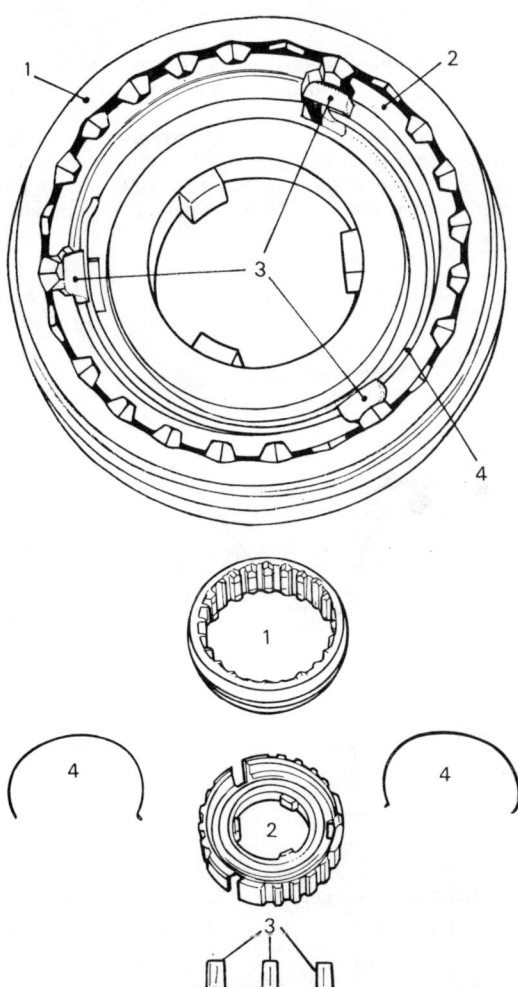

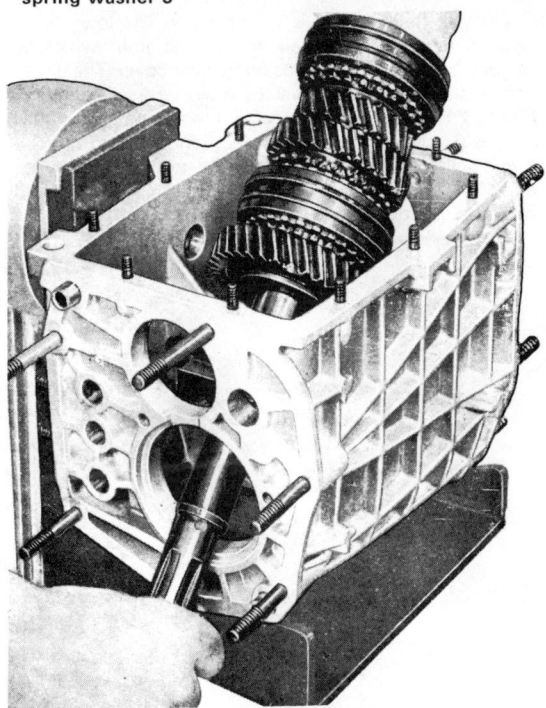

FIG 6:21 Inserting the mainshaft assembly in the gearcase

FIG 6:19 Sliding sleeve and hub assembly

Key to Fig 6:19 1 Sleeve 2 Hub 3 Dogs 4 Retaining springs

6:6 Replacing worn parts

As a general rule, it is not advisable to repair or recondition worn parts. Most of the gearbox components are readily available from the Fiat agents and it is good practice to replace parts worn or suspect during a major overhaul as the slight additional cost more than compensates for the extra trouble in having to dismantle a second time because the suspect part has let you down.

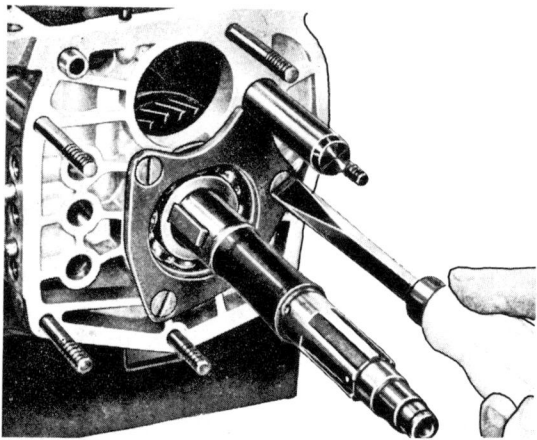

FIG 6:22 Fitting and securing bearing retainer plate

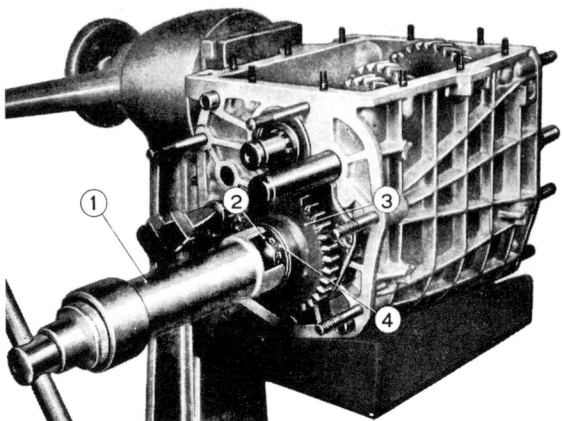

FIG 6:23 Use of tool A.70158 1 to fit snap ring 2, and spring washer 4, retaining the reverse driven gear 3

6:7 Gearchange servicing and adjustment

The gearchange lever is in two parts. The lower stud lever is mounted in a ball and socket joint which is secured by three nuts to bolts on the rear cover. The upper part is secured to the lower by a sleeve assembly (see **FIG 6:24**) comprising a shoulder block, and two rubber bushes 6, surrounding the stublever and secured to it by a split collet 2, held closed around the groove at the upper end of the stub lever by the upper rubber bush. Movement of the collet down the stub lever is prevented by this

groove while the bush is held in place by the lever jacket 5, embracing the spring ring 4, abutting onto the lower rubber bush.

The component parts of the ball and socket mechanism are shown in **FIG 6:25**. The ball itself is housed in a socket formed by the two half-covers 10 and 5, with intervening gasket 6, and a lower gasket through which

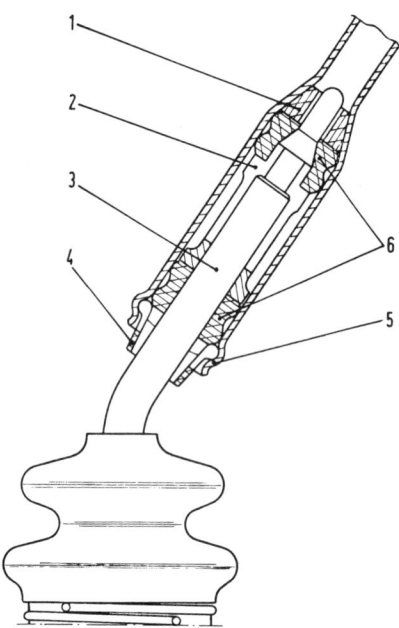

FIG 6:24 Section through gearlever joint

Key to Fig 6:24   1 Shoulder block   2 Split collet spacer
3 Stub lever   4 Spring ring   5 Lever jacket
6 Rubber bushes

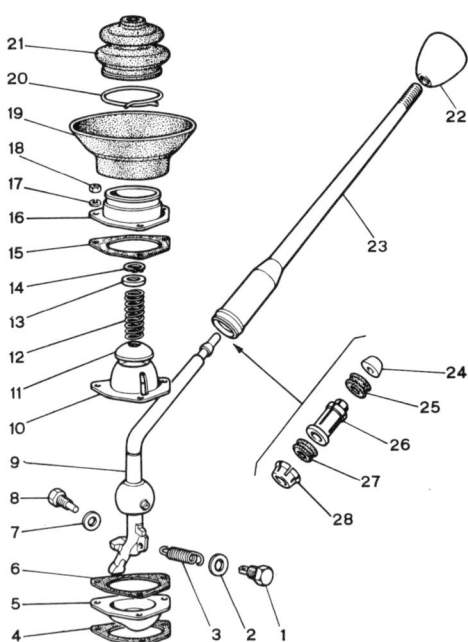

FIG 6:25 Components of gearshift assembly

Key to Fig 6:25   1 Spring anchor screw   2 Washer
3 Tension spring   4/6 Gaskets   5 Lower half-cover
7/8 Stop screw and washer   9 Gearlever stub and ball
10 Upper half-cover   11 Dome washer   12 Compression
spring   13/14 Washer and snap ring   15 Gasket
16 Flange and collar   17/18 Nuts and washers   19 Rubber
grommet   20 Spring ring   21 Rubber boot   22 Knob
23 Shaft   24 Shoulder block   25 Rubber bush   26 Split
collet spacer   27 Rubber bush   28 Spring ring

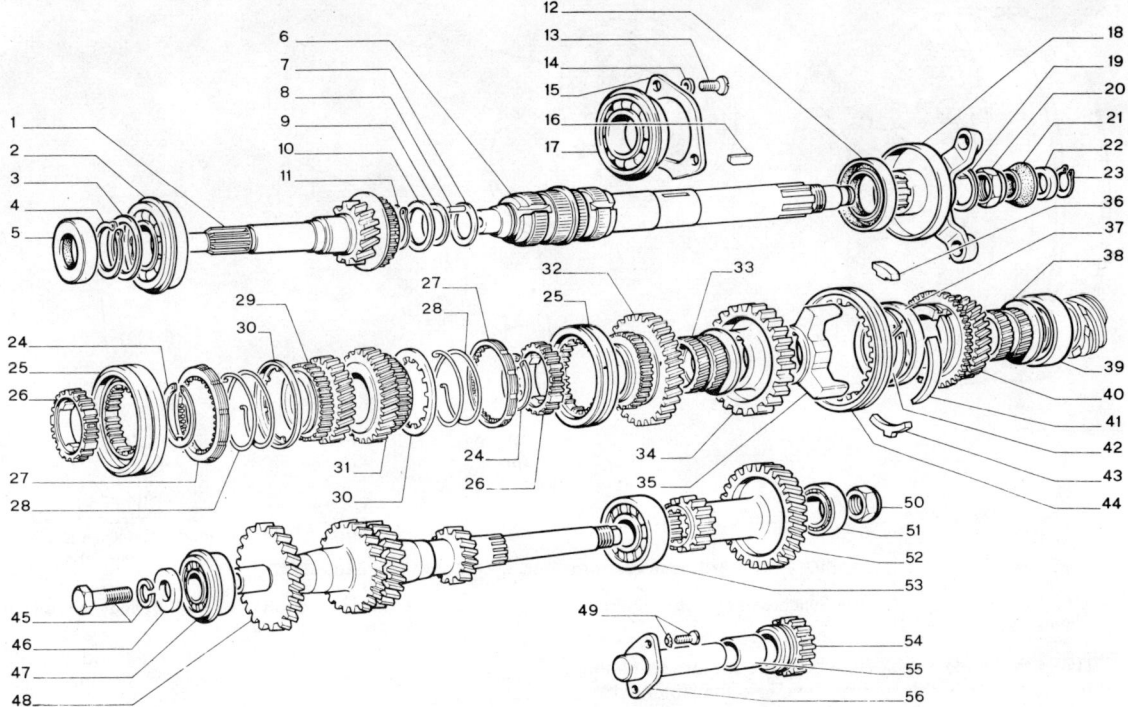

FIG 6:26   Fivespeed gearbox components

Key to Fig 6:26   1 Constant mesh and fourth gearshaft   2 Front ballbearing   3 Spring washer   4 Snap ring   5 Gasket
6 Mainshaft   7 Thrust washer   8 Needle rollers   9 Thrust washer   10 Spring washer   11 Snap ring   12 Gasket
13 Plate fixing screws   14 Toothed washers   15 Bearing retainer plate   16 Woodruff key   17 Intermediate ballbearing
18 Joint sleeve   19 Lockwasher   20 Nut   21 Seal ring   22 Positioning ring   23 Snap ring   24 Snap ring   25 Sliding sleeves,
1st, 2nd, 3rd and 4th gears   26 Sliding sleeve hubs   27 Synchronizing ring   28 Springs   29 3rd speed gear   30 Cup
31 2nd speed gear   32 1st speed gear   33 1st speed gear bushing   34 Reverse gear   35 Sliding sleeve hub, 5th speed gear
36 Stop plate   37 5th speed gear synchronizing ring   38 5th speed gear bushing   39 Rear roller bearing   40 5th speed gear
41 Spring   42 Snap ring   43 Thrust plate   44 5th gear sliding sleeve   45 Screws and spring washer, locking bearing
46 Plain washer   47 Front ballbearing, countershaft   48 Countershaft and gears for 1st, 2nd, 3rd and constant mesh   49 Screws
and toothed washer fixing reverse gearshaft   50 Nut   51 Rear ballbearing   52 Reverse and 5th speed gears   53 Intermediate roller
bearing   54 Reverse gear   55 Reverse gear bushing   56 Reverse gearshaft

it is bolted to the cover. A slot in the upper half-cover
allows the pin on the ball of the lever 9, to move up or
down from a central position, determined by the upward
pressure of the ball against the upper plate effected by the
spring 12, acting on the washer 13 and snap ring 14, the
side pressure of the spring 3, and the abutment of the stop
immediately above the spring lug on the side of the lower
half-cover. (This can be seen more clearly by a study of
FIG 6:3). The stop on the other side, butting against
the stop screw 8, against the tension of the spring 3,
positions the lower end in the gear striker rod slots for
engagement of the first and second gears.

Selection of the reverse gear is by downward pressure
of the gearlever, moving the ball clear of the upper plate
with the spring 12, compressed and enabling the stop to
clear the lip of the lower half-cover. The end of the gearlever is then in the slot of the reverse striker rod and the
reverse intermediate gear can be moved into mesh with
the layshaft and mainshaft gears.

The ball and socket assembly is protected by a rubber
boot 21, encircling the flange 16, and secured by spring
ring 20, this flange and collar providing the housing for
the spring and dome washer. The surrounding grommet

19, encloses the spring ring and provides a protective
feature to the assembly.

**To disconnect the upper half of the gearlever
from the lower,** ease the lever jacket over the lip of the
spring ring. The upper half can then be pulled off and the
rest of the joint assembly dismantled into its component
parts.

To disconnect the lower half for dismantling,
first remove the rear cover and disconnect the spring as
described earlier, unscrew the three nuts attaching the
lever assembly to the rear cover and extract. The mechanism will then dissemble into its component parts.

Reassembly and reinstallation is a reversal of this
procedure.

6:8   Reinstallation

Place the gearbox on the support, A.70509, on a
hydraulic jack and position it under the car. Raise the jack
until the gearbox is level with the engine at the front and
propeller shaft at the rear. This will entail the unit being
inclined slightly to the rear.

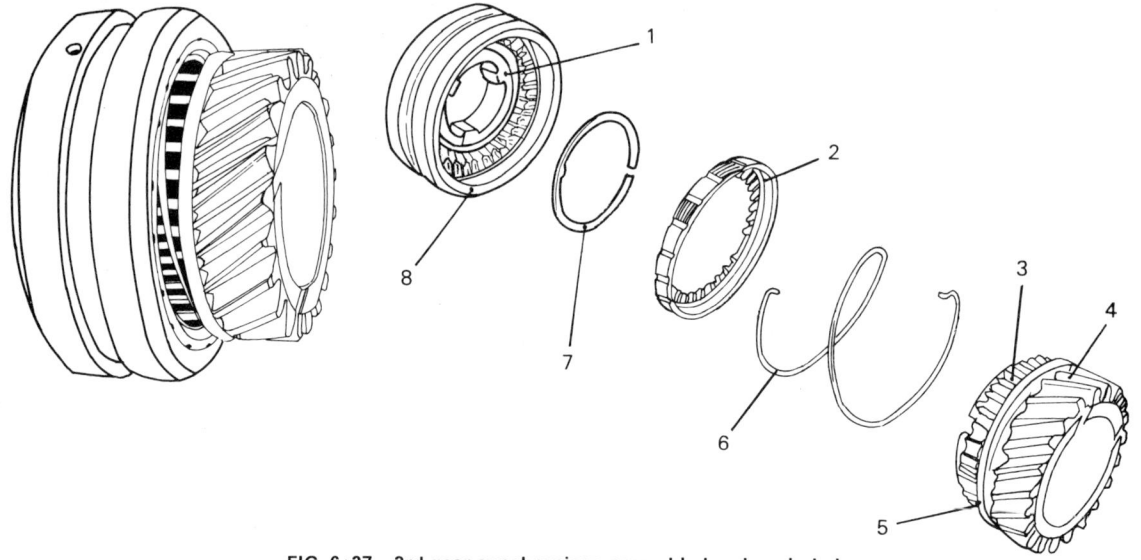

FIG 6:27   3rd gear synchronizer, assembled and exploded

Key to Fig 6:27   1 Hub   2 Synchronizing ring   3 Blocker ring   4 3rd gear pinion   5 Cup ring   6 Spring   7 Circlip
8 Sliding sleeve

Using the guide pin, A.70081, centre the driven plate of the clutch, insert the gearshaft end into the clutch with the friction ring in between, gently push home and secure in place by the studs holding the bellhousing to the crankcase.

Fix the starter motor to the bellhousing with the three bolts and integral spring washers. Secure the starter

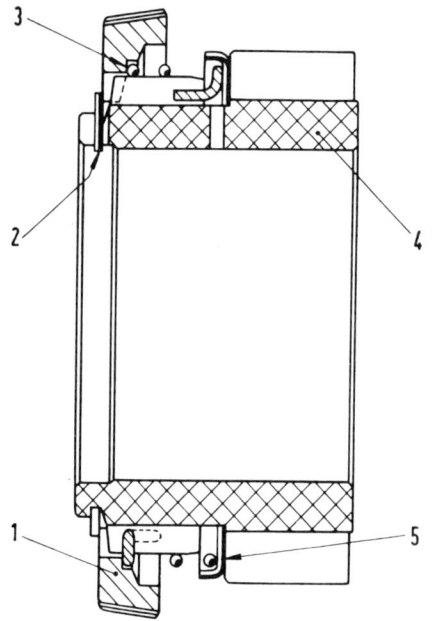

FIG 6:28   Section through 3rd gear and synchronizer

Key to Fig 6:28   1 Synchronizing ring   2 Circlip
3 Spring   4 3rd gear pinion   5 Cup ring

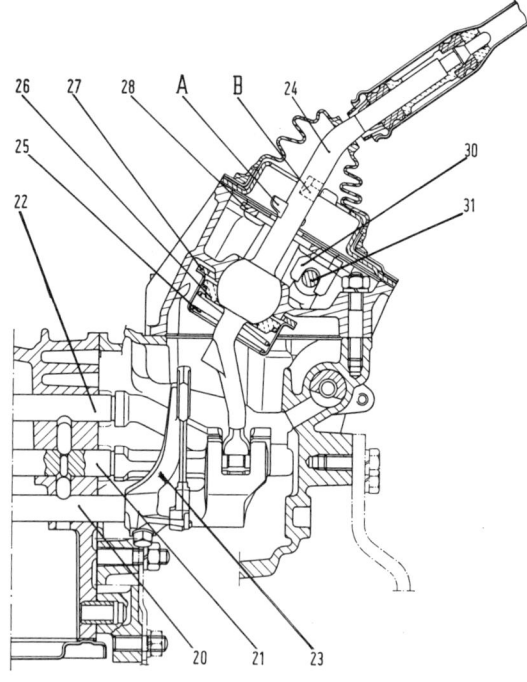

FIG 6:29   Section through selector and gearlever assembly. Early type

Key to Fig 6:29   A Stop dog   **B** Reverse stop   20 5th and reverse selector bar   21 3rd and 4th selector bar   22 1st and 2nd selector bar   23 5th reverse selector fork   24 Gearlever   25 Reverse spring   26 Gearlever ball socket   27 Ball socket retaining plate   28, 30 Gearlever guide plate   31 Spring spindle for 1st, 2nd, 5th and reverse

motor heat shield to the exhaust manifold. Connect the heavy current starter cable to the starter motor and the light current solenoid cable to the solenoid terminal.

Recouple the speedometer drive cable to the gearbox and screw home the retaining ring.

Lift the gearbox and refit the rear crossmember for supporting the gearbox and bolt to the car floor with the two bolts, spring washers and flat washers, tightened to a torque of 11 lb ft.

Reinstall the upper part of the gearshift lever.

Reconnect the flexible coupling on the propeller shaft to the spider on the mainshaft and secure with the self-locking nuts.

Reconnect the clutch withdrawal cable and adjust for clutch pedal free play.

Reinstall the flywheel cover using the lefthand rear bolt to secure the heavy duty earth return lead as well.

Fix the exhaust pipe support collar to the bracket on the gearbox cover.

Lower the hydraulic jack and remove. Lower the car to the floor.

6:9 Fivespeed transmissions

The internal components of the fivespeed gearbox fitted to later cars are shown in **FIG 6:26** for comparison with the fourspeed box shown in **FIG 6:18**. The fifth speed is in effect an overdrive with a step-up ratio of

.881:1, engaged by moving the gearlever into the opposite to reverse through the gate.

On these gearboxes, and also on later versions of the fourspeed boxes, an improved type of synchronizer is used as shown in **FIG 6:27**. This consists of a sliding sleeve 8 with hub 1, and synchronizing ring 2 and spring 6.

The sliding sleeve rotates with the hub and therefore with the mainshaft while the internal teeth on the synchronizing ring engage with the blocker ring 3 of the gear 4 which runs freely on the mainshaft. When the sleeve is moved it contacts the synchronizing ring at the outer end of the blocker ring through the thrust of the spring 6 between the cup ring 5 and the synchronizing ring. The friction between the cones of the synchronizing ring and the sleeve brings the parts to the same rotational speed and gear engagement is smoothly effected.

Care must be taken on reassembly to ensure that the returned ends of the spring are inserted in the slots in the blocker ring without affecting the normal diameter of the coil before fitting the circlip (see **FIG 6:28**).

Gear shift mechanism:

Up to chassis No. 0005752 the gearlever mechanism was of the type illustrated in **FIG 6:29** but later cars are fitted with the modified pattern shown in **FIG 6:30** in which the operation is effected through a remote control instead of the direct selection of the earlier type.

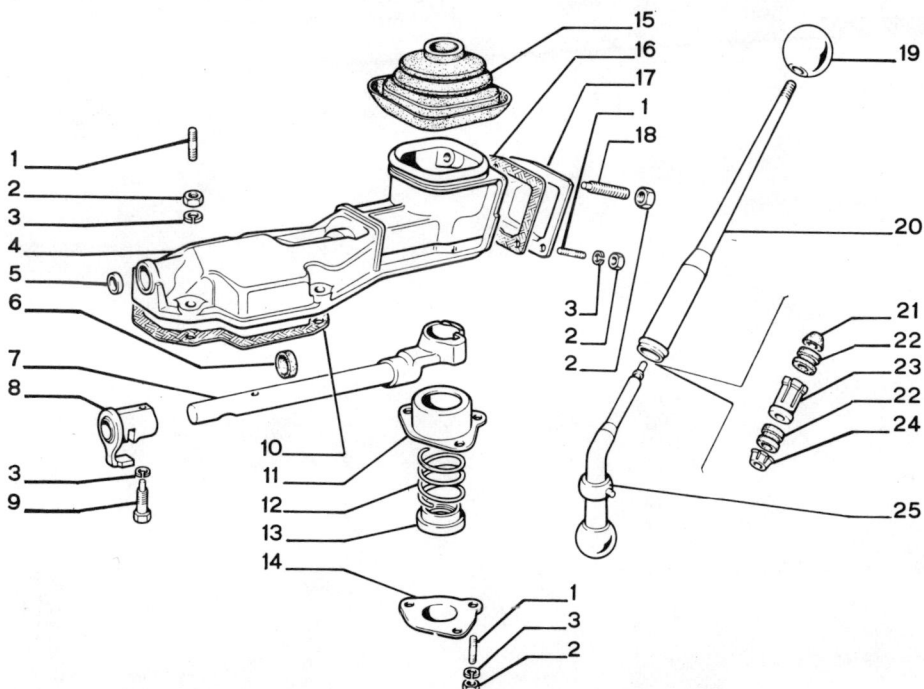

FIG 6:30   Later type gearshift mechanism

Key to Fig 6:30   1 Studs   2 Nuts   3 Spring washers   4 Support   5 Plug   6 Gasket   7 Gear selector and actuating bar   8 Dog   9 Screw   10 Gasket   11 Cover, spring retaining   12 Reverse stiffening spring   13 Upper ball socket, pivot lever   14 Lower ball socket, pivot lever   15 Boot   16 Gasket   17 Cover   18 Pin   19 Grip   20 Lever jacket   21 Pad   22 Resilient bushings   23 Spacer   24 Snap ring, lever jacket   25 Pivot lever, gearshift

6:10 Special tools

In the foregoing procedure, the work is facilitated if the special tools designed for the Fiat 124 series of engines are used. Not all the tools will readily be available from a Fiat agent but they can either be obtained or loaned from the servicing agent or garage who will quote a price for the securement or loan.

The special tools are:

A.40085	Universal puller.
A.55035	Wrench for gearbox attachment nuts.
A.70025	Tool for removal of coupling on propeller shaft.
A.70081	Guide pin for clutch driven plate.
A.70158	Tool for fitting spring washers of Belleville type.
A.70509	Support fitting for gearbox on jack.
A.81101	Pliers for fitting snap rings.
Arr.22204	Universal stand for gearbox dismantling.
Arr.22206.12	Attachment for gearbox to Arr.22204.

6:11 Fault diagnosis

(a) Jumping out of gear

1 Weak detent springs
2 Detent springs in wrong positions
3 Broken or missing detent ball
4 Synchronizing rings worn
5 Selector forks loose on striker rods
6 Worn shift forks
7 Worn sliding sleeve

(b) Noisy gearchange

1 Synchronizing rings worn
2 Broken dog springs
3 Clutch not disengaging
4 Wrong selection of gears

(c) Stiff gearchange

1 Tight gearlever ball in socket
2 Selector rod bent
3 Selector rod tight in bushings
4 Sliding sleeves tight on shaft

(d) 'Sloppy' gearlever

1 Ballsocket too loose
2 Gearlever spring disconnected or broken

(e) Noisy forward gears

1 Excessive wear on helical gears
2 Worn tooth wheels

(f) Noisy reverse gear

1 Worn gearteeth
2 Worn bore on intermediate gear

(g) Clicking noise from gearbox

1 Broken ball in a bearing
2 Broken or chipped gear tooth
3 Broken dog spring

CHAPTER 7

PROPELLER SHAFT, REAR AXLE, REAR SUSPENSION

7:1 Description of propeller shaft

The propeller shaft connecting the gearbox to the differential of the rear axle is in two parts coupled by a universal joint. The forward section is tubular and terminates in a flexible coupling on the gearbox mainshaft. The rear section is solid and is supported within a housing in a ballbearing on a central cushioned bracket adjacent to the universal joint and terminates, at the differential pinion shaft with a splined coupling sleeve.

A diagrammatic section through the propeller shaft and couplings is shown in **FIG 7:1**. The forward flexible joint comprises a central flexible unit 3, interconnecting the gearbox mainshaft spider 12, and the propeller shaft spider and sleeve 4, by the bolts 2 and 10. A centring ring on the stub end of the gearbox mainshaft 1, is a close fit into a bushing 11, in the propeller shaft spider which is internally splined to take the matching splined end of the propeller shaft 7. A grease plug 5, seal 8, and cover 9, ensures that sliding action within the sleeve can take place and is efficiently lubricated.

The foward propeller shaft terminates at the universal joint between the two halves which comprises coupling forks 13 and 15, mounted on a common spider 24, in needle bearings secured by a snap ring 25.

The rear propeller shaft 20, is supported in a ballbearing 16, mounted in the end cap 19, of the tubular cover 21, and this, in turn, is supported in a rubber pad 17, within a shell 18, welded to the cover which is secured to the car deck by nuts and bolts 32. The ballbearing is held in place by the snap ring 23.

The rear end of the propeller shaft is splined and terminates in a coupling sleeve 31, mating it with the differential bevel pinion shaft 28, the sleeve itself butting on to the end of the propeller shaft where it is held by the spring 30, within the cover flange 27.

7:2 Dismantling and reassembling the propeller shaft

First fit tool A./0025 to the flexible coupling (see **FIG 7:2**) and remove the sliding sleeve from the coupling by unbolting the three nuts and bolts 1. Remove the brake hose retaining clip from the cover of the rear shaft and, after plugging the outlet from the brake fluid reservoir, disconnect the hose from the rear brake pipe. Release the pipe from the two clips welded to the rear shaft cover.

Remove the four bolts and washers securing the rear shaft cover to the differential housing. Disconnect the handbrake return spring (see **FIG 7:3**) from the central

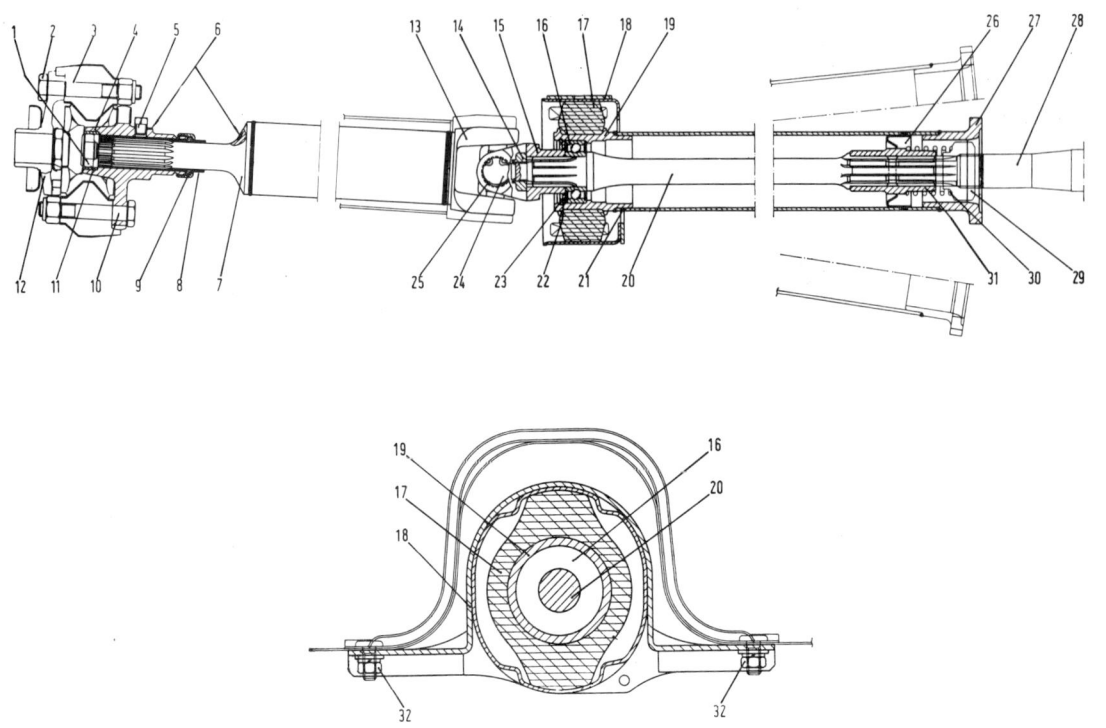

FIG 7:1 Sections through propeller shaft and pillow block

Key to Fig 7:1 1 Gearbox mainshaft   2 Mainshaft spider securing bolts   3 Flexible unit   4 Propeller shaft spider   5 Grease plug   6 Reference marks   7 Forward section of shaft   8 Seal   9 Cover   10 Propeller shaft spider securing bolts   11 Bush   12 Mainshaft spider   13 Universal coupling fork   14 Coupling fork retaining nut   15 Universal coupling fork   16 Ballbearing   17 Rubber pad   18 Pillow block shell   19 Shaft cover end cap   20 Rear section of shaft   21 Tubular shaft cover   22 Bearing shield   23 Snap ring   24 Coupling pin   25 Needle bearing   26 Shield   27 Cover flange   28 Bevel pinion shaft   29 Bevel pinion locknut   30 Spring   31 Bevel pinion coupling sleeve   32 Pillow block mounting studs

support bracket and unscrew the four nuts and washers 1, securing it to the chassis floor. Lower and slide the propeller shaft assembly towards the front of the car to disengage it from the bevel shaft, taking care not to lose the spring, lower away and transfer to the bench.

Remove the spider from the universal joint. This is a simple operation involving the removal of the snap ring and withdrawal of the needle bearings with their cups and sealing washers. **Care must be taken not to lose or mislay the needle bearing rollers which are quite small and to ensure that the correct number are present when reassembling.**

The propeller shaft will now be in two parts. Taking, first, the rear part, unscrew the fixing nut 14 (see **FIG 7:1**) remove the fork 15 and then the bearing snap ring 23. The shaft and bearing can then be removed from the tubular cover 21. Extract the ballbearing 16, from the end of the shaft.

On the front half, unscrew the cover 9, from the sleeve 4 and slide the sleeve clear of the shaft.

Clean all parts free from dirt and grease and examine for signs of excessive wear. Check the two bare shafts for out-of-truth and balance either by mounting them on centres or by rolling them on knife edges on a level surface plate. Check out-of-centre with a dial gauge. It should not exceed .02 inch at the centre.

If the out-of-centre is in excess of this limit, straighten in a press or change to a new shaft. **Do not attempt to straighten by hammering.** If a new shaft is fitted, it must be balanced. Balancing of an existing shaft is not necessary, providing that the assembly is made with the reference marks 6, coinciding, as the shafts will have been balanced at the factory.

After inspection and replacement of worn or damaged parts, the shaft can be reassembled. This is a reversal of the dismantling process with particular attention to the fitting of the needle bearings to the universal joint, the mating of reference marks and the tightening of the coupling fork nut 14 to a torque of 87 lb ft and staking with a centre punch. Charge the front sleeve with grease through plug 5.

Should it be necessary to replace the rubber pad or bearing on the pillow block, these can be released by removal of the snap ring 23, with expanding pliers A.81102.

Installation in the car is, again, a simple reversal of the removal process but, when fitting the pillow block to the chassis, do not tighten the nuts 1 (see **FIG 7:3**) until the lateral clearance between the tubular cover of the rear half of the propeller shaft and the housing of the pillow block has been adjusted, with the car unladen, so that the distance on the left, viewed from the rear, is about 1 mm more than that on the right. That is to say, the shaft should be offset within the housing by about .02 inch to the left. In this position, tighten the nuts securing the body to the chassis. After reconnecting the hydraulic brake lines, bleed the system as described in **Chapter 10**.

7:3 Description and construction of the rear axle

The rear axle is of the semi-floating type, the wheels being directly mounted on the shafts. The wheel hubs are constructed as part of the shaft which is supported at the outer end in ballbearings within the axle housing and at the inner end entirely by the side gears of the differential. The outer end inner bearing rings are a shrink fit on the shaft.

The differential case is carried in a pair of tapered roller bearings adjusted by retaining rings. The crownwheel, bolted to the differential casing, is carried in two tapered roller bearings. Similarly, the pinion shaft is also mounted in tapered roller bearings and, in each case, precise engagement is ensured by adjustment with shims and thrust washers.

A section through the rear axle assembly is shown in **FIG 7:4**. The axle shaft 1, is carried on ballbearing 2, secured by snap ring 3, within the housing 4, at the wheel end. The inner ring of the ballbearing abuts the collar 5, which is a shrink fit of the shaft, the housing being made oiltight by the oil seal 6.

The brake disc 7, is secured to the hub by a pair of spigot studs 9, which are reinforced by the wheel studs 10, holding the wheel 11, in place and providing between them the means of transmitting the braking torque applied by the disc brakes 8, to the road wheel and tyres.

At the inner end, the axle shaft splines are inserted in the side bevels 12, within the differential housing 13. This housing is supported, on taper roller bearings 14, which are adjusted and secured within the axle casing 17, by the bearing adjuster ring 15, and its locking plates 16 and bolts.

The differential casing 18, secured to the rear axle banjo by the studs and washers 19, supports the bevel drive shaft 20, and pinion 21, on a pair of tapered roller bearings 26. The drive from the bevel 21, is transmitted to the crownwheel 22, bolted to the differential housing 13, by the studs 23. The free bevels 24, mounted on the shaft 25, within the housing provide the link between the two shafts enabling the car to corner without wheelspin. Adjustment of mesh between the pinion 21, and crownwheel 22, is by means of the thrust washer 27.

7:4 Lubrication and servicing parts without axle removal

Normal servicing of the rear axle shaft and differential is limited to checking the level of the oil in the differential casing and refreshing, if necessary, with SAE 90 EP oil. This is done through the top filler plug hole and the level should reach the bottom of the plug hole. This check should be carried out every 6000 miles and at 18,000 miles it is advisable to drain the casing and completely renew the oil. The quantity for a complete renewal is 5 pints.

This lubricant supplies all the differential gears and bearings and those of the bevel shaft and pinion. It is prevented by the oil seal from reaching the outer ball-bearings on the axle halfshafts and these are packed with grease at the assembly stage. If it should be necessary to renew the grease, the halfshaft must be withdrawn, after

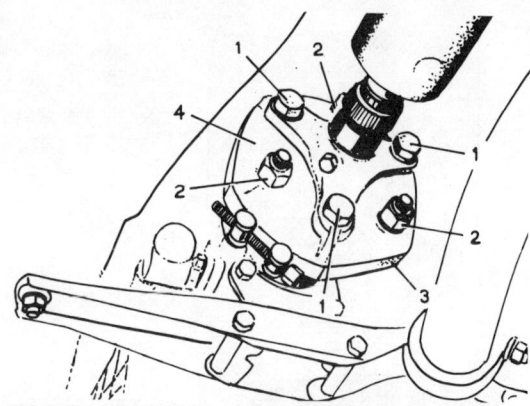

FIG 7:2 View of forward universal joint showing the flexible unit 4, spider securing bolts 1 and 2 and the special tool A.70025, 3. The gearbox support beams and fixing is also visible

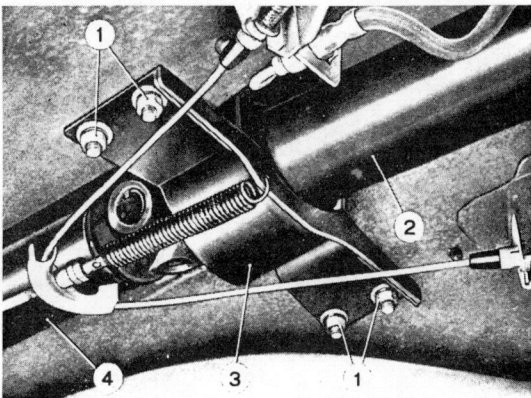

FIG 7:3 View of pillow block 3, with mounting nuts 1, rear propeller shaft 2, forward propeller shaft 4

removing the retaining clip (see **FIG 7:6**), by means of the percussion puller, A.47017 (see **FIG 7:7**) sufficiently to gain access to the bearing.

7:5 Axle removal

To remove the axle and housing from the car, first remove the rear wheel hub caps and loosen the studs securing the wheels to the wheel hubs. Raise the car on a jack and support it on stands D.15051. These give access to the axle when the jack is removed. Remove the two wheels.

Plug the brake fluid reservoir outlet and disconnect the brake hose from the pipe. Remove the propeller shaft as already explained and disconnect the handbrake cable from both disc brake assemblies. Uncouple the two trailing arms from the stabilizer bar, uncouple the link to the control rod of the brake regulator and, with the axle housing supported on the jack, remove the upper fixing nuts of the shock absorber with special wrench A.57070.

Unbolt the axle from the anchor arms (item 1) and also from the sway bar (item 4). Lower the hydraulic jack and the axle housing will come away with it. Transfer to the bench or stand for dismantling.

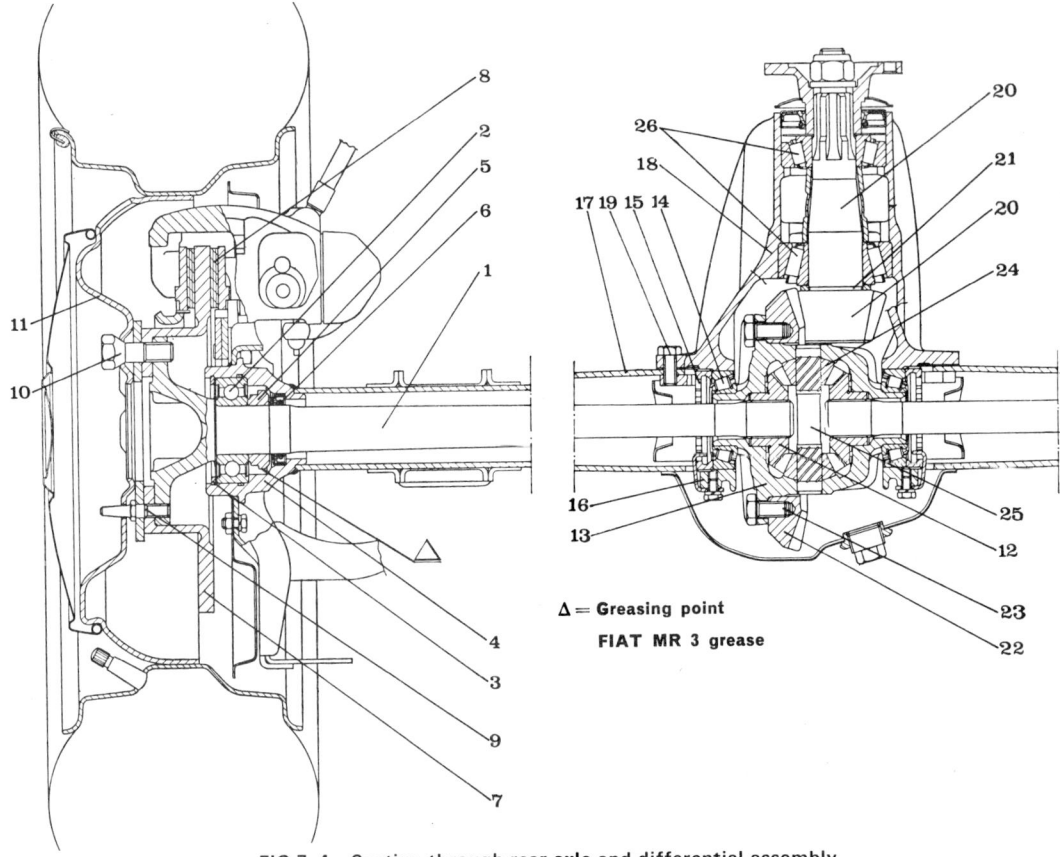

FIG 7 : 4 Section through rear axle and differential assembly

Δ = **Greasing point**

FIAT MR 3 grease

Key to Fig 7 : 4   1 Rear axle shaft   2 Ballbearing   3 Snap ring   4 Bearing housing   5 Collar   6 Oil seal   7 Brake disc   8 Disc brake gear   9 Spigot stud   10 Wheel securing stud   **11** Wheel   12 Side bevels   13 Differential housing   14 Taper roller bearings   15 Bearing adjuster ring   16 Locking plates   **17** Axle casing   18 Differential casing   19 Stud and washer   20 Bevel drive shaft   21 Pinion   22 Crownwheel   23 Crownwheel securing studs   24 Free bevels   25 Free bevel shaft   26 Taper roller bearings

Commence dismantling by removing the hydraulic pipe three-way union together with the piping and unions at the brake ends from the casing to which it is attached by clips welded to the casing. The union is attached by a bolt.

Remove the drain plug from the differential casing and drain the oil. This may be used again if in good condition. Disconnect the brake hoses from the anchor clips, remove the splitpins from the caliper retaining blocks, slide out the blocks and extract calipers, friction pads and springs. Unbolt and remove the caliper support brackets. Withdraw the two spigot studs and remove the brake disc from the axle shaft hub.

Extract the snap ring from its seating behind the hub with pliers A.81114 (see **FIG 7 : 6**) and withdraw the axle shaft by means of the percussion puller A.47017 (see **FIG 7 : 7**), together with dust shield 6, bearing 7, and retaining ring 8 (see **FIG 7 : 5**). Remove the differential carrier assembly by extracting the eight bolts and washers securing it to the axle housing.

Clean and examine the axle housing for signs of damage, distortion or faulty welds. If any are evident or suspected, hand over to the Fiat agent who will have the

necessary equipment to check and correct misalignments.

Check the condition of the two axle shafts together with the ballbearing, retaining collar, dust shield and snap ring. If the bearing needs replacement, it will be necessary first to remove the retaining collar. As this is a shrink fit, it must be removed in a hydraulic press using a special tool A.74108 to support the collar while the shaft is pushed through. **Once removed, the collar must not be used a second time. A new collar must be fitted.**

To replace the bearing and a new collar, first clean the shaft and examine for signs of scoring or damage. If any are present, replace the shaft. Check also the condition of the splines at the other end.

Assemble the snap ring, dust shield, and bearing on the axle in that order and mount vertically in a hydraulic press on sole plate A.74017/1 (see **FIG 7 : 9**). Heat the new collar in an oven until it is around 300°C and then, using special pliers A.60183 to grip the collar around the groove, transfer it to the shaft, grooved end up, slip the sleeve A.74017/2 over the shaft and apply pressure to force it home hard against the inner ring of the ballbearing. Maintain the pressure until cool.

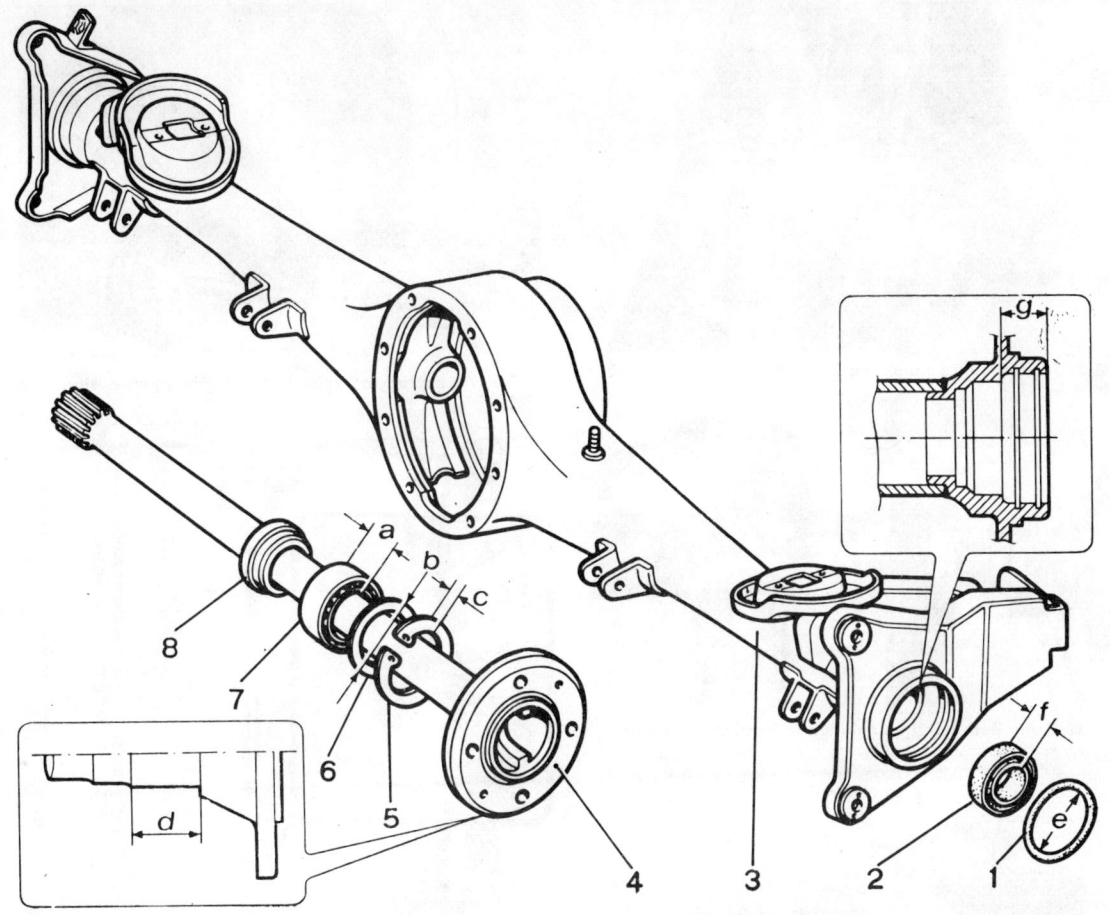

FIG 7:5   Rear axle housing and axle shaft

Key to Fig 7:5   1 O-ring   2 Oil seal   3 Axle housing   4 Axle shaft   5 Snap ring   6 Dust shield   7 Ballbearing
8 Retaining ring

Dimension in inches (mm)	Up to 069548	After 06949
a	.63 (16)	.82 (21)
b	2.42 (61.5)	2.53 (64.5)
c	.078 (2)	.102 (2.6)
d	1.22 (31)	1.35 (34.5)
e	2.44 (62)	2.55 (65)
f	.393 (10)	.314 (8)
g	.866 (22)	1.082 (27.5)

7:6 Dismantling and replacing differential

Attach the differential assembly, removed from the axle housing, to support bracket Arr.22206/4 mounted on stand Arr.22204. This will enable all the component parts to be inspected visually and dismantled as required with the minimum of difficulty. The parts, as viewed from the open end of the differential casing, are shown in **FIG 7:10**. The same parts, dismantled into their separate components, are shown in **FIG 7:13**.

Remove the bolts and spring washers 15, to release the locking plates 16 and 17, from the differential case bearing caps 28, at each side. (The single and double tooth locking plates, by transposition when fixing, enable the bearing retaining plate to be adjusted by half slots). Remove the studs and spring washers 20, to release the bearing caps

28, and extract the differential housing 12, complete with side gears 8, and bearing retaining rings 14, free bevels 9, and shaft 10, and the crownwheel 11.

Dismantle the assembly by unbolting the crownwheel from the housing, sliding the bearing retaining rings clear of the side gears and extracting the free bevels by driving out the shaft with a drift. By rotating one side bevel and holding the other stationary, the free bevels will move round to the openings through which they can be extracted. The side bevels and thrust washers will then be able to collapse inwards for extraction through the same openings.

To dismantle the bevel shaft and pinion assembly, fit ring-tool A.55075 to the nut 27, bolt tool A.70130 to the casing with the splined collar over the end of the shaft and loosen and remove the nut (see **FIG 7:11**).

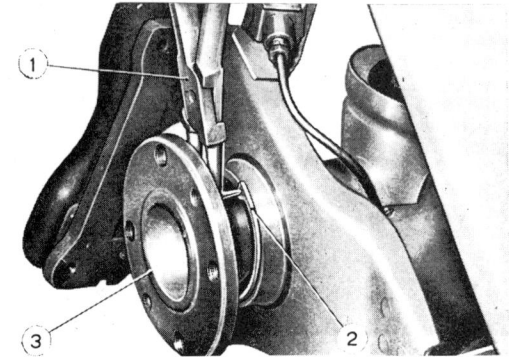

FIG 7:6   Removing snap ring 2, from axle shaft 3, with pliers A.81114, 1

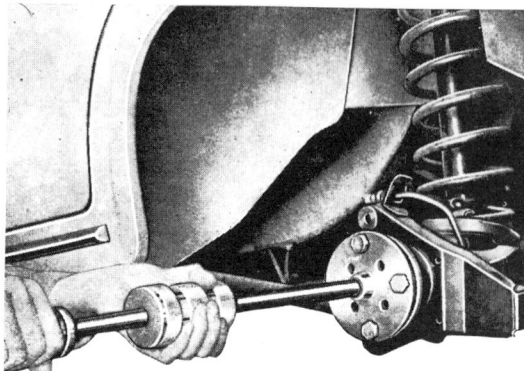

FIG 7:7   Extracting axle shaft from housing with puller A.47017

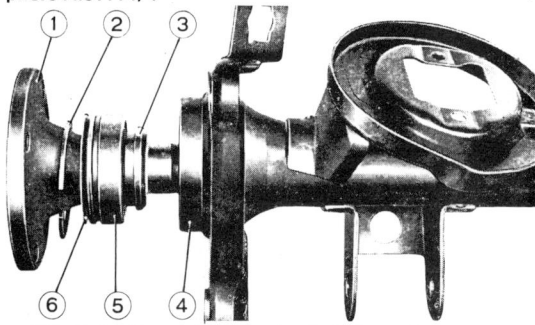

FIG 7:8   Removing an axle shaft from the housing

Key to Fig 7:8   1 Axle shaft   2 Snap ring   3 Bearing retaining collar   4 Axle housing   5 Ballbearing   6 Dust shield

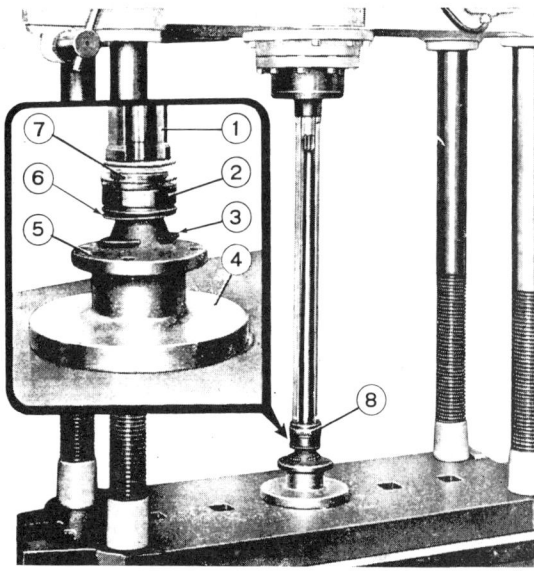

FIG 7:9   Use of sleeve A.74107/2 to fit bearing retaining collar in hydraulic press

Key to Fig 7:9   1 Sleeve A.74107/2   2 Ballbearing   3 Snap ring   4 Soleplate A.74107/1   5 Axle shaft flange   6 Dust shield   7 Bearing retaining collar   8 Collar holder A.74107/4

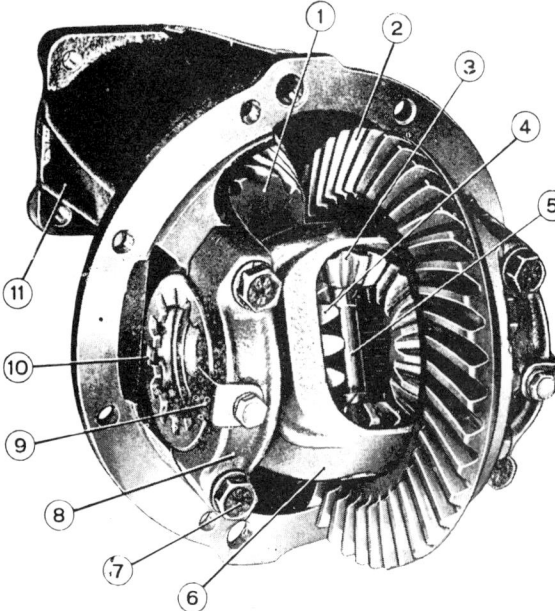

FIG 7:10   Differential casing and components unbolted from axle shaft casing

Key to Fig 7:10   1 Pinion   2 Ring gear   3 Pinion gear   4 Side gear   5 Pinion gear shaft   6 Differential case   7 Differential case bearing cap screw   8 Differential case bearing cap   9 Ring lock plate   10 Bearing retaining ring   11 Differential housing

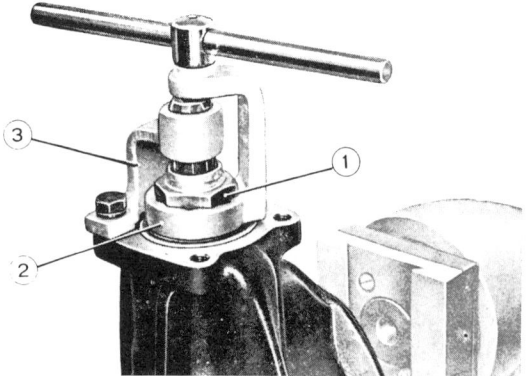

FIG 7:11   Removing bevel pinion nut 1, with ring tool A.55075, 2 and shaft retaining tool A.70130 3

Withdraw the pinion complete with shaft, thrust ring 6, front roller bearing 5, inner ring and collapsible spacer 26. From the opposite end, withdraw the spacer 1, oil seal 2, oilslinger 3, and bearing inner ring and race 4. The outer rings must be withdrawn by means of a drift. Using a universal puller, extract the inner ring and roller bearings from the pinion shaft and from the differential side gears.

Clean and examine all parts for signs of wear or damage and replace as necessary. Always replace the oil seals regardless of condition and take care to insert them the right way round.

The crownwheel and bevel are supplied in matched pairs and the replacement of one must always be accompanied by the replacement of the other by the matched counterpart.

Reassembly of the differential:

First assemble the side gears in the differential housing with thrust washers in position, insert the free bevels on opposite sides and turn one side bevel on the other to rotate the free bevels until their centres are opposite the holes in the housing for insertion of the shaft. Insert the shaft and check that the end play on each side gear is not greater than .02 inch. If it is, dismantle and replace the thrust washers by the next thicker size. **The thrust washers are supplied in four thicknesses ranging from .076 inch to .082 inch.** If the play is still excessive with the thickest washer in place, the gears are worn and must be replaced.

Bolt the crownwheel to the differential housing, tightening the bolts to a torque of 72 lb ft, and then, with tool A.70152, fit the inner races to the side gears. The housing assembly is then complete.

Correct meshing of bevel pinion and crownwheel is ensured by the choice of thrust ring inserted between the pinion and rear roller bearing. This thrust washer is shown at 6 in **FIG 7:13**. The selection of the correct thickness is a procedure calling for some care and the use of a dial gauge

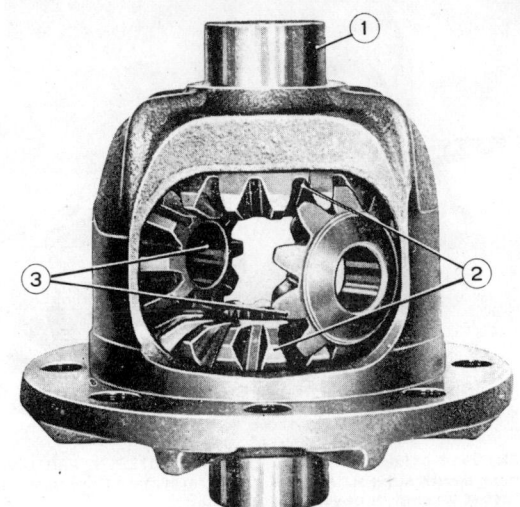

FIG 7:12 Relative positions of pinion gears in differential housing

Key to Fig 7:12   1 Differential housing   2 Side bevels
3 Free bevels

with a dummy pinion A.70129. Procedure is as follows:

First examine the pinion and shaft for its individual marking (see **FIG 7:15**). This gives a figure, preceded by a + or − sign, in addition to the serial procedure and matching number.

The next step is to install the dummy pinion in the differential casing and to adjust the dial gauge (see **FIG 7:14**). **First, zero the indicator by setting it on a surface plate with the dial indicator support detached from the dummy pinion and placed flat on the plate.**

Mount the dummy pinion in the casing with both roller bearings in position. This is shown diagrammatically in

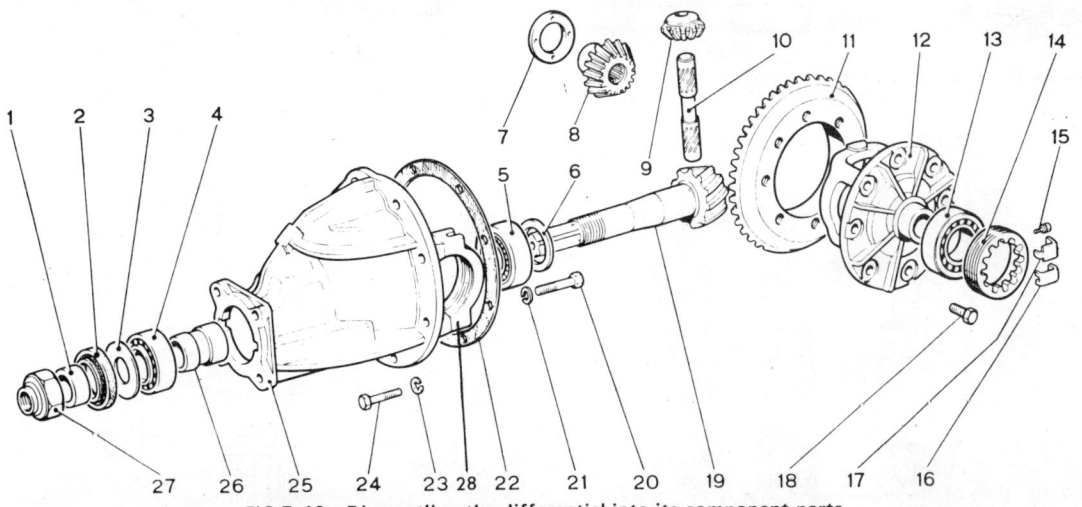

FIG 7:13   Dismantling the differential into its component parts

Key to Fig 7:13   1 Spacer   2 Oil seal   3 Oil slinger   4 Ballbearing   5 Front roller bearing   6 Thrust ring   7 Side bevel thrust ring   8 Side bevel   9 Free bevel   10 Free bevel shaft   11 Crownwheel   12 Differential housing   13 Ballbearing 14 Bearing retaining ring   15 Lockplate stud and washer   16/17 Lockplates   18 Crownwheel securing stud   19 Bevel shaft and pinion   20/21 Bearing cap bolts and washers   22 Gasket   23/24 Differential casing to axle housing studs and washers 25 Differential casing   26 Collapsible spacer   27 Bevel pinion nut   28 Bearing cap

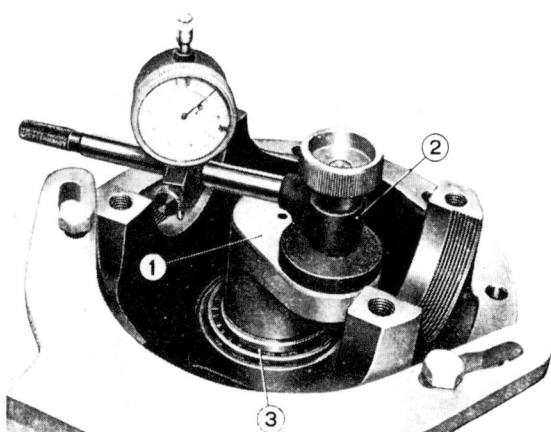

FIG 7:14 Use of dummy pinion A.70129, 1 and dial gauge with support A.95690, 2, to determine thickness of thrust washer in bevel rear bearing 3

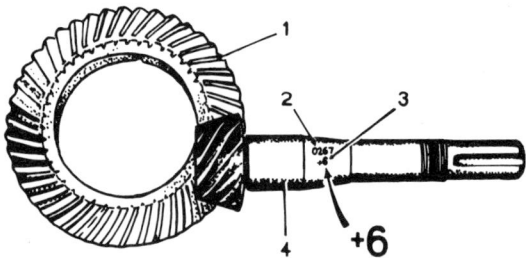

FIG 7:15 Crownwheel and pinion showing position of production serial number 2 and difference figure 3 on crownwheel 1 and bevel shaft 4 matched pair

FIG 7:16 (a). Attach the indicator support and gauge in position on the dummy pinion with the sensor in contact, first with one and then with the other face of the differential sleeve housing. To the mean value of these two readings, in hundredths of a millimetre, add or subtract the figure stamped on the pinion shaft according to the sign preceding the figure. The result is the thickness of the thrust washer to be fitted behind the pinion (see FIG 7:16(b)).

Reinstall the pinion and shaft in the reverse order of dismantling with the selected thrust washer in place (seventeen thicknesses of washer, from 2.55 to 3.35 mm in steps of .05 mm are available) and remount the differential housing with the bearing adjuster rings in place and secured in their seating by the bearing caps. When tightening the nut on the end of the bevel pinion shaft, apply a torque of about 140 lb ft (see FIG 7:17).

This value is approximate and the actual tightening must be such that the turning torque of the shaft without the pinion in mesh with the crownwheel is between 1.2 and 1.5 lb ft measured with dynamometer A.95697 as shown in FIG 7:18. If the torque cannot be achieved within 25 lb ft of the nut tightening torque, the thrust washer must be exchanged for the next size up or down.

With the differential housing in place and the bearing cap nuts tightened to a torque of 36 lb ft the next step is to preload the bearings and adjust the backlash between the gears.

Install the fixture A.95688 as shown in FIG 7:20 attaching it to the differential casing by support stud 1 and screw 6, inserted into the locking plate screw holes in the bracket cap. Move the lefthand gauge 9, on its support 7, until the cranked arm 5, is touching the side of the bracket cap. Lock the gauge on the shaft in this position by screw 8.

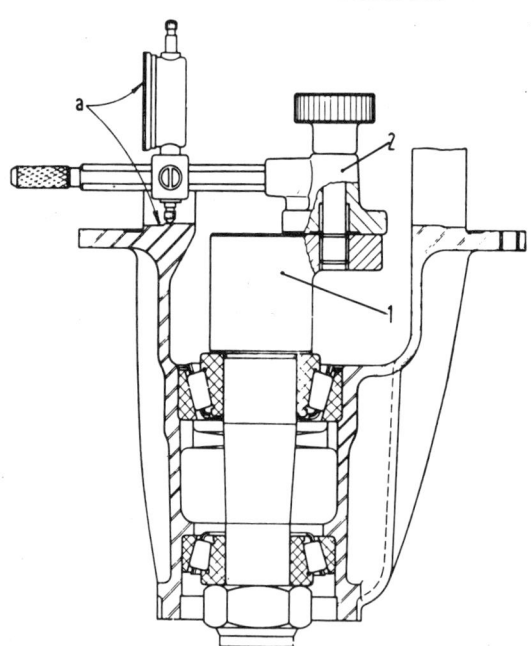

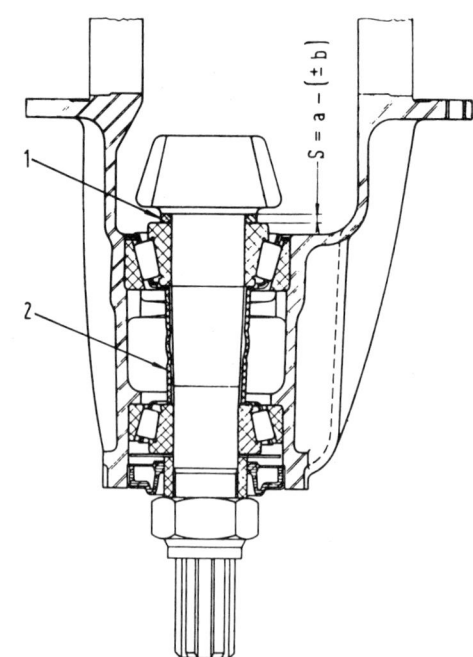

FIG 7:16 Diagrammatic section showing, left, position of dummy pinion with, right, the corresponding position of real thrust washer 1 on pinion shaft 2. Thickness of washer, S, is the dial gauge reading, a, less the figure, b, on the bevel shaft

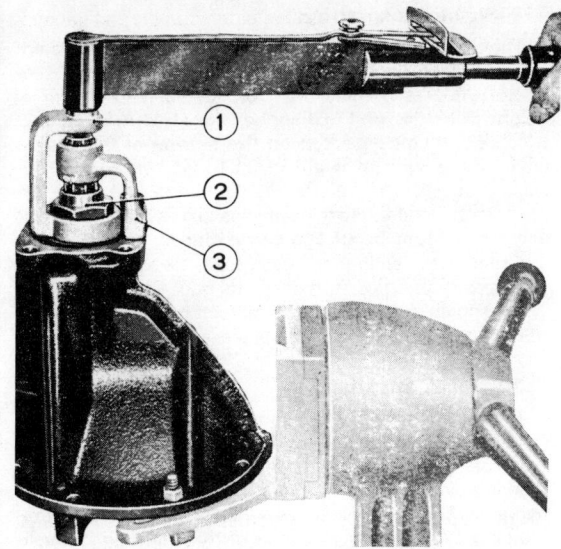

FIG 7:17 Fitting the bevel pinion nut with a torque spanner A.70130 set to 140 lb ft prior to preloading

Key to Fig 7:17 1 Ring nut 2 Bevel pinion nut 3 Shaft retainer

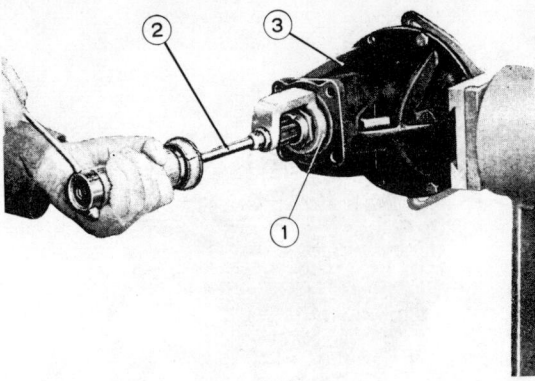

FIG 7:18 Use of dynamometer to determine pre-loading torque on bevel pinion shaft mounting

Key to Fig 7:18 1 Sleeve A.55075 2 Dynamometer A.95697 3 Differential carrier

Using wrench A.55015, tighten the bearing retaining rings alternately until the backlash on the crownwheel is about .004 inch measured on the righthand gauge, without any preloading. This is, in effect, a centring stage for the differential housing in relation to the drive pinion.

Now tighten the two bearing retaining rings, each by the same amount, until the lefthand gauge 9, shows an increase of .0063 to .0078 inch in distance D (see **FIG 7:19**). Again check that the backlash is of the same order and then lock both rings in place by means of the locking plates after removal of the attachment.

7:7 Axle replacement

The axle replacement can now be commenced. First, mount the differential assembly to the axle shaft casing with the gasket 22 (see **FIG 7:13**) in position and tighten the eight bolts to a torque of 22 lb ft. Fit the oil seal and O-ring in their seats in the axle housing, push the axle shaft home, charge the outer ballbearing with grease and fit into the housing, at the same time meshing the splines at the inner end with those in the side bevels of the differential. Fit the dust cover in place and secure with the snap ring.

Secure the brake discs to the axle shaft stub with the two spigot screws, refit the caliper support brackets, tightening the bolts to a torque of 25 lb ft and remount the disc brakes assemblies. Reclip the hydraulic pipes in place and reconnect the brake flexible tubes.

7:8 Rear suspension

A general view of the rear suspension, from beneath from the front of the car is shown in **FIG 7:23**. The suspension comprises a pair of coil springs combined with hydraulic shock absorbers, two anchor rods, a sway bar and a transverse stabilizer bar. The springs are seated on rubber ring pads on the body at the upper end and to

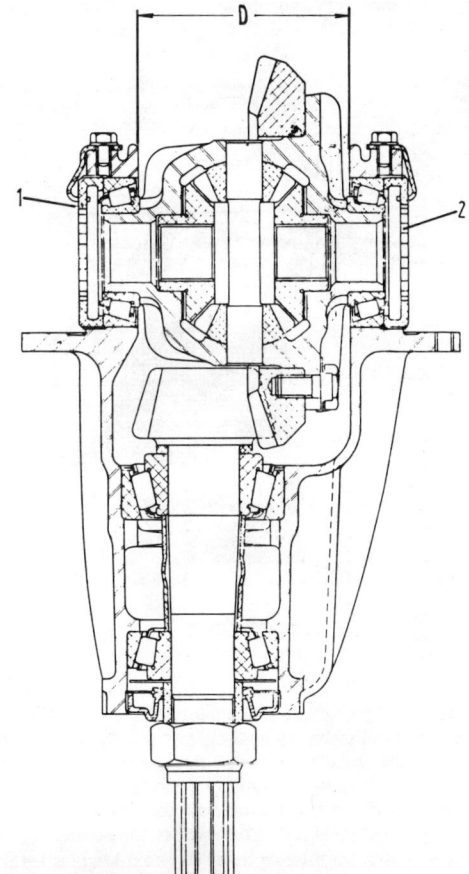

FIG 7:19 Preloading check dimension on differential casing roller bearings

Key to Fig 7:19 1 Bearing retaining ring 2 Bearing retaining ring

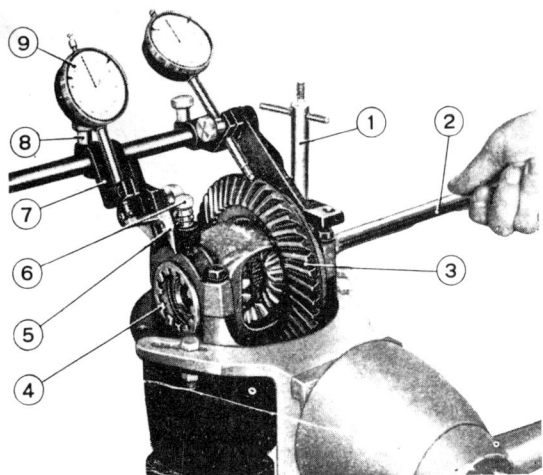

FIG 7:20 Adjusting the backlash

Key to Fig 7:20   1/6 Support stud and screw   2 Wrench
A.55015   3 Crownwheel   4 Bearing retaining ring
5 Cranked arm   7 Dial gauge bracket   8 Clamping screw
9 Dial gauge

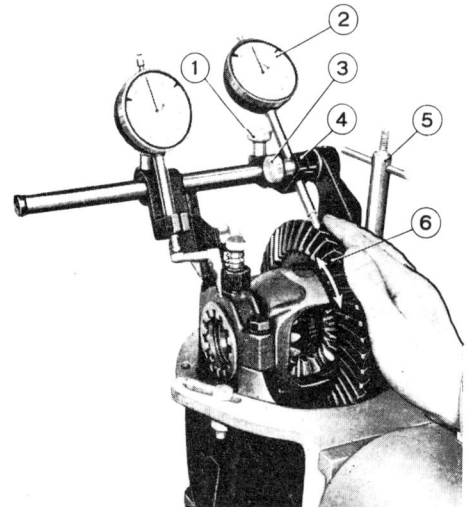

FIG 7:21   Checking backlash on bevel gears

Key to Fig 7:21   1 Clamping screw   2 Dial gauge
3 Clamping screw   4 Clamp   5 Support stud
6 Crownwheel

two plates welded to the axle arms on the lower end. The
anchor rods and the sway bar are solidly connected
through rubber bushes between the axle casing and the
body in lateral and end-to-end directions.

An exploded view of the rear suspension is shown in
FIG 7:24. The first stage of removal of the suspension is
the same as that for the rear axle. The next stage is for the
removal of the coil springs and shock absorbers from the
axle shaft casings. This is done by unbolting and removing
the shock absorbers from the lower mounting plate. The
shock absorbers and springs will then come away with
the ring pads and upper seating ring.

7:9 Suspension springs

The coil suspension springs for the Coupé are separated
into two classes according to their developed compressed
length under a nominal load of 507 lb. Those with a
height in excess of 11.61 inches are class A, identified
by a yellow stripe painted on the outside of the centre
coils. Those with a height of 11.61 inches or less are
class B and bear a green stripe painted on the inside of
the centre coils. **Both springs in a suspension
assembly must be of the same class.**

Examine the springs removed from the suspension for
cracks or signs of distortion or fatigue. Change both if
either should appear less than perfect. Inspect the condition of the ring pads and change these too if at all suspect.

7:10 Shock absorbers

FIG 7:25 shows a diagrammatic section through a
shock absorber. It comprises a cylindrical body formed by
two coaxial tubes 14 and 15, of which the inner is the
working cylinder and the outer a reservoir casing for the
hydraulic fluid not immediately being utilized within the
working cylinder. The capacity of this reservoir is small
since it comprises the annular space between the two
cylinders only.

The third, outer cylinder 13, attached to the piston rod 2,
serves to protect the working parts and reservoir from
damage by stones and mud thrown up from the road.

The working cylinder is closed at the top by an extension
of the bush 11, held in place by clamping ring 3, screwed
into the reservoir cylinder, through the sealing washer 9,
seal housing 4, and clamping ring washer. The piston rod
passing through the bush is made oiltight by the combination of seal, housing 4, packing 5, and spring 8, the

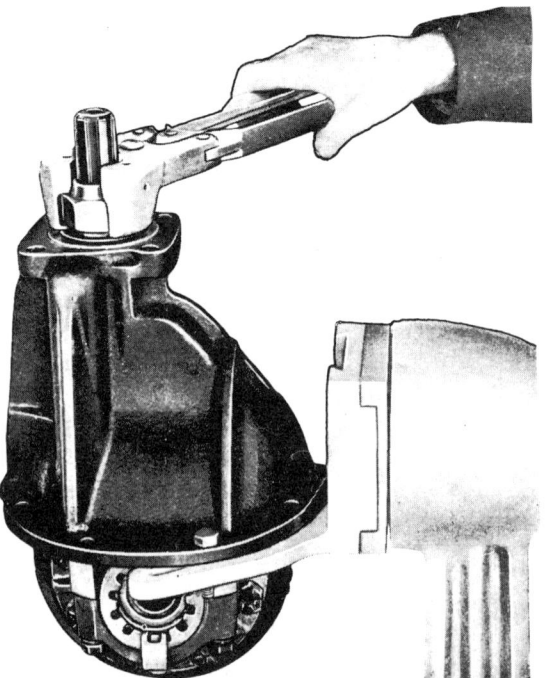

FIG 7:22   Use of tool A.74126/6 to stake bevel pinion
fixing nut

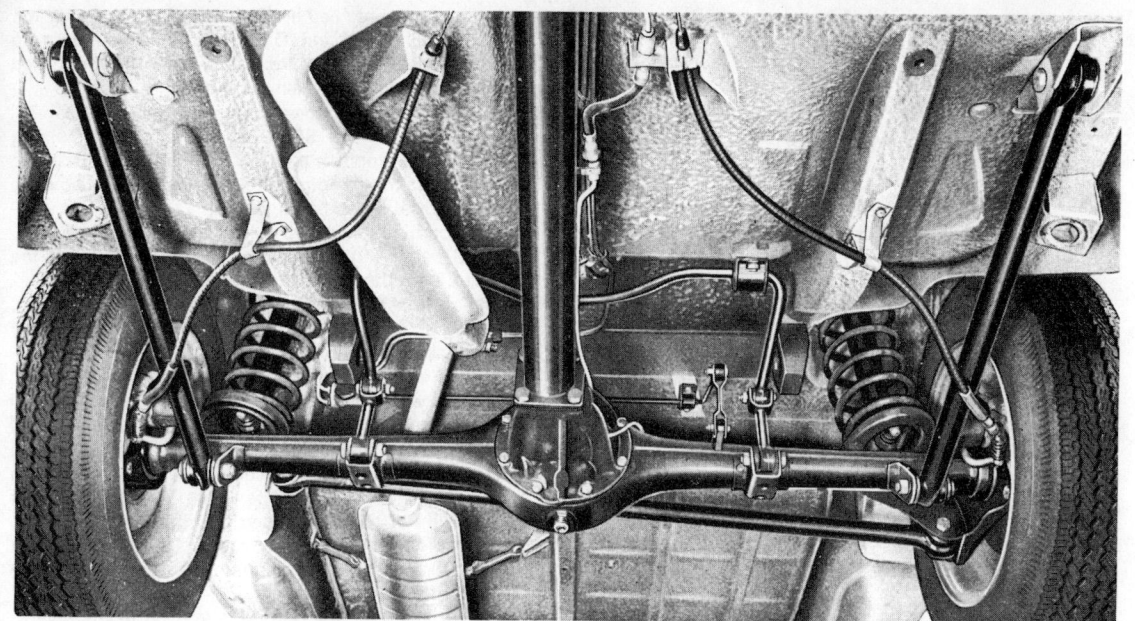

FIG 7:23 Forward underside view of rear suspension (early models)

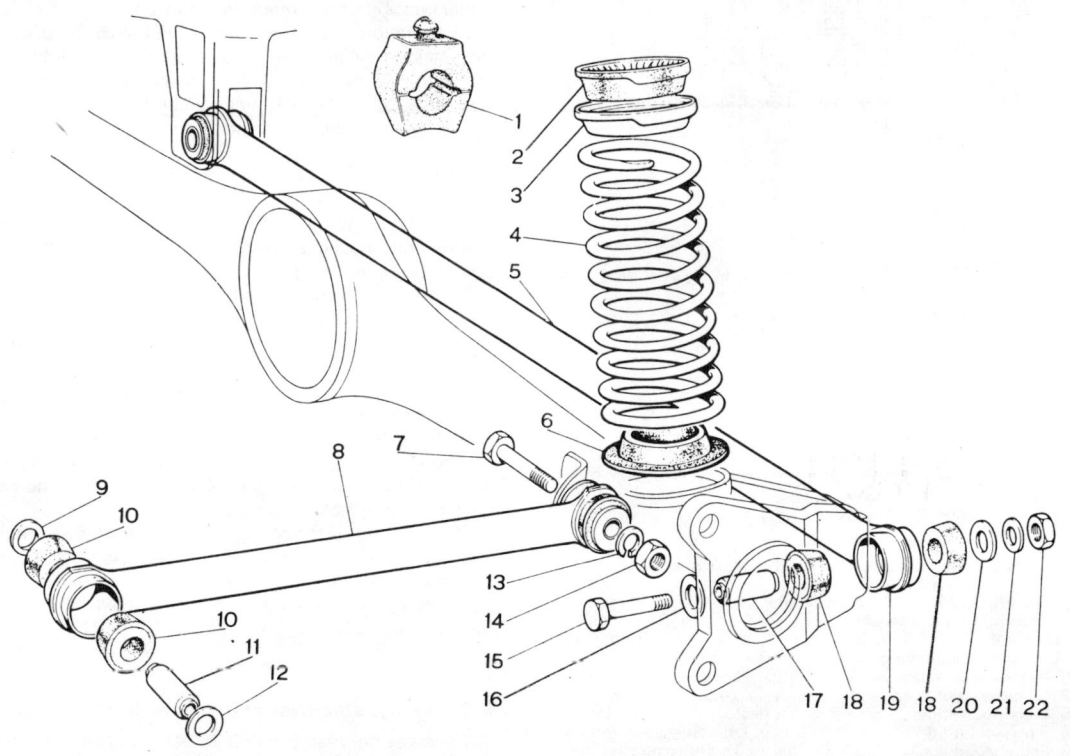

FIG 7:24 Exploded view of rear suspension

Key to Fig 7:24 1 Rubber pad   2 Upper ring pad   3 Seating ring   4 Coil spring   5 Sway bar   6 Lower ring pad
7/13/14 Anchor bar fixing bolt nut and washer   8 Anchor bar   9 to 12 Bushing assembly for anchor bar   15 to 22 Bushing
assembly for sway bar

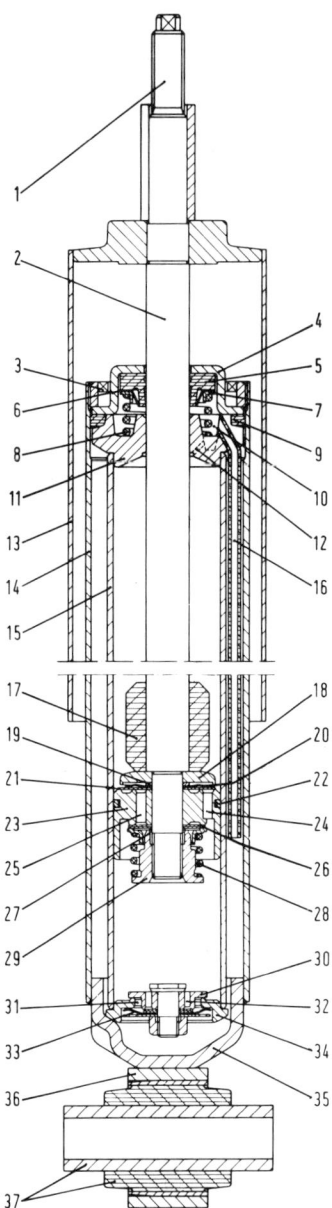

FIG 7:25 Section through shock absorber

Key to Fig 7:25 1 Upper shaft end 2 Piston rod
3 Clamping ring and washer 4 Seal housing
5 Rod seal 6 Tab spring 7 Spring cup
8 Gasket packing spring 9 Sealing washer
10 Vapour drain chamber 11 Upper sealing bush
12 Capillary duct 13 Outer cylinder 14 Reservoir cylinder
15 Working cylinder 16 Drain passage 17 Buffer
18 Flow limiting disc 19 Lift adjustment washer
20 Star shaped spring 21 Outer transfer port
22 Compression ring 23 Piston 24 Outer transfer port
25 Inner transfer port 26 Valve 27 Control spring guide cup
28 Control spring 29 Mounting plug
30 Compensating valve 31 Annular passage 32 Flow orifice
33 Compression valve 34 Carrier plug 35 Lower cap
36 Lower fixing eye 37 Fixing eye bushes

whole being maintained in close contact with the piston rod by the clamping ring. Oil or vapour leakage past the seal is transferred back to the reservoir through the capillary duct 12, and drain passage 16.

The reservoir casing, being secured to the lower cap 35, and mounting shank 36, enables the same clamping pressure to be applied, through the working cylinder, to the lower seal in the form of the carrier plug 34, housing the compensating and compression valve. This is a concentric combination of two valves, the first, compression, valve 33, permitting the restricted flow of fluid through the orifices 32, on the downstroke while sealing off the compensating flow passages and the second, compensating, valve 30, opening to allow free return of fluid through the annular passage 31, on the upstroke.

The piston rod 2, terminates within the cylinder in the piston 23, with compression ring 22, which is provided with transfer ports 24 and 25, enabling the hydraulic fluid to pass from one side to the other at a controlled rate as the piston is moved in either direction. This control is applied on the downstroke by the upper valve 21, opened against the pressure of the star shaped spring 20, to enable the flow, restricted by the limiting disc 18, lift adjustment washer 19, and the dimensions of the passage to pass through the outer transfer port 21.

On the upstroke, the control is applied in the reverse direction by the valve 26, sealing off the transfer port 25, opening against the pressure of the control spring 28, and guide cup 27, on the mounting plug 29.

In operation, the spaces above and below the piston in the working cylinder are always full with hydraulic fluid, the piston, in the dormant state, taking up a position midway between the two extremes according to the degree of compression of the suspension springs by the load in the car.

When the vehicle is in motion, the effect of the shock absorber is to impart a delaying effect on the transmission of road shocks to the body and, as a result, vertical oscillations are reduced while roll, pitch and yaw are almost completely eliminated.

Dismantling a shock absorber is not an operation that the normal owner driver can undertake successfully. It is usually better to fit a new or reconditioned shock absorber which can readily be obtained from the Fiat agent.

To reinstall a shock absorber, fit the lower rubber ring on the upper shank of the unit, extend the shock absorber and then insert it into the centre of the coil spring in place on the lower ring pad 6 (see **FIG 7:24**) and bolt into place on the spring seating plates of the axle housing with the fixing bolts supplied.

Over the top of the spring, fit the upper seating ring 3, and ring pad 2. Raise the hydraulic jack with the suspension and back axle into position, with the extended shock absorber upper shank inserted in the holes in the body, for final reinstallation.

7:11 Sway, stabilizer and anchor bars

The sway bar (see 5 in **FIG 7:24**), comprises a hollow steel bar terminating in sockets for attachment to the rear axle and chassis by means of bolt 17, rubber bushes 18, and washer and nut 20 and 22. The bars must be straight, free from damage or cracks and measure 39.78 inches between the eye centres.

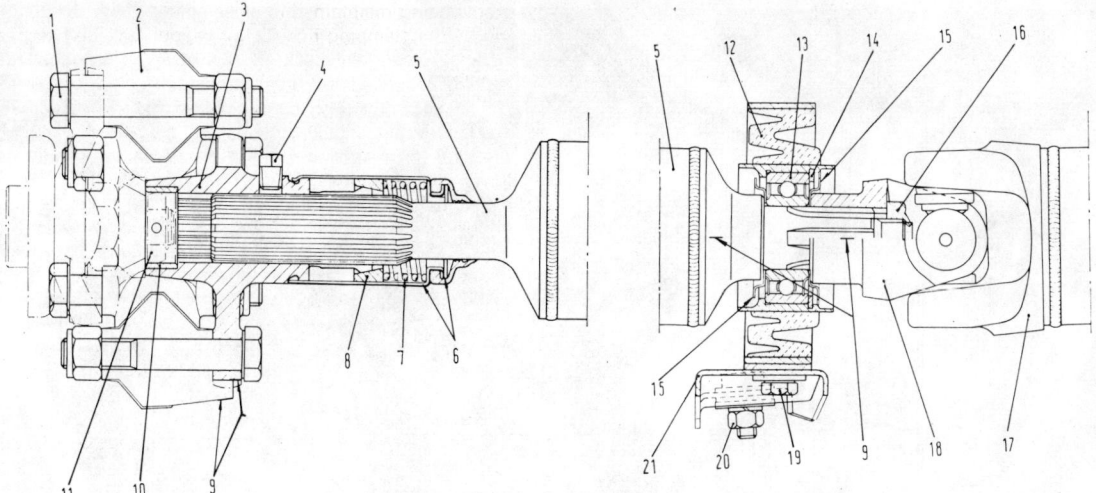

FIG 7:26 Section through front flexible joint and centre pillow block (later type)

Key to Fig 7:26   1 Flexible joint-to-transmission mounting screw and nut   2 Flexible joint   3 Slip sleeve
4 Lubrication hole plug   5 Propeller shaft front section   6 Seal and housing   7 Spring   8 Cone ring
9 Assembly reference marks   10 Location bushing   11 Location ring   12 Centre pillow block   13 Ballbearing
14 Bearing snap ring   15 Bearing shields   16 Nut   17 Propeller shaft rear section   18 Universal joint yoke
19 Crossmember-to-underbody nuts   20 Pillow block-to-crossmember screws   21 Crossmember

The anchor bars, similarly, are hollow steel bars terminating in sockets for attachment to the axle shaft brackets at one end and chassis brackets at the rear, also by means of bolts and rubber bushes. These too must be straight, free from cracks or damage and measure 23 inches between the eye centres.

The stabilizer bar is a double cranked, solid steel bar secured to the chassis by rubber bushed brackets the ends of which are linked to brackets on the axle housing by means of steel links forked at one end for engagement with the bar and bushed at the other for connection to the axle housing brackets. The coupling, in each case, is by means of bolts and nuts inserted in rubber bushings. The bar must not be distorted and the links must be straight and free from damage and, when mounted in position, the alignment of the axle shaft and the bottom level of the chassis must be parallel.

All four bars, their location and fixing can be seen in **FIGS 7:23** and **7:24**.

7:12 Reinstallation of rear axle

With all sub-assemblies completed and the rear axle housing in place on the jack, partially raised to permit the entry of the shock absorber shafts into the body holes, connect the anchor bars and sway bars to their respective mounting brackets but do not, at this stage, tighten the nuts. Fix the stabilizer bar to the chassis by means of the bushed brackets but do not tighten the nuts. Install the connecting links between the end of the stabilizer bar and the axle housing brackets.

Reconnect the brake regulator linkage.

Reinstall the propeller shaft assembly not forgetting to insert the compression spring 30 (see **FIG 7:1**) in the line between the locking nut 29 and coupling sleeve 31.

Secure at both ends. Tighten the upper fixing nuts on the shock absorbers within the car body.

Connect the hydraulic brake hoses and bleed the system. Couple the handbrake linkage and adjust. Fit the rear wheels in position with the studs fingertight, remove the stands and lower the car to the ground. Tighten the wheel nuts.

With rear tyre pressures set at 22 lb load the car so that the distance between the jacking point and the level ground at the rear is 8.3 inches and at the front 7.2 inches. Tighten the anchor bar and sway bar nuts to a torque of 72 lb ft and the stabilizer bracket and link nuts to a torque of 25 lb ft. This completes the rear suspension installation.

7:13 Modifications

Propeller shaft:

On Sport models from No. 1759184 and Coupé models from 0066059 a new type of propeller shaft is fitted as illustrated in **FIG 7:26** from which it will be seen that the splined front section includes a slip yoke and that a universal joint is now fitted to the rear section.

Rear suspension:

A modified suspension layout employing four reaction struts as shown in **FIG 7:27** has been in use on later models as listed above.

7:14 Fault diagnosis

(a) Rear of car out of level

1 Uneven tyre pressures
2 Weak or broken spring
3 Faulty shock absorber
4 Bent sway bar

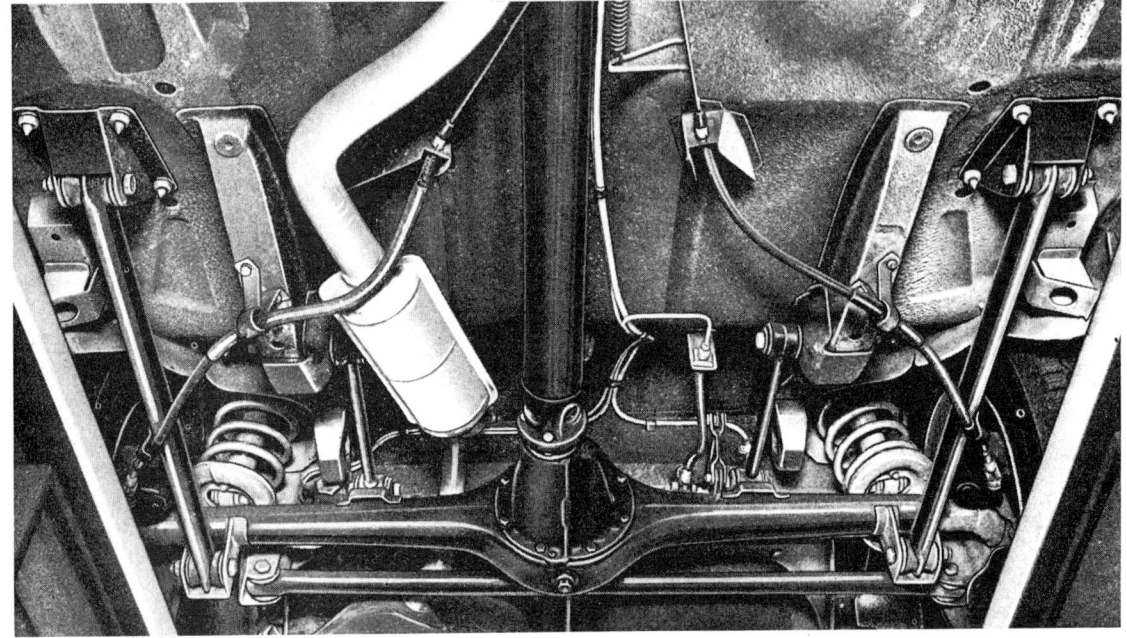

FIG 7:27   Four reaction strut suspension seen from front of car (later models)

(b) Uneven tyre wear

1 Unbalanced tyre pressures
2 Weak or broken spring on one side
3 Faulty shock absorber on one side

(c) Excessive road vibration

1 Faulty shock absorbers
2 Wheels out of balance
3 Loose couplings on sway bar (worn bushes)

4 Loose coupling on anchor bar (worn bushes)
5 Loose couplings on stabilizer bar (worn bushes)
6 Propeller shaft out of balance
7 Loose or worn pillow block

(d) Car pulls to one side

1 Flat tyre
2 Uneven tyre pressures
3 One brake shoe binding
4 Bent anchor bar

CHAPTER 8

FRONT SUSPENSION AND HUBS

8 : 1 Description of system

The front suspension comprises a fairly conventional arrangement of wishbone swinging arms with independent coil spring, hydraulic shock absorbers and a stabilizer bar. The upper and lower arms support the steering knuckles in ball joints permanently lubricated for life, the joints being housed in cups attached to the arms by rivets.

The upper and lower arms swing on pivot pins in compressed 'live' rubber bushes, the pins being bolted, at the upper end to the chassis and at the lower end to a crossmember which also supports the engine. Each coil spring is located between the lower arm and the car body and encircles the shock absorber which is connected between the lower arm and a fixing hole in the chassis and serves as a suspension damper and spring retaining member at the same time.

The wheels are mounted on stub axles integral with the knuckle arms through taper roller bearing hubs which also support the brake disc. The brakes are of the hydraulic-operated disc pattern. Details of the steering linkage and gearbox are given in **Chapter 9**.

8 : 2 Routine maintenance

The suspension is designed for minimum maintenance and the only servicing that is required is to repack the wheel hub bearings with grease every 12,000 miles. This necessitates withdrawal of the hub and invariably involves replacement of the oil seal.

8 : 3 Front hub removal and replacement

The cross section through the front wheel and suspension in **FIG 8 : 1** illustrates the main features and components as they appear in position. Dealing, first, with hub withdrawal, raise the car on stands and remove the wheels.

Unbolt and remove the disc brake assembly. **It is not necessary to disconnect the hydraulic system for a simple hub removal but only for a full suspension dismantling.** Unscrew the two spigot studs and remove the disc from the hub. With percussion tool A.47014, remove the hub cap (see **FIG 8 : 2**). Remove the nut and spring washer fixing the hub to the knuckle. **The right-hand hub has a lefthand thread.**

With puller A.47015, withdraw the hub (see **FIG 8 : 3**). With puller A.47001 withdraw the inner race from the stub axle. The outer roller bearing and inner bearing outer ring will have come away with the hub (see **FIG 8 : 4**). Remove the oil seal.

Examine all surfaces and parts for signs of wear or scoring. Light scoring can be removed with a smooth file

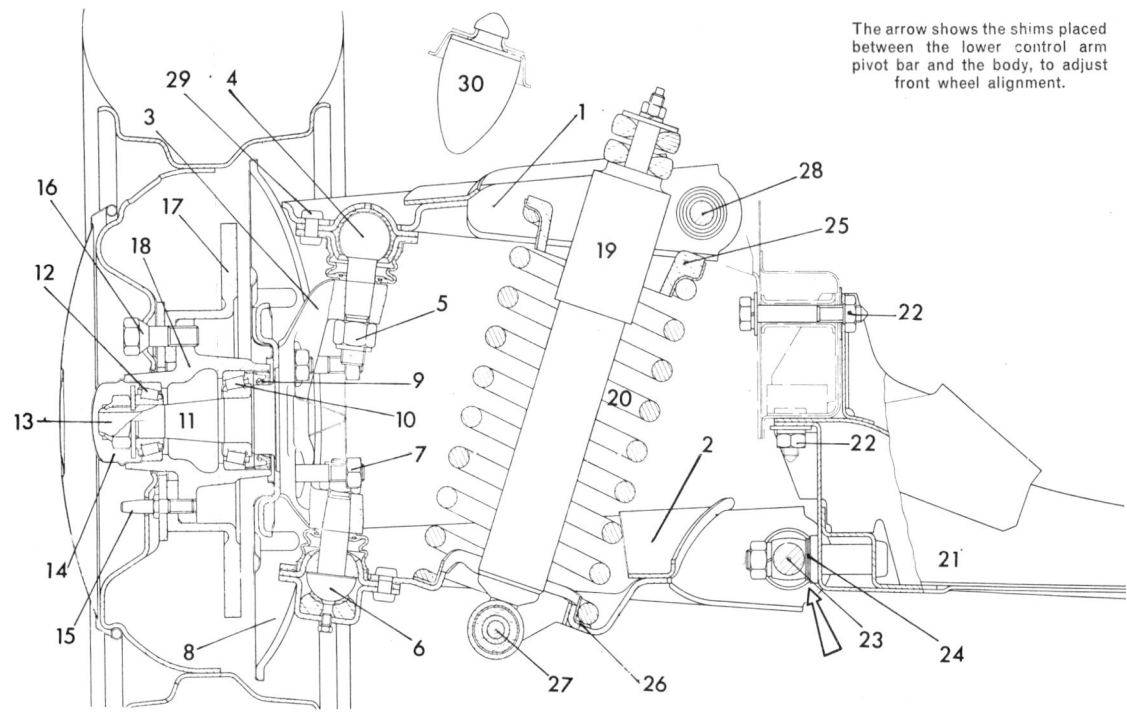

The arrow shows the shims placed between the lower control arm pivot bar and the body, to adjust front wheel alignment.

FIG 8 : 1 Diagrammatic section through lefthand front suspension

Key to Fig 8 : 1 1 Upper swing arm 2 Lower control arm 3 Steering knuckle 4 Upper ball joint 5 Knuckle pin nut 6 Lower ball joint 7 Steering arm bolt 8 Brake disc guard 9 Oil seal 10 Inner roller bearing 11 Stub axle 12 Outer roller bearing 13 Hub nut and washer 14 Hub cap 15 Spigot stud 16 Wheel stud 17 Brake disc 18 Hub 19 Shock absorber 20 Suspension spring 21 Crossmember 22 Crossmember bolts 23 Lower arm mounting pin 24 Shims 25 Spring cup and seating pad 26 Seating pad 27 Shock absorber lower bolt 28 Upper arm fixing bolt 29 Ballcup rivet 30 Bumper

or fine stone. If the scoring is deep, renew the part. Remove all traces of old grease and dry all surfaces.

If it is necessary to replace the bearing, extract the outer ring with a suitable tool and refit the new one. Fit both bearings to the hub, fill the inner chamber with Fiat MR.3, or equivalent, grease (about 3 oz evenly spread around the interior) and insert the spacer and a new oil seal. **The spacer is an additional feature fitted on all cars after May 1966.**

Attach the brake disc to the hub with the two spigot screws and mount the assembly on to the stub axle. Fix the outer bearing thrust washer, inserting the tab in the groove on the axle, apply the nut and tighten to a torque of 15 lb ft while swinging the hub in either direction (see **FIG 8 : 5**). This ensures that the bearing is properly seated.

Unscrew the nut and retighten to a torque of 5 lb ft. Make a mark on the washer at midpoint of one nut face (see **FIG 8 : 6**) and slacken one half face (30 deg.). Secure the nut in this position by crimping with tool A.74126 (see **FIG 8 : 7**), fill the cap with grease and force home with drift A.74088.

Refit the disc brake gear, tightening the fixing bolts to a torque of 15 lb ft, and replace the wheels and caps.

8 : 4 Removing coil springs

Lift the front of the car and support it on stands A.15051 or their equivalent to give access to the underside of the car when the jack is removed. Remove the front wheels

and, working from inside the car, disconnect the upper end of the shock absorbers. To prevent the shank from turning while undoing the nut, hold the shank with wrench A.57070. Remove the bolt and nut securing the bottom end of the shock absorber to the lower swinging arm and remove the shock absorber through the lower arm aperture.

Compress the spring with tool A.74174 (see **FIG 8 : 8**).

Unbolt the stabilizer bar from the control arm, plug the outlet from the hydraulic brake fluid reservoir and uncouple the brake hoses from the hydraulic pipelines (see **FIG 8 : 9**).

Disconnect the tie rod from the steering arm with puller A.47044 (see **FIG 8 : 10**), unscrew and remove the bolt securing the upper swinging arm to the body and remove the two nuts attaching the lower swinging arm to the crossmember. **Note the number and position of the shims inserted on the bolt behind the pin for refitting at a later stage.**

Transfer the wishbone and spring assembly to the bench and unscrew the spring-containing tool A.74174 to release the spring pressure. Expand the wishbones and remove the spring.

Reassembly is a simple reversal of these instructions.

The suspension springs do differ slightly between the Coupé and Spyder, so refer to **Technical Data** for the part numbers and dimensions. The Coupé springs will be marked with white and blue stripes but in addition a yellow

FIG 8:2 Removing wheel hub cap with percussion drawer A.47014

FIG 8:3 Removing front wheel hub 1 with puller A.47015, 2

or green daub of paint is used to classify the tension of the spring under a predetermined load. Nominally, the length of the spring under a load of 507 lb (230 kg) should be 11.6 inch. If the length is above this a daub of yellow paint is used, if it is below the nominal length then a daub of green paint is used.

In the event of renewal, both front springs must be changed, irrespective of the condition of the other and in the case of the Coupé, both springs must have the same daub of colour.

Both springs in an assembly must be of the same class.

Examine the springs after extraction and replace if cracked, deformed or otherwise suspect, replacing the rubber seating pads at the same time.

8:5 Dismantling the suspension

The procedure so far has involved the transfer to the bench of the wishbone and knuckle rod assembly for spring extraction. The next step is to dismantle and inspect the wishbone assembly. Remove the four nuts 1 (see **FIG 8:11**) securing the steering arm to the steering knuckle. This will also release the brake caliper bracket and brake disc guard.

Remove the nuts securing the two knuckle pins to the steering knuckle (see **FIG 8:12**) and, with tool A.47042 inserted as shown (see **FIG 8:13**) force the lower knuckle pin out of its seating to free the arm assembly from the steering knuckle. With the assistance of a distance piece, the same procedure can be repeated to release the upper swinging arm from the knuckle (see **FIG 8:14**).

The three parts can now be inspected separately. First, thoroughly clean the arms and examine them for signs of damage, cracking or distortion. A special gauge, A.95716, is available for this purpose and it should be possible to insert without effort the gauge pin in one of the three holes in the upper platform, according to which is being examined (see **FIG 8:15**). If the distortion is slight, the arm may be straightened; otherwise replace the complete arm. **Do not use any arm in which cracks are evident.**

Examine the bushes and replace any which are worn or hardened. The mounting pin of the lower, or control, arm is secured in place in the arm by the bushes and, to renew the bushes, they must be extracted by pushing the bush out in a press, using the mounting pin as a drift, against a hollow mandrel, A.47045 (see **FIG 8:16**). The second bush is removed by reversing the arm.

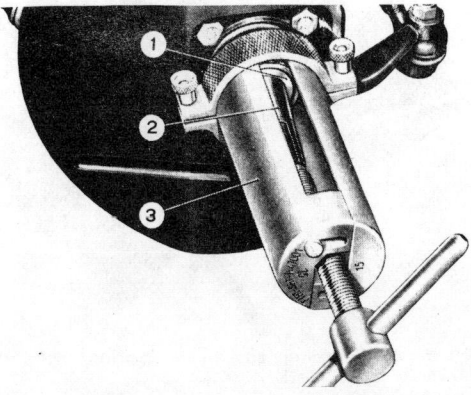

FIG 8:4 Removing inner race 1 from stub axle 2 with puller A.47001, 3

FIG 8:5 Tightening stub axle bearing fixing nut with torque wrench

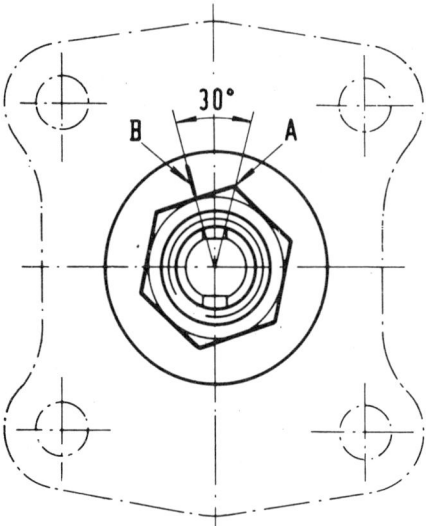

Nut tightened with a torque of 5 lb ft (.7 kgm)

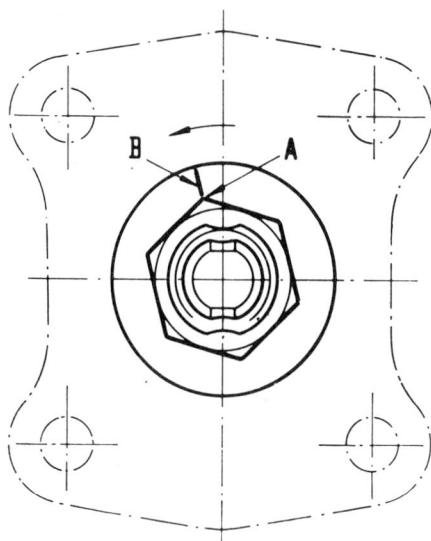

Nut unscrewed by 30 deg.

FIG 8:6 Diagram showing the two stages in wheel hub nut tightening. For the right front hub, the unscrewing is in the reverse direction as it is a lefthand thread

Renewal of the bush is with the assistance of tool A.74177. This is in two parts. The arm and pin are first fitted to part 2, held in a vice, the bushes are applied to the ends of the pin where they protrude through the arm eyes and then forced home by the second part of the tool. This is then removed and the fixing nut applied and tightened (see **FIG 8:17**).

Removal and reinstallation of the bushes in the upper arm is by means of tool A.47046. Extraction is effected by placing the head outside the arms and insertion by placing it inside (see **FIG 8:18**).

Check the condition of the ball joints riveted to each arm. If they are worn or seized or are not secure in the arm, change the whole arm. **Do not attempt to renew the ball joint.** The collapsible rubber sealing bushes can be renewed if they are torn or hardened.

Examine the steering knuckles and steering arms for signs of wear, damage or distortion. The knuckle can be checked for distortion in tool A.96006 (see **FIG 8:19**). Replace if at all suspect.

8:6 Reassembly of the control arms

Reassembly is a simple reversal of the dismantling procedure. When tightening the self-locking nuts to the knuckle pins, use new self-locking nuts and tighten to a torque of 73 lb ft.

The torque for tightening the two short and two long stud nuts attaching the steering arm is 44 lb ft and they are locked in place by means of the tab strips.

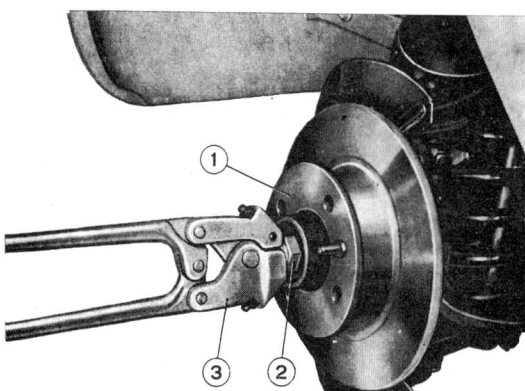

FIG 8:7 Use of crimping tool A.74126 to secure wheel hub nut

Key to Fig 8:7 1 Brake disc   2 Axle nut   3 Tool A.47126

FIG 8:8 Compressing suspension spring with tool A.74174

Key to Fig 8:8 1 Upper plate of A.74174   2 Lower plate   3 Crank

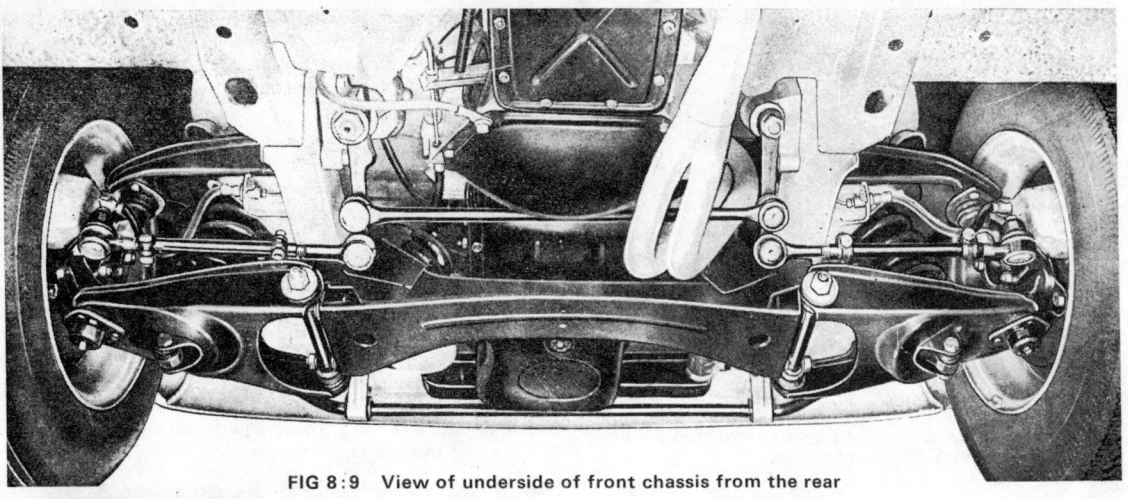

FIG 8:9　View of underside of front chassis from the rear

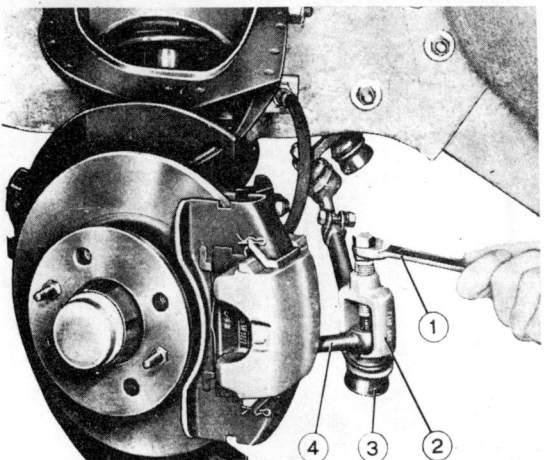

FIG 8:10　Removing steering arm pin 3 from arm 4 with puller A.47044, 2 and spanner 1

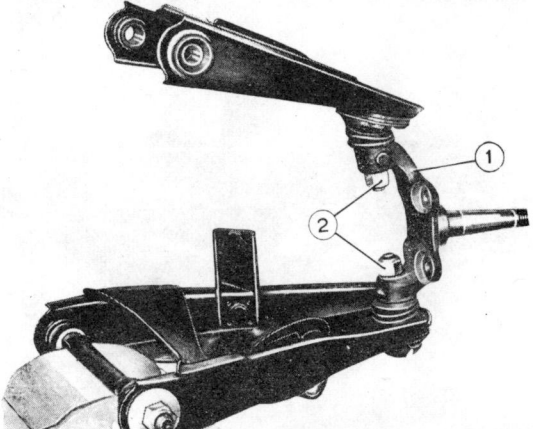

FIG 8:12　Second stage of dismantling wishbone assembly showing steering knuckle 1 and knuckle pin securing nuts 2

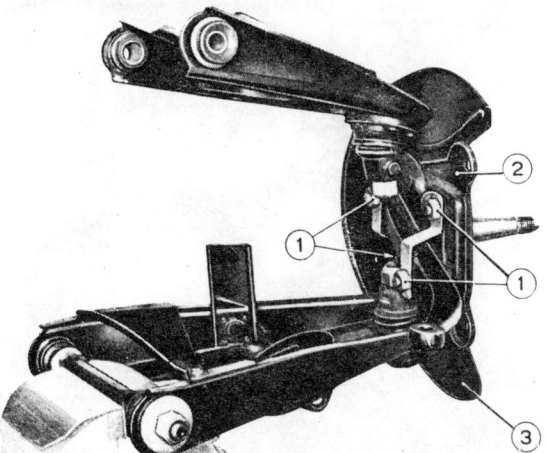

FIG 8:11　First stage in dismantling wishbone assembly showing brake disc guard nuts 1, brake caliper bracket 2 and brake disc guard 3

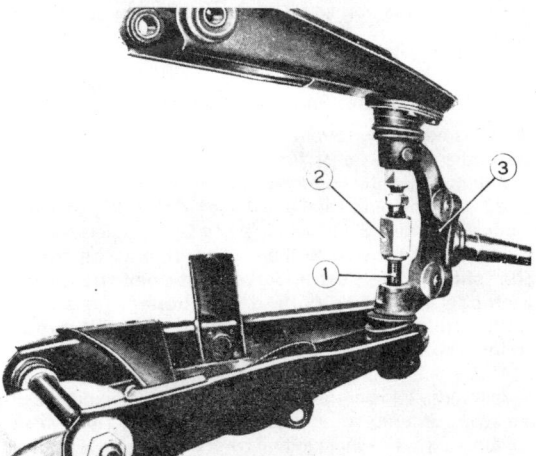

FIG 8:13　Third stage of dismantling wishbone assembly showing use of puller A.47042 to remove lower knuckle pin 1 from steering knuckle 3

FIG 8:14 Fourth stage of dismantling wishbone assembly showing removal of upper knuckle pin 2 from knuckle 3 by puller A.47042 and spacer 1

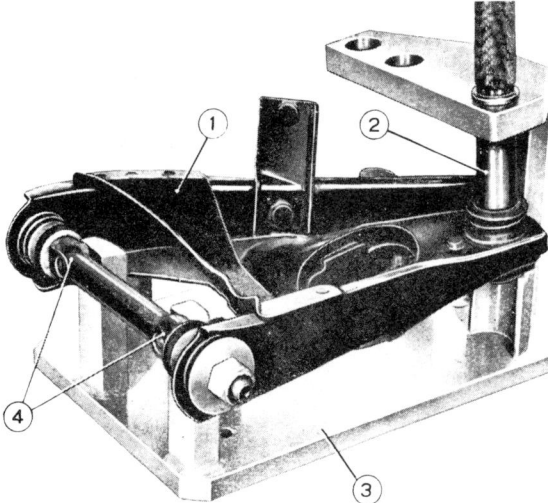

FIG 8:15 Checking control arm in check jig A.95716

Key to Fig 8:15 1 Lower control arm 2 Locating pin for knuckle pin 3 Jig A.95716 4 Positions of centring pins in gauge

8:7 Crossmember and stabilizer bar

If it is necessary to remove the crossmember (see **FIG 8:9**) the engine must first be disconnected from the mounting pads and supported on bar A.70526 as in **FIG 8:20**. The one horizontal bolt 1 (see **FIG 8:21**) and two vertical stud nuts 2, at each side can be extracted and the crossmember lowered to the ground. **It may be found that shims have been inserted between the crossmember and body behind the upper horizontal fixing bolt. Preserve these and reinstall when fixing the crossmember back in place.**

After examining the crossmember for signs of damage or distortion, transfer the unit to a surface plate and check the swing arm mounting studs for alignment. There are a number of ways of checking this or the Fiat agent will have a special jig A.74170 designed for the purpose. Slight deformations may be corrected, otherwise change the crossmember.

Remove the stabilizer bar from the chassis and check the alignment of the ends. Misalignment should be not greater than .02 inch. Straighten, if the deformation is slight, or change. Check and renew the rubber mounting bushes as necessary.

8:8 Reinstalling the suspension

First, refit the crossmember if it has been dismantled, tightening the nuts to a torque of 25 lb ft and ensuring that the shims between the sides and the chassis have been reinserted as before dismantling. Reconnect the support pads to the engine mounting and remove the support bar. Tightening torque for the nuts securing the support pads is 22 lb ft. Reinstall the stabilizer bar.

Reinstall the right and left wishbone assemblies in position, securing the lower arm mounting pin to the crossmember with the same number of shims behind the pin as at dismantling. These may be changed later when adjusting camber and castor angles.

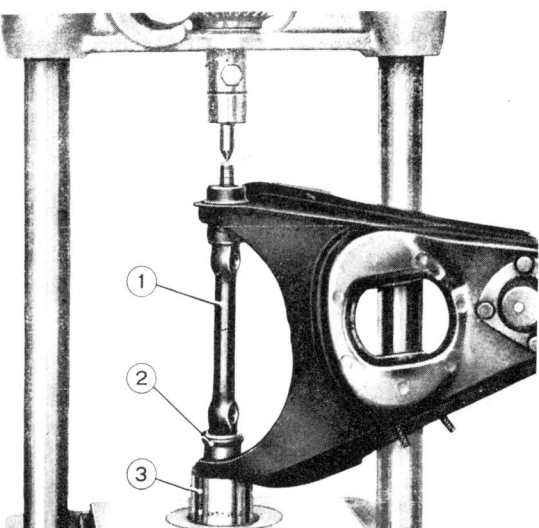

FIG 8:16 Removal of bush 2 from lower control arm by using mounting pin 1 as drift against mandrel A.47045 in an hydraulic press

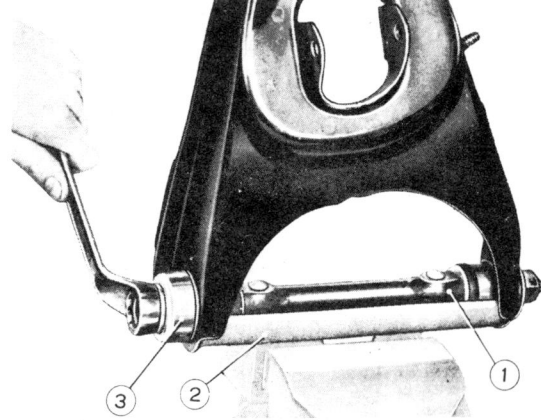

FIG 8:17 Inserting new bushes into control arm pin 1 with support tool A.74177/2, 2 and collar A.74177/1, 3

Fit the coil spring to the lower control arm and compress it to reduce height with tool A.74174 as in **FIG 8:22.** Adjust height until it is possible to connect the upper arm to its body mounting, insert the bolt and washers with nut but do not tighten. Attach the stabilizer arms to the lower control arms. Connect the steering arm to the steering side arms and tighten the nut to 15 lb ft torque. Recouple the hydraulic brake connections and bleed the system.

Release the spring carefully until it seats on the lower control arm and then free and remove the tool. Install the shock absorbers, replace the wheel and lower the car to the ground. Transfer to a flat level surface, adjust the tyre pressures to 20 lb/sq in at front and 23 lb/sq in at the rear and the load the car until the distance between the front jack pads and ground is 7.16 inches and between the rear jack pad and ground, 8.31 inches.

Tighten the top arm nut to 72 lb ft torque, the lower arm mounting pin nuts to 44 lb ft torque and the lower arm-to-bearing pin nuts to 72 lb ft torque.

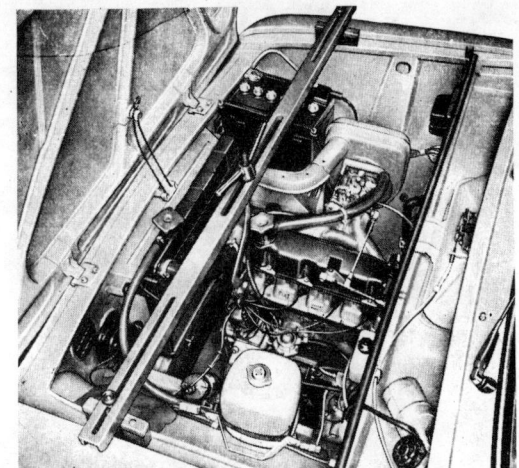

FIG 8:20 Use of bar A.70526 to support engine while crossmember is removed from car

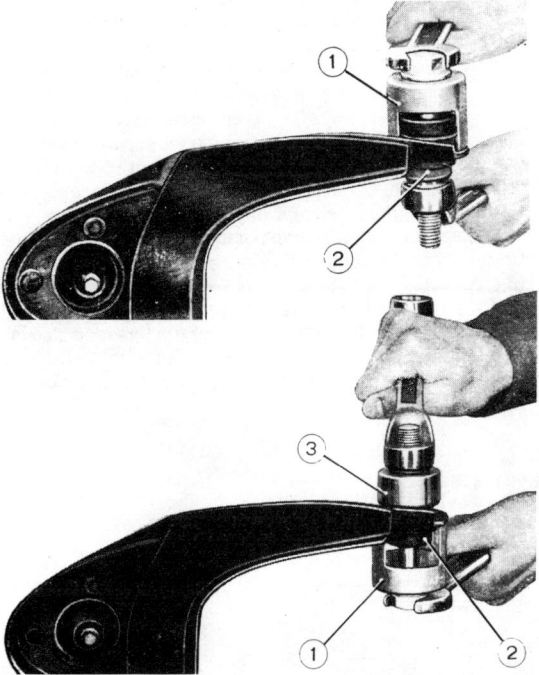

FIG 8:18 Use of tool A.47046, 1 to extract bush (above) and insert new bush (below). In each case the bush is marked 2 and the collar for insertion is marked 3

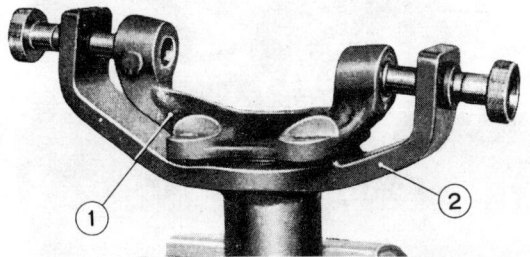

FIG 8:19 Checking steering knuckle 1 in jig A.96006, 2 for distortion

FIG 8:21 End view of crossmember 4 in position to show the horizontal fixing bolt 1, vertical fixing studs 2 and the mounting pin studs with shims 3

8:9 Front wheel alignment

Before attempting to align the front wheels, it is necessary to ensure that the steering has been overhauled and is free from wear or play beyond the permitted tolerances. That is to say, although the technique is described here, it follows naturally the maintenance procedures outlined in this and the succeeding Section.

The alignment can be set up with the car laden or unladen but the values here given are those for the laden state as set in the last Section, so that the procedure follows in sequence.

Two special tools are required; a pair of platforms with graduated quadrants and a pendulum goniometer for checking castor and camber angles, and an adjustable track width gauge with dial type indicator for checking toe-in. The Fiat tools are Ap.5106 for the first and Ap.5107 for the second but alternative tools which can serve the same function are, of course, permissible.

To set the castor angle, mount the front wheels on the graduated quadrants with the rear wheels on pads of

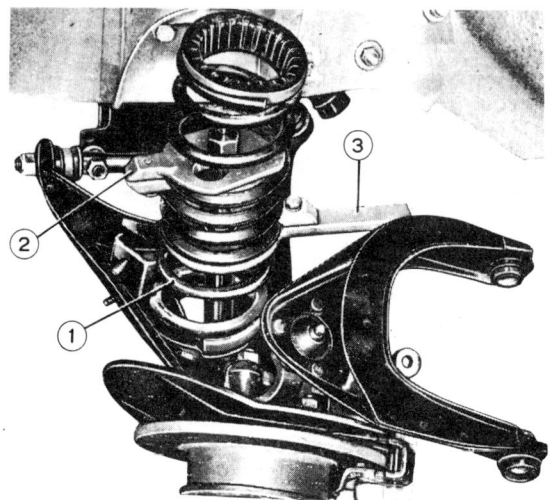

FIG 8:22 Collapsing spring 1 by clamping it between upper plate 2 and lower plate 3 of tool A.74174

equivalent thickness to maintain the car level. With the wheels centred to driving straight-ahead, set the quadrants at zero degrees against the adjustable pointer (see **FIG 8:23**).

Clamp the goniometer support to the rim of the front wheel and secure the instrument to it so that the mounting shaft is in line with the wheel centre. Turn the wheel outward by 20 deg. as measured on the quadrant. Set the movable scale on the goniometer to zero against the pointer.

Now move the steering so that the wheel is pointing 20 deg. in the opposite direction; that is, through a total angle on the quadrant of 40 deg. The goniometer reading must be between 3 deg. 25 min and 4 deg. 0 min.

To adjust castor angle transfer shims from the forward mounting stud to the rear to increase, and from the rear to the front to decrease, castor angle on the lower arm mounting pin (see **FIG 8:21**) and resecure the nuts with a torque of 43 lb ft. This necessitates the raising of the car on a jack, the removal of the wheel and shock absorber and the use of tool A.74174 to restrain the suspension spring while the transfer of shims is being made.

To check the camber angle, use the same set-up with the wheels pointing straight-ahead and read the angle direct from the camber scale on the goniometer. This should lie between 0 deg. 10 min and 0 deg. 50 min **and must be the same on both front wheels.**

To correct camber angle, make a similar adjustment to the shims as for castor, but now add the same number of shims to both studs to reduce camber angle **or** remove the same number from both to increase camber angle.

The procedure for measuring and adjusting the front wheel alignment or toe-in is as follows:

Measure the distance between the inner sides of the wheel rims at the front of each wheel and at wheel centre height. Mark the two points of reference.

Roll the car forward by exactly one half of a wheel revolution so that the reference marks are now at the back of the wheels and again measure the distance between them. The amount by which the second measurement is greater than the first is the amount of toe-in.

For this check the vehicle should be loaded, the Coupé with three persons and 110 lb of luggage, and the Sport (Spyder) with two persons and 44 lb of luggage. Under these conditions toe-in should be .12±.04 inch (3±1 mm).

If the toe-in as measured is outside these limits it will be necessary to adjust it by means of the threaded sleeves on the steering side rods, making sure that the two sleeves are each turned in the appropriate direction by the same amount.

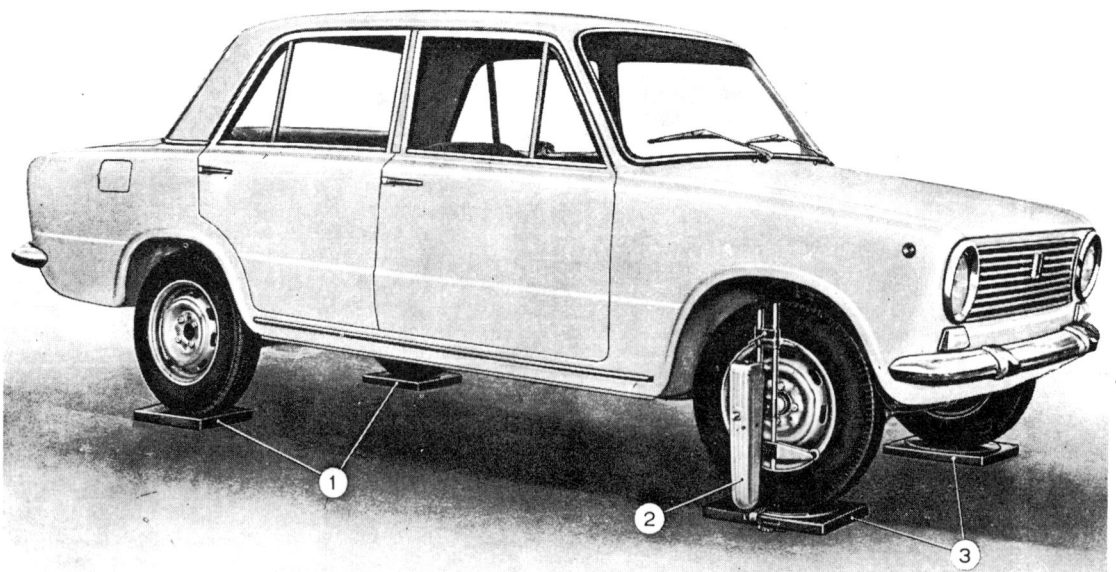

FIG 8:23 Alignment checks on quadrants 3 and pads 1 with goniometer 2 installed for camber and castor checks (124 Saloon used for illustration only)

8:10 Fault diagnosis

(a) Wheel bounce

1 Faulty or worn tyre
2 Uneven tyre pressures
3 Tyre pressures too high
4 Weak coil spring
5 Shock absorber not working
6 Wheel or tyre out of alignment

(b) Excessive tyre wear

1 Incorrect camber setting
2 Excessive acceleration and braking
3 Tyre pressure too low
4 Cornering too sharp or too fast
5 Excessive wheel bearing play
6 Brakes out of adjustment

(c) Pulls to one side, normal running

1 Tyres unevenly inflated
2 Slow puncture in one tyre
3 Flat tyre

4 Steering arms bent
5 Unevenly worn tyres
6 One front brake binding

(d) Pulls to one side when braking

1 Brakes out of adjustment
2 Tyres unevenly worn or inflated

(e) Car weaves at speed

1 Excessive play in steering
2 One wheel loose on hub
3 Excessive play in wheel bearings
4 Wheels out of alignment

(f) Noisy suspension

1 Faulty shock absorbers
2 Loose absorber mountings
3 Worn spring seatings
4 Play in swinging arm bushes
5 Play in stabilizer bar mountings

NOTES

CHAPTER 9

THE STEERING GEAR

9:1 Description

The steering gear employed on both cars is of the worm and roller type with a ratio of 1 : 16.4. The layout is shown in **FIG 9 : 1**. The pitman arm 1 is keyed to the roller shaft in the gearbox 2 and actuates a transverse idler arm rod 7 which in turn operates at its other end an idler arm 3. It will be seen that at their outer ends the pitman arm and the idler arm are connected to the two track rods, linking with the steering knuckles on the front wheels. Also visible in the illustration are the adjusting sleeves on the two track rods by which the front wheel alignment is set.

A hydraulic damper 4 is included in the idler arm bracket bolted to the sidemember opposite to the steering box which, by absorbing vibration, prevents road shocks from damaging the assembly or being transmitted to the steering wheel. This arrangement permits simple change-over from right- to lefthand drive and vice versa.

The steering column is attached to the underside of the dashboard by four nuts and bolts passing through adjusting slots in the guide bracket. It is carried in two ball-bearings, and in order to provide a satisfactory driving attitude on the roadster is equipped with a pair of universal joints which enable the steering wheel position to be lowered. Details of this steering column assembly and its mounting are shown in **FIG 9 : 2**.

9:2 Routine maintenance and adjustment

Providing that the oil seals and protective gaiters on the ball joints and steering box are intact, the steering can be considered as lubricated for life. Inspection of the gaiters at regular intervals is, therefore, the only servicing required unless sloppy steering has been traced to wear in the steering box or in the ball joints and not, as may be more likely, to hub bearing wear. **Worn ball joints must be replaced, not rectified.** Play in the steering box can be adjusted as an extension of the initial setting-up, the details of which are given in **Section 9 : 5**.

9:3 Removing the steering gear

The initial step in dismantling the steering is to remove the steering wheel. First, however, disconnect and remove the battery. This is to prevent inadvertent earths on the wiring to the direction indicator and dipswitch on the column and to the horn button circuit. Now prise off the central motif and cover on the steering wheel to reveal the nut securing the wheel to the column. Using wrench A.57005, unscrew and remove the nut. The steering wheel can now be taken off.

Loosen and remove the four screws retaining the half covers of the direction indicator switch and dismantle the

FIG 9:1   View of steering linkage on car

Key to Fig 9:1   1 Steering arm   2 Steering box   3 Idler arm   4 Idler arm bracket (hydraulic damper)   5 End of righthand track rod   6 Adjusting sleeve of righthand track rod   7 Idler arm rod   8 End of lefthand track rod   9 Adjusting sleeve of lefthand track rod

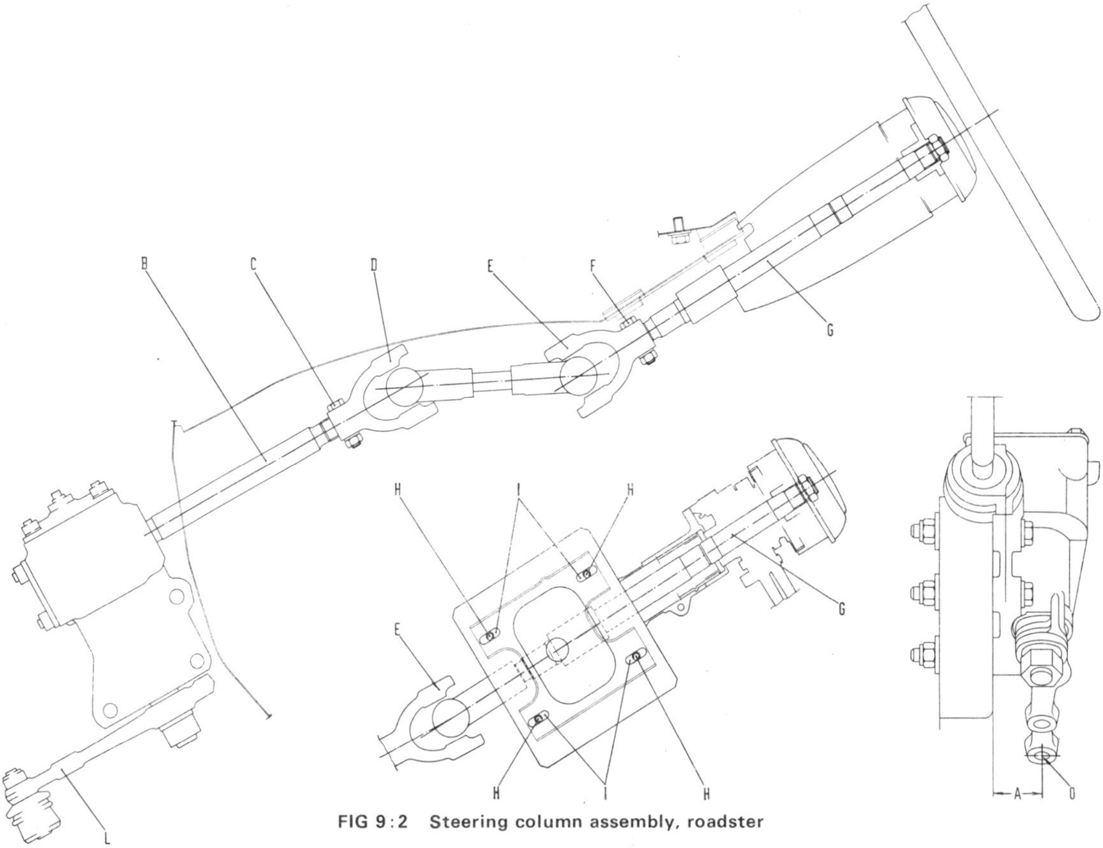

FIG 9:2   Steering column assembly, roadster

Key to Fig 9:2   B Lower steering column   C Lower universal joint fork bolt   D and E Universal joint forks   F Upper steering column universal joint fork bolt   G Upper steering column   H Steering column guide bracket fixing screws   I Slots   L Steering arm   O Centre of steering arm eye

A=42.5 mm (1.67 in) approx. This dimension must be respected when fitting steering assembly to car

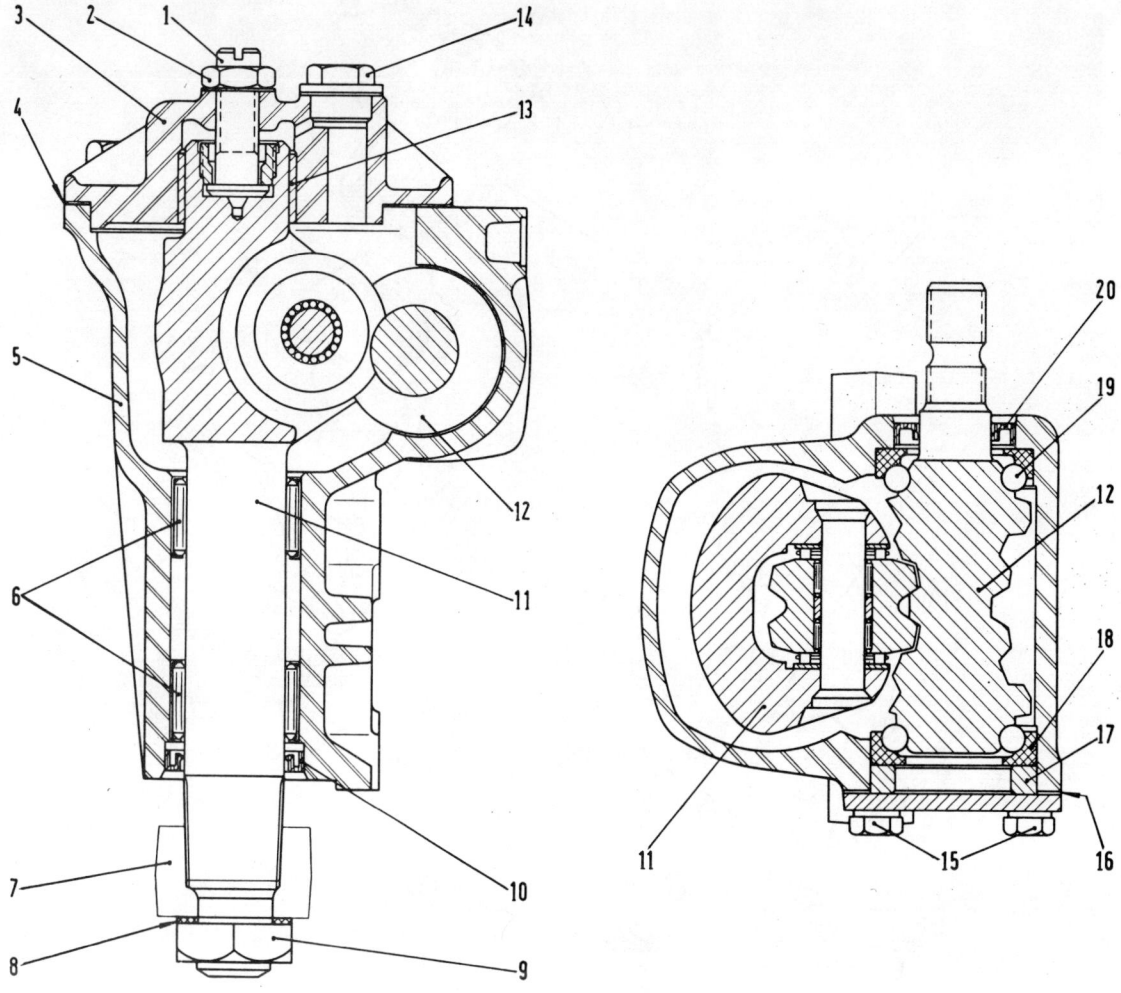

FIG 9:3 Sectional views of steering gear type 4167806

Key to Fig 9:3 1 Adjusting screw 2 Locknut 3 Steering housing cover 4 Gasket 5 Steering gear housing 6 Needle roller bearings 7 Pitman arm 8 Lock plate 9 Nut, pitman arm to roller shaft 10 Seal 11 Roller shaft 12 Steering column 13 Bushing 14 Oil filler plug 15 Worm screw thrust cover screws 16 Shims 17 Spacer 18 Bearing cap 19 Ballbearing 20 seal

covers. Unscrew the switch retaining collar on the bracket, disconnect the cables and remove the direction indicator switch. Unscrew the threaded ring retaining the ignition switch to the column bracket, extract the four nuts and bolts and working either from within the engine compartment or through the hole in the floor at the base of the column revealed by removal of the rubber boot, release the bolts C and F and extract the steering column from the car (see **FIG 9:2**).

Raise the front of the car on stands to gain access to the underside. Working from beneath the car, loosen and remove the three bolts securing the steering box to the side beams, extract the steering arm pins on the pitman arm with puller A.47004 (see **FIG 8:10**) and remove the steering box. It may be found that shims have been inserted at position S where the steering box abuts the side beam. These are to correct any misalignment that would have imposed abnormal stresses on the box and made steering stiff. Check the number and position when dismantling and replace them as before when reinstalling the steering box.

Dismantle the idler rod and side arm assembly together with the idler arm by withdrawing the ball joint pins, again with puller A.47004 and unbolt the idler arm bracket from the opposite side beam. Transfer all parts to the bench for examination and rectification.

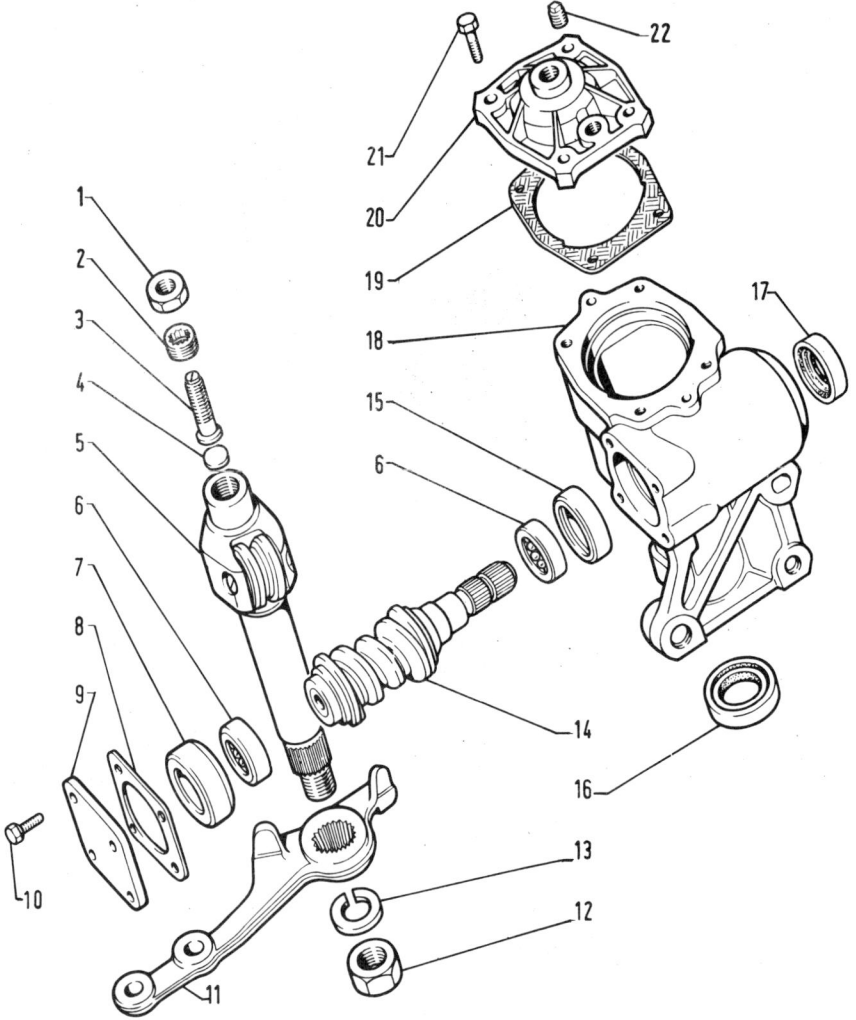

FIG 9:4   Exploded view of steering type 4169064

Key to Fig 9:4   1 Adjusting screw nut   2 Screw ring   3 Adjusting screw   4 Plug   5 Roller shaft   6 Ballbearings   7 Bearing retainer   8 Shims   9 Worm screw thrust cover   10 Cover screws   11 Pitman arm   12 Nut, pitman arm to roller shaft   13 Washer   14 Worm screw   15 Bearing retainer   16 Roller shaft seal   17 Steering column seal   18 Steering gear housing   19 Gasket   20 Steering housing upper cover   21 Upper cover screws   22 Oil filler plug

9:4 Servicing the steering box

Two types of steering gears are fitted in production and they are illustrated in **FIGS 9:3** and **9:4** and before commencing to dismantle the box it should be cleaned and drained of oil through the filler plug hole.

Unscrew the nut 9 and locking washer 8 to release the pitman arm and pull it off the roller shaft 11 using tool A.47043 as shown in **FIG 9:5**.

Remove the four nuts and lift off the cover 3 together with the roller shaft 11. Extract and examine the oil seal 10.

Remove the four nuts and washers securing the worm thrust coverplate 15 and shims 16 to the steering box. Take off the cover and note the number of shims for later replacement. The worm screw assembly may now be pushed through the aperture together with the top and bottom bearings. Extract the oil seal 20.

Carefully examine all parts for wear and in particular check that the contact faces of both worm and roller are not pitted or scored. If the shims have been correctly fitted the two components will have meshed comfortably in the middle. Replace any items showing excessive wear or damage.

9:5 Reassembly and adjustment

Reassembly of the steering box is a reversal of the dismantling procedure, care being taken to ensure that all parts are lightly lubricated and that the same number of shims are refitted in the same positions as before removal. Tighten up all nuts and check that there is no end play on the worm shaft, then measure the turning torque with a dynamometer as shown in **FIG 9:6**. This should be between .1 and .5 lb ft and if necessary may

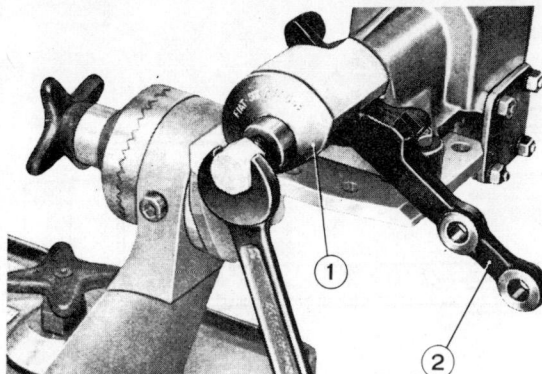

FIG 9:5 Removing the pitman arm **2** from roller shaft using tool A.47043 **1**

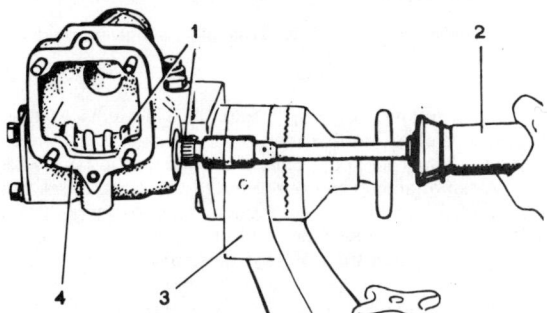

FIG 9:6 Checking the turning torque of wormshaft

Key to Fig 9:6 1 Wormshaft 2 Tool A95697 3 Stand 4 Steering box

be adjusted by changing the number of shims at 16, increasing the number to reduce the torque and removing one or more to increase it. It is recommended that the oil seal at 20 should be renewed and care must be taken to see that it is inserted the right way as shown.

To adjust the backlash in the worm shaft first set the gear in the midway position. This is done by turning the steering column from lock to lock, counting the number of turns and dividing by two and positioning the column accordingly.

Temporarily fit the pitman arm to the shaft so that its centre line is parallel with the base of the steering box (see **FIG 9:8**) and rotate the steering column in one direction by a quarter of a turn at a time, checking the clearance at each step and reducing it to a minimum by means of the adjusting screw. Repeat this by turning the column in the opposite direction.

If it is found that meshing is tight at one end and too slack at the other it indicates that the worm is not properly centred. This must be corrected by adjusting the shims under the worm shaft coverplate and behind the inner bearing.

When the adjustments are completed lock the adjusting screw with the locknut 2 and fill the steering box with the recommended grade of oil. The steering box is reinstalled by bolting it in place, not omitting any shims which were present before removal.

9:6 Refitting the steering column

Having firmly secured the steering box, set the pitman arm (L in **FIG 9:2**) in the middle of its stroke at which point the centre of the eye O will be 1.67 inch (42.5 mm) from the face of the steering box on the body.

Fit the fork E to the upper part of the steering column and tighten the screw F.

Fit the fork D to the column B and fix the guide bracket to the instrument panel with the screws H without tightening them so as to enable the bracket to be slid into position.

Temporarily fit the steering wheel and turn it from side to side a few times to get the assembly settled in position when the bracket fixing screws may be secured.

Check carefully to see that the universal joints where fitted do not tend to bind the movement of the column and that there is no play between the bracket and the column at the bearing on the steering wheel side and then tighten the bolt C. A section through the upper steering column is given in **FIG 9:9** and it is stressed that the bearing retaining spring 5 must be in good condition since it takes up any play between the balls and races of the upper steering column bearings.

FIG 9:7 Fitting steering box cover, showing fitting of adjusting disc 4

Key to Fig 9:7 1 Adjusting screw locknut 2 Roller shaft adjusting screw 3 Roller shaft 4 Adjusting screw plate 5 Studs 6 Lockwashers

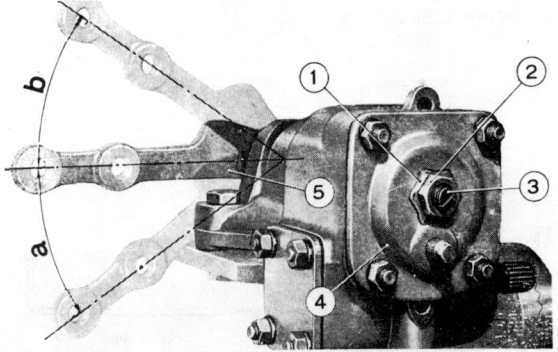

FIG 9:8 Adjusting worm to roller backlash

Key to Fig 9:8 1 Lockwasher 2 Adjusting screw locknut 3 Adjusting screw 4 Steering box cover 5 Drop arm
$a = b = 30° 40' \pm 1° 40'$

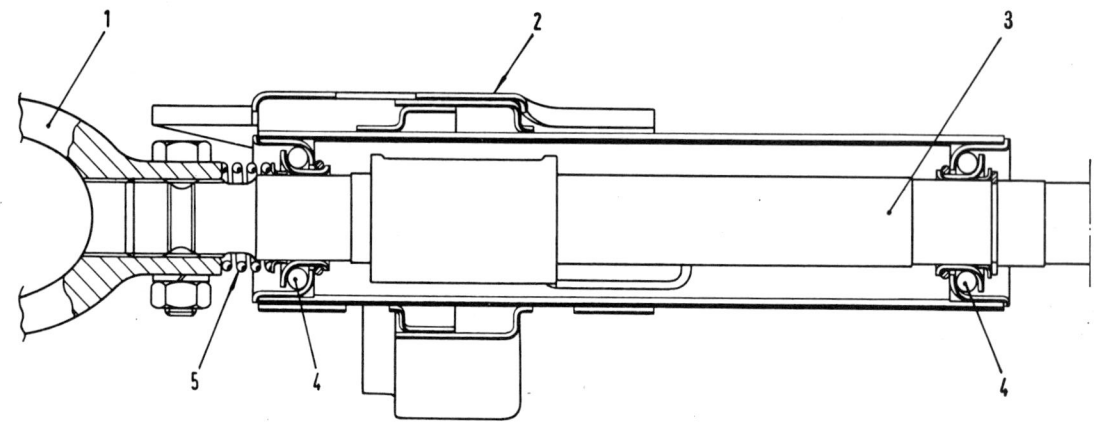

FIG 9:9 Section through upper steering column

Key to Fig 9:9 1 Fork   2 Upper steering column bracket   3 Upper steering column   4 Ballbearings   5 Bearing retaining spring

9:7 Steering links and adjustment

The idler arm rod is of fixed length and is connected between the inner eyes of the pitman and idler arms by ball pin joints. These joints are integral with the idler arm rod and if for any reason a defective joint is due to be renewed the whole rod must be replaced (see **FIG 9:10**).

The two side rods are provided with adjustable heads terminating in ballpin joints to permit adjustment of both toe-in and centring of the steering. The centre section is split and is provided with a clamp at either end and is threaded to accept the head sections. The threads at each end are reversed so that turning of the centre section extends or contracts the effective length without detaching the pin-joints from the steering arm, relay arm or pitman arm. Renewal of a pin-joint necessitates the replacement of only one head but it is important when replacing, to ensure that the new part is threaded the right way round.

When setting up for the first time, the wheel must be centred for straight-ahead and the side arms adjusted so that both front wheels are pointing straight-ahead and are parallel. This must be checked with a gauge before toe-in is adjusted, using the same gauge, as outlined in **Chapter 8, Section 8:9**.

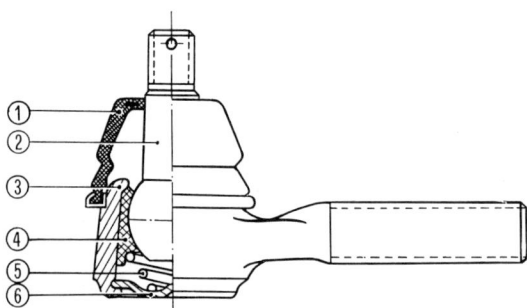

FIG 9:10 Section through ballpin joint on idler arm rod

Key to Fig 9:10   1 Rubber boot   2 Ballpin   3 Socket
4 Spherical bush   5 Spring   6 Coverplate

After setting, securely clamp the side-arms in their positions checking that the slots in the sleeves and those in the clamps are in the same plane and on the same side.

When attaching the pin-joints to the arms, check the type of nut used (nut and cotter of self-locking). If the latter, use a new self-locking nut and do not re-use the old one. Tighten the nut, regardless of type, to a torque of 25 lb ft.

Neither the idler rod nor side rods must be bent. If the side rods are bent, replace them. Slight bending of the idler rod can be corrected in a press or vice but not by hammering. If the bend is appreciable, replace the rod. Never apply a hammer to any part of the steering linkage. Extract the ballpins with the proper extractor A.47004. As most parts are hardened, the use of a hammer may introduce cracks which, though not noticed at the time, may result in failure while on the road with disastrous possibilities.

9:8 Fault diagnosis

(a) Loose steering

1 Slack front wheel bearings
2 Faulty ballpin joints in steering linkage
3 Play in steering box gearing
4 Play in steering box mounting

(b) Heavy steering

1 Seized roller shaft in bushing
2 Seized relay lever in bushing
3 Worm and roller set too close

(c) Play in steering

1 Worn roller or worm
2 End play in roller shaft
3 Loose steering column clamp
4 Loose steering box mounting
5 Loose pin joints

(d) Persistent front tyre squeal

1 Bent track rod
2 Loose side rod

CHAPTER 10

THE BRAKING SYSTEM

10:1 Description

The braking system follows conventional practice with hydraulically operated disc brakes on all four wheels and a cable operated handbrake on the rear wheels only. A brake regulating valve, operated mechanically by the pitch of the body on the suspension, reduces the effect of braking on the rear wheels, according to the severity of retardation, to minimise the chances of rear wheel skids. A Master-Vac servo unit is connected directly between the brake pedal and the master cylinder and, by using the depression in the inlet manifold, reduces the pressure exerted by the driver in applying the brakes.

The general arrangement of the braking system is shown in **FIG 10:1**. The master cylinder 23, deriving its fluid from the reservoir 5, is operated by the foot pedal via a short coupling and pushrod. Separate outlets from the master cylinder are coupled, via the hydraulic lines, to the brake cylinders of the wheels. The stoplight transducer 6, is mechanically linked to the footbrake and switches on the stoplights 9, when the brake is applied and the ignition switch is turned on.

The handbrake, located centrally between the two front seats, applies the rear brakes through cables and levers.

10:2 Routine maintenance

Normal servicing of the hydraulic system is confined to checking the level of the brake fluid in the reservoir at regular intervals and topping up with the approved grade (Fiat blue label) of fluid as necessary. The level must never be allowed to fall below that which would enable air to enter the hydraulic lines or braking will become spongy and inefficient. The system will then have to be bled.

The capacity of the master cylinder is sufficient to supply, at a single stroke, enough hydraulic fluid to all cylinders regardless of pad wear. As the rear wheel brakes are self compensating, there is no indication of brake pad wear at either foot or handbrake. Wear can be determined only by measuring pad thickness at the periodical disc and caliper overhauls. This should be at the 12,000 mile check and pads must be replaced when their thickness is

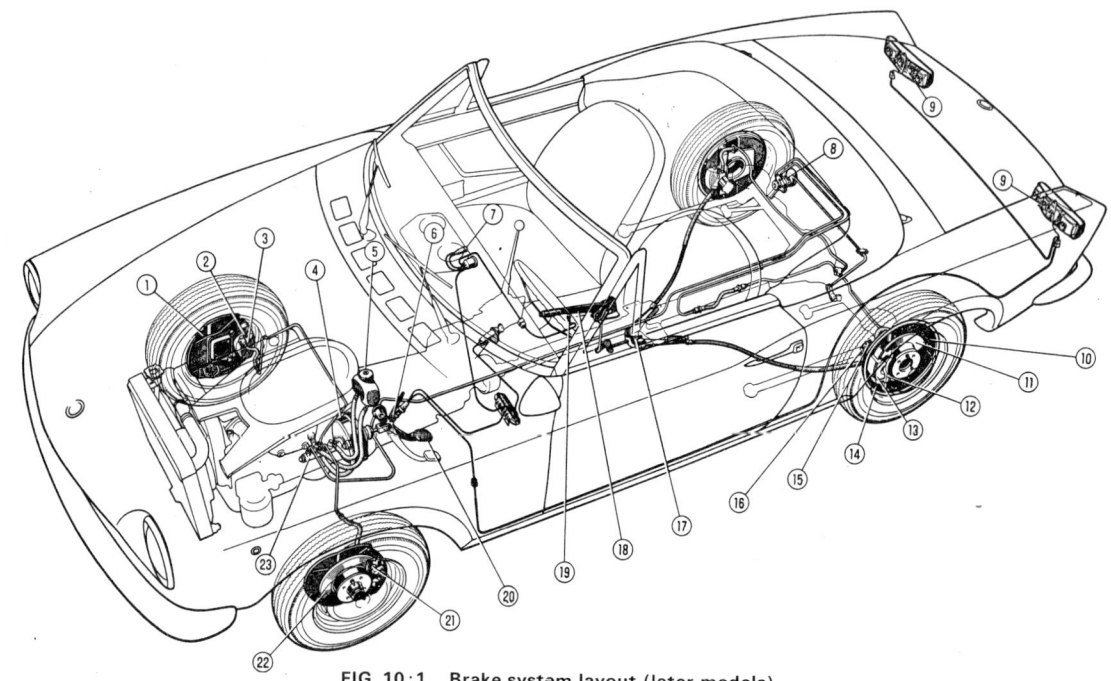

FIG 10:1   Brake system layout (later models)

Key to Fig 10:1   1 Front brake splash shield   2 Front brakes bleeding connection   3 Front brake caliper   4 Vacuum servo unit
5 Dual brake fluid reservoir (front and rear brakes)   6 Mechanically operated stoplight switch   7 Handbrake (on) light indicator
8 Braking regulator on rear brake circuit   9 Stoplights   10 Rear brake splash shield (rear)   11 Rear brake disc   12 Caliper bracket
13 Rear brake caliper   14 Rear brake splash shield (front)   15 Rear brakes bleeding connection   16 Parking brake
17 Parking brake cable tensioner   18 Parking brake hand lever   19 Press-switch for handbrake (on) indicator   20 Hydraulic
brake pedal   21 Friction pad holder   22 Front brake disc
23 Dual-piston master cylinder

below .079 inch or there is indication that they will reach this figure before the next check is due.

A check of the brake regulator setting and linkage should be carried out at the same time.

10:3 The master cylinder (early type)

The master cylinder is shown in diagrammatic section in **FIG 10:2**. The main body 1, houses a cylinder within which is the piston 6, and return spring 12, together with the fluid inlet port 4, and union seating 3, and the outlet

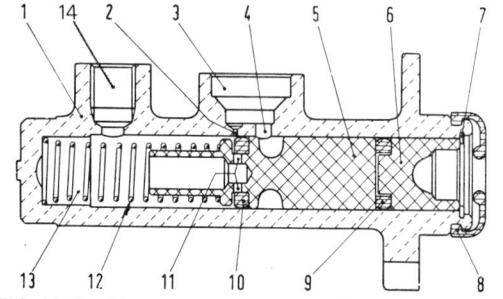

FIG 10:2 Diagrammatic section through master cylinder (early type)

Key to Fig 10:2   1 Cylinder body   2 Compensating port
3 Fluid inlet seating   4 Feed port   5 Valve carrier
6 Piston   7 Snap ring   8 Rubber boot   9 Sealing ring
10 Valve ring   11 Valve port   12 Return spring
13 Pressure chamber   14 Outlet union seating

union seating 14. The piston is separated from the valve carrier 5, by a sealing ring 9, and is operated by the brake pedal pushrod through the rubber boot 8. The snap ring 7, retains the piston within the body at the limit of its travel when the footbrake is off.

In the fully retracted position, fluid enters the cylinder through the feed port 4, and past the relaxed valve ring 10, to fill the hydraulic lines and brake cylinders. On application of the footbrake, the valve body 5, moving forward, pushes the valve ring first towards the compensating port 2, returning the excess fluid to the reservoir and leaving a measured quantity within the braking system when it is sealed by passage of the ring over 2. Increased pressure now has the effect of tightly sealing the chamber by the fluid passing through the port 11, behind the valve to force it outwards onto the cylinder walls. All further pressure is then communicated direct to the hydraulic lines and brake cylinders without loss. Each time the footbrake is released, the piston is returned by the spring 12, to its original position enabling the fluid from the reservoir to enter and make good any leakage from the hydraulic lines or brake cylinders and to compensate for pad wear.

10:4 Disc brakes

The disc brakes on the front wheels are of the non-compensating pattern and comprise a simple hollow piston 4 (see **FIG 10:3**) within the cylinder 5, of the caliper body 1, sealed against fluid leakage by the oil seal

3, and against the ingress of dirt by rubber boot 2. Forward motion of the piston is communicated to one brake pad 6, while the reaction to the pressure on the brake disc pulls the caliper body and the opposing pad 7, within the caliper bracket into contact with the opposite face of the disc, the two gripping it firmly between them.

On the rear brakes, an additional feature is the compensating piston and mechanical linkage for handbrake operation. This comprises a nut 14 (see **FIG 10:4**) rotating within the piston on a ball thrust bearing 13, on its five start internal thread engaged with the male thread on the butt of the handbrake plunger 11. A spring 15, tightly coiled around the nut and anchored at one end to the hydraulic piston, permits rotation in one direction to unscrew the nut on the butt while preventing counter-rotation in the other. Each time the handbrake is applied by operation of the cam lever 9, the full mechanical thrust of the butt-and-nut combination is applied, through the piston wall, to the brake pad. On the return stroke, the piston is gripped by the seal 3, and apart from a slight movement to free the pads from the disc, further withdrawal of the plunger 11, only serves to rotate the nut, fractionally extending the length of the combination to give reduced travel on the cam lever for the next braking application.

10:5 Dismantling and reassembling the master cylinder

First, plug the fluid outlet from the reservoir by a small hardwood plug. **Do not use a softwood plug or one of material that will break and permanently choke the line.** Unscrew the union from the reservoir at the master cylinder then unscrew and remove the union to the brake lines. This is a three-way unit secured to the master cylinder body by a single hexagon-headed bolt

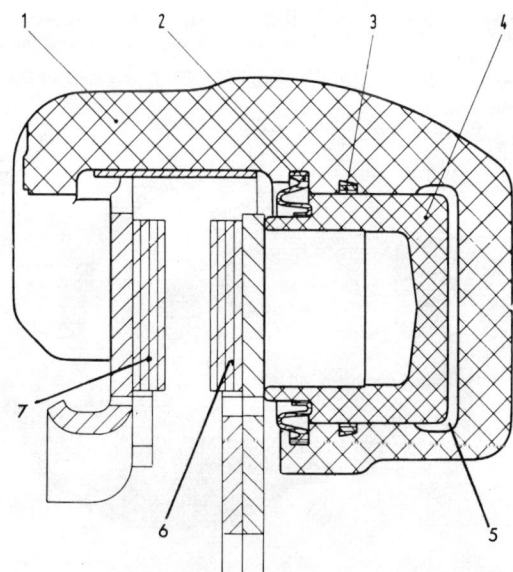

FIG 10:3   Diagrammatic section through front caliper

Key to Fig 10:3   1 Caliper body   2 Piston protection cap 3 Seal   4 Piston   5 Cylinder   6 Moving friction pad   7 Fixed friction pad

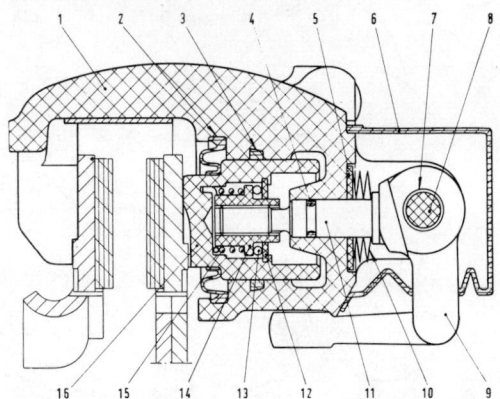

FIG 10:4   Diagrammatic section through rear caliper

Key to Fig 10:4   1 Caliper body   2 Piston protection cap 3 Seal   4 Plunger seal   5 Spring thrust washer 6 Handbrake link boot 7 Bush or needle bearing 8 Pivot pin 9 Cam lever   10 Plunger return spring   11 Handbrake plunger   12 Spun-in disc   13 Ball thrust bearing   14 Nut 15 Spring   16 Piston

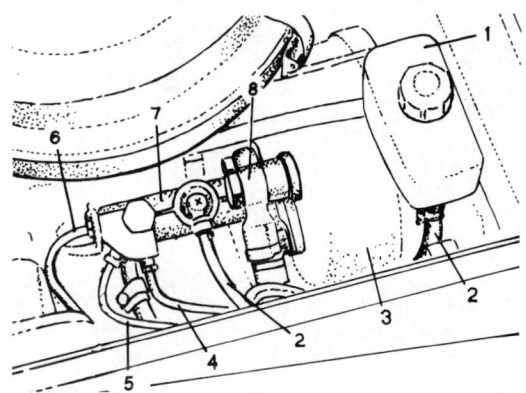

FIG 10:5   Master-Vac servo-system on vehicle

Key to Fig 10:5   1 Brake fluid reservoir   2 Pipeline from reservoir to master cylinder   3 Master-Vac servo unit   4 Pressure line to left front wheel   5 Pressure line to right front wheel   6 Pressure line to rear wheels 7 Master cylinder   8 Vacuum line

(see **FIG 10:5**). Loosen and remove the two nuts and bolts attaching the master cylinder to the servo unit. The cylinder can then be transferred to the bench for dismantling.

Remove the rubber boot 8 (see **FIG 10:2**) and extract the snap ring 7, with round nosed pliers. Push the piston forward to expel any trapped fluid from the outlet union into a convenient receptacle. Do not use this fluid again.

Withdraw the component parts, all of which can be identified from the diagram, from the cylinder body and inspect for wear or signs of deterioration. The cylinder bore, in particular, must be mirror smooth without any roughness or scoring. Replace as necessary.

Clean all parts in a special brake fluid (Fiat blue label) and reassemble in the correct order with new oil seals and

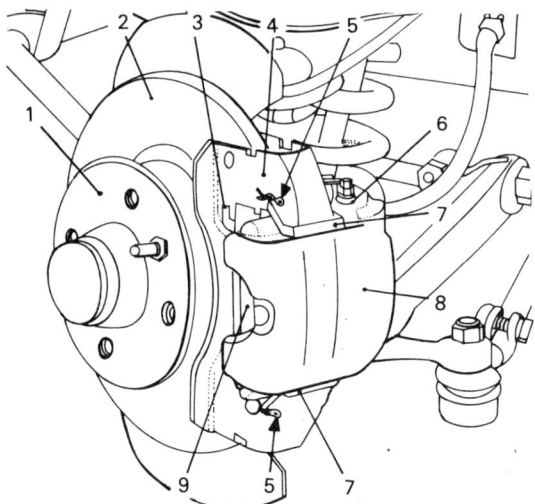

FIG 10:6 Brake assembly showing disc brake components

Key to Fig 10:6 1 Plate 2 Brake disc 3 Friction pad locking spring 4 Caliper support bracket 5 Cotterpins 6 Bleed connection 7 Caliper locking blocks 8 Caliper body 9 Friction pad

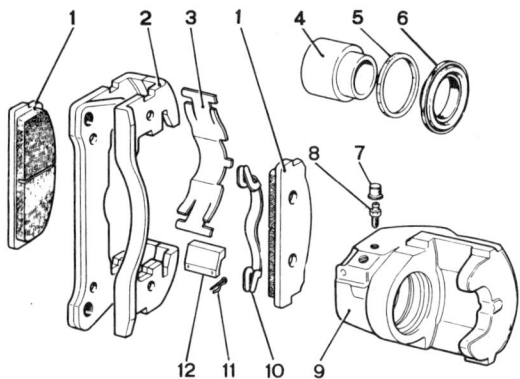

FIG 10:7 Components of front disc brake assembly

Key to Fig 10:7 1 Friction pad 2 Caliper bracket 3 Flat caliper retaining spring 4 Piston 5 Seal 6 Piston protection cap 7 Bleed connection 8 Bleed nipple cover 9 Caliper body 10 Friction pad locking spring 11 Cotter pin 12 Caliper locking block

rubber boot. **Take care to ensure that at no time do the seals come into contact with petrol, paraffin or other mineral base fluid.** Finally, remount in the car and reconnect to the hydraulic lines.

10:6 Servicing the front brakes

A general view of the front brake assembly is shown in **FIG 10:6** and a diagrammatic view of the component parts, dismantled in **FIG 10:7**.

To remove the brake assembly, first plug the outlet from the brake fluid reservoir and disconnect the flexible hydraulic brake line at the bracket (see **FIG 10:6**). Clean the brake assembly with hot water and a soap base detergent, rinse clean with more hot water and dry off with an air jet.

Chock the rear wheels, raise the front on a jack and

remove the wheels. Remove the cotter pins 11, locking plates 12, the caliper body 9, flat spring 3, friction pads 1, and pad locking springs 10, in that order. These operations are illustrated in **FIGS 10:8** to **10:10.** Unbolt and remove the caliper bracket 2 (see **FIG 10:11**).

Check the runout of the brake disc with a dial gauge. This must not exceed .006 inch (see **FIG 10:12**). If the runout is excessive or the disc surfaces are deeply scored, the discs must be replaced or reground, always providing that the latter operation does not reduce the disc thickness below .375 inch.

On the bench, dismantle the caliper assemblies and examine for signs of wear or scoring on the cylinder inner surfaces. Renew all oil seals and rubber boots and any other part that shows signs of excessive wear or corrosion.

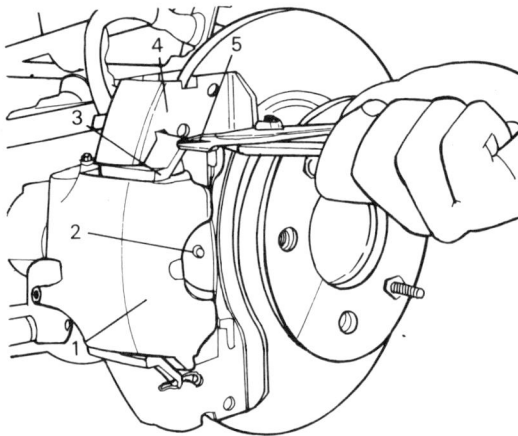

FIG 10:8 Dismantling disc brake. Stage 1, removing locking block with curved pliers

Key to Fig 10:8 1 Caliper body 2 Brake pad 3 Locking block 4 Caliper support bracket 5 Curved pliers

FIG 10:9 Dismantling disc brake. Stage 2, removing caliper body

Key to Fig 10:9 1 Caliper body 2 Piston 3 Friction pad anchor spring 4 Brake disc 5 Caliper support bracket 6 Friction pad 7 Radial flat spring fixing caliper

Reassemble after washing in brake fluid and refit the protecting cap 6.

Check the pad thickness and if it is below the specified minimum thickness of .079 inch, or is likely to fall below this thickness before the next maintenance, renew the pads.

Always refit the pads in the same position; that is, the outer and inner pads must not be transposed, so mark them on dismantling to ensure that they go back correctly. When renewing pads, remember that two types are supplied, identified by a black or orange paint stripe on the rear. All brake pads on a car must be of the same type and bear the same colour stripe.

Reassemble the brake assembly in the reverse order to dismantling and check that the distance between the inner faces of the pads is not less than .42 inch. Reconnect the hydraulic line, unplug the brake fluid reservoir and bleed the brake cylinders.

FIG 10:12 Checking runout on brake disc

Key to Fig 10:12 1 Magnetic bracket A.95684 2 Brake disc 3 Dial gauge

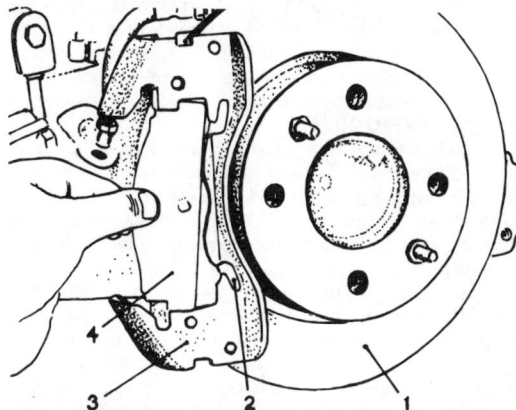

FIG 10:10 Dismantling disc brake. Stage 3, removing friction pad

Key to Fig 10:10 1 Brake disc 2 Friction pad locking spring 3 Caliper support bracket 4 Friction pad

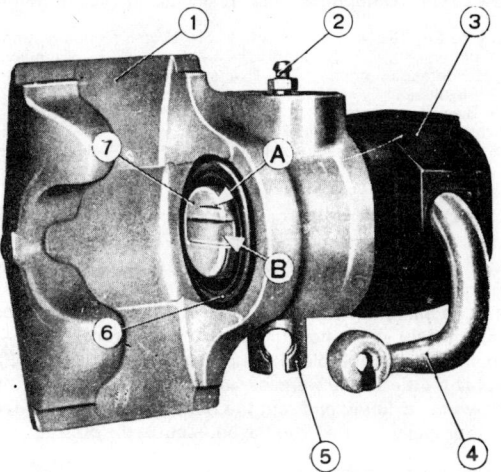

FIG 10:13 Component parts of rear brake caliper showing position of reference mark **A**, and friction pad slot **B**, before assembly

Key to Fig 10:13 1 Caliper body 2 Bleed connection 3 Handbrake link boot 4 Cam lever 5 Cable sleeve anchorage 6 Piston protection cap 7 Piston

10:7 Servicing the rear brakes

The procedure for dismantling the rear brake assemblies is similar to that already described for the front assemblies with the additional step of disconnecting the handbrake cable from the lever arm and anchorage (see **FIG 10:13**). The component parts, when dismantled, are shown in **FIG 10:14**.

After inspection and replacements of oil seals, boots and other parts necessitated by wear or corrosion, fit the piston with self-adjusting nut and washer into the cylinder, lubricating it with a smear of brake fluid, after inserting the sealing ring 3 (see **FIG 10:4**). **The piston and nut assembly is made with the securing ring 12, spun into place to make an integral unit. Do not attempt to dismantle but renew as one unit if necessary.**

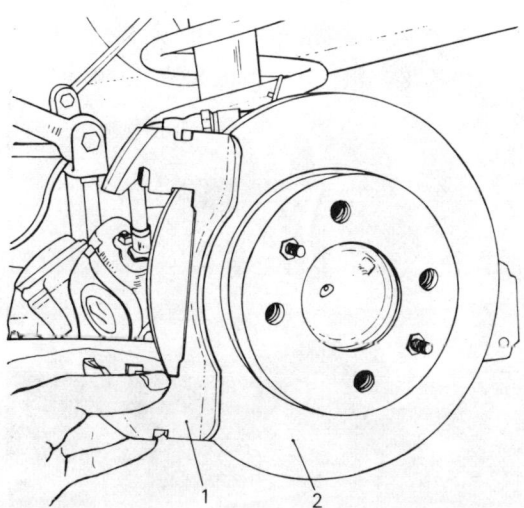

FIG 10:11 Dismantling disc brake. Stage 4, removing caliper bracket

Key to Fig 10:11 1 Caliper support bracket 2 Brake disc

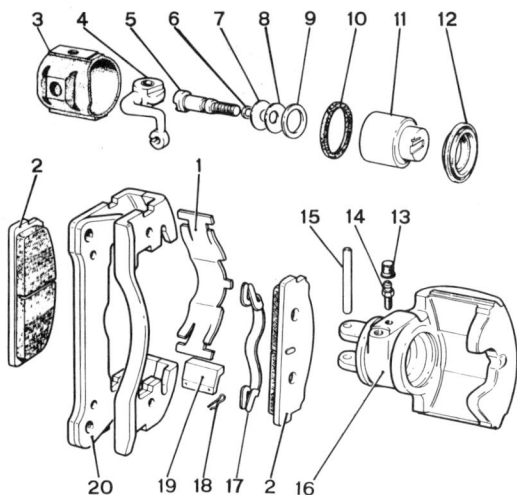

FIG 10:14 Components of rear disc brake assembly

Key to Fig 10:14   1 Flat caliper retaining spring
2 Friction pad   3 Handbrake link boot   4 Cam lever
5 Handbrake plunger   7/8 Disc springs   9 Thrust washer
10 Piston seal   11 Piston   12 Piston protection cap
13 Bleed nipple cover   14 Bleed nipple   15 Cam lever
pivot pin   16 Caliper body   17 Friction pad locking spring
18 Cotter   19 Caliper locking block   20 Caliper bracket

Install the handbrake cam lever, smearing the contact faces of the cam lever 9, and plunger 11, with SP.323 or equivalent grease and replace the gaiter 6. Rotate the piston in the cylinder so that the butt and piston length is at its minimum and rotate a little further until the pad engagement slot is horizontal with the reference mark **A,** on the side of the bleed connection (see **FIG 10:13**). Apply a little SP.323 grease around the piston where it enters the cylinder and refit the boot 2, ensuring that the lip is properly inserted into the undercut in the body.

Remount onto the caliper bracket and complete the assembly of the brakes as for the front. Reconnect the hydraulic lines and bleed. Apply the footbrake a few times, reconnect the handbrake cable and adjust the handbrake.

10:8 Brake regulator

The rear wheel brake regulator comprises a piston operated by a torsion bar, within a cylinder the movement of which varies the flow of hydraulic fluid to the rear brake cylinders according to the degree of braking effort applied to the car by application of the footbrake.

The general arrangement of the brake regulator is shown, as it appears from the rear underside of the car, in **FIG 10:15** the same view being illustrated diagrammatically in **FIG 10:16**. Application of the brakes tends to make the car body move forward on the suspension resulting in the rear of the chassis lifting away from the axle. This is translated as a downward pull by the rear axle case on the link 6, coupled to the long cranked end of the torsion bar 5. At the opposite end, the short crank which has been bearing on the end of the regulator piston moves away from it and the piston now moves with it under the pressure of the hydraulic fluid from the master cylinder (see **FIG 10:17**).

Up to this moment, the piston has been positioned by the torsion bar crank so that there is a free flow around its head and the piston seal 6, is clear from the transfer ports in the slotted ring 7. That is to say, any brake pressure applied is transmitted equally to all four brake cylinders.

Now, however, the piston, moving outwards, first closes the main transfer route around the head and under the piston seal, then, by taking the seal with it, closes the more restricted transfer ports in the slotted ring. Any further increases in pressure from the master cylinder cannot be applied to the rear brake cylinders but only to the front. The rear brakes are still held partially on since the hydraulic fluid already trapped in the lines cannot return.

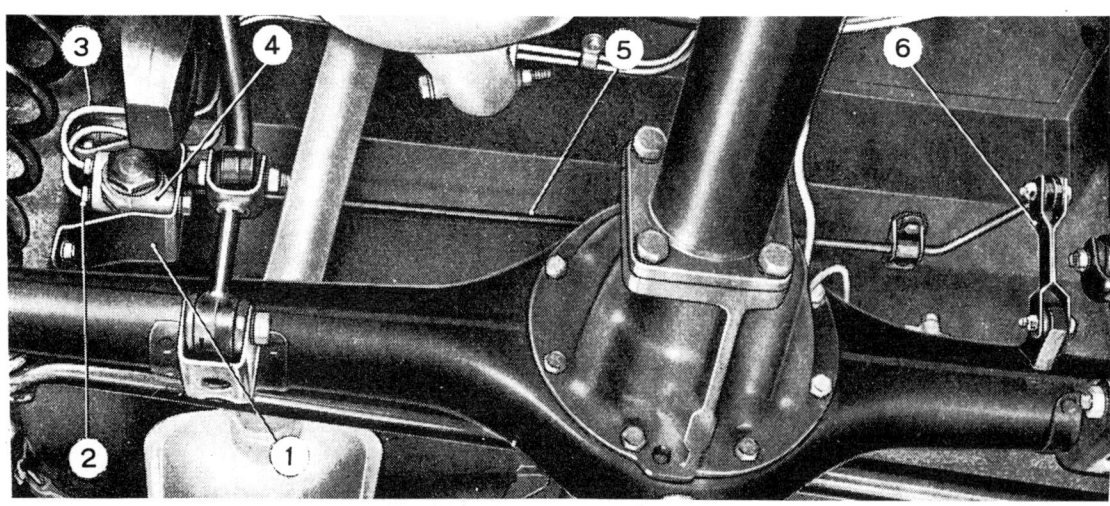

FIG 10:15   Brake regulator installation on rear axle

Key to Fig 10:15   1 Regulator bracket   2 Hydraulic line couplings   3 Hydraulic lines   4 Brake regulator   5 Torsion bar
6 Bar-to-axle housing link

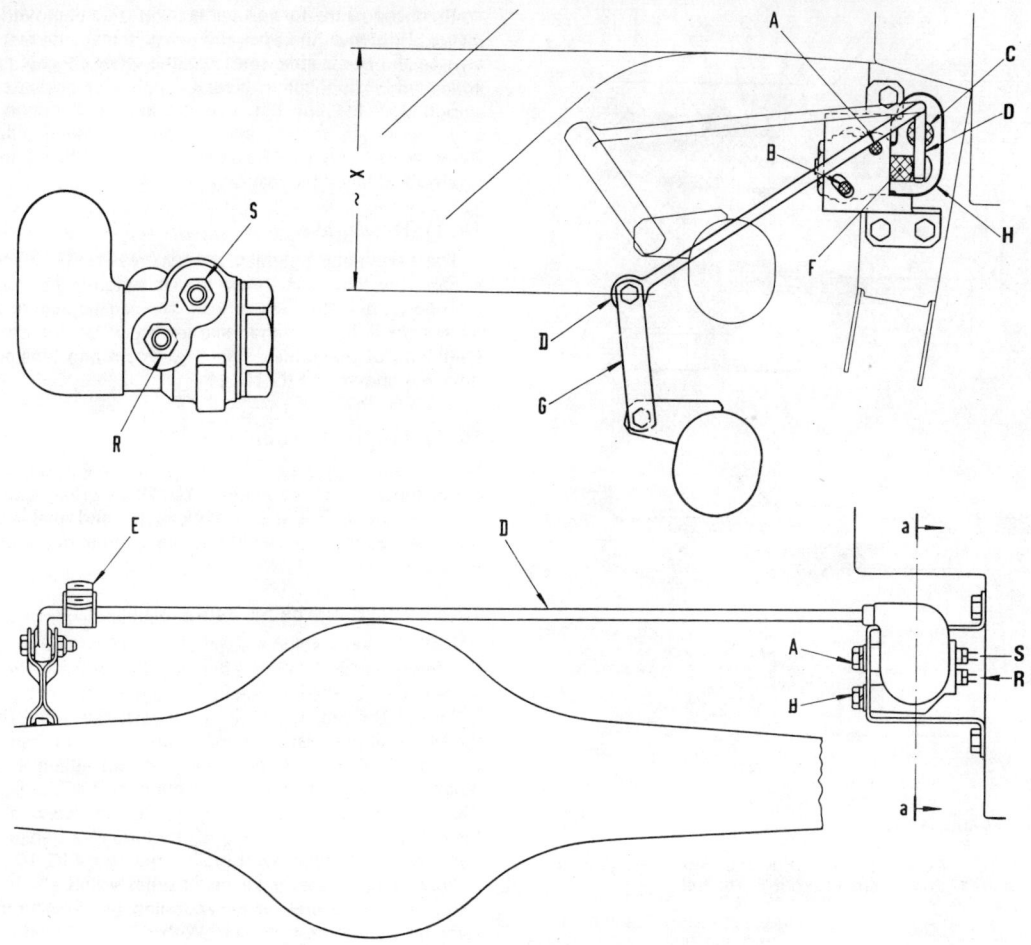

FIG 10:16   Installation details of brake regulator

Key to Fig 10:16   A Upper body support screw   **B** Lower body support screw   **C** Torsion bar bearing pin   **D** Torsion bar   **DD** Cranked ends of torsion bar   **E** Torsion bar support bracket   **F** Regulator piston   **G** Link   **H** Regulator boot   **R** Delivery pipe from master cylinder   **S** Delivery pipe to rear brake cylinders   **X** Setting distance for regulator installation=5.75 inches on Coupé, 3.74 inches on Spyder   Light outline represents torsion bar position when not braking

As retardation decreases, the body returns to an even keel and the torsion bar re-exerts pressure on the piston to re-open, first, the main transfer route around the head and under the seal and then, by moving the seal clear from the transfer ports in the slotted ring, the secondary route. Braking pressure is once again equalized on all four cylinders.

10:9 Dismantling the regulator

Plug the outlet to the fluid reservoir and disconnect the two hydraulic lines to the brake regulator. Raise the rear of the car on jacks, permitting the weight to be taken from the suspension and providing working room beneath the car. Disconnect the upper end of the link 6 (see **FIG 10:15**) from the torsion bar, unscrew the hydraulic unions 2, and unbolt the torsion bar bracket from the chassis. Now unbolt the regulator mounting bracket 1, from the car and transfer regulator and torsion bar to the bench. Remove gaiter and bar.

Remove the endplug and washer from the regulator. This will release the slotted ring 7, retaining plate 8, and its retaining spring 9. Now extract the piston 2, with seal 6, to free the fluid seal 4, thrust washer 5, and spring.

Wash all parts in clean brake fluid and examine for signs of wear or deterioration. Renew the seals. Finally reassemble in the reverse order.

10:10 Installing the regulator

Fix the regulator to the bracket, the bracket to the car and the torsion bar to the body with its own bracket. Do not tighten the two screws holding the regulator onto the bracket at this stage. It will be noticed that one, the upper, is close fit in the hole in the bracket while the other, the lower, is in a slotted hole.

Raise the long cranked end of the torsion bar until it is $5\frac{3}{4}$ inches from the underside of the body. Holding it in this position, raise the boot at the regulator end and turn the regulator about the upper screw until the short

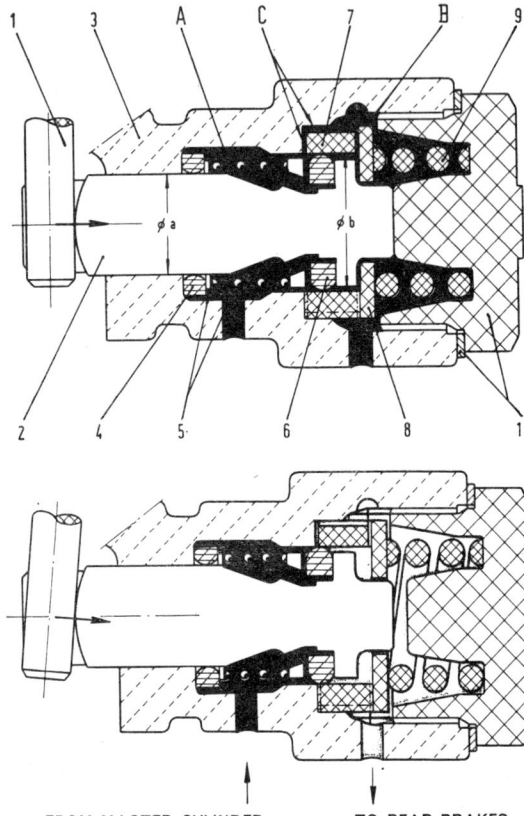

FIG 10:17 Sections through brake regulator while at rest, above, and when braking hard, below

FROM MASTER CYLINDER   TO REAR BRAKES

Key to Fig 10:17   1 Torsion bar   2 Piston   3 Pressure regulator body   4 Seal   5 Rest ring and spring for seal 6 Seal   7 Slotted ring   8 Washer   9 Piston spring 10 Plug with washer   · **A** Normal pressure chamber **B** Chamber for pressure regulation   **C** Slots on ring 7, for passage of fluid between the chambers

FIG 10:18 Handbrake adjuster showing adjusting bar 1, with adjusting nut 3, and locknut 4. The handbrake return spring 2, is secured to the propeller shaft pillow bracket

cranked end of the torsion bar is in light contact with the piston. Tighten both upper and lower bracket screws and replace the boot, after smearing the inner contact areas with a rubber lubricating grease.

Recouple the link between the axle and torsion bar and reconnect the hydraulic lines to the regulator. Remove the plug in the fluid reservoir, lower the car to the ground and bleed the rear brakes.

10:11 Handbrake

The handbrake operates the two rear brakes through a cable system and, once set, it requires no further attention since the rear wheels are self-adjusting. Any excess travel in the handbrake lever can be due only to stretching of the cables. The adjustment and tensioning device is shown in **FIG 10:18**.

10:12 Footbrake support

The general arrangement of the footbrake and clutch pedal support is shown in **FIG 10:19** as a diagrammatic exploded view. This is self-explanatory and enables the dismantling and reassembly to be carried out without difficulty.

10:13 Bleeding the hydraulic brakes

If the braking is spongy, indicating that there is air in the hydraulic system, or after any brake servicing, the system must be bled. Procedure is as follows:

Top up the brake fluid reservoir with new fluid. Clean the bleed nipple dust caps and the area around them free from dirt and dust. Remove the cap and attach a short length of rubber tube with screw coupling (A.72206) into the bleed connection. Loosen the bleed screw a few turns and insert the free end of the tube in a transparent container partly filled with brake fluid (see **FIG 10:20**).

Now depress the brake pedal quickly and allow it to return slowly several times, watching the tube until no bubbles emerge from its end. With the pedal held down retighten the bleed screw, remove the connection and replace the dust cap. Top up the fluid in the reservoir and transfer to the next wheel.

Providing that the fluid in the container is clean to start with, it and the fluid bled from the system may be re-used for topping up the reservoir but only after it has stood for a while to allow trapped air to escape.

10:14 Master-Vac brake booster

This is a vacuum powered hydraulic unit which utilizes the vacuum in the engine inlet manifold to reduce the pedal effort required to apply the brakes. The installation is shown diagrammatically in **FIG 10:21** and the complete assembly of master cylinder and power section is illustrated in the sectional view of **FIG 10:22**.

When the brake pedal is applied the valve operating rod 18 is moved to the left and closes the vacuum port 8. Further movement opens the atmosphere port 19 and air is admitted to chamber B. Since a vacuum is maintained in the chamber A the pressure differential across the piston 6 will cause it to move to the left and with it the hydraulic piston pushrod 4 and piston 27 and its associated components. Hydraulic fluid in the master cylinder 29 is forced under pressure through the port 31 to the wheel cylinders and applies the brakes. At the same time the

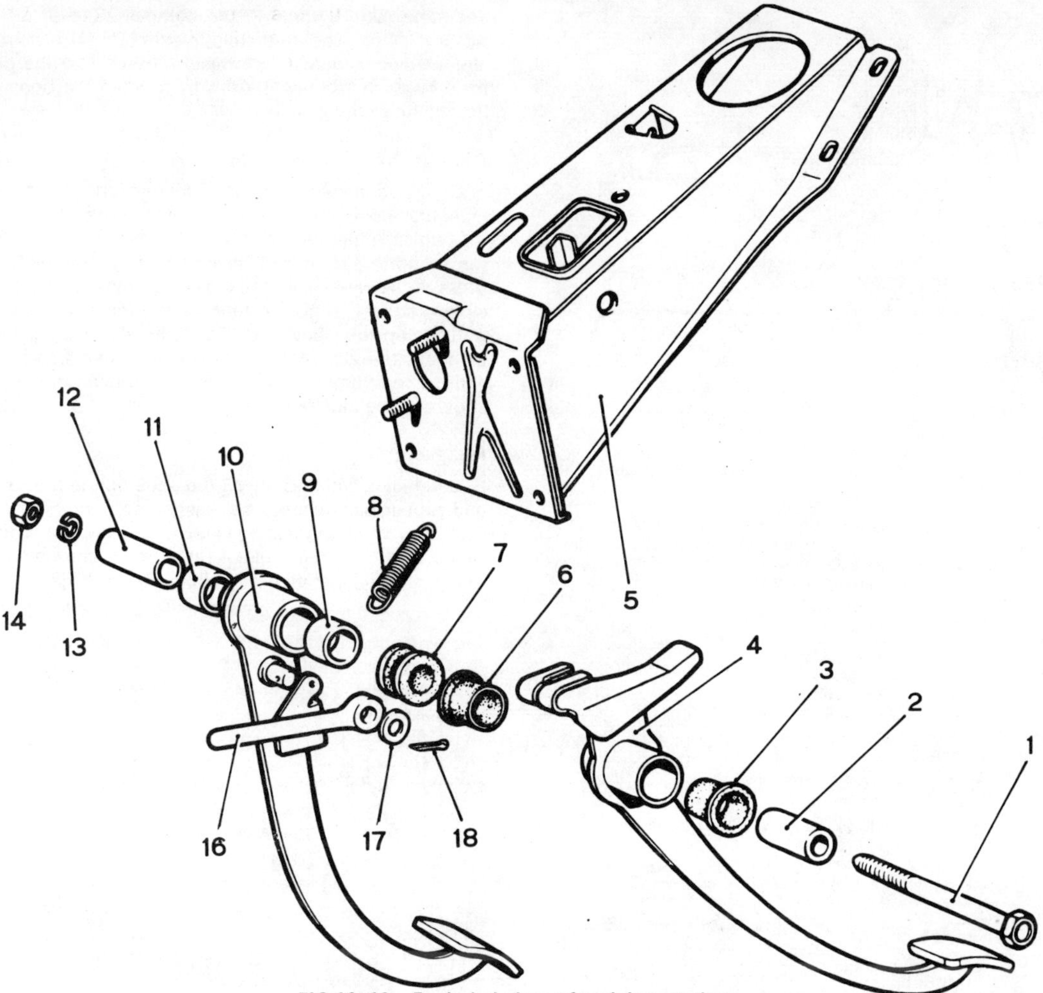

FIG 10:19 Exploded view of pedal mountings

Key to Fig 10:19 1 Pedal pivot pin 2 Clutch pedal spacer 3/6 Bushes 4 Clutch pedal 5 Support bracket 67/12 Spacers
8 Brake pedal return spring 9/11 Bushes 13/14 Nut and washer 15 Master cylinder 16 Pushrod 17/18 Washer and cotter

reaction disc 23 is subjected to pressure and through the valve plunger 23 moves the valve to the right to close off the atmosphere port 19. The valve plunger then reaches a lap position in which both the atmosphere and vacuum ports are closed.

Further pressure on the valve rod 18 will again open the port to atmosphere and cause the power piston 6 to move to the left and increase the pressure on the hydraulic fluid to the brakes.

Reducing pressure on the valve rod allows the poppet assembly 11 to move to the right, opening the vacuum port 10. Air is removed from chamber B reducing the pressure differential across the piston which moves back towards the right and reduces the pressure applied to the brakes.

In the event of using the brakes when the engine is not running or the vacuum system has failed the brakes may still be applied by direct mechanical contact from the

FIG 10:20 Bleeding the hydraulic braking system

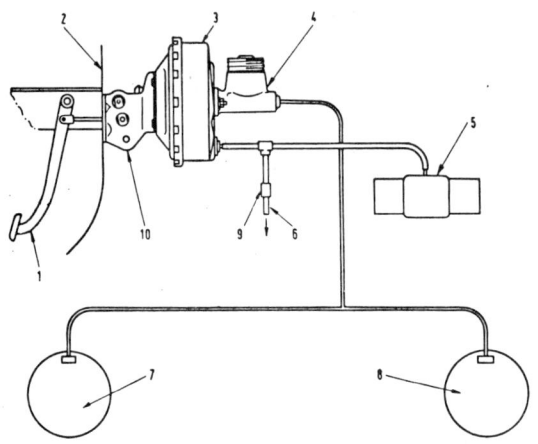

FIG 10:21 Master-Vac installation diagram

Key to Fig 10:21 1 Brake pedal 2 Firewall
3 Master-Vac power section 4 Master cylinder
5 Vacuum reservoir 6 Intake manifold vacuum pipe
7 Rear wheel brakes 8 Front wheel brakes 9 Vacuum
check valve 10 Mounting bracket

operating rod 18 through the plunger 23, disc 24 and pushrod 4 to the hydraulic piston 27. Under these circumstances more effort must be exerted by the driver for a given amount of braking than when the booster is functioning normally.

Dismantling (see FIG 10:23):

Before commencing to dismantle the Master-Vac mark the two shells to ensure correct reassembly. Remove the two securing nuts and lift off the master cylinder. Hold the mounting plate in a vice and using a suitable bar, press in the rear shell 2 at the same time turning it anti-clockwise to line up the tabs on the rear shell with the notches on the front shell. Carefully relieve the pressure to avoid the abrupt separation of the two halves. The various components may now be withdrawn in the order shown in the illustration.

Reassembly:

Carefully clean and dry all the parts noting that plastic and rubber parts should be washed only in white spirit. Check for wear and damage and renew any part which is found to be unserviceable. All the rubber components in the master cylinder assembly should be renewed.

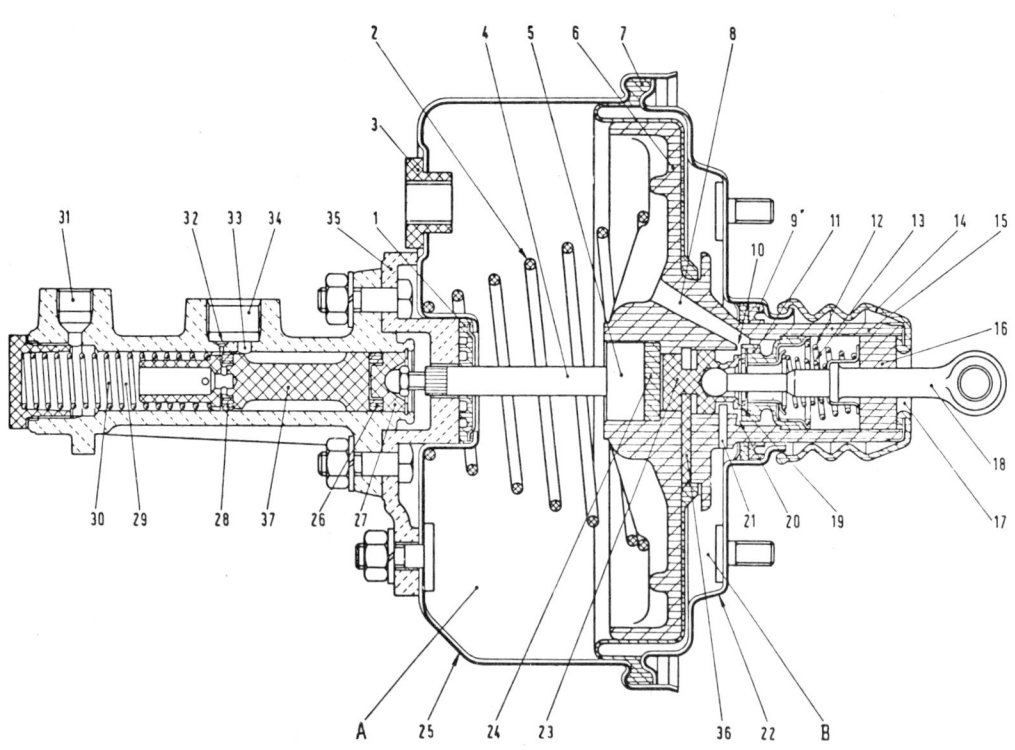

FIG 10:22 Sectional view of Master-Vac assembly

Key to Fig 10:22 1 Front shell vacuum seal 2 Power piston return spring 3 Vacuum port 4 Hydraulic piston pushrod
5 Pushrod plunger 6 Power piston 7 Power piston diaphragm 8 Vacuum passage 9 Rear shell vacuum seal
10 Vacuum port 11 Poppet assembly 12 Valve return spring 13 Poppet return spring 14 Dust guard of piston guide tube (15)
15 Piston guide tube 16 Air cleaner filter 17 Atmosphere inlet 18 Valve operating rod 19 Atmosphere port
20 Vacuum port 21 Control vacuum passage 22 Rear shell 23 Valve plunger 24 Reaction disc 25 Front shell
26 Secondary cup 27 Hydraulic piston 28 Primary cup 29 Master cylinder 30 Hydraulic piston return spring
31 Hydraulic port to wheel cylinders 32 Compensating port 33 Fluid inlet port 34 Hydraulic port from fluid reservoir
35 Mounting plate 36 Valve plunger retaining plate 37 Floating cup carrier **A** Front chamber **B** Rear chamber

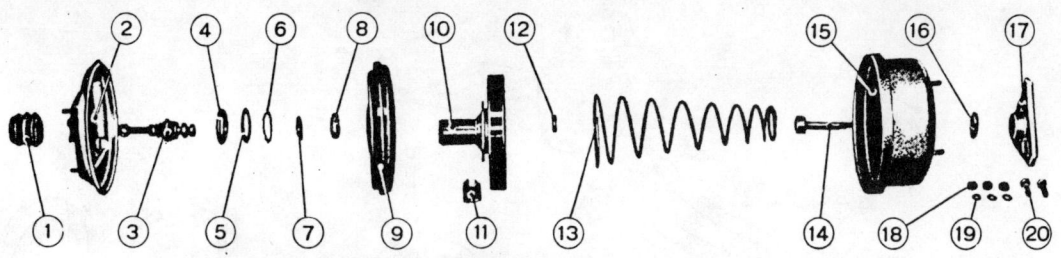

FIG 10:23   Components of power section

Key to Fig 10:23   1 Dust guard   2 Rear shell   3 Valve operating rod, poppet and valve plunger assembly   4 Rear seal
5 Backing ring   6 Holding ring   7 Air cleaner filter cup   8 Air cleaner filter   9 Diaphragm   10 Power piston
11 Valve rod, poppet and valve plunger assembly retaining plate   12 Reaction disc   13 Piston return spring   14 Hydraulic
piston pushrod   15 Front shell   16 Front seal   17 Master cylinder mounting plate   18 Mounting plate nuts   19 Lockwasher
20 Master cylinder mounting screws

Fit the seal 4, the backing ring 5 and the holding ring 6 on the rear shell 2. Apply a little 'Rubber Grease' to the outer and inner faces of the power piston guide tube and insert the valve operating rod, poppet and plunger assembly 3 in the tube and secure with the retaining plate 11.

Fit the diaphragm 9 on the hub of the piston, apply a little 'Rubber Grease' on the diaphragm rib and fit the assembly to the rear shell. Fit a new reaction disc 12 after coating it with 'Rubber Grease'.

Fit the seal 16 to the front shell, then attach the mounting plate 17. Hold the mounting plate in a vice,

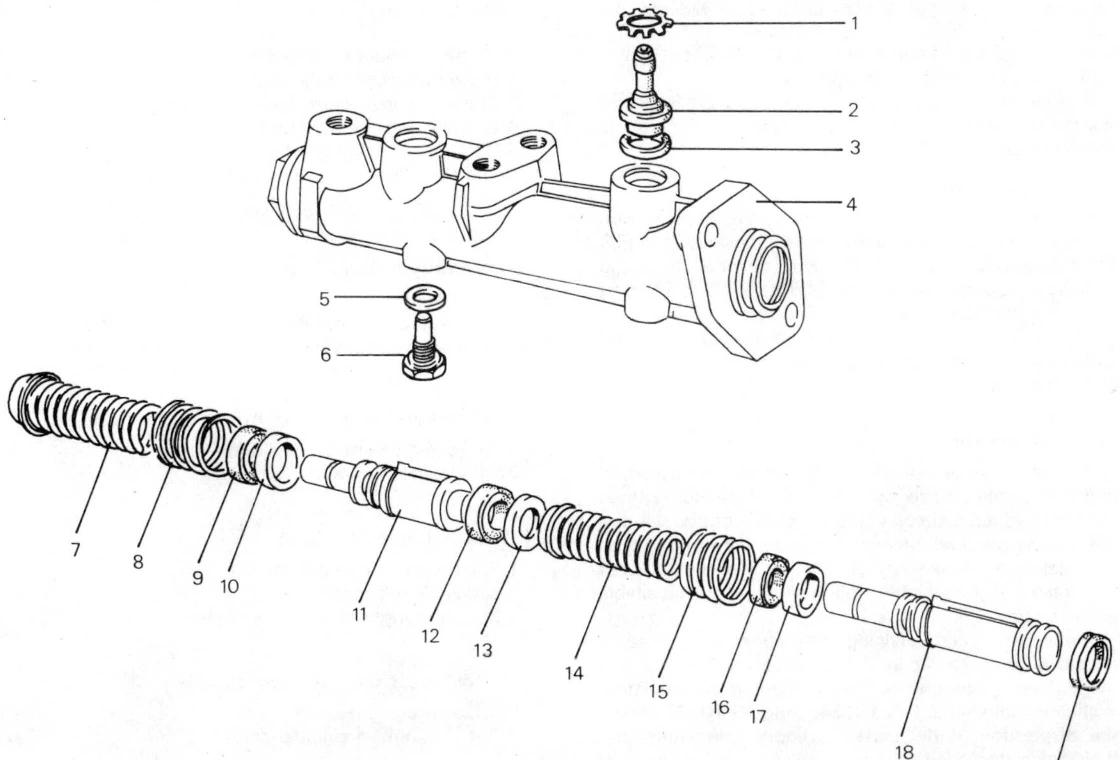

FIG 10:24   The components of dual master cylinder

Key to Fig 10:24   1 Star washer   2 Fluid inlet valve   3 Seal   4 Master cylinder body   5 Washer   6 Plug   7 Spring   8 Spring
9 Seal   10 Washer   11 Secondary piston (rear brakes)   12 Seal   13 Washer   14 Spring   15 Spring   16 Seal   17 Washer
18 Primary piston (front brakes)   19 Seal

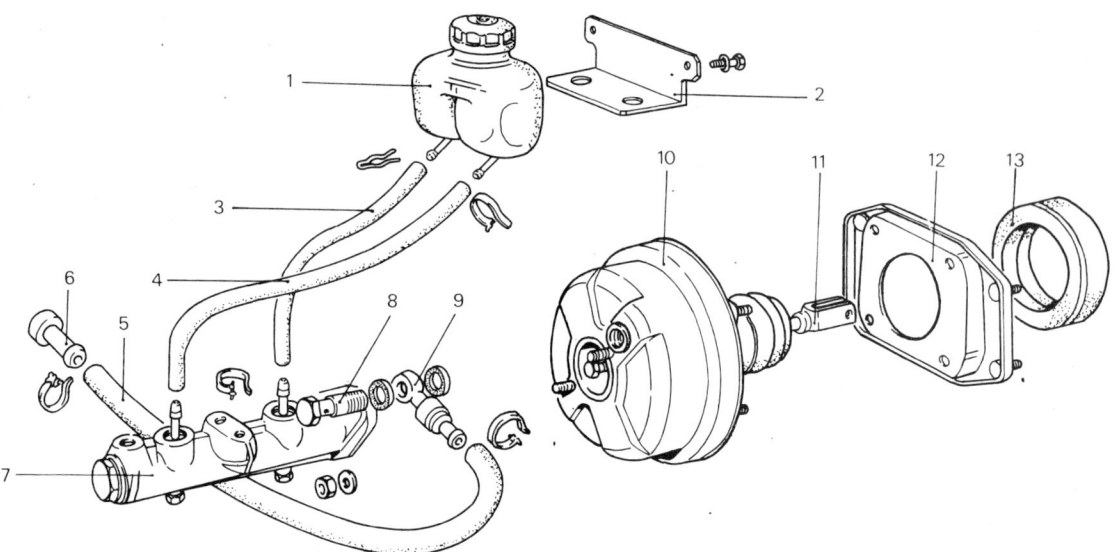

FIG 10:25 The master cylinder and vacuum servo unit showing connections and mountings

Key to Fig 10:25 1 Fluid reservoir 2 Mounting bracket 3 Supply hose for front brake circuit 4 Supply hose for rear brake circuit 5 Vacuum hose 6 Manifold union 7 Master cylinder 8 Banjo union bolt 9 Vacuum non-return valve and banjo union 10 Servo unit 11 Fork to brake pedal 12 Mounting bracket 13 Mounting ring

insert the pushrod 14 and apply a coat of 'Rubber Grease' on the face of the pushrod plunger.

Position the return spring 13 and recouple the front and rear shells ensuring that the two locating marks coincide Refit the master cylinder and tighten.

Adjusting the brake booster:

Adjustment is made by means of an adjusting screw on the end of the pushrod 4. In the released position (see **FIG 10:22**) the top edge of the master cylinder mounting plate 35 should protrude .051 to .059 inch (1.3 to 1.5 mm) from the end of the pushrod adjusting screw.

After adjustment the screw thread should be coated with a sealing compound in order to avoid the possibility of the screw working loose.

10:15 Dual braking system

In 1969 a dual braking system was introduced in which a tandem master cylinder is used providing three separate hydraulic circuits, one for each front wheel and one for the two rear wheels. The advantage of this type of installation, shown in **FIG 10:1** is that, in the event of a failure in one circuit, full braking is still available on two wheels.

Maintenance and servicing instructions are the same as those given earlier in this chapter modified to suit the different components. The tandem master cylinder is shown exploded in **FIG 10:24**, and **FIG 10:25** shows the disposition of the master cylinder, servo unit and their associated connections.

10:16 Fault diagnosis

(a) Brake locked on

1 Swollen brake pads through oil contamination
2 Damage to hydraulic lines closing them

3 Master cylinder compensating hole blocked
4 Master cylinder piston seized
5 Brake or pedal return springs broken
6 Dirt choking the hydraulic system
7 Bent regulator torsion bar

The term 'locked on' covers full or partial application of the brakes.

(b) Spongy brake action

1 Air in hydraulic lines or master cylinder
2 Use of wrong hydraulic fluid
3 Fluid level in reservoir low causing (1)

(c) Pedal yields under continued pressure

1 Faulty seals in master cylinder
2 Faulty seals in brake cylinders

(d) Unbalanced braking

1 Fluid leaks in one cylinder
2 Unevenly worn tyres
3 Seized plunger in one brake cylinder

(e) Reservoir empties too quickly

1 Leaks in pipelines
2 Deterioration of cylinder seals

(f) Brake failure

1 Broken hydraulic line
2 Empty fluid reservoir
3 Ruptured master cylinder seal
4 Ruptured brake cylinder seal

CHAPTER 11

THE ELECTRICAL EQUIPMENT

11 : 1 Description

The electrical system employed on both Sport and Coupé models is a conventional 12-volt layout with negative earthing. The battery, housed on the righthand side of the engine compartment is charged by an alternator with an external voltage regulator, driven by the same belt as drives the cooling fan from the crankshaft.

Wiring diagrams with colour codes will be found in Technical Data at the end of the book to enable faults to be found and rectified, but although information is given for a number of servicing operations, in the absence of accurate testing equipment, it may be preferable to enlist the aid of the service station or take advantage of the exchange service available.

The instrument panel of the Sport is illustrated in **FIG 11 : 1** and shows the position of most of the electrical controls and instruments available to the driver.

11 : 2 The battery

The battery is a six-cell lead/acid type with a capacity of 48 amp/hr at a 20 hour discharge rate. That is to say, a fully charged battery discharging at 2.4 amps through a resistor will become completely discharged in 20 hours.

The dimensions of the battery are 10.25 inches long by 6.75 inches wide by 8.875 inches high and the total weight with electrolyte is about 47.5 lb. It is stored in the righthand side of the engine compartment and is secured on a bracket by tie rods (see **FIG 11 : 2**).

New Fiat batteries are supplied dry charged and only require filling with 1.28 sg battery acid and a short period of rest before installation in the vehicle. Batteries of other makes with comparable capacities and dimensions can be used if Fiat batteries are not available.

The terminal posts are provided with terminal clamps for the heavy current starter connections. The positive clamp also serves as the terminal of the cable supplying other services and the charging current.

To remove the battery from the vehicle, first slacken and then remove the terminal clamps from the terminal posts. Loosen the nuts on the tie rods, swing the metal bar clear of the battery edge and lift the battery out.

To reinstall the battery, after lowering it in place and securing by the bar and tie rods, clean the interior surface of the terminal clamps and the exterior surface of the pillars, fit the clamps in place, tighten down and then lightly smear the surfaces with vaseline to inhibit acid creep and corrosion.

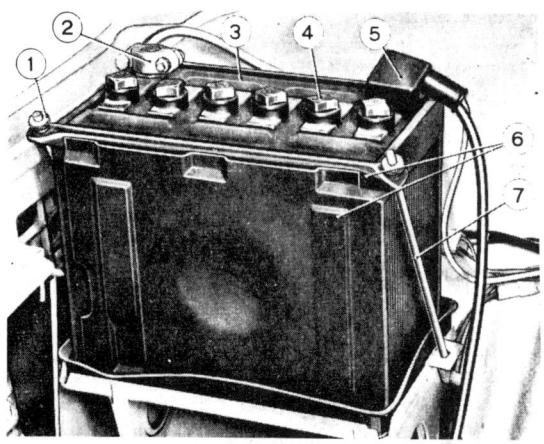

FIG 11 : 1   Instruments and controls. Sport (early models)

Key to Fig 11 : 1   1 Switch for outside lights   2 Instrument panel   3 Control knob for intensity of instrument panel and side lamps   4 Instrument panel light on/off switch   5 Adjustable air diffusers to direct air onto windscreen or inside car   6 Internal rear-view mirror   7 Screen wiper on/off switch   8 Screen wiper speed control   9 Glove-box knob   10 Ventilation air intake control   11 Heater control lever   12 Three-position selector for controlling ventilation fan   13 Cigar lighter   13 Cigar lighter   14 Heater (air control lever)   15 Choke control knob   16 Key-switch to control ignition, indications, starting and anti-theft device   17 Horn button   18 Direction indicator control   19 Dipper switch   20 Lefthand pocket   21 Clutch pedal   22 Brake pedal   23 Accelerator pedal   24 Gearlever   25 Ashtray   26 Emergency and parking brake   27 Righthand pocket

FIG 11 : 2   Battery in position on car

Key to Fig 11 : 2   1 Knurled nut on tie rod   2 Earth cable end on negative terminal of battery   3 Sealing compound   4 Filler plug   5 Cable end of positive lead   6 Battery retaining clamp   7 Tie rod

Do not attempt to loosen heavy duty clamps from battery terminals by twisting or with the clamp not eased . open. Damage to the battery case can result. Always use a proper spanner to loosen or tighten clamp nuts, never hammer or pliers.

A battery which will provide an adequate level of light from the car lamps, but which will not turn the starter motor may have one faulty or sulphated cell. Although a Hydrometer test may disclose the bad cell, the best check is with a cell tester which monitors the across-cell voltage while drawing a substantial current (of the order of starting current) from the battery.

Routine maintenance is confined to regular checks of acid level in the battery cells, topping up to regular checks of acid level in the battery cells, topping up with distilled water as necessary and maintaining the surfaces of the battery dry, clean and free from corrosion.

11 : 3 The alternator

The Fiat Alternator Type A 12M.124/12/42 M is illustrated in the exploded diagram of **FIG 11 : 3** and is a three phase self-rectifying unit incorporating rotating field windings in a stationary armature.

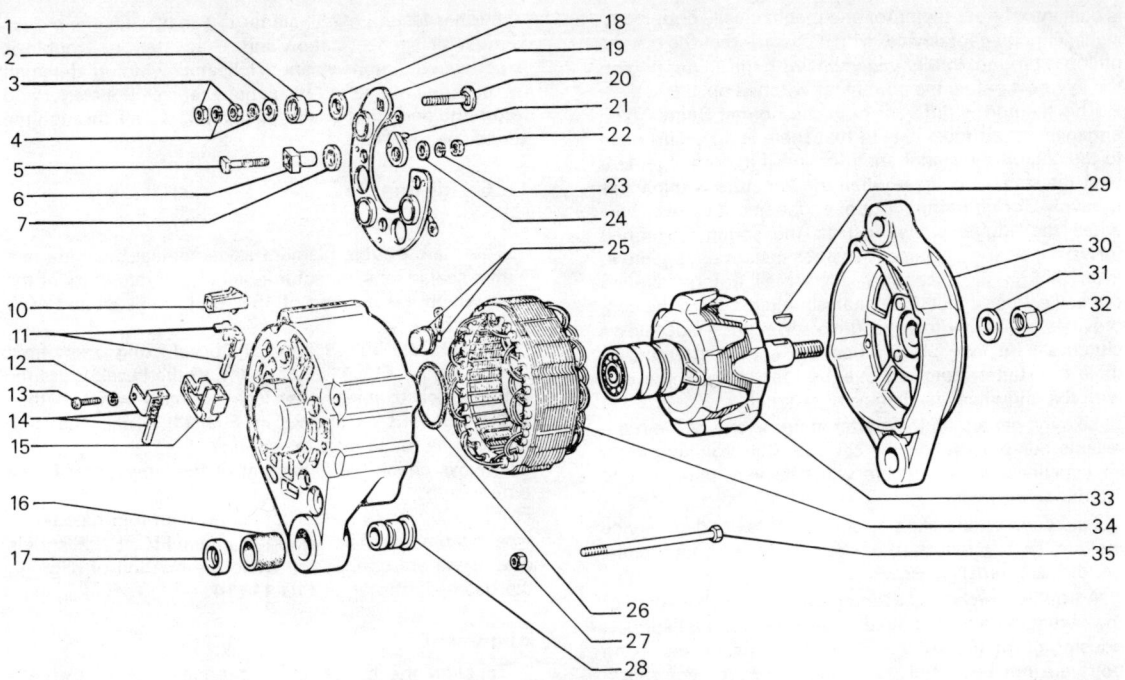

FIG 11 : 3   Exploded view of alternator

Key to Fig 11 : 3   1 Insulator   2 Washer   3 Nut   4 Locking washer   5 Bolt   6 Insulator   7 Insulator   10 Coupling
11 Carbon brush   12 Locking washer   13 Bolt   14 Carbon brush   15 Brush holder   16 Bush   17 Washer   18 Insulator
19 Plate   20 Bolt   21 Insulator   22 Nut   23 Spring washer   24 Washer   25 Rectifier   26 Sealing ring   27 Nut   28 Boss
29 Key   30 End bracket   31 Spacer   32 Nut   33 Rotor   34 Stator   35 Bolt

Silicone diodes contained within the slip ring end cover in a three-phase bridge circuit between the stator and output terminals provide rectification of the generated current. The brush gear is also mounted in the slip ring end cover and comprises two brushes which bear against the slip rings in the rotor assembly.

Since the alternator is self-limiting as regards current output, the only additional regulator required is to control the voltage. This is done by a dual vibrating contact type unit RC 1/12 B. A warning lamp on the instrument panel lights up if the alternator should fail to charge.

11 : 4 Alternator maintenance

The alternator requires very little maintenance and no lubrication is provided for as the bearings are packed with grease 'for life'.

The tension of the drive belt should be checked occasionally and adjusted if necessary as described earlier in **Chapter 4**. The connections should be kept tight and clean and the outside of the unit should be kept free of oil and dirt particularly around the ventilating slots in the cover.

It is essential that the following precautions are taken when working on an alternator charging system, otherwise irreparable damage may be caused.

1 Always observe the correct polarity when connecting any components in the system.

2 Do not disconnect the battery or any wires in the system while the engine is running.

3 Do not attempt to polarize the alternator.

4 If using an outside source of power ensure that it is correctly connected and do not start the engine with the charger connected.

In the event of unsatisfactory operation, it is recommended that the alternator be removed and taken to a service station for testing or replacement. It is, however, a simple matter to check on the brushgear and to clean the faces of the slip rings before doing so.

The unit is removed by disconnecting the battery and then the cables from the alternator. Release the securing bolts, move the alternator inwards to release the drive belt and lift it away from the engine.

Check that the springs are holding the brushes firmly in contact with the slip rings and that they move freely in their holders. Renew any brush that is worn to less than $\frac{3}{8}$ inch.

Cleaning with a cloth moistened with petrol should be sufficient, but if the slip rings are very dirty very fine emery cloth may be used, preferably while spinning in a lathe.

11 : 5 The starter motor

Two types of starter motors are used on these cars, but differ only in minor points of specification so that a description of one will suffice for both. From the views given in **FIG 11 : 5** it will be seen that the solenoid starter switch is built into the starter motor and mechanically coupled to a gear engagement device, which ensures that the driving pinion is brought into engagement with the starter ring on the flywheel before the current is switched on.

This method is different from the normal Bendix type engagement on most cars in that there is no worm drive to the cog on the starter shaft forcing it into engagement with the starter ring gear when the armature commences to revolve, or returning it out of engagement by overdrive when the engine starts. Instead the spring-cushioned forward meshing movement ensures instant engagement, even though the stationary gears may not be aligned correctly, while a clutch mechanism integral with the cog, provides a positive forward drive for starting but allows clutch slip to take place when the engine attempts to drive the starter motor on overrun. Jamming of the cog with the ringwheel, is, therefore, avoided.

Like the generator, the starter motor is one of the more reliable components on the car and little trouble should be experienced through life with the very minimum of attention.

Faults which are likely to arise after extended service include switch failure, breakage of springs and commutator and brush wear.

A trouble which has arisen on occasions is breakage of the casting where it is bolted to the bell mouthed support housing of the gearbox. This can occur only if the fixing bolts are not tight and periodical checks of the starter mounting tightness is recommended.

Dismantling the starter is a simple task. Procedure is as follows.

First, disconnect the battery positive connection. Then disconnect the heavy duty lead to the starter motor, the red lead to terminal 50, the solenoid connection, and then unbolt the starter from the bell mouth housing and transfer to the bench.

Disconnect the lead from the solenoid winding to its terminal by unscrewing the fixing nut. Unscrew the three nuts securing the solenoid in position on the motor and remove the solenoid.

Remove the cover from the commutator end of the motor and disconnect the positive brush from the winding lead. Lift both brushes and retain in the holders as already described for the generator. Remove the nuts on the through tie rods at the commutator end and slide the end plate clear from the body. Take care not to lose the thrust washers.

Remove the splitpin and pivot pin from the drive engagement lever, out of the casing together with the thrust washers. Remove fork from the engagement sleeve. The armature assembly will then appear as in **FIG 11 : 6**. If it is necessary to dismantle the drive, remove the washers 8, expand and extract the snap ring 7, and slide off the remainder.

After examination and replacements where necessary, the reassembly is a straight reversal of the above order. When reassembling the drive, lubricate the splines with Fiat VS.10W oil, or equivalent, and the spindle bushes with engine oil. After reassembly, check the current taken by the starter when running free from the engine. This should be less than 25 amps at 12-volt. If a large enough ammeter and shunt is available, check the stall current, 325 amps with an external resistance of .021 ohm.

Further testing of the starter is a matter for the manufacturer or service station and, if any serious trouble is experienced (such as an overheated winding detected by the smell of charred insulation) replace the starter and return the damaged one to the manufacturers through the service agent.

11:6 Lighting

(a) Headlamps:

These are double filament asymmetrical beam pattern with a sealed lens/reflector assembly for rear entry of the bulb which has a rating of 45W on high beam and 40W anti-dazzle.

To replace a bulb, remove the bezel fixing screw from the lug 6 (see **FIG 11 : 7**) and lift off the bezel. Press the spring catch to release the lens assembly which is then pulled forward as shown in **FIG 11 : 8** and the bulb released by unclipping the springs.

Always check the alignment of the lamps after fitting a new bulb.

From 1970 Coupé models are fitted with four halogen type headlamps. The wiring diagram **FIG 13 : 3** shows how these are connected, while the method of aligning the beams is shown in **FIG 11 : 14**.

Alignment:

To align the lamps, stand the car squarely on level ground in front of a wall at a distance of 16 feet, checking that the tyres are correctly inflated.

Draw two vertical lines 49 inches apart (see A in **FIG 11 : 9**) and equidistant from the centre line of the car. Draw a horizontal line b–b 4 inches less than the height of the lamp centres from the ground.

Switch on the low beam and adjust the headlamp screws 3 and 7 until the horizontal line between the dark and lighted areas is on the line b–b and the upward divergence commences at P as shown.

Check the high beam, but no further adjustment should be necessary.

(b) Direction indicator and side lamps

These are housed in a rectangular mounting below the headlamp or bumper and access is obtained by unscrewing the front glass cover as shown in **FIG 11 : 10**. The more recent Coupé models have the lights housed inside the re-styled front bumper. The side lamps on the inside are rated at 5W and the direction indicator bulb is 20W.

Side indicator repeaters are single filament 3W bulbs mounted on the side of the wing and retained in the holder by the rubber shield attaching it to the rear of the lens from behind the panel.

(c) Rear stop and direction indicator lamps:

These are housed in a double rectangular mounting as shown in **FIG 11 : 11** with the lenses held in place by a single central screw. The direction lamp is a single filament 20W bulb while for tail and stop lamps a double filament 5/20W bulb is used. Later models of the Coupe have a three-lamp rear light cluster mounted vertically in the rear edges of the wings.

The flasher unit for the direction indicator lamps is a sealed unit for which no adjustment is provided. In the event of failure a replacement unit should be obtained.

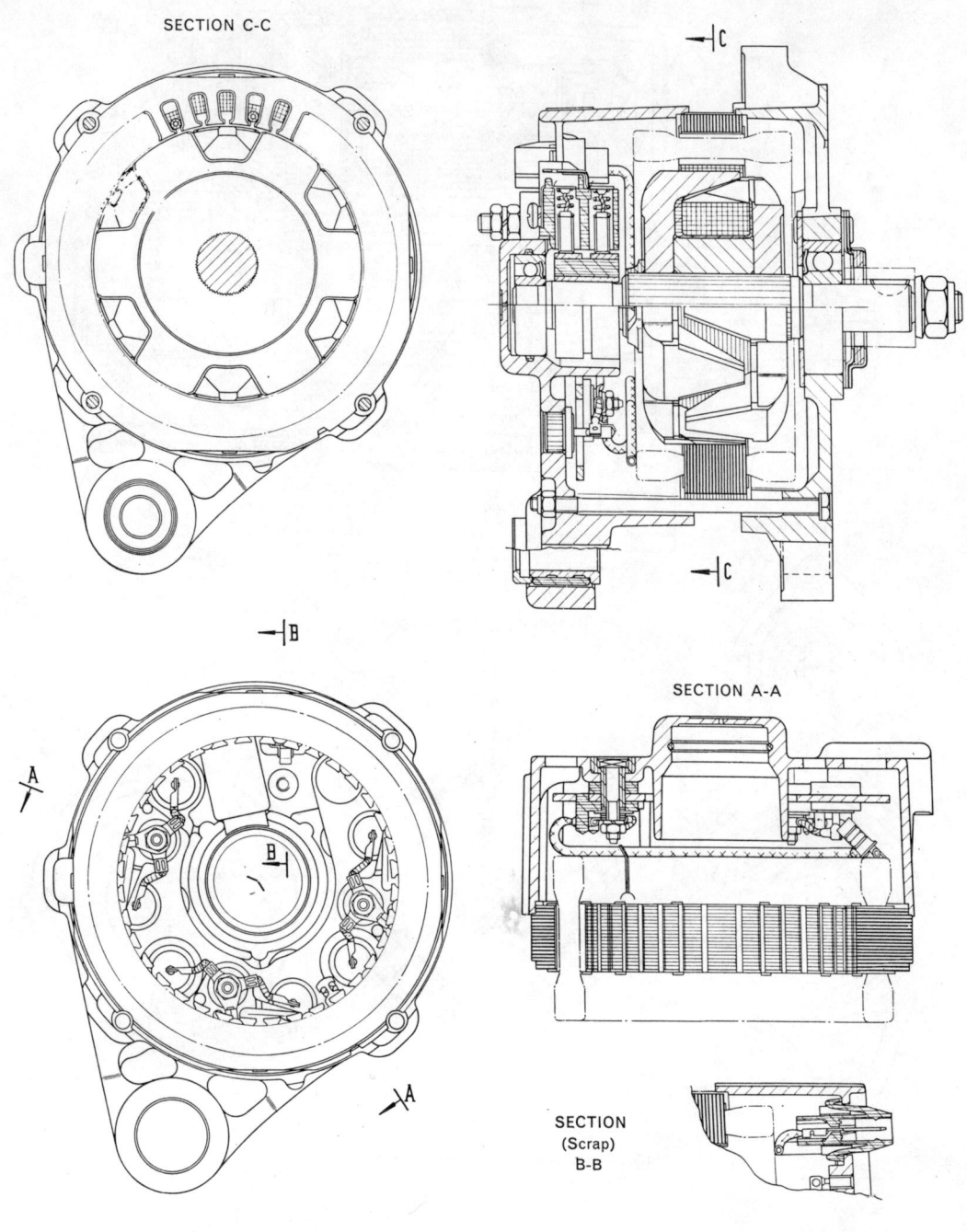

SECTION C-C

SECTION A-A

SECTION
(Scrap)
B-B

FIG 11 : 4 Sectional views of alternator

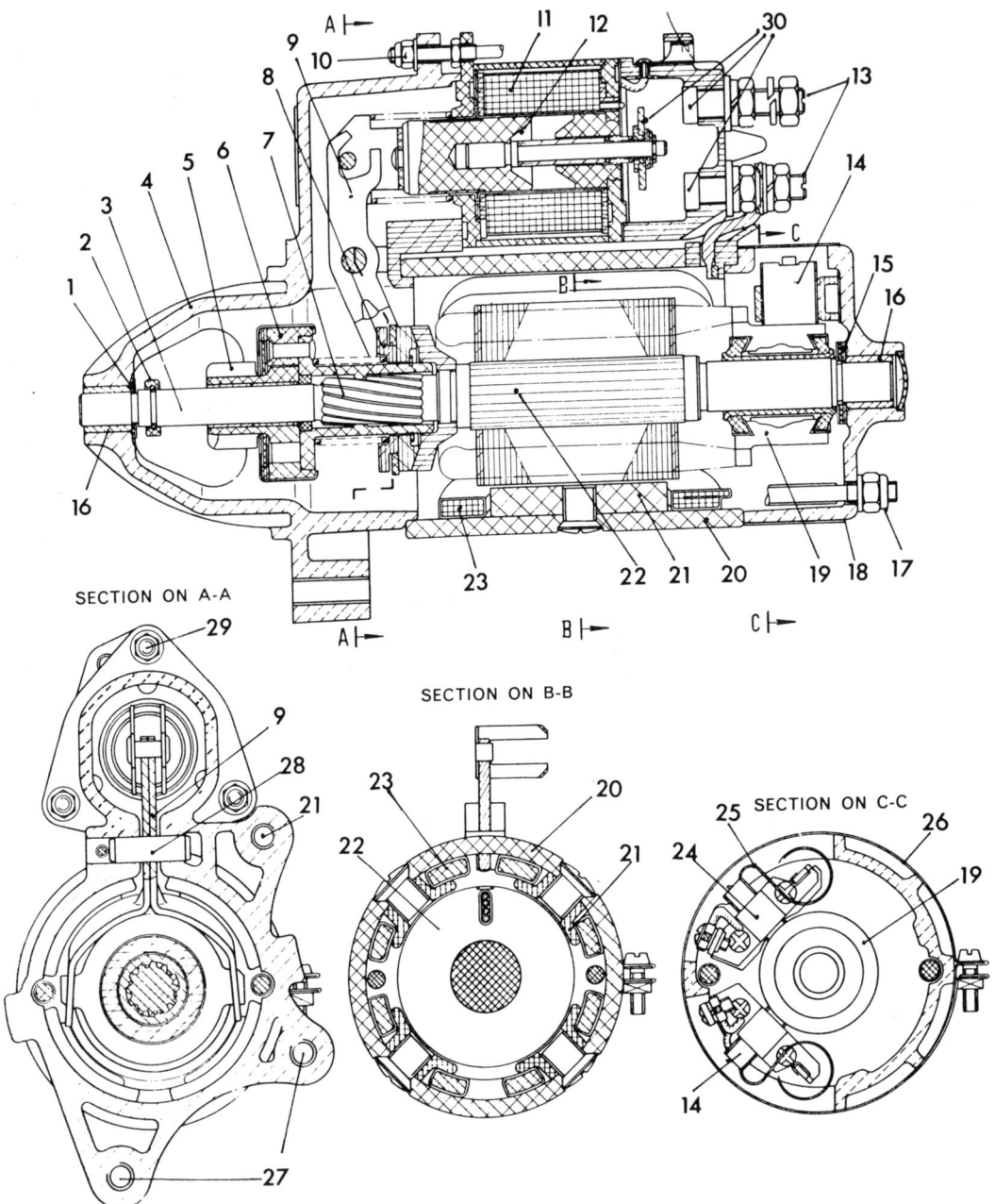

SECTION ON A-A

SECTION ON B-B

SECTION ON C-C

FIG 11:5   Section through starter motor

Key to Fig 11:5   1 Washers   2 Snap ring   3 Armature shaft   4 Mounting end plate   5 Engagement drive pinion   6 Clutch
7 Splines   8 Sleeve   9 Operating lever   10 Solenoid attachment nuts   11 Solenoid winding   12 Solenoid armature   13 Heavy
current terminals   14 Brush   15 Washers   16 Bush   17 Through-bolt and nut   18 Commutator end plate   19 Commutator
20 Body housing   21 Polepiece   22 Armature winding and laminations   23 Field coil   24 Brush holder   25 Brush spring
26 Commutator end cover   27 Holes for fixing to bellhousing   28 Pivot pin   29 Solenoid attachment bolts   30 Heavy duty
switch contacts

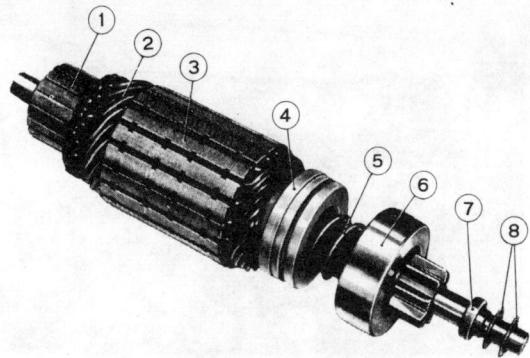

FIG 11 : 6   Starter motor armature and drive

Key to Fig 11 : 6   1 Commutator   2 Armature windings
3 Armature   4 Engaging sleeve   5 Sleeve spring   6 Pinion
and freewheel complete   7 Stop ring   8 Thrust washers

FIG 11 : 7   Headlamp with bezel removed (Spyder)

Key to Fig 11 : 7   1 Spring clip for clamping headlamp unit
2 Bezel retaining lug   3 Beam adjusting screw, horizontal
direction   4 Earth lead of headlamp unit   5 Locating pin
of headlamp unit   6 Bezel fixing screw lug   7 Vertical
adjusting screw

FIG 11 : 8   Removing headlamp beam unit (Spyder)
Key to Fig 11 : 8   1 Socket   2 Bulb retaining spring
3 Lens/reflector assembly   4 Bulb

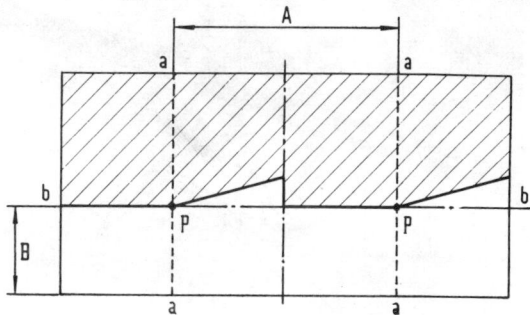

FIG 11 : 9   Headlamp alignment

Key to Fig 11 : 9   **A**=49 inches   **B**=Height of headlamp
centre less 4 inches
Lefthand drive shown. Mirror image for righthand drive

(d) Number plate lamps:

Two lamps are fitted to the rear bumper for the
illumination of the number plates. These are 5W and
may be replaced by removing the screw and pulling off
the fitting as shown in **FIG 11 : 12**.

There are in addition to the above sundry lights and
warning lamps of which details will be found in the wiring
diagram, including lights which are illuminated when
either the engine or luggage compartment lids are
opened.

11 : 7 Horns

Two tuned horns are fitted at the front of the car behind
the grille and are operated by a pneumatic compressor
motor through a remote control relay actuated by the
horn button on the steering wheel.

In the event of failure to operate check on the contact
at the horn button and at the relay. Examine also for

FIG 11 : 10   Removing righthand side lamp lens (Spyder)

Key to Fig 11 : 10   1 Righthand direction indicator bulb
2 Righthand side lamp bulb   3 Lens of righthand front
lamp

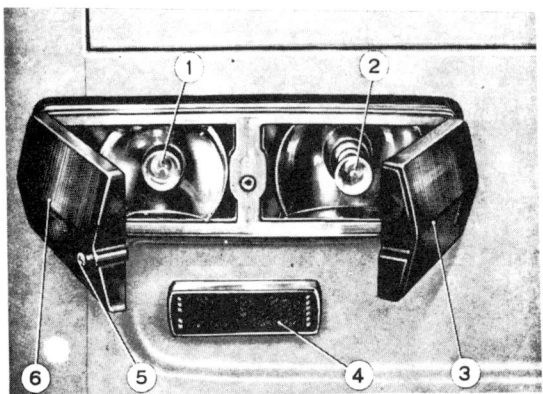

FIG 11:11   Rear lamp assembly

Key to Fig 11:11   1 Direction indicator bulb   2 Double filament bulb of parking and stoplight   3 Lens of double filament bulb   4 Reflector   5 Lens plate screws 6 Direction indicator light lens

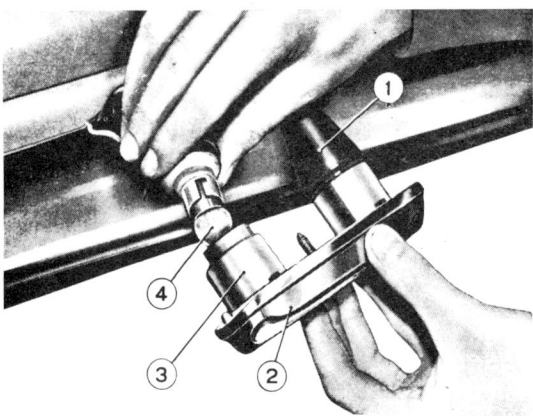

FIG 11:12   Number plate lamp

Key to Fig 11:12   1 Dust protector on lampholder 2 Body and lens   3 Lampholder socket   4 Bulb

faulty connections or breaks in the wiring. The internal mechanism of the horns and relay should not be dismantled but new units fitted.

11:8 Windscreen wipers

The double arm wipers are controlled by an on-off switch in the centre of the facia panel and a rotary rheostat by which the speed may be adjusted.

The spray type windscreen washer is operated by a pedal pump, the use of which also switches on the wipers at the same time.

11:9 Fuel gauge and transmitter

The fuel gauge transmitter in the petrol tank comprises a sealed chamber in which is contained the calibrated wire wound resistor and contact arm, the latter directly linked to the float arm, and an additional contact to operate the low fuel warning light on the instrument panel when the level falls below one gallon approximately.

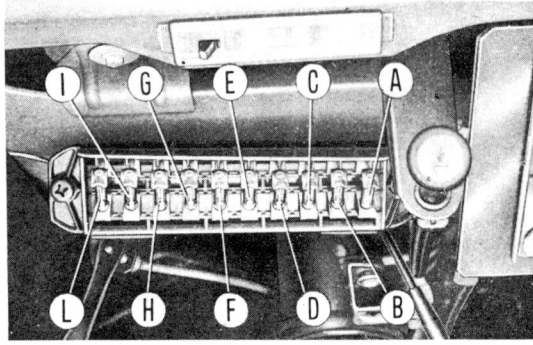

FIG 11:13   Fuseboard below facia panel. Circuits protected

Key to Fig 11:13   A* (16 amp) Interior lights, electro-pneumatic horn, inspection lamp socket, cigar lighter
B Engine compartment lights, instrument panel lights, direction lamps and indicators, stoplights, windscreen wiper, ventilation fan motor
C Lefthand headlamp, main beam, headlamp main beam indicator lamp
D Righthand headlamp, main beam
E Lefthand anti-dazzle beam
F Righthand anti-dazzle beam
G Lefthand side lamp, side lamp indicator lamp, righthand tail lamp, lefthand number plate lamp, cigar lighter spot lamp, luggage compartment light, back-up lights
H Righthand front side lamp, lefthand tail lamp, righthand number plate lamp,
I Oil pressure gauge and low oil-pressure warning light, temperature gauge, fuel gauge and reserve warning light, electro-magnetic fan-clutch, engine speed indicator, glove compartment light
L Voltage regulator, alternator field winding

*Circuits protected by this fuse are not controlled from the ignition switch

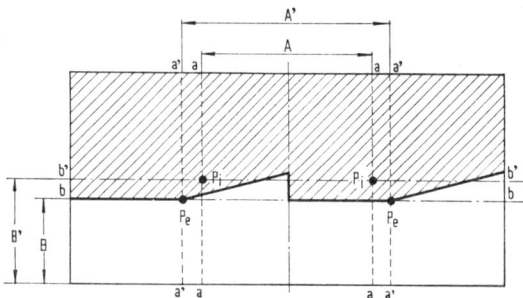

FIG 11:14   Headlamp alignment. Coupé models with four lamp installation (lefthand drive shown)

Key to Fig 11:14   A 32.83 inches   A' 46.06 inches B=C—3.93 inches (new car), C—3.15 inches (settled car) B≐C—1.57 inches   C Height of headlamp centre above ground   Vehicle to be unladen 15 feet from screen

The sealed chamber is welded to the petrol suction tube and the connections are brought to a socket outlet on the supporting flange for gauge and tube.

In the event of failure of the transmitter, do not attempt to break the seal of the unit but replace the whole assembly. The indicator is a calibrated voltmeter in series with the transmitter rheostat and is coupled to it via the pink and red/grey cables. The low fuel indicator is the grey/red connection.

11:10 Fuse board

The fuse board is located beneath the dashboard adjacent to the steering column. There are ten fuses on the standard models (one 16 amp and nine 8 amp). They are of the replaceable cartridge type and the circuits protected by each fuse will be found in the appropriate wiring diagram.

It will be seen that the high beam and low beam circuits are separately fused. If one beam fails to light check the fuse before replacing the bulb.

The battery charging circuit alternator, ignition starting, and no-charge indicator are not protected by fuses.

All fused circuits, apart from the inside lights and horn, controlled from position 2 are dead unless the ignition switch is in position 1, 2 or 3 and are available only in position 3 with the engine switched off and the ignition key withdrawn.

If a fuse has blown, check the circuit for the fault before replacing the fuse.

11:11 Fault diagnosis

(a) Battery discharged

1 Internal fault—replace battery
2 External wiring fault—check circuits
3 Generator not charging—check regulator and cut-out
4 Ignition left on overnight

(b) Battery does not start engine

1 Faulty cell
2 Low state of charge
3 Faulty battery connection

(c) Battery charging too low

1 Faulty regulator
2 Slipping belt
3 Loose battery connection

(d) Ignition warning light does not extinguish

1 Loose or broken belt
2 Faulty regulator
3 Loose alternator or battery connection
4 Faulty alternator

(e) Lamps do not light

1 Fuse blown
2 Faulty earth connection
3 Break in wiring circuit
4 Burnt-out lamp

With double filament lamps, one filament may burn out without affecting the other. The bulb must be replaced.

(f) Horn does not blow

1 Faulty earth at horn button
2 Faulty horn relay
3 Fault in horn
4 Loose connection or break in wiring

(g) Windscreen wiper inoperative

1 Faulty earth at wiper motor
2 Fault on dashboard switch
3 Fuse No. 1 blown
4 Open circuit in wiring
5 Fault in wiper motor or internal switch

(h) Fuel gauge inoperative

1 Faulty transducer
2 Sticking float arm
3 Punctured float
4 Loose connection or break in wiring
5 Fuse No. 1 blown

(j) Low oil indicating with normal oil level

1 Faulty transducer
2 Earth fault on line
3 Oil pump not working or blocked
4 Oil pressure valve failure
5 Clogged filter

(k) Direction indicators not working

1 Fuse No. 1 blown
2 Faulty flasher unit
3 Faulty column switch
4 Open circuit in wiring

Always check fuses and lamp bulbs before suspecting other faults. Then check for good earth connection and return. A good earth to adjacent metal is not always a good system earth through corrosion in adjacent metal bodywork.

NOTES

CHAPTER 12

THE BODYWORK

12:1 Bodywork finish

The body structure is made up from pressed steel sections joined together by spot welding. Damage to any section which is too great for local rectification can be dealt with by replacing the section in the chassis and body, and spot welding it into position. As this is a procedure entailing, in most cases, the realignment of the chassis or its assembly in a special jig, the work should not be attempted by the owner-mechanic but placed with a Fiat repair agent who is in possession of the necessary jigs and tools.

The enamel finish is of a durable nature and will last for many years if kept reasonably clean by washing and polishing. **Do not attempt to wipe road dust from the body with a dry cloth or its high polish will be impaired by fine scratches.** Always wash the dirt away by copious flushing with water from a jet or hose using a soft sponge or brush to loosen the dirt while it is under the flow of water. The use of a soapy detergent in the water can also help but it must be flushed with clean water afterwards and dried off with a chamois leather. Finally, polish with a soft cloth.

The protective film of wax should be renewed from time to time. There are two good indications of wax surface deterioration. The first is when water sprayed onto the surface tends to wet it evenly all over. Water should run off or, at least, stand on the surface in separate globules. The second is the 'feel' of the polishing cloth after drying. If it slips easily over the surface with no effort, the wax film is intact. If there is the slightest feel of 'drag', either the film has deteriorated and you are down to the base enamel or the film is contaminated by ingrained dirt and must be renovated.

Renovation is in two stages. The first is the removal of the old film with its ingrained dirt by means of a cutting compound; the second is the replacement by a new coating of wax. Many excellent proprietary cutting compounds and cleaners are on the market and can be used safely so long as the instructions are followed. The separate compounds, cutter and wax polish, are to be preferred but the polishing can then be a long and arduous task which, however, pays good dividends in the final appearance. Combined cleaners and polishers are an acceptable second best. The cleaners and the combined products will show some colour on the applicator cloth when used. This is the old film being removed and need cause no alarm that the enamel is being eroded.

Most products are now based on silicones and should not be allowed to contaminate the glass of windscreens

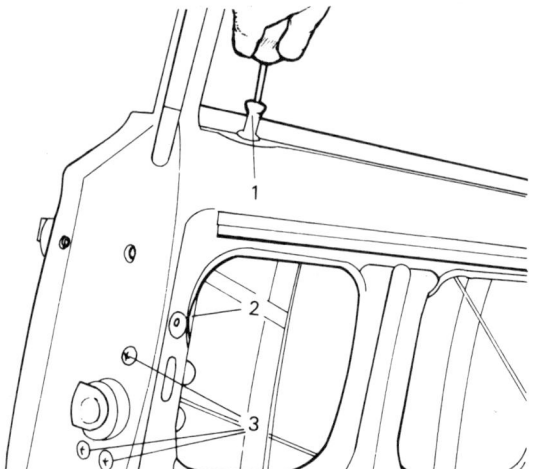

FIG 12:1 Door lock with panel removed to show, locking plunger 1, operating rod 2, and fixing screw 3

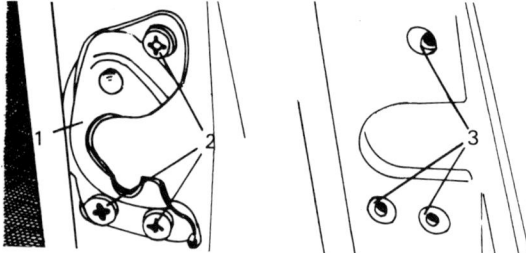

FIG 12:2 Door latch plate 1, showing fixing screws 2, and rear screw plate 3

and windows. The presence of silicone on glass is to make it water-repellent and the action of the windscreen wipers is then to smear rather than clear the area of vision. The film is difficult to remove but a windscreen can be renovated by the use of non-abrasive cleaning powders and plenty of water or by a metal polish. Prevention is, however, better than cure.

It is not generally known that chrome plating is porous and, despite its high polish, water can penetrate through it to the metal beneath, causing pitting, bubbling and even stripping of the metal over large areas. After cleaning with metal polish, always use body wax to close the pores and seal them against the ingress of water. On a new car, it is a good practice to smear all exposed chrome surfaces with a warm solution of lanolin in white spirit and allow it to stand for a few hours. The solution can be made up by a chemist. Afterwards, clean off the wax and polish. What is left in the pores will give protection for many years despite the use of chrome polishes.

Tar can be removed by the use of a little butter on a soft cloth finishing off with an application of wax. Bird droppings should be removed as soon as possible. Wipe off with a very wet cloth, applied with a rotary motion and little pressure, until it is clear. Renew the wax. Most bird droppings have constituents which eat through the wax and affect the colour of the enamel beneath, leaving a lighter coloured area.

12:2 Upholstery and trim

Clean the imitation leather panels and trim with a wet cloth and soap or soap liquid. Allow to stand for a few minutes, wipe clean with a new cloth and finish off with a dry one. **Do not use spirit cleaners, ammonia or soda in any form.**

Brush out the interior and the upholstery at frequent intervals. Use a vacuum cleaner, if possible, on the upholstery and to extract dirt from the crevices and from the floor under the mats. Dull or dirty upholstery can be refreshed by brushing with a soapy solution in the direction of the grain, raising a foam, wiping clear with a clean dry cloth and, after the surface is completely dry, brushing against the grain to raise the nap.

12:3 Locks and hinges

Locks and hinges must be kept in good condition and oiled regularly. Be sparing with the oil, however, as excess can spoil not only the adjacent fabric but also the clothes of those using the car.

The doors are secured by locks which are operated by a handle from the outside and a lever from the inside. A safety plunger is provided on each door to secure the lock from the inside. The locks are retained in position

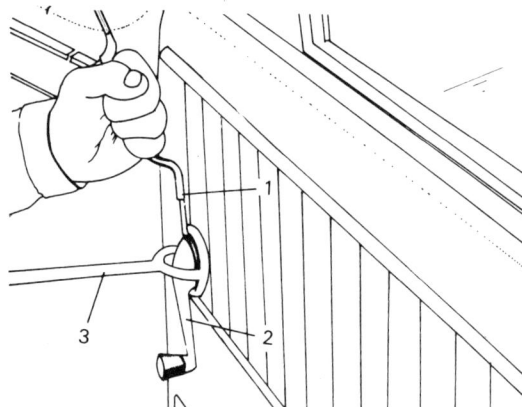

FIG 12:3 Removing window winding handle 2, with tool A.78025 1, to hold the escutcheon back permitting removal of the pin by tool A.78007, 3

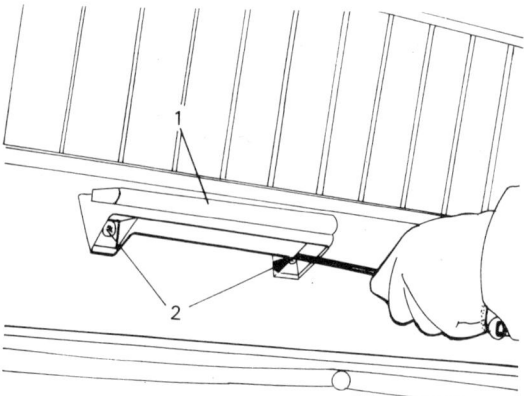

FIG 12:4 Removing armrest 1, from door by extracting fixing screws 2

by three screws 3 (see **FIG 12:1**) and a check on the tightness of these should be made from time to time. The lock latch plate is secured to the door jamb by three screws (see **FIG 12:2**) and these must also be tightened and adjusted so as to hold the door closed without rattle but without the need for excessive slamming to close. When properly adjusted, the joint between the door and the adjacent panel should be flush.

The hinges, locks and latch plates are all secured by Philips screws of the self-tapping variety with a cruci-form slot to take the special driver head. When tightening, keep pressure on the head firm or the driver and the screw head may be damaged. In the case of the latch plate, the screws fit into a threaded plate at the rear of the door jamb metalwork and not into the metal itself.

12:4 Window raising gear

The windows are raised by a cord-type regulator from the handle passing through the panel trim. To gain access to the mechanism, first, push back the trim around the handle to expose the securing pin (see **FIG 12:3**) push out the pin and remove the handle, circular plate and spring at the rear. Next, unscrew the armrest (see **FIG 12:4**) and lever off the remote control door handle escutcheon plate (see **FIG 12:5**). With a screwdriver

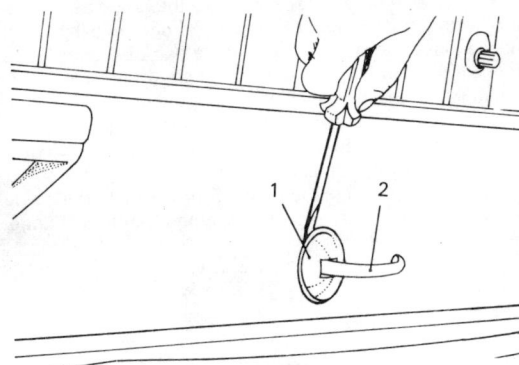

FIG 12:5 Easing escutcheon plate 1, from door panel around the remote lock handle 2

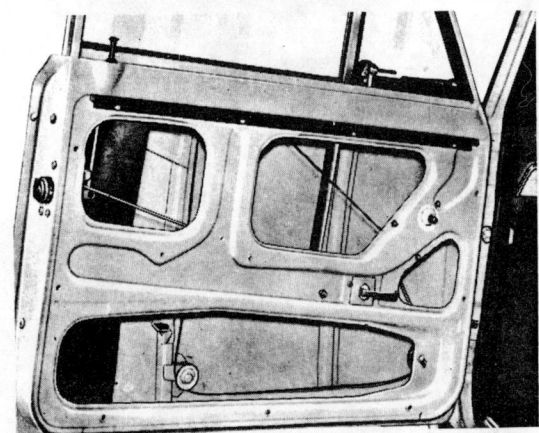

FIG 12:6 View of the interior of the door with panel removed showing window raising cord

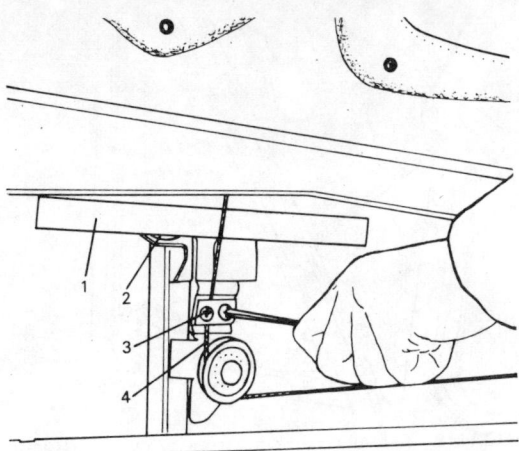

FIG 12:7 Window glass support channel 1, secured to cord 4, by clamp 3. In the lowered position, channel comes to rest on pad 2

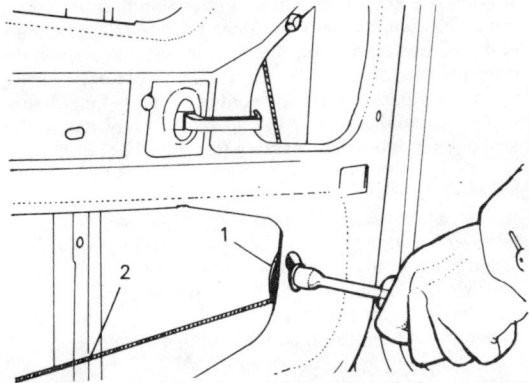

FIG 12:8 Adjusting the tension of the window support cord 2, by positioning pulley 3, in slot and securing

inserted between the panel and the metalwork adjacent, ease the panel away from the door, slide it clear from the door handle and remove to expose the interior mechanism (see **FIG 12:6**).

The glass is supported on a horizontal frame of channel section 1 (see **FIG 12:7**) which is attached by a clip 3, to the raising and lowering cord 4, passing around pulleys and the boss of the winding handle. The cord is tensioned by the lower pulley adjacent to the door hinges which is adjustable in a slot in the door and secured by a nut (see **FIG 12:8**).

To replace the glass, first remove the quarter light by extracting the fixing screw (see **FIG 12:9**) and removing, then lower the window, release the clip from the cable and take the window glass and support channel out as one piece.

12:5 Reglazing front and rear screens

Sport:

The windscreen is secured in place by a special weatherstrip. To remove, just push the glass out by applying firm pressure around the edge of the weather-strip.

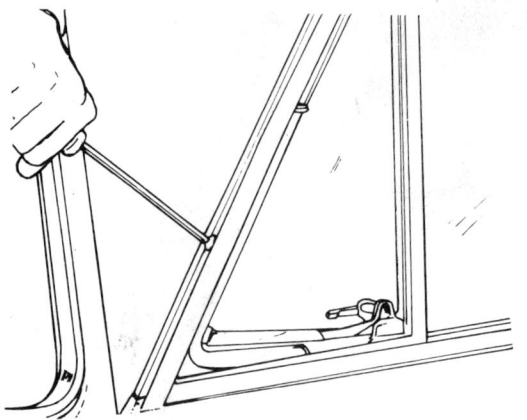

FIG 12:9 Removing fixing screw prior to extracting the quarter light

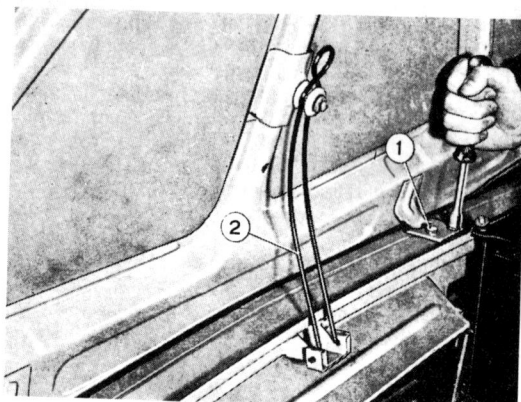

FIG 12:10 Boot hinges and spring prop 2. To remove, unscrew the fasteners 1, and extract prop by pinching lower end

To replace, fit the weatherstrip to the glass all round and insert a cord in the outer groove bringing both ends out at the centre lower side. Clean the body flanges, then, with one person holding the glass in position against the opening from the outside and the two cord ends inside, the second person pulls the cord to ease the inner flange of the weatherstrip over the lip of the body flange. No sealing compound is necessary (see **FIG 12:12**).

Coupé:

The windscreen and the rear lights are secured to the body by a bonding process using a thermo-electric sealing compound with the trade name 'Solbit' which consists of a neoprene strip 8 mm in diameter containing a resistor wire for connection to a 24-volt supply in order to soften the Solbit strip prior to fitting and setting.

To replace a glass it is first necessary to remove the outer trim moulding and the inner linings, preferably using the pair of tools A.78032 and all traces of broken glass or old adhesive. Then clean the contour flange and check the trim moulding clips, replacing any which may be defective.

Place the two rubber spacers from the Solbit pack onto the bottom flange, about 8 inches in from the pillars then fit the glass into its opening using a pair of suction grips for easier handling. It will be helpful in accurately locating the glass to stick short lengths of masking tape across the gap between glass and surround as shown in **FIG 12:11** and then cutting along the glass edge to give reference points for final fitting.

Apply a thin coat of the primer $\frac{3}{8}$ inch wide to the inside edge of the glass and the opening contour flange.

FIG 12:11 Fitting a new windscreen on Coupé model. Arrows indicate masking tape locating strips

Expose the two ends of the reel of Solbit, connect to a 24-volt supply and allow the current to flow for one minute to pre-heat and dry up the compound.

Now place the strip around the inner edge of the glass with a slight protrusion, starting from one of the bottom corners at the spacer and twisting the two ends together when they meet. Lift the glass onto the spacer in the position as marked and pass the current through the resistor wire for two minutes, pushing the glass well into the softened strip until an adhesive coat $\frac{1}{4}$ inch wide is obtained on the glass edge. The use of the gauge A.96801 will assist in ensuring an accurate fit of both windscreen and rear window.

Note that the time available for positioning the glass is 5 to 6 minutes and as soon as the specified width of adhesive has been obtained stop pressing the glass but keep the heat on for one hour. Disconnect the electricity and trim off the wires and allow the glass to cool.

A water test should be made and any leaks sealed with scraps of Solbit previously trimmed off.

Replace the outer trim mouldings.

12:6 Compartment lids and locks

The bonnet over the engine compartment is hinged at the front and is fitted with a spring prop to hold it open in the vertical position (see **FIG 12:10**). The rear catch is released by cable from a lever adjacent to the steering column in the car.

The boot lid is also hinged and secured in the open position by similar methods and is latch closed by a spring latch which, on early cars can be locked by a key inserted into a barrel lock incorporated in the release button. On later cars 1973, the boot lid is locked automatically when the lid is closed and a key is required to open it. The latch plate is adjustable to ensure rattle proof closing.

12:7 Instrument panel and trim

The instrument panel trim is attached to the lower part of the dashboard at eight places, by four screws immediately below the panel and by four nuts which are reached through the glove compartment and instrument cluster aperture.

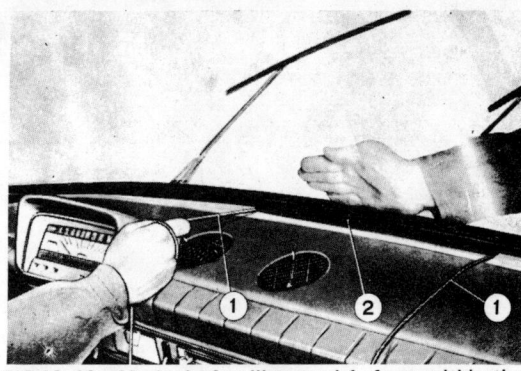

FIG 12:12   Method of pulling cord 1, from within the car to fit the weatherstrip 2, when reglazing the windscreen

To remove the trim:

First extract the screw in each windscreen pillar through the side pillar trim and slide the trim upwards to free it from the panel. Remove the two half-collars of the direction indicator lever on the steering column. Next, remove the instrument cluster, disengaging it from the speedometer drive and from the rear electrical connections.

Remove the switches controlling the side, rear and headlamps, the instrument cluster lights and the windscreen wiper.

Disconnect the glove compartment light.

Now remove the four screws attaching the lower part of the trim to the dashboard and the four nuts securing the upper part. In addition, take out the two screws securing the glove compartment partition to the panel. Ease the trim away from the dash and, from behind, disconnect the flexible cables from the air conditioning control levers. The panel trim is now free.

To reinstall, reverse the above procedure.

As with all internal working involving the electrical circuits, while the lighting cables are isolated by the ignition switch being in the O position, it is a wise precaution to isolate the battery positive by removing the terminal clamp.

NOTES

APPENDIX

GENERAL DESCRIPTION

TECHNICAL DATA

Engine   Fuel system   Ignition system   Cooling system
Clutch   Gearbox   Front suspension   Rear suspension
Steering   Braking system   Electrical equipment
Capacities   Torque loadings

WIRING DIAGRAMS

HINTS ON MAINTENANCE AND OVERHAUL

GLOSSARY OF TERMS

INDEX

NOTES

TECHNICAL DATA

Dimensions are in inches unless otherwise stated

ENGINE

Number of cylinders	4
Firing order	1–3–4–2
Position of No. 1	Front
Bore and stroke, 1438 cc	80 x 71.5 mm
1592 cc	80 x 79.2 mm
1608 cc	80 x 80 mm
1756 cc	84 x 79.2 mm
Compression ratio, 1438 cc	8.9:1
1592 cc	9.8:1
1608 cc	9.8:1 or 8.5:1
1756 cc	9.8:1

Cylinder bore diameter:

1438 cc, 1592 cc, 1608 cc	80.00 to 80.05 mm in .01 mm steps
1756 cc	84.00 to 84.05 mm in .01 mm steps

Pistons:

Diameter 1438 cc, 1608 cc, Class A	3.14606 to 3.14646
Class C	3.14685 to 3.14724
Class E	3.14764 to 3.14803
1592 cc, Class A	3.1476 to 3.1479
Class C	3.1483 to 3.1487
Class E	3.1491 to 3.1496
1756 cc, Class A	3.3047 to 3.3050
Class C	3.3055 to 3.3059
Class E	3.3062 to 3.3066
Oversizes available	.008, .016, .023

Clearance in cylinder bore:

1438 cc, 1608 cc	.0031 to .0039 at 2.05 inch from piston crown
1592 cc	.002 to .0028 at .906 inch from bottom of skirt
1756 cc	.0016 to .0024 at 1.18 inch from bottom of skirt

Gudgeon pin bore:

1438 cc, 1608 cc, Class 1	.86543 to .86559
Class 2	.86559 to .86575
Class 3	.86575 to .86590
1592 cc, 1756 cc, Class 1	.8660 to .8661
Class 2	.8661 to .8662

Gudgeon pin diameter:

1438 cc, 1608 cc, Group 1	.86496 to .86512
Group 2	.86512 to .86528
Group 3	.86528 to .86543
1592 cc, 1756 cc, Class 1	.8658 to .8659
Class 2	.8659 to .8660
Oversize available	.0079

Clearance in piston:

1438 cc, 1608 cc	.00031 to .00102
1592 cc, 1756 cc	.0001 to .0003

Clearance in small end:

1438 cc, 1608 cc	.00039 to .00165 interference
1592 cc, 1756 cc	.0004 to .0006

Piston rings:
Clearance in groove 1438 cc, 1608 cc:
Compression ring	...	...	...	...	.002 to .003
Top oil control ring	...	...	...	...	.001 to .0015
Bottom oil control ring		...	...	...	.001 to .002

Clearance in groove 1592 cc, 1756 cc:
Compression ring	...	...	...	...	.0015 to .003
Top oil control ring	...	...	...	...	.001 to .003
Bottom oil control ring		...	...	...	.001 to .002

Gap in bore, 1438 cc, 1608 cc:
Compression ring	...	...	...	...	.012 to .018
Top oil control ring	...	...	...	...	.008 to .014
Bottom oil control ring		...	...	...	.008 to .014

Gap in bore 1592 cc:
Compression ring	...	...	...	...	.012 to .018
Top oil control ring	...	...	...	...	.008 to .020
Bottom oil control ring		...	...	...	.008 to .020

Gap in bore 1756 cc:
Compression ring	...	...	...	...	.012 to .018
Top oil control ring	...	...	...	...	.012 to .018
Bottom oil control ring		...	...	...	.010 to .016

Crankshaft:
1438 cc, 1608 cc:
Journal diameter	...	...	...	...	1.999 to 1.9998
Crankpin diameter	...	...	...	...	1.791 to 1.792
Big-end bearing clearance	...	...	...	.001 to .003
End float	...	...	...	...	.0025 to .010

1592 cc, 1756 cc:
Journal diameter	...	...	...	2.0860 to 2.0868
Crankpin diameter, Class A	...	...	...	1.9997 to 2.0001
Class B	...	...	...	1.9993 to 1.9997
Big-end bearing clearance, Class A	...	...	.0018 to .0031
Class B	...	...	.0019 to .0032
End float	...	...	...	...	.002 to .012
Journal and crankpin undersizes	...	...	.01, .02, .03, .04
Main bearing clearance	...	...	...	.002 to .0037
Thrust rings, thickness...	...	...	...	.091 to .093
oversize ...	...	...	...	.096 to .098

Camshaft:
Bearing bore diameter:
Front	...	...	...	...	1.1814 to 1.1824
Middle...	...	...	...	...	1.8031 to 1.8042
Rear	...	...	...	...	1.8189 to 1.8198

Journal diameter:
Front	...	...	...	...	1.1788 to 1.1795
Middle...	...	...	...	...	1.8013 to 1.8020
Rear	...	...	...	...	1.8171 to 1.8178

Bearing clearance:
Front	...	...	...	...	.0019 to .0035
Middle...	...	...	...	...	.0011 to .0027
Rear	...	...	...	...	.0011 to .0027

Auxiliary drive shaft:
Journal diameter:
Front	...	...	...	...	1.8903 to 1.8913
Rear	...	...	...	...	1.5326 to 1.5336

Bush bore:
Front	...	...	...	...	1.8930 to 1.8938
Rear	...	...	...	...	1.5354 to 1.5362

Bearing clearance:
- Front ... ... .0018 to .0036
- Rear ... ... .0018 to .0036

Valves and guides:

1438 cc, 1608 cc:
- Stem diameter, inlet ... ... .3140 to .3146
- exhaust ... ... .3137 to .3143
- Guide bore ... ... .3158 to .3165
- Clearance, inlet ... ... .0012 to .0026
- exhaust ... ... .0015 to .0028
- Head diameter, inlet 1.629
- exhaust 1.417

1592 cc, 1756 cc:
- Stem diameter ... ... .3139 to .3146
- Guide bore ... ... .3158 to .3165
- Clearance ... ... .0012 to .0026
- Head diameter, inlet ... ... 1.6613 to 1.6771
- exhaust ... ... 1.4115 to 1.436

- Width of seat in head ... ... .079
- Angle of seat in head ... ... 45 deg. ± 5'
- Valve seat angle ... ... 45 deg. 30' ± 5'

Valve springs:
- Length at load, outer ... ... 1.417 at 85.8 lbs
- inner ... ... 1.22 at 32.8 lbs

Valve working clearance, cold:
- 1438 cc, 1608 cc ... ... .017 to .019
- 1592 cc, 1756 cc ... ... .017 to .023

Valve timing clearance ... ... .031

Oil pump pressure:
- 1438 cc, 1608 cc ... ... 50 to 70 lb/sq inch
- 1592 cc to 1756 cc ... ... 57 to 85 lb/sq inch

FUEL SYSTEM

Carburetter, 1438 cc:

Type — *Weber 34 DFH*

	Primary barrel	Secondary barrel
Barrel diameter	1.338	1.338
Venturi diameter	.944	1.023
Main jet	.049	.047
Idling jet	.017	.023
Main air jet	.070	.059
Idling air jet	.047	.027
Pump jet	.015	—
Extra fuel device: air jet	.051	.049
fuel jet	.043	.075
mixture jet	.043	.075
Float level: from cover face to float	.236	
travel	.335	

Type (from Engine No. 43458) — *Weber 34 DHS/1-/3*

	Primary barrel	Secondary barrel
Barrel diameter	1.338	1.338
Venturi diameter	.944	1.023
Main jet	.049	.047
Idling jet	.017	.023
Main air jet	.070	.067
Idling air jet	.047	.027

Pump jet ...	.015	—
Extra fuel device: air jet ...	.051	.049
fuel jet ...	.043	.075
mixture jet ...	.043	.075
Emulsion tube ...	F34	F34
Float level: from cover face to float ...	.256
travel ...	.335

Carburetter (1600 model):

Type — Weber 40 IDF

	Primary barrel	Secondary barrel
Barrel diameter ...	1.5757	1.575
Venturi diameter ...	1.260	1.260
Auxiliary venturi ...	.177	.177
Main jet ...	.047	.047
Idling jet ...	.021	.021
Starting jet ...	.035	
Main air jet ...	.083	.083
Idling air jet ...	.045	.045
Pump jet ...	.015	—
Float level ...	.394	

Type — Solex C40 P11 6

	Primary barrel	Secondary barrel
Barrel diameter ...	1.575	1.575
Venturi diameter ...	1.260	1.260
Main jet ...	.055	.055
Idling jet ...	.021	.021
Starting jet ...	.047	
Main air jet ...	.067	.067

Type 1971-72 (USA) — Weber 28/36 DHSA2

	Primary barrel	Secondary barrel
Barrel diameter ...	28 mm	36 mm
Venturi diameter ...	23	28
Main jet ...	1.25	1.55
Idling jet ...	.50	.70
Main air jet ...	1.95	1.50
Idling air jet ...	1.60	.70
Pump jet ...	.50	
Float level. Top of float to cover ...	6	

Carburetter (1973 models):

Type — Weber 34 DMS

	Primary barrel	Secondary barrel
Venturi diameter ...	24 mm	26 mm
Main jet ...	1.25	1.55
Idle jet ...	.50	.70
Main air jet ...	1.80	1.80
Pump jet ...	.50	
Emulsion tube ...	F61	F61
Auxiliary venturi ...	4.50	4.50
Needle valve ...	1.75	
Float level ...	7 mm (gauge A 95129)	

Type — Solex C34 EIES 5

	Primary barrel	Secondary barrel
Venturi diameter ...	24	27
Auxiliary venturi ...	4.5	4.5
Main jet ...	1.25	1.50
Idle jet ...	.47	.80

Main air jet	1.50	1.50
Idle air jet	.90	1.10
Emulsion tube	3.50	3.50
Float level		20.5 mm (gauge A.95139)
Idle mixture adjust. orifice	1.60	—
Pump jet	.55	—

IGNITION SYSTEM

Distributor:

1438 cc, 1608 cc:
- Early type ... ... Marelli S124A
- Later type ... ... Marelli S124B

Automatic centrifugal advance:
- Early type ... ... Marelli 20 deg.
- Later type ... ... 24 deg.
- Contact breaker gap ... ... .016 to .018

1592 cc, 1756 cc:
- Type 4-speed transmission ... ... Marelli S147L
- 5-speed transmission ... ... Marelli S147H
- Automatic centrifugal advance ... ... 28 deg. ± 2 deg.
- Contact breaker gap ... ... .0145 to .017
- Dwell ... ... 52 deg. to 58 deg.
- Ignition cut-out set at ... ... 6500 ± 100 rev/min
- Static advance ... ... 10 deg. BTDC
  (1970-71 5 deg. BTDC)

Coil:

1438 cc, 1608 cc ... ... Marelli BZR 202A or
Martinetti G37 SU

1592 cc, 1756 cc ... ... Marelli BES 200A or
Martinetti G37 SU

Spark plugs:
- Marelli ... ... CW8 LP
- Champion N6Y
- Bosch W230T30
- Gap ... ... .019 to .023

COOLING SYSTEM

Type	Centrifugal pump with electro-magnetic fan
Thermostat, starts to open	189°F or 87°C
Minimum valve travel at 212°F	.295
Fan, air gap	.0098 to .0137

CLUTCH

Type	Single dry plate, diaphragm spring
Facing diameter, outside	7.87 (1972 on 8.46)
inside	5.59 (1972 on 5.71)
Pedal free travel	.984
Withdrawal flange travel	.31

GEARBOX

Type	4 or 5 speed forward and reverse. Synchromesh on all forward gears

Ratios:

4 speed:
- 1st 3.75:1
- 2nd 2.30:1
- 3rd 1.49:1
- 4th 1:1
- Reverse 3.87:1

5 speed, 1438 cc early:

1st	...	...	...	...	... 3.42:1
2nd	...	...	...	...	... 2.10:1
3rd	...	...	...	...	... 1.36:1
4th	...	...	...	...	... 1:1
5th	...	...	...	...	... .912:1
Reverse	...	...	...	...	... 3.526:1

5 speed, 1438 cc later:

1st	...	...	...	...	... 3.79:1
2nd	...	...	...	...	... 2.17:1
3rd	...	...	...	...	... 1.41:1
4th	...	...	...	...	... 1:1
5th	...	...	...	...	... .913:1
Reverse	...	...	...	...	... 3.65:1

5 speed, others:

1st	...	...	...	...	... 3.66:1
2nd	...	...	...	...	... 2.10:1
3rd	...	...	...	...	... 1.36:1
4th	...	...	...	...	... 1:1
5th	...	...	...	...	... .881:1
Reverse	...	...	...	...	... 3.53:1

FRONT SUSPENSION

Type	Independent swinging arms, coil springs, telescopic hydraulic dampers	
Springs (model and part No.):	*Coupé (4181023)*	*Spyder (4151714)*
Number of turns	7.75	7.5
Wire diameter	.492	.51
Inside diameter	3.54	3.54
Direction	Clockwise	Clockwise
Free length	14.52	13.54
Length under load	8.82 (992 lb)	8.82 (900 lb)

REAR SUSPENSION

Type	Coil spring with 2 (or 4) control struts and stabilizer bar	
Dampers	Hydraulic telescopic	
Springs (model and part No.):	*Coupé (4166468)*	*Spyder (4152192)*
Number of turns	7¾	7
Wire diameter	.466	.464
Inside diameter	4.01	4.01
Direction	Clockwise	Clockwise
Free length	17.52	16.33
Length under load	11.6 (507 lb)	11.6 (441 lb)

STEERING

Type	Worm and roller
Ratio	1:16.4
Kingpin inclination	6 deg.
Castor (loaded)	3 deg. 30'
Camber (loaded)	0 deg. 30' ± 20'
Toe-in (loaded) 1438 cc, 1608 cc	.118 ± .039
1592 cc, 1756 cc	.118 ± .079

BRAKING SYSTEM

Type	Hydraulic servo assisted discs on four wheels
Disc diameter	8.93
Thickness: nominal	.39
minimum	.35
Run-out maximum	.0059
Friction pads:	
Minimum thickness	.079
Fluid	FIAT blue label

ELECTRICAL EQUIPMENT

Battery:	
Voltage	12-volt
Capacity	48AH
Dimension	$10\frac{1}{4}$ x $6\frac{3}{4}$ x $8\frac{7}{8}$
Alternator: Type	A 12 M 124/12/42M
Output	770 watts
Cut-in speed at 12V	1000 rev/min
Maximum current	53 amp
Regulator: Type 1438 cc	RC 1/12B
1608 cc, 1592 cc, 1756 cc ...	RC 2/12B
Starter motor:	
Type	E100-1.3/12
Nominal output	1.3KW
Direction	Clockwise
Drive	Pre-engage, electro-magnetic
Current	280A
Torque	6.5 lb ft
Type	E84-0.8/12 Var.4
Nominal output	.8KW
Direction	Clockwise
Drive	Pre-engage, electro-magnetic
Current	160A

CAPACITIES

	Imperial	USA
Fuel	10 gallons premium	$11\frac{1}{2}$ gallons
Radiator	1.6 gallons	8 quarts
Oil sump and filter	6.6 pints 20W-40	4 quarts
Transmission	2.9 pints ZC90	$3\frac{1}{2}$ pints
Rear axle	2.5 pints	$3\frac{1}{5}$ pints

TORQUE LOADINGS (lb ft)
ENGINE 1438 cc, 1608 cc

Crankshaft bearing cap	59.8
Cylinder head bolts	55.7
Cylinder head extension stud	21
Big-end bearing cap	38
Flywheel bolts	58
Camshaft gear screws	35
Timing belt idler lock	34
Fan drive pulley nut	88
Manifold stud nut	18
Sump bolts	6
Alternator upper screw	32
Alternator lower screw	50

ENGINE 1592 cc, 1756 cc

Front bearing cap screw	57.8
Main bearing caps self-locking screw	83
Engine breather mounting screw	18
Cylinder head hold-down screw	54
Nut, cylinder head extension stud	18
Nut, intake manifold to cylinder head stud	18
Nut, exhaust manifold to cylinder head stud	18
Con-rod bearing cap screw nut	47
Flywheel to crankshaft screw	61.5
Camshaft sprocket screw	86.8
Tensioner nut	32.5
Alternator and water pump drive pulley nut	180.3
Self-locking nut with nylon, alternator lower support stud	32.5
Alternator upper bracket screw	40
Alternator lower mounting nut	50.6
Self-locking nut with nylon, alternator to upper bracket	32.5
Spark plug	28.9
Oil pressure switch 12 volts—Var. 7	25
Electric heat gauge sending unit Var. 9 (water temperature) ...	36

TRANSMISSION

Clutch to flywheel	18
Transmission to engine	61
Front bearing to countershaft	68
Lower cover to central bore...	7
Rear bearing to countershaft	86
Selector fork	9
Flex joint to spider	72
U/J to rear propeller shaft	87
Rear shaft to axle housing	50
Bearing to level pinion	108 to 166
Differential cage bearing cap	36
Crownwheel to cage	72

CHASSIS

Differential to housing	31
Brake caliper plate	40
Wheel to hub	51
Crossmember to sidemember	69
Control arm to crossmember	72
Shock absorber lower mounting	43
Steering arm to knuckle	43
Steering box to body	29
Steering wheel to column	36
Steering arm to roller shaft	174
Ball end pins to arm	25
Engine support bracket	18
Support bracket to pad	22
Transmission to pad	18
Pad to crossmember	18

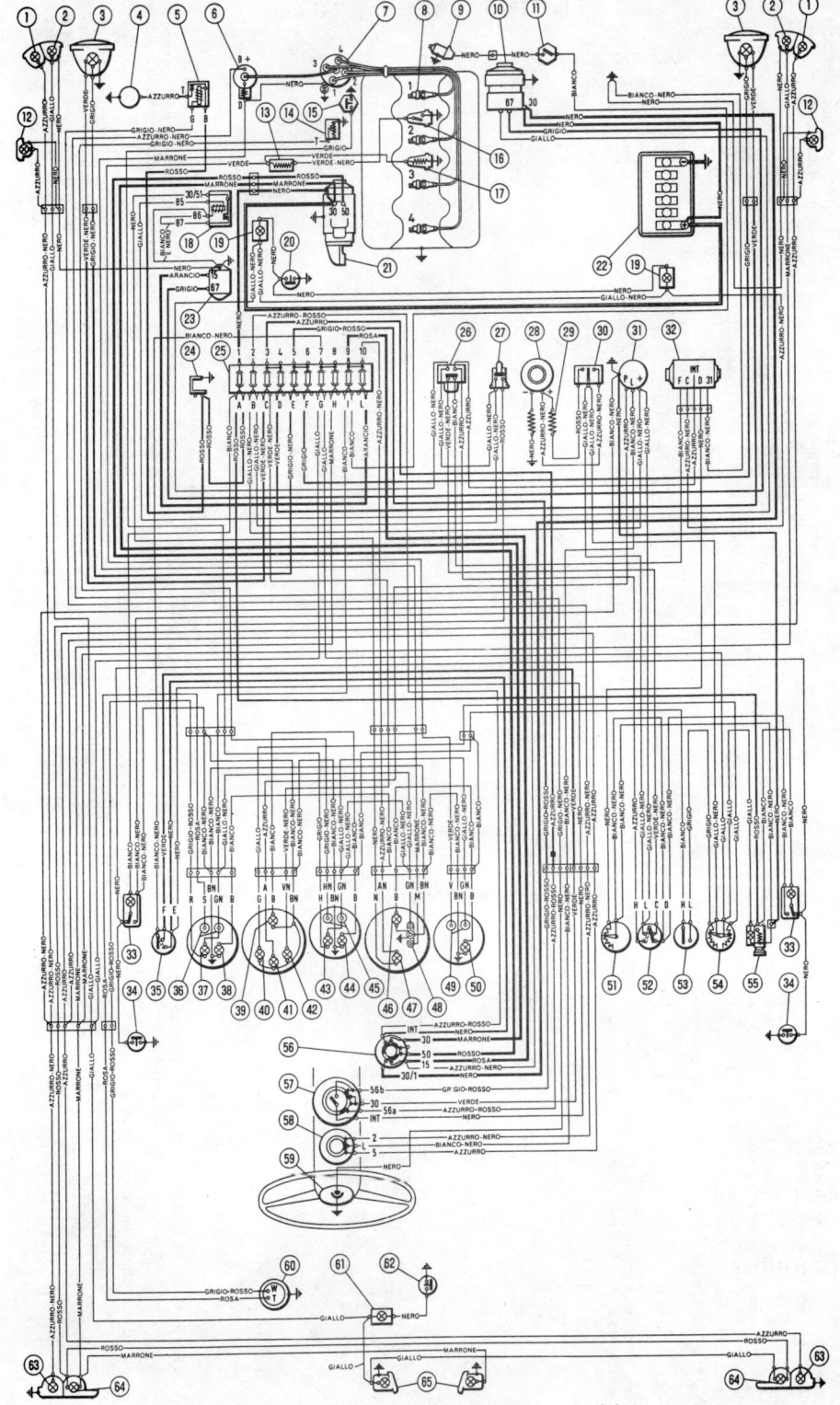

FIG 13:1   Wiring diagram for Sports model

FIAT 124 SPORT

Key to Fig 13:1   1 Front direction lamps   2 Front lamps   3 Headlamps; main beam and anti-dazzle   4 Horn compressor motor   5 Remote control of two-tone horns 6 Ignition coil   7 Ignition distributor   8 Sparking plugs   9 Electromagnetic fan-clutch brush   10 Alternator   11 Thermostatic switch controlling radiator fan-clutch 12 Side direction lamps   13 Temperature gauge extra resistor   14 Oil gauge sender   15 Low oil pressure warning sender   16 Temperature gauge thermal switch: shifts gauge pointer to red end of scale (dangerous water temperature) irrespective of impulses from sender 17   17 Temperature gauge sender   18 Relay switch for warning light 47 19 Engine compartment lamps   20 Push switch for engine compartment lights   21 Starter motor   22 Battery   23 Voltage regulator   24 Single-pole socket for inspection lamp   25 Fuses   26 Pedal switch, windscreen washer and wiper   27 Push switch for stoplights   28 Ventilation fan motor, two-speed   29 Ventilation fan motor extra resistor   30 Three-position ventilation fan selector switch   31 Direction indicator flasher   32 Screen wiper motor   33 Dashboard lamps with built-in switches   34 Push switches for courtesy lights   35 Outside lighting switch   36 Fuel gauge   37 Reserve warning lamp   38 Fuel gauge light   39 Speedometer light 40 Side lamps indicator (green)   41 Direction indicator repeater light (green)   42 Main beam repeater light (blue)   43 Low oil pressure indicator light (red)   44 Oil gauge lamp   45 Oil pressure gauge   46 Engine-speed indicator lamp   47 Warning light, no battery charge   48 Engine-speed indicator   49 Temperature gauge 50 Temperature gauge indicator lamp   51 Screen-wiper motor rheostat   52 Screen-wiper motor on-off switch   53 Selector switch for outer lighting and anti-dazzle lights and side lamps repeater rheostat   54 Instrument panel lights switch flashes   58 Direction indicator switch   55 Cigar lighter (with spot lamp)   56 Ignition, services and starting switch   57 Selector switch for outer lighting and anti-dazzle light push switch   63 Rear direction lamps   64 Tail and stop lamps   65 Number plate lamps   59 Horn button   60 Fuel gauge sender   61 Luggage compartment light   62 Luggage compartment

NOTE: The symbol — means that the cable carries a numbered ring or sleeve

Colour code

Key to colour code   Viola=Violet   Blu=Blue   Rosa=Rose   Azzurro=Light blue   Giallo=Yellow   Nero=Black   Verde=Green   Bianco=White   Grigio=Grey
Rosso=Red   Marrone=Brown   Arancio=Orange

Key to Fig 13:2   1 Front parking and direction indicator lamps   2 Headlamps, main beam and anti-dazzle   3 Horn compressor motor   4 Remote control of two-tone horns   5 Ignition coil   6 Ignition distributor   7 Sparking plugs   8 Electromagnetic fan-clutch brush   9 Alternator   10 Thermostatic switch controlling radiator fan-clutch   11 Side direction lamps   12 Temperature gauge extra resistor   13 Oil gauge sender unit   14 Low oil pressure indicator sender unit   15 Temperature gauge thermal switch: shifts gauge pointer to red end of scale (dangerous water temperature) irrespective of impulses from sender 16   16 Temperature gauge sender unit   17 Relay switch for warning light 37   18 Engine compartment lamps   19 Push switch for engine compartment lights   20 Starter motor   21 Battery   22 Voltage regulator   23 Inspection lamp socket   24 Fuses   25 Pedal switch, windscreen washer and wiper   26 Push switch for stoplights   27 Ventilation fan motor, two-speed   28 Ventilation fan motor extra resistor   29 Three-position ventilation fan selector switch   30 Direction indicator flasher   31 Windscreen wiper motor   32 Side lamps indicator (green)   33 Direction indicator repeater light (green)   34 Main beam repeater light (blue)   35 Speedometer light   36 Engine-speed indicator light   37 Warning light, no-battery charge   38 Engine-speed indicator   39 Fuel gauge   40 Reserve warning lamp   41 Fuel gauge light   42 Low oil pressure warning light (red)   43 Oil gauge light   44 Oil gauge   45 Temperature gauge light   46 Temperature gauge   47 Windscreen wiper motor rheostat   48 Screen-wiper motor switch   49 Instrument panel lights and side lamps repeater rheostats   50 Instrument panel lights switch   51 Glove compartment lamp with built-in switch   52 Outside lighting switch   53 Key-type switch for ignition, services and starting   54 Push switches for courtesy lights   55 Selector switch for outer lighting and anti-dazzle flashes   56 Direction indicator switch   57 Horn button   58 Cigar lighter (with spot lamp)   59 Front interior lamp with built-in switch   60 Rear interior lamps with built-in switch   61 Back-up lamps push switch   62 Fuel gauge sender unit   63 Luggage compartment light   64 Luggage compartment light push switch   65 Rear direction lamps   66 Tail and stop lamps   67 Back-up lamps   68 Number plate lamps

NOTE: The symbol   means that the cable carries a numbered ring or sleeve

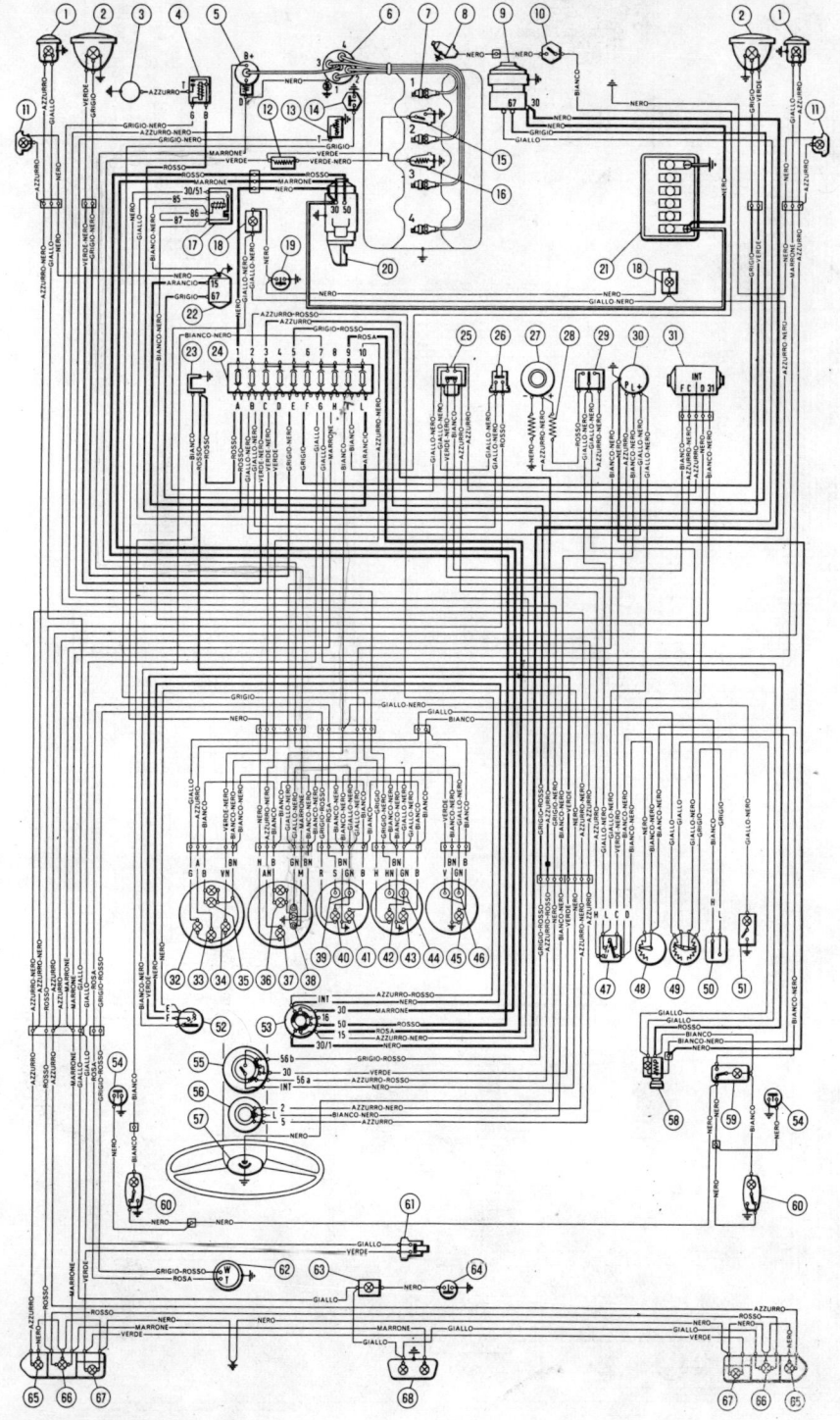

FIG 13 : 2   Wiring diagram for Coupé model

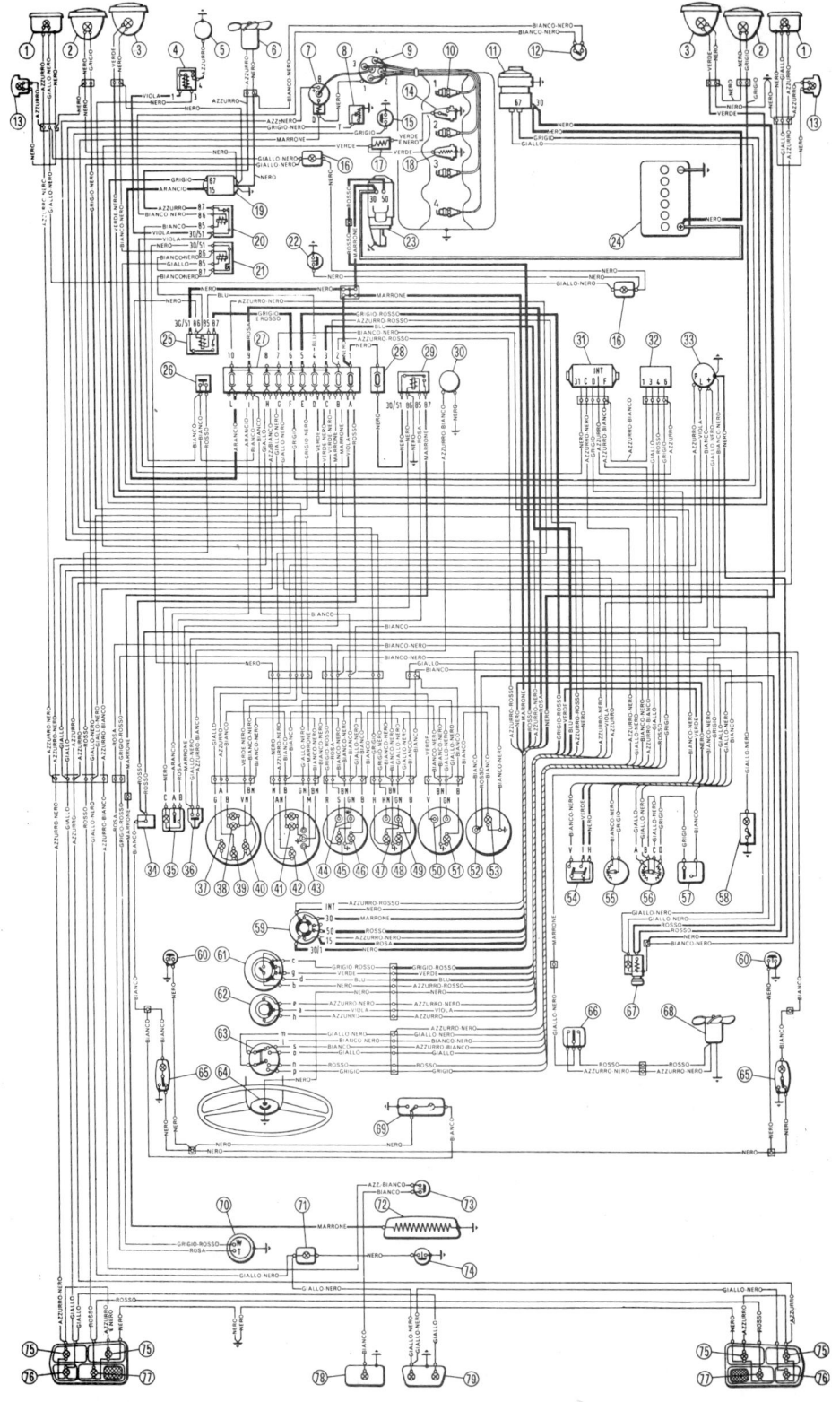

FIG 13:3   Wiring diagram for 1600 Coupé (1970 model)

Key to Fig 13:3 1 Front parking and direction lights 2 Low-beams (halogen lamps) 3 High-beams (halogen lamps) 4 Electropneumatic horns relay 5 Electropneumatic horns compressor 6 Radiator fan motor 7 Ignition coil 8 Oil pressure gauge sending unit 9 Ignition distributor 10 Spark plugs 11 Alternator 12 Thermal switch for motor 6 13 Direction indicator side repeaters 14 Thermal switch for water thermometer: shifts gauge pointer to end of scale (dangerous water temperature) irrespective of pulses from sender 18 15 Low oil pressure indicator sending unit 16 Engine compartment lights 17 Water thermometer additional resistor 18 Water thermometer sending unit 19 Voltage regulator 20 Motor 6 control relay 21 Engine compartment lights press switch 22 Relay for indicator 42 23 Starting motor 24 Battery 25 Relay for turning on high and low beams simultaneously 26 Stop lights press switch 27 Protection fuses 28 Protection fuse for demister 72 (optional) 30 Windshield washer electropump 31 Windshield wiper motor 32 Windshield washer intermittent operation device 33 Direction indicators flasher 34 Inspection lamp socket 35 Switch with built-in light indicator for demister 72 (optional) 36 Windshield washer electropump press button 37 Parking lights 'on' indicator (green light) 38 Speedometer light 39 Direction indicator tell-tale light (green light) 40 High-beam 'on' indicator (blue light) 41 Engine tachometer light 42 Battery no-charge warning light (red light) 43 Engine tachometer 44 Fuel gauge 45 Low fuel indicator light 46 Fuel gauge light 47 Low oil pressure warning light (red light) 48 Oil gauge light 49 Oil gauge 50 Water thermometer 51 Water thermometer light 52 Electric clock 53 Electric clock light 54 Outer lighting two-position switch 55 Windshield wiper speed control rheostat 56 Instrument and indicator lights rheostat 57 Instrument lights switch 58 Glove compartment light with built-in switch 59 Key switch for ignition, services and starting 60 Press switch on doors for lights 65 61 Front outer lights and light flashers selector switch 62 Direction indicator selector switch 63 Windshield wiper three-position switch 64 Electropneumatic horns button 65 Rear interior lights with built-in switch 66 Three-position switch for air conditioner electrofan 67 Electric cigarette lighter, with spot light 68 Electrofan two-speed motor 69 Front interior light with built-in switch 70 Fuel gauge sending unit 71 Luggage compartment light 72 Rear window demister (optional) 73 Back-up light press switch 74 Luggage compartment light press switch 75 Rear direction indicator lights 76 Rear parking lights 77 Stop lights 78 Back-up light 79 License plate lights

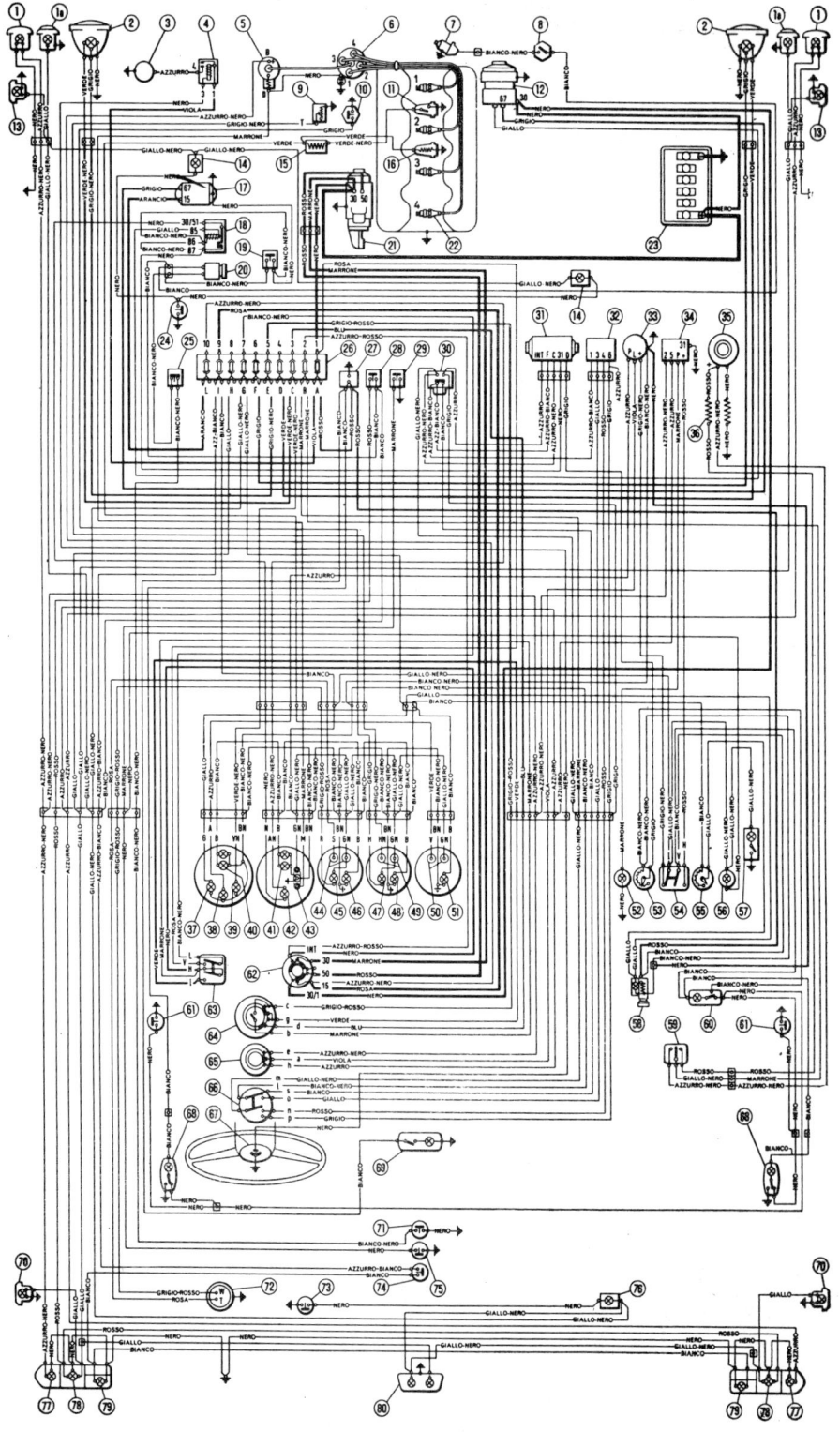

FIG 13:4 Wiring diagram for 1400 Coupe 1969-72

See key on page 154

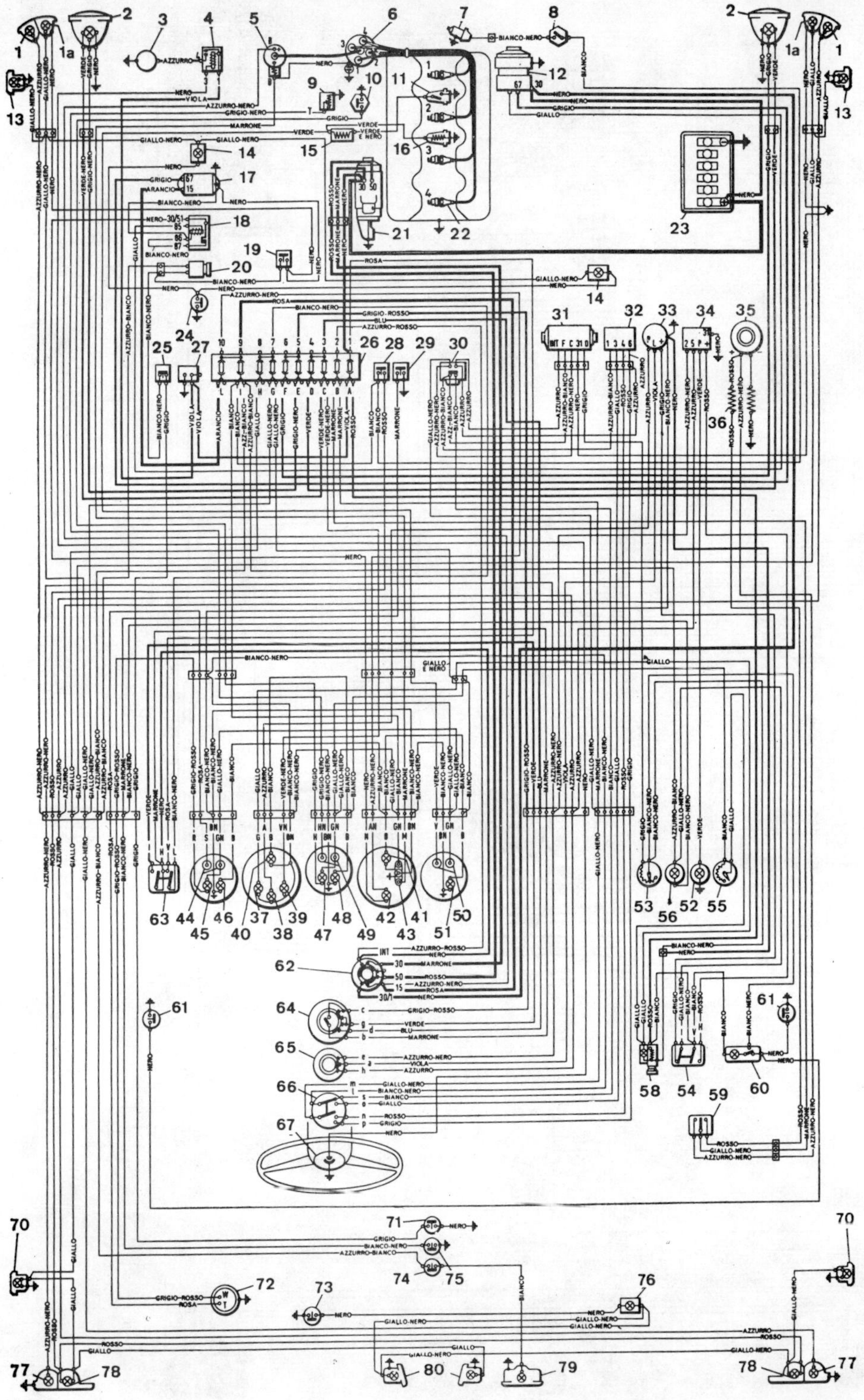

FIG 13:5   Wiring diagram for Spider 1969-72

See key on page 154

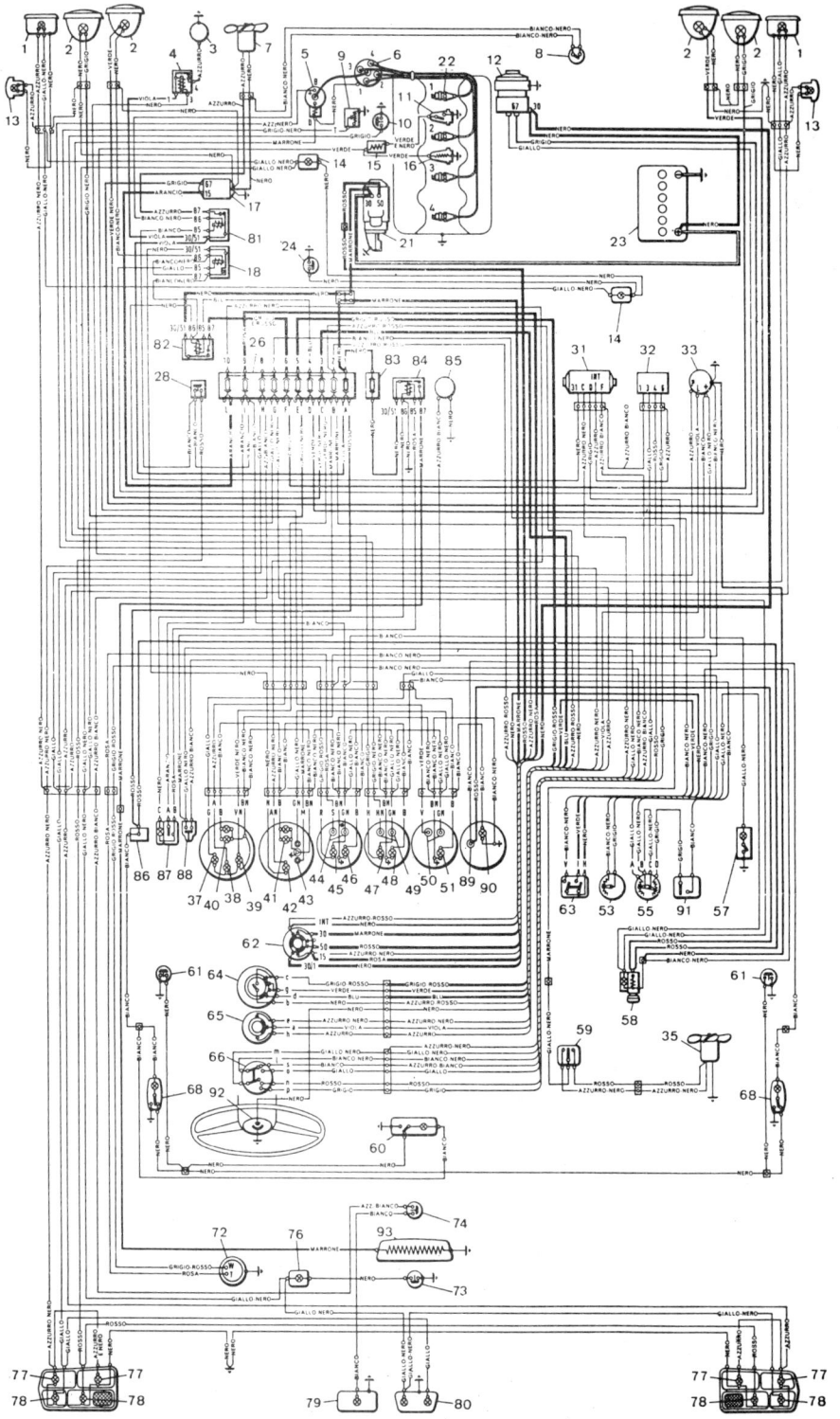

FIG 13:6   Wiring diagram for 1600/1800 Coupe 1972 on

See key on page 154

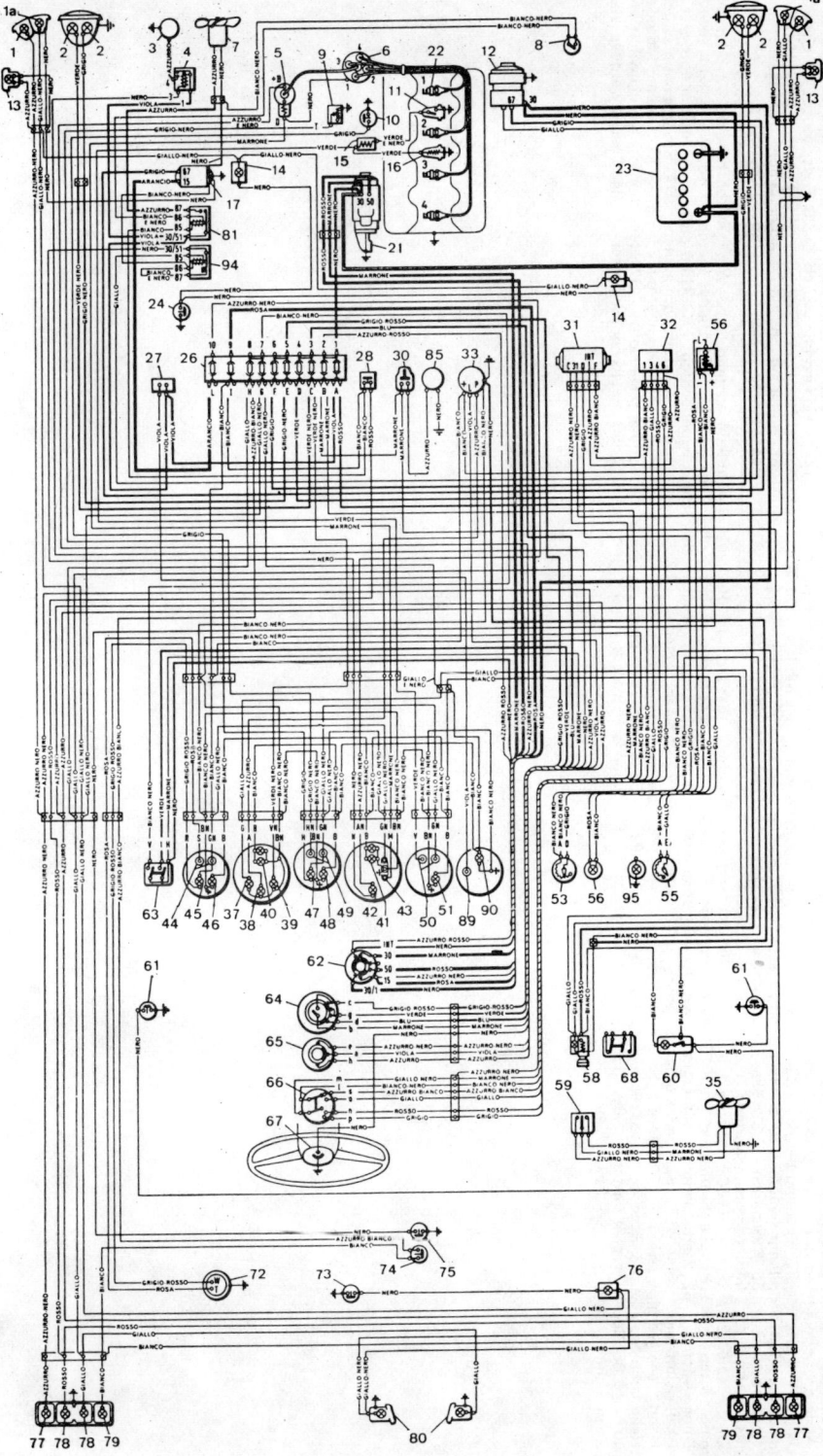

FIG 13:7 Wiring diagram for 1600/1800 Spider 1972 on

See key on page 154

FIAT 124 SPORT

Key to Figs 13:4, 13:5, 13:6 and 13:7   1 Front flashers   1a Side lamps   2 Head lamps   3 Horn compressor   4 Horn relay   5 Coil   6 Distributor   7 Fan
8 Fan switch   9 Oil gauge transmitter   10 Oil warning transmitter   11 Coolant warning switch   12 Alternator   13 Side repeaters   14 Engine compartment lamp
15 Additional coolant resistor   16 Coolant temperature transmitter   17 Voltage regulator   18 Warning lamp relay   19 Fast idle switch   20 Emission control electrovalve   21 Starter   22 Sparking plugs   23 Battery   24 Engine compartment lamp switch   25 Clutch pedal switch (emission control)   26 Fuses   27 Inspection
lamp socket   28 Stop lamp switch   29 Brake warning switch   30 Washer switch   31 Wiper motor   32 Wiper interrupter switch   33 Flasher switch   34 Flasher unit
35 Heater blower   36 Resistance   37 Side lamp warning (green)   38 Flasher warning (green)   39 Headlamp warning (blue)   40 Speedometer light   41 Rev
counter light   42 Charging system warning (red)   43 Rev counter   44 Fuel gauge   45 Fuel level warning   46 Fuel gauge light   47 Oil pressure warning (red)
48 Oil pressure gauge light   49 Oil pressure gauge   50 Coolant temperature gauge   51 Light for 50   52 Hazard light warning   53 Wiper motor rheostat   54 Hazard
warning switch   55 Panel light rheostat   56 Brake system warning   57 Glove box light and switch   58 Cigar lighter   59 Heater switch   60 Interior light (front)
61 Door switches   62 Starter switch   63 Lighting switch   64 Headlamp flasher   65 Flasher switch   66 Screen wiper switch   67 Horn push   68 Interior light (rear)
69 Rear-vision-mirror lamp   70 Side repeater lamps (rear)   71 Gearbox switch (emission control)   72 Fuel tank unit   73 Boot light switch   74 Reverse lamp switch
75 Hand brake warning switch   76 Boot light   77 Rear flashers   78 Rear and stop lamps   79 Reversing lamps   80 Number plate lamp   81 Cooling fan relay
82 Head lamp relay   83 Fuse for heated rear window   84 Relay for 93   85 Screen wash pump   86 Inspection lamp take-off   87 Heated rear window switch and
warning   88 Screen washer switch   89 Clock   90 Clock light   91 Panel lamp switch   92 Horn push   93 Rear window heater   94 Charge warning relay
95 Spare warning lamp   96 Spare switch

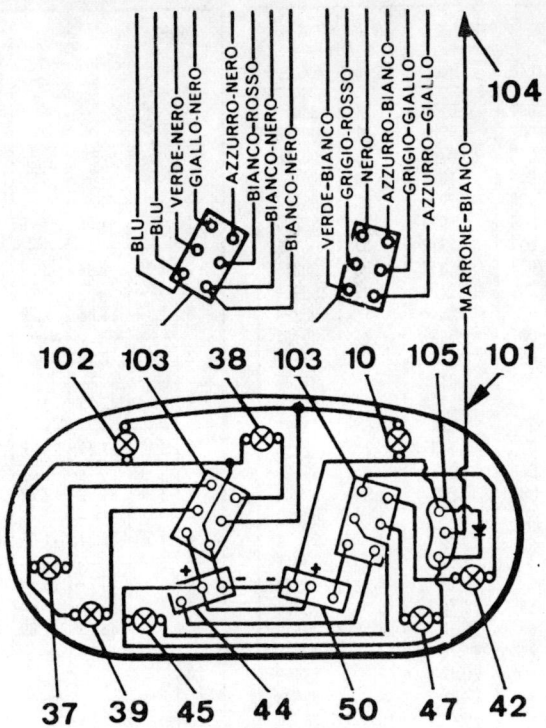

BLU
BLU
VERDE-NERO
GIALLO-NERO
AZZURRO-NERO
BIANCO-ROSSO
BIANCO-NERO
BIANCO-NERO

VERDE-BIANCO
GRIGIO-ROSSO
NERO
AZZURRO-BIANCO
GRIGIO-GIALLO
AZZURRO-GIALLO

MARRONE-BIANCO

104

102 103 38 103 10 105 101

37 39 45 44 50 47 42

FIG 13:8 Additional wiring for electronic rev-counter

Key to Fig 13:8   101 Rev counter lead from engine
102 Instrument panel lamps   103 Connectors   104 To
terminal D on coil or terminal 1 on electronic ignition assembly
105 Electronic rev-counter

Inches	Decimals	Milli-metres	Inches to Millimetres — Inches	Inches to Millimetres — mm	Millimetres to Inches — mm	Millimetres to Inches — Inches
1/64	.015625	.3969	001	.0254	.01	.00039
1/32	.03125	.7937	.002	.0508	.02	.00079
3/64	.046875	1.1906	.003	.0762	.03	.00118
1/16	.0625	1.5875	.004	.1016	.04	.00157
5/64	.078125	1.9844	.005	.1270	.05	.00197
3/32	.09375	2.3812	.006	.1524	.06	.00236
7/64	.109375	2.7781	.007	.1778	.07	.00276
1/8	.125	3.1750	.008	.2032	.08	.00315
9/64	.140625	3.5719	.009	.2286	.09	.00354
5/32	.15625	3.9687	.01	.254	.1	.00394
11/64	.171875	4.3656	.02	.508	.2	.00787
3/16	.1875	4.7625	.03	.762	.3	.01181
13/64	.203125	5.1594	.04	1.016	.4	.01575
7/32	.21875	5.5562	.05	1.270	.5	.01969
15/64	.234375	5.9531	.06	1.524	.6	.02362
1/4	.25	6.3500	.07	1.778	.7	.02756
17/64	.265625	6.7469	.08	2.032	.8	.03150
9/32	.28125	7.1437	.09	2.286	.9	.03543
19/64	.296875	7.5406	.1	2.54	1	.03937
5/16	.3125	7.9375	.2	5.08	2	.07874
21/64	.328125	8.3344	.3	7.62	3	.11811
11/32	.34375	8.7312	.4	10.16	4	.15748
23/64	.359375	9.1281	.5	12.70	5	.19685
3/8	.375	9.5250	.6	15.24	6	.23622
25/64	.390625	9.9219	.7	17.78	7	.27559
13/32	.40625	10.3187	.8	20.32	8	.31496
27/64	.421875	10.7156	.9	22.86	9	.35433
7/16	.4375	11.1125	1	25.4	10	.39370
29/64	.453125	11.5094	2	50.8	11	.43307
15/32	.46875	11.9062	3	76.2	12	.47244
31/64	.484375	12.3031	4	101.6	13	.51181
1/2	.5	12.7000	5	127.0	14	.55118
33/64	.515625	13.0969	6	152.4	15	.59055
17/32	.53125	13.4937	7	177.8	16	.62992
35/64	.546875	13.8906	8	203.2	17	.66929
9/16	.5625	14.2875	9	228.6	18	.70866
37/64	.578125	14.6844	10	254.0	19	.74803
19/32	.59375	15.0812	11	279.4	20	.78740
39/64	.609375	15.4781	12	304.8	21	.82677
5/8	.625	15.8750	13	330.2	22	.86614
41/64	.640625	16.2719	14	355.6	23	.90551
21/32	.65625	16.6687	15	381.0	24	.94488
43/64	.671875	17.0656	16	406.4	25	.98425
11/16	.6875	17.4625	17	431.8	26	1.02362
45/64	.703125	17.8594	18	457.2	27	1.06299
23/32	.71875	18.2562	19	482.6	28	1.10236
47/64	.734375	18.6531	20	508.0	29	1.14173
3/4	.75	19.0500	21	533.4	30	1.18110
49/64	.765625	19.4469	22	558.8	31	1.22047
25/32	.78125	19.8437	23	584.2	32	1.25984
51/64	.796875	20.2406	24	609.6	33	1.29921
13/16	.8125	20.6375	25	635.0	34	1.33858
53/64	.828125	21.0344	26	660.4	35	1.37795
27/32	.84375	21.4312	27	685.8	36	1.41732
55/64	.859375	21.8281	28	711.2	37	1.4567
7/8	.875	22.2250	29	736.6	38	1.4961
57/64	.890625	22.6219	30	762.0	39	1.5354
29/32	.90625	23.0187	31	787.4	40	1.5748
59/64	.921875	23.4156	32	812.8	41	1.6142
15/16	.9375	23.8125	33	838.2	42	1.6535
61/64	.953125	24.2094	34	863.6	43	1.6929
31/32	.96875	24.6062	35	889.0	44	1.7323
63/64	.984375	25.0031	36	914.4	45	1.7717

UNITS	Pints to Litres	Gallons to Litres	Litres to Pints	Litres to Gallons	Miles to Kilometres	Kilometres to Miles	Lbs. per sq. In. to Kg. per sq. Cm.	Kg. per sq. Cm. to Lbs. per sq. In.
1	.57	4.55	1.76	.22	1.61	.62	.07	14.22
2	1.14	9.09	3.52	.44	3.22	1.24	.14	28.50
3	1.70	13.64	5.28	.66	4.83	1.86	.21	42.67
4	2.27	18.18	7.04	.88	6.44	2.49	.28	56.89
5	2.84	22.73	8.80	1.10	8.05	3.11	.35	71.12
6	3.41	27.28	10.56	1.32	9.66	3.73	.42	85.34
7	3.98	31.82	12.32	1.54	11.27	4.35	.49	99.56
8	4.55	36.37	14.08	1.76	12.88	4.97	.56	113.79
9		40.91	15.84	1.98	14.48	5.59	.63	128.00
10		45.46	17.60	2.20	16.09	6.21	.70	142.23
20				4.40	32.19	12.43	1.41	284.47
30				6.60	48.28	18.64	2.11	426.70
40				8.80	64.37	24.85		
50					80.47	31.07		
60					96.56	37.28		
70					112.65	43.50		
80					128.75	49.71		
90					144.84	55.92		
100					160.93	62.14		

UNITS	Lb ft to kgm	Kgm to lb ft	UNITS	Lb ft to kgm	Kgm to lb ft
1	.138	7.233	7	.967	50.631
2	.276	14.466	8	1.106	57.864
3	.414	21.699	9	1.244	65.097
4	.553	28.932	10	1.382	72.330
5	.691	36.165	20	2.765	144.660
6	.829	43.398	30	4.147	216.990

HINTS ON MAINTENANCE AND OVERHAUL

There are few things more rewarding than the restoration of a vehicle's original peak of efficiency and smooth performance.

The following notes are intended to help the owner to reach that state of perfection. Providing that he possesses the basic manual skills he should have no difficulty in performing most of the operations detailed in this manual. It must be stressed, however, that where recommended in the manual, highly-skilled operations ought to be entrusted to experts, who have the necessary equipment, to carry out the work satisfactorily.

Quality of workmanship:

The hazardous driving conditions on the roads to-day demand that vehicles should be as nearly perfect, mechanically, as possible. It is therefore most important that amateur work be carried out with care, bearing in mind the often inadequate working conditions, and also the inferior tools which may have to be used. It is easy to counsel perfection in all things, and we recognize that it may be setting an impossibly high standard. We do, however, suggest that every care should be taken to ensure that a vehicle is as safe to take on the road as it is humanly possible to make it.

Safe working conditions:

Even though a vehicle may be stationary, it is still potentially dangerous if certain sensible precautions are not taken when working on it while it is supported on jacks or blocks. It is indeed preferable not to use jacks alone, but to supplement them with carefully placed blocks, so that there will be plenty of support if the car rolls off the jacks during a strenuous manoeuvre. Axle stands are an excellent way of providing a rigid base which is not readily disturbed. Piles of bricks are a dangerous substitute. Be careful not to get under heavy loads on lifting tackle, the load could fall. It is preferable not to work alone when lifting an engine, or when working underneath a vehicle which is supported well off the ground. To be trapped, particularly under the vehicle, may have unpleasant results if help is not quickly forthcoming. Make some provision, however humble, to deal with fires. Always disconnect a battery if there is a likelihood of electrical shorts. These may start a fire if there is leaking fuel about. This applies particularly to leads which can carry a heavy current, like those in the starter circuit. While on the subject of electricity, we must also stress the danger of using equipment which is run off the mains and which has no earth or has faulty wiring or connections. So many workshops have damp floors, and electrical shocks are of such a nature that it is sometimes impossible to let go of a live lead or piece of equipment due to the muscular spasms which take place.

Work demanding special care:

This involves the servicing of braking, steering and suspension systems. On the road, failure of the braking system may be disastrous. Make quite sure that there can be no possibility of failure through the bursting of rusty brake pipes or rotten hoses, nor to a sudden loss of pressure due to defective seals or valves.

Problems:

The chief problems which may face an operator are:
1 External dirt.
2 Difficulty in undoing tight fixings
3 Dismantling unfamiliar mechanisms.
4 Deciding in what respect parts are defective.
5 Confusion about the correct order for reassembly.
6 Adjusting running clearances.
7 Road testing.
8 Final tuning.

Practical suggestion to solve the problems:

1 Preliminary cleaning of large parts—engines, transmissions, steering, suspensions, etc.,—should be carried out before removal from the car. Where road dirt and mud alone are present, wash clean with a high-pressure water jet, brushing to remove stubborn adhesions, and allow to drain and dry. Where oil or grease is also present, wash down with a proprietary compound (Gunk, Teepol etc.,) applying with a stiff brush—an old paint brush is suitable—into all crevices. Cover the distributor and ignition coils with a polythene bag and then apply a strong water jet to clear the loosened deposits. Allow to drain and dry. The assemblies will then be sufficiently clean to remove and transfer to the bench for the next stage.

On the bench, further cleaning can be carried out, first wiping the parts as free as possible from grease with old newspaper. Avoid using rag or cotton waste which can leave clogging fibres behind. Any remaining grease can be removed with a brush dipped in paraffin. If necessary, traces of paraffin can be removed by carbon tetrachloride. Avoid using paraffin or petrol in large quantities for cleaning in enclosed areas, such as garages, on account of the high fire risk.

When all exteriors have been cleaned, and not before, dismantling can be commenced. This ensures that dirt will not enter into interiors and orifices revealed by dismantling. In the next phases, where components have to be cleaned, use carbon tetrachloride in preference to petrol and keep the containers covered except when in use. After the components have been cleaned, plug small holes with tapered hard wood plugs cut to size and blank off larger orifices with grease-proof paper and masking tape. Do not use soft wood plugs or matchsticks as they may break.

2 It is not advisable to hammer on the end of a screw thread, but if it must be done, first screw on a nut to protect the thread, and use a lead hammer. This applies particularly to the removal of tapered cotters. Nuts and bolts seem to 'grow' together, especially in exhaust systems. If penetrating oil does not work, try the judicious application of heat, but be careful of starting a fire. Asbestos sheet or cloth is useful to isolate heat.

Tight bushes or pieces of tail-pipe rusted into a silencer can be removed by splitting them with an open-ended hacksaw. Tight screws can sometimes be started by a tap from a hammer on the end of a suitable screwdriver. Many tight fittings will yield to the judicious use of a hammer, but it must be a soft-faced hammer if damage is to be avoided, use a heavy block on the opposite side to absorb shock. Any parts of the steering system which have been damaged should be renewed, as attempts to repair them may lead to cracking and subsequent failure, and steering ball joints should be disconnected using a recommended tool to prevent damage.

3 If often happens that an owner is baffled when trying to dismantle an unfamiliar piece of equipment. So many modern devices are pressed together or assembled by spinning-over flanges, that they must be sawn apart. The intention is that the whole assembly must be renewed. However, parts which appear to be in one piece to the naked eye, may reveal close-fitting joint lines when inspected with a magnifying glass, and, this may provide the necessary clue to dismantling. Left-handed screw threads are used where rotational forces would tend to unscrew a right handed screw thread.

Be very careful when dismantling mechanisms which may come apart suddenly. Work in an enclosed space where the parts will be contained, and drape a piece of cloth over the device if springs are likely to fly in all directions. Mark everything which might be reassembled in the wrong position, scratched symbols may be used on unstressed parts, or a sequence of tiny dots from a centre punch can be useful. Stressed parts should never be scratched or centre-popped as this may lead to cracking under working conditions. Store parts which look alike in the correct order for reassembly. Never rely upon memory to assist in the assembly of complicated mechanisms, especially when they will be dismantled for a long time, but make notes, and drawings to supplement the diagrams in the manual, and put labels on detached wires. Rust stains may indicate unlubricated wear. This can sometimes be seen round the outside edge of a bearing cup in a universal joint. Look for bright rubbing marks on parts which normally should not make heavy contact. These might prove that something is bent or running out of truth. For example, there might be bright marks on one side of a piston, at the top near the ring grooves, and others at the bottom of the skirt on the other side. This could well be the clue to a bent connecting rod. Suspected cracks can be proved by heating the component in a light oil to approximately 100°C, removing, drying off, and dusting with french chalk, if a crack is present the oil retained in the crack will stain the french chalk.

4 In determining wear, and the degree, against the permissible limits set in the manual, accurate measurement can only be achieved by the use of a micrometer. In many cases, the wear is given to the fourth place of decimals; that is in ten-thousandths of an inch. This can be read by the vernier scale on the barrel of a good micrometer. Bore diameters are more difficult to determine. If, however, the matching shaft is accurately measured, the degree of play in the bore can be felt as a guide to its suitability. In other cases, the shank of a twist drill of known diameter is a handy check.

Many methods have been devised for determining the clearance between bearing surfaces. To-day the best and simplest is by the use of Plastigage, obtainable from most garages. A thin plastic thread is laid between the two surfaces and the bearing is tightened, flattening the thread. On removal, the width of the thread is compared with a scale supplied with the thread and the clearance is read off directly. Sometimes joint faces leak persistently, even after gasket renewal. The fault will then be traceable to distortion, dirt or burrs. Studs which are screwed into soft metal frequently raise burrs at the point of entry. A quick cure for this is to chamfer the edge of the hole in the part which fits over the stud.

5 **Always check a replacement part with the original one before it is fitted.**

If parts are not marked, and the order for reassembly is not known, a little detective work will help. Look for marks which are due to wear to see if they can be mated. Joint faces may not be identical due to manufacturing errors, and parts which overlap may be stained, giving a clue to the correct position. Most fixings leave identifying marks especially if they were painted over on assembly. It is then easier to decide whether a nut, for instance, has a plain, a spring, or a shakeproof washer under it. All running surfaces become 'bedded' together after long spells of work and tiny imperfections on one part will be found to have left corresponding marks on the other. This is particularly true of shafts and bearings and even a score on a cylinder wall will show on the piston.

6 Checking end float or rocker clearances by feeler gauge may not always give accurate results because of wear. For instance, the rocker tip which bears on a valve stem may be deeply pitted, in which case the feeler will simply be bridging a depression. Thrust washers may also wear depressions in opposing faces to make accurate measurement difficult. End float is then easier to check by using a dial gauge. It is common practice to adjust end play in bearing assemblies, like front hubs with taper rollers, by doing up the axle nut until the hub becomes stiff to turn and then backing it off a little. Do not use this method with ballbearing hubs as the assembly is often preloaded by tightening the axle nut to its fullest extent. If the splitpin hole will not line up, file the base of the nut a little.

Steering assemblies often wear in the straight-ahead position. If any part is adjusted, make sure that it remains free when moved from lock to lock. Do not be surprised if an assembly like a steering gearbox, which is known to be carefully adjusted outside the car, becomes stiff when it is bolted in place. This will be due to distortion of the case by the pull of the mounting bolts, particularly if the mounting points are not all touching together. This problem may be met in other equipment and is cured by careful attention to the alignment of mounting points.

When a spanner is stamped with a size and A/F it means that the dimension is the width between the jaws and has no connection with ANF, which is the designation for the American National Fine thread. Coarse threads like Whitworth are rarely used on cars to-day except for studs which screw into soft aluminium or cast iron. For this reason it might be found that the top end of a cylinder head stud has a fine thread and the lower end a coarse thread to screw into the cylinder block. If the car has mainly UNF threads then it is likely that any coarse threads will be UNC, which are not the same as Whitworth. Small sizes have the same number of threads in Whitworth and UNC, but in the $\frac{1}{2}$ inch size for example, there are twelve threads to the inch in the former and thirteen in the latter.

7 After a major overhaul, particularly if a great deal of work has been done on the braking, steering and suspension systems, it is advisable to approach the problem of testing with care. If the braking system has been overhauled, apply heavy pressure to the brake pedal and get a second operator to check every possible source of leakage. The brakes may work extremely well, but a leak could cause complete failure after a few miles.

Do not fit the hub caps until every wheel nut has been checked for tightness, and make sure the tyre pressures are correct. Check the levels of coolant, lubricants and hydraulic fluids. Being satisfied that all is well, take the car on the road and test the brakes at once. Check the steering and the action of the handbrake. Do all this at moderate speeds on quiet roads, and make sure there is no other vehicle behind you when you try a rapid stop.

Finally, remember that many parts settle down after a time, so check for tightness of all fixings after the car has been on the road for a hundred miles or so.

8 It is useless to tune an engine which has not reached its normal running temperature. In the same way, the tune of an engine which is stiff after a rebore will be different when the engine is again running free. Remember too, that rocker clearances on pushrod operated valve gear will change when the cylinder head nuts are tightened after an initial period of running with a new head gasket.

Trouble may not always be due to what seems the obvious cause. Ignition, carburation and mechanical condition are interdependent and spitting back through the carburetter, which might be attributed to a weak mixture, can be caused by a sticking inlet valve.

For one final hint on tuning, never adjust more than one thing at a time or it will be impossible to tell which adjustment produced the desired result.

NOTES

GLOSSARY OF TERMS

Allen key — Cranked wrench of hexagonal section for use with socket head screws.

Alternator — Electrical generator producing alternating current. Rectified to direct current for battery charging.

Ambient temperature — Surrounding atmospheric temperature.

Annulus — Used in engineering to indicate the outer ring gear of an epicyclic gear train.

Armature — The shaft carrying the windings, which rotates in the magnetic field of a generator or starter motor. That part of a solenoid or relay which is activated by the magnetic field.

Axial — In line with, or pertaining to, an axis.

Backlash — Play in meshing gears.

Balance lever — A bar where force applied at the centre is equally divided between connections at the ends.

Banjo axle — Axle casing with large diameter housing for the crownwheel and differential.

Bendix pinion — A self-engaging and self-disengaging drive on a starter motor shaft.

Bevel pinion — A conical shaped gearwheel, designed to mesh with a similar gear with an axis usually at 90 deg. to its own.

bhp — Brake horse power, measured on a dynamometer.

bmep — Brake mean effective pressure. Average pressure on a piston during the working stroke.

Brake cylinder — Cylinder with hydraulically operated piston(s) acting on brake shoes or pad(s).

Brake regulator — Control valve fitted in hydraulic braking system which limits brake pressure to rear brakes during heavy braking to prevent rear wheel locking.

Camber — Angle at which a wheel is tilted from the vertical.

Capacitor — Modern term for an electrical condenser. Part of distributor assembly, connected across contact breaker points, acts as an interference suppressor.

Castellated — Top face of a nut, slotted across the flats, to take a locking splitpin.

Castor — Angle at which the kingpin or swivel pin is tilted when viewed from the side.

cc — Cubic centimetres. Engine capacity is arrived at by multiplying the area of the bore in sq cm by the stroke in cm by the number of cylinders.

Clevis — U-shaped forked connector used with a clevis pin, usually at handbrake connections.

Collet — A type of collar, usually split and located in a groove in a shaft, and held in place by a retainer. The arrangement used to retain the spring(s) on a valve stem in most cases.

Commutator — Rotating segmented current distributor between armature windings and brushes in generator or motor.

Compression ratio — The ratio, or quantitative relation, of the total volume (piston at bottom of stroke) to the unswept volume (piston at top of stroke) in an engine cylinder.

Condenser — See capacitor.

Core plug — Plug for blanking off a manufacturing hole in a casting.

Crownwheel — Large bevel gear in rear axle, driven by a bevel pinion attached to the propeller shaft. Sometimes called a 'ring gear'.

'C'-spanner — Like a 'C' with a handle. For use on screwed collars without flats, but with slots or holes.

Damper — Modern term for shock-absorber, used in vehicle suspension systems to damp out spring oscillations.

Depression — The lowering of atmospheric pressure as in the inlet manifold and carburetter.

Dowel — Close tolerance pin, peg, tube, or bolt, which accurately locates mating parts.

Drag link — Rod connecting steering box drop arm (pitman arm) to nearest front wheel steering arm in certain types of steering systems.

Dry liner — Thinwall tube pressed into cylinder bore

Dry sump — Lubrication system where all oil is scavenged from the sump, and returned to a separate tank.

Dynamo — See Generator.

Electrode — Terminal, part of an electrical component, such as the points or 'Electrodes' of a sparking plug.

Electrolyte — In lead-acid car batteries a solution of sulphuric acid and distilled water.

End float — The axial movement between associated parts, end play.

EP — Extreme pressure. In lubricants, special grades for heavily loaded bearing surfaces, such as gear teeth in a gearbox, or crownwheel and pinion in a rear axle.

Fade	Of brakes. Reduced efficiency due to overheating.	**Journals**	Those parts of a shaft that are in contact with the bearings.
Field coils	Windings on the polepieces of motors and generators.	**Kingpin**	The main vertical pin which carries the front wheel spindle, and permits steering movement. May be called 'steering pin' or 'swivel pin'.
Fillets	Narrow finishing strips usually applied to interior bodywork.	**Layshaft**	The shaft which carries the laygear in the gearbox. The laygear is driven by the first motion shaft and drives the third motion shaft according to the gear selected. Sometimes called the 'countershaft' or 'second motion shaft.
First motion shaft	Input shaft from clutch to gearbox.		
Fullflow filter	Filters in which all the oil is pumped to the engine. If the element becomes clogged, a bypass valve operates to pass unfiltered oil to the engine.		
FWD	Front wheel drive.	**lb ft**	A measure of twist or torque. A pull of 10 lb at a radius of 1 ft is a torque of 10 lb ft.
Gear pump	Two meshing gears in a close fitting casing. Oil is carried from the inlet round the outside of both gears in the spaces between the gear teeth and casing to the outlet, the meshing gear teeth prevent oil passing back to the inlet, and the oil is forced through the outlet port.		
		lb/sq in	Pounds per square inch.
		Little-end	The small, or piston end of a connecting rod. Sometimes called the 'small-end'.
		LT	Low Tension. The current output from the battery.
Generator	Modern term for 'Dynamo'. When rotated produces electrical current.	**Mandrel**	Accurately manufactured bar or rod used for test or centring purposes.
Grommet	A ring of protective or sealing material. Can be used to protect pipes or leads passing through bulkheads.	**Manifold**	A pipe, duct, or chamber, with several branches.
		Needle rollers	Bearing rollers with a length many times their diameter.
Grubscrew	Fully threaded headless screw with screwdriver slot. Used for locking, or alignment purposes.	**Oil bath**	Reservoir which lubricates parts by immersion. In air filters, a separate oil supply for wetting a wire mesh element to hold the dust.
Gudgeon pin	Shaft which connects a piston to its connecting rod. Sometimes called 'wrist pin', or 'piston pin'.		
Halfshaft	One of a pair transmitting drive from the differential.	**Oil wetted**	In air filters, a wire mesh element lightly oiled to trap and hold airborne dust.
Helical	In spiral form. The teeth of helical gears are cut at a spiral angle to the side faces of the gearwheel.	**Overlap**	Period during which inlet and exhaust valves are open together.
Hot spot	Hot area that assists vapourisation of fuel on its way to cylinders. Often provided by close contact between inlet and exhaust manifolds.	**Panhard rod**	Bar connected between fixed point on chassis and another on axle to control sideways movement.
		Pawl	Pivoted catch which engages in the teeth of a ratchet to permit movement in one direction only.
HT	High Tension. Applied to electrical current produced by the ignition coil for the sparking plugs.	**Peg spanner**	Tool with pegs, or pins, to engage in holes or slots in the part to be turned.
Hydrometer	A device for checking specific gravity of liquids. Used to check specific gravity of electrolyte.	**Pendant pedals**	Pedals with levers that are pivoted at the top end.
Hypoid bevel gears	A form of bevel gear used in the rear axle drive gears. The bevel pinion meshes below the centre line of the crownwheel, giving a lower propeller shaft line.	**Phillips screwdriver**	A cross-point screwdriver for use with the cross-slotted heads of Phillips screws.
		Pinion	A small gear, usually in relation to another gear.
		Piston-type damper	Shock absorber in which damping is controlled by a piston working in a closed oil-filled cylinder.
Idler	A device for passing on movement. A free running gear between driving and driven gears. A lever transmitting track rod movement to a side rod in steering gear.	**Preloading**	Preset static pressure on ball or roller bearings not due to working loads.
		Radial	Radiating from a centre, like the spokes of a wheel.
Impeller	A centrifugal pumping element. Used in water pumps to stimulate flow.		

Radius rod	Pivoted arm confining movement of a part to an arc of fixed radius.
Ratchet	Toothed wheel or rack which can move in one direction only, movement in the other being prevented by a pawl.
Ring gear	A gear tooth ring attached to outer periphery of flywheel. Starter pinion engages with it during starting.
Runout	Amount by which rotating part is out of true.
Semi-floating axle	Outer end of rear axle halfshaft is carried on bearing inside axle casing. Wheel hub is secured to end of shaft.
Servo	A hydraulic or pneumatic system for assisting, or, augmenting a physical effort. See 'Vacuum Servo'.
Setscrew	One which is threaded for the full length of the shank.
Shackle	A coupling link, used in the form of two parallel pins connected by side plates to secure the end of the master suspension spring and absorb the effects of deflection.
Shell bearing	Thinwalled steel shell lined with anti-friction metal. Usually semi-circular and used in pairs for main and big-end bearings.
Shock absorber	See 'Damper'.
Silentbloc	Rubber bush bonded to inner and outer metal sleeves.
Socket-head screw	Screw with hexagonal socket for an Allen key.
Solenoid	A coil of wire creating a magnetic field when electric current passes through it. Used with a soft iron core to operate contacts or a mechanical device.
Spur gear	A gear with teeth cut axially across the periphery.
Stub axle	Short axle fixed at one end only.
Tachometer	An instrument for accurate measurement of rotating speed. Usually indicates in revolutions per minute.

TDC	Top Dead Centre. The highest point reached by a piston in a cylinder, with the crank and connecting rod in line.
Thermostat	Automatic device for regulating temperature. Used in vehicle coolant systems to open a valve which restricts circulation at low temperature.
Third motion shaft	Output shaft of gearbox.
Threequarter floating axle	Outer end of rear axle halfshaft flanged and bolted to wheel hub, which runs on bearing mounted on outside of axle casing. Vehicle weight is not carried by the axle shaft.
Thrust bearing or washer	Used to reduce friction in rotating parts subject to axial loads.
Torque	Turning or twisting effort. See 'lb ft'.
Track rod	The bar(s) across the vehicle which connect the steering arms and maintain the front wheels in their correct alignment.
UJ	Universal joint. A coupling between shafts which permits angular movement.
UNF	Unified National Fine screw thread.
Vacuum servo	Device used in brake system, using difference between atmospheric pressure and inlet manifold depression to operate a piston which acts to augment brake pressure as required. See 'Servo'.
Venturi	A restriction or 'choke' in a tube, as in a carburetter, used to increase velocity to obtain a reduction in pressure.
Vernier	A sliding scale for obtaining fractional readings of the graduations of an adjacent scale.
Welch plug	A domed thin metal disc which is partially flattened to lock in a recess. Used to plug core holes in castings.
Wet liner	Removable cylinder barrel, sealed against coolant leakage, where the coolant is in direct contact with the outer surface.
Wet sump	A reservoir attached to the crankcase to hold the lubricating oil.

NOTES

INDEX

Alfa Romeo Giulia 1600,
1750, 2000 1962 on
Aston Martin 1921-58
Auto Union Audi 70, 80,
Super 90, 1966-72
Audi 100 1969 on
Austin, Morris etc.
1100 Mk. 1 1962-67
Austin, Morris etc. 1100
Mk. 2, 3, 1300 Mk. 1, 2, 3
America 1968 on
Austin A30, A35, A40
Farina 1951-67
Austin A55 Mk. 2, A60
1958-69
Austin A99, A110 1959-68
Austin J4 1960 on
Austin Allegro 1973 on
Austin Maxi 1969 on
Austin, Morris 1800
1964 on
Austin, Morris 2200 1972 on
Austin Kimberley, Tasman
1970 on
Austin, Morris 1300, 1500
Nomad 1969 on
BMC 3 (Austin A50, A55
Mk. 1, Morris Oxford
2, 3 1954-59)
Austin Healey 100/6,
3000 1956-68
Austin Healey, MG
Sprite, Midget 1958 on
Bedford CA Mk. 2 1964-69
Bedford CF Vans 1969 on
Bedford Beagle HA Vans
1964 on
BMW 1600 1966 on
BMW 1800 1964-71
BMW 2000, 2002 1966 on
Chevrolet Corvair 1960-69
Chevrolet Corvette V8
1957-65
Chevrolet Corvette V8
1965 on
Chevrolet Vega 2300
1970 on
Chrysler Valiant V8
1965 on
Chrysler Valiant Straight
Six 1963 on
Citroen DS 19, ID 19
1955-66
Citroen ID 19, DS 19, 20,
21 1966 on
Citroen Dyane Ami 1964 on
Daf 31, 32, 33, 44, 55
1961 on
Datsun Bluebird 610 series
1972 on
Datsun Cherry 100A, 120A
1971 on
Datsun 1000, 1200 1968 on
Datsun 1300, 1400, 1600
1968 on
Datsun 240C 1971 on

Datsun 240Z Sport 1970 on
Fiat 124 1966 on
Fiat 124 Sport 1966 on
Fiat 125 1967-72
Fiat 127 1971 on
Fiat 128 1969 on
Fiat 500 1957 on
Fiat 600, 600D 1955-69
Fiat 850 1964 on
Fiat 1100 1957-69
Fiat 1300, 1500 1961-67
Ford Anglia Prefect 100E
1953-62
Ford Anglia 105E, Prefect
107E 1959-67
Ford Capri 1300, 1600 OHV
1968 on
Ford Capri 1300, 1600,
2000 OHC 1972 on
Ford Capri 2000 V4, 3000 V6
1969 on
Ford Classic, Capri
1961-64
Ford Consul, Zephyr,
Zodiac, 1, 2 1950-62
Ford Corsair Straight
Four 1963-65
Ford Corsair V4 1965-68
Ford Corsair V4 2000
1969-70
Ford Cortina 1962-66
Ford Cortina 1967-68
Ford Cortina 1969-70
Ford Cortina Mk. 3
1970 on
Ford Escort 1967 on
Ford Falcon 6 1964-70
Ford Falcon XK, XL
1960-63
Ford Falcon 6 XR/XA
1966 on
Ford Falcon V8 (U.S.A.)
1965-71
Ford Falcon V8 (Aust.)
1966 on
Ford Pinto 1970 on
Ford Maverick 6 1969 on
Ford Maverick V8 1970 on
Ford Mustang 6 1965 on
Ford Mustang V8 1965 on
Ford Thames 10, 12,
15 cwt 1957-65
Ford Transit V4 1965 on
Ford Zephyr Zodiac Mk. 3
1962-66
Ford Zephyr Zodiac V4,
V6, Mk. 4 1966-72
Ford Consul, Granada
1972 on
Hillman Avenger 1970 on
Hillman Hunter 1966 on
Hillman Imp 1963-68
Hillman Imp 1969 on
Hillman Minx 1 to 5
1956-65
Hillman Minx 1965-67

Hillman Minx 1966-70
Hillman Super Minx
1961-65
Jaguar XK120, 140, 150,
Mk. 7, 8, 9 1948-61
Jaguar 2.4, 3.4, 3.8 Mk.
1, 2 1955-69
Jaguar 'E' Type 1961-72
Jaguar 'S' Type 420
1963-68
Jaguar XJ6 1968 on
Jowett Javelin Jupiter
1947-53
Landrover 1, 2 1948-61
Landrover 2, 2a, 3 1959 on
Mazda 616 1970 on
Mazda 808, 818 1972 on
Mazda 1200, 1300 1969 on
Mazda 1500, 1800 1967 on
Mazda RX-2 1971 on
Mazda R100, RX-3 1970 on
Mercedes-Benz 190b,
190c, 200 1959-68
Mercedes-Benz 220
1959-65
Mercedes-Benz 220/8
1968 on
Mercedes-Benz 230
1963-68
Mercedes-Benz 250
1965-67
Mercedes-Benz 250
1968 on
Mercedes-Benz 280
1968 on
MG TA to TF 1936-55
MGA MGB 1955-68
MGB 1969 on
Mini 1959 on
Mini Cooper 1961-72
Morgan Four 1936-72
Morris Marina 1971 on
Morris (Aust) Marina
1972 on
Morris Minor 2, 1000
1952-71
Morris Oxford 5, 6 1959-71
NSU 1000 1963-72
NSU Prinz 1 to 4 1957-72
Opel Ascona, Manta
1970 on
Opel GT 1900 1968 on
Opel Kadett, Olympia 993 cc
1078 cc 1962 on
Opel Kadett, Olympia 1492,
1698, 1897 cc 1967 on
Opel Rekord C 1966-72
Peugeot 204 1965 on
Peugeot 304 1970 on
Peugeot 404 1960 on
Peugeot 504 1968 on
Porsche 356A, B, C 1957-65
Porsche 911 1964 on
Porsche 912 1965-69
Porsche 914 S 1969 on
Reliant Regal 1952-73

Renault R4, R4L, 4 1961 on
Renault 5 1972 on
Renault 6 1968 on
Renault 8, 10, 1100 1962-71
Renault 12, 1969 on
Renault 15, 17 1971 on
Renault R16 1965 on
Renault Dauphine
Floride 1957-67
Renault Caravelle 1962-68
Rover 60 to 110 1953-64
Rover 2000 1963-73
Rover 3 Litre 1958-67
Rover 3500, 3500S 1968 on
Saab 95, 96, Sport
1960-68
Saab 99 1969 on
Saab V4 1966 on
Simca 1000 1961 on
Simca 1100 1967 on
Simca 1300, 1301, 1500,
1501 1963 on
Skoda One (440, 445, 450)
1955-70
Sunbeam Rapier Alpine
1955-65
Toyota Carina, Celica
1971 on
Toyota Corolla 1100,
1200 1967 on
Toyota Corona 1500 Mk. 1
1965-70
Toyota Corona Mk. 2
1969 on
Triumph TR2, TR3, TR3A
1952-62
Triumph TR4, TR4A
1961-67
Triumph TR5, TR250,
TR6 1967 on
Triumph 1300, 1500
1965-73
Triumph 2000 Mk. 1, 2.5 PI
Mk. 1 1963-69
Triumph 2000 Mk. 2, 2.5 PI
Mk. 2 1969 on
Triumph Dolomite 1972 on
Triumph Herald 1959-68
Triumph Herald 1969-71
Triumph Spitfire, Vitesse
1962-68
Triumph Spitfire Mk. 3, 4
1969 on
Triumph GT6, Vitesse
2 Litre 1969 on
Triumph Stag 1970 on
Triumph Toledo 1970 on
Vauxhall Velox, Cresta
1957-72
Vauxhall Victor 1, 2, FB
1957-64
Vauxhall Victor 101
1964-67
Vauxhall Victor FD 1600,
2000 1967-72

Continued on following page

Vauxhall Victor 3300,
  Ventora 1968-72
Vauxhall Victor FE
  Ventora 1972 on
Vauxhall Viva HA 1963-66
Vauxhall Viva HB 1966-70

Vauxhall Viva, HC Firenza
  1971 on
Volkswagen Beetle 1954-67
Volkswagen Beetle 1968 on
Volkswagen 1500 1961-66

Volkswagen 1600 Fastback
  1965-73
Volkswagen Transporter
  1954-67
Volkswagen Transporter
  1968 on

Volkswagen 411 1968-72
Volvo 120 series 1961-70
Volvo 140 series 1966 on
Volvo 160 series 1968 on
Volvo 1800 1960-73